# SLEEPING WITH THE FBI

# SLEEPING WITH THE FBI

*Sex, Booze, Russians and the
Saga of an American Counterspy
Who Couldn't*

**Russell Warren Howe**

National
Press
Books

Washington, D.C.

Library of Congress Cataloging-in-Publication Data

Howe, Russell Warren, 1925-
Sleeping with the FBI: sex, booze, Russians and the saga of
an American counterspy who couldn't
Russell Warren Howe.
400 pp., 156 x 22.5 cm.
Includes index.
ISBN 0-915765-62-4: $23.95
1. Espionage, Soviet—United States—History—20th century.
2. Espionage, Soviet—California—Los Angeles Region—
History—20th century.
3. United States—Foreign relations—Soviet Union.
4. Soviet Union—Foreign relations—United States.
5. United. Federal Bureau of Investigation—History.
6. Miller, Richard W.
7. Ogorodnikova, Svetlana.
8. Spies—Soviet Union—Biography.
9. Spies—United States—Biography.
I. Title.
E183.8.S65H73  1993
327.1247073—dc20
92-46161        CIP

Cover image of Richard Miller © 1989 *Los Angeles Times*.

PRINTED IN THE UNITED STATES OF AMERICA

*Plea bargaining is one of the great abominations of the American criminal justice system.*

*In fact, it is a double abomination, because it lets people guilty of egregious crimes get off with minor punishment and it pressures innocent people to plead guilty to crimes they never committed out of fear that they will get harsh punishment if they fight for their rights.*

Carl T. Rowan, Syndicated column, February 22, 1988

*I cannot speak of the record of the FBI in checking crime in the United States. I had nothing to do with that side of its activities. But I had a great deal to do with its counter-espionage work, and its record in that field was more conspicuous for failure than for success. Hoover did not catch MacLean or Burgess; he did not catch Fuchs, and would not have caught the rest if the British had not caught Fuchs and worked brilliantly on his tangled emotions; he did not catch Lonsdale; he did not catch Abel for years, and then only because Haynanen delivered him up on a platter; he did not even catch me. If ever there was a bubble reputation, it is the FBI's.*

Kim Philby, *My Silent War*

# CONTENTS

# Foreword

Shortly before one a.m. on October 3, 1984, Richard William Miller was arrested at his home in Bonsall, California, by some of his colleagues in the Federal Bureau of Investigation. He was taken briefly to the FBI office in San Diego, then to the local metropolitan detention center.

The decision of William Webster, then Director of the FBI, to overrule Miller's supervisor, Richard Bretzing, and the head of internal security at Justice, John Martin, had caught everybody flat-footed. Bretzing had dismissed Miller from the Bureau, and Bretzing and Martin had intended to leave it at that. Then, Webster had ordered Miller arrested for espionage. Assistant Federal Attorney Russell Hayman had been aroused from home late on October 2, to pay a midnight visit to a magistrate's home to get the arrest warrant. Hayman took off for San Diego at seven a.m. in an FBI helicopter, and arraigned Miller in court that morning.

When the news hit the radio bulletins, there was a celebration party at the Soviet consulate-general in San Francisco. The party was for the KGB Rezident, Aleksandr Vasiliyevich Grishin, who had just brought off a stunning victory.

Most readers of spy fiction would love to do what their favorite characters do—a solo operation that works. At forty-eight, Richard William Miller had had the opportunity to try. He was a member of the Foreign Counter-Intelligence (FCI) unit of the Los Angeles office of the FBI. He was also a member of its "double agent" program. And he badly needed to redeem a mediocre career.

Like Len Deighton's character Bernard Samson, Miller was overweight. Like Samson, he was considered an outsider by his colleagues, and had few friends within the FCI—the FBI's equivalent of MI-5.

As Samson does regularly, Miller disobeyed orders. He kept his superiors in the dark about what he was doing. He used his own network: In place of Samson's shadowy friends in Berlin, he found a compliant Russian swallow in West Hollywood, an official FBI "asset" and informant named Svetlana Ogorodnikova, to whom he made love every time they met. Through her, he made unauthorized contact with The Enemy—which was to lead to her and her husband's arrest for complicity. Miller also took on, as legman, a small-time private eye.

*11*

Like Samson, Miller was suspected by his colleagues of being a mole. And, like Samson, he finally went to his superior and reported what he had done; he asked for permission to go to Vienna with Svetlana to meet a GRU general. Like Samson, he was berated for having broken the rules.

From that point on, *nothing* happened as in a Deighton novel. Samson is always reluctantly forgiven, because of his successes. But Miller hadn't really yet succeeded in anything, nor was he likely to. Grishin had been on to Miller at once, just as he had been on to a similarly ham-fisted operation—this one, authorized—by one of Miller's colleagues, John Hunt, the year before. Grishin had decided to teach Miller, and the "traitorous" Russian swallow, a lesson—by setting them up for the FBI.

Using language so suspicious as to be frankly hilarious, Grishin had made a series of "instruction" calls to Svetlana on a line he knew was bugged by the FBI—always at the same hour and on the same day of the week, so that the FBI couldn't miss. As readers will see, the situation wasn't helped by the fact that the Joint Intelligence Center at the Pentagon, distrusting both FBI security and competence, withheld most of its "take" of the consulate-general's traffic from the Bureau, while the San Francisco office of the FBI similarly often left its counterpart in Los Angeles in the dark about what it knew. When the FBI arrested its own man and its own swallow, Grishin savored a triumph of audacity and gall. He went home to head a geographic division of S Directorate of the First Chief Directorate of the KGB, in charge of all nondiplomatic spies in his division.

This is the author's sixteenth book, and his third on a miscarriage of justice. The others were *Mata Hari—The True Story* and *The Hunt For "Tokyo Rose"*. In nearly all judicial scandals of this sort, there are invariably "flags" which show the investigator that the central character is innocent, and encourage him to push his research further. In the Miller case, his exposure of himself to the FBI cameras doing the surveillance of the Soviet consulate-general in San Francisco made his own intention clear—even, alas, to the Russians!

The second "flag", which seems fairly clearly to indicate that the Ogorodnikovs also were not KGB officers or agents, is the fact that they have never been "traded".

They are the only nondiplomatic Russians convicted of espionage in the United States in recent decades who have not simply been exchanged for Americans fortuitously arrested in Russia.

The third oddity in the affair is that Grishin always called Mrs. Ogorodnikova on a telephone line which he and she knew was monitored, and that, although he was a "legal" (a diplomat), he returned home without waiting to be declared persona non grata; he thus not only directed heightened prosecutorial attention to the Miller-Ogorodnikova case, but also sacrificed Moscow's chance to expel an American "spook" of equally high grade from the Soviet Union. This Grishin ploy could only have been a part of his overall strategy.

The narrative of this book is drawn from the FBI files, from the records of the three trials, and from interviews with all involved—the three defendants, their friends, their lawyers, their lawyers' investigators, Justice Department officials, the prosecuting attorneys, intelligence analysts who have reconstructed Grishin's modus operandi and strategy, and others. For obvious reasons, I have used pseudonyms for two Western intelligence analysts, for their "cover" firm, and for the firm's owner.

With Svetlana, I have sometimes taken the liberty of correcting both her syntax and her neglect of compound tenses where this creates confusion in the chronology. I have sometimes inserted articles—*a* and *the*—which Russian, like other Asian languages, does not have. I have edited her a little, adding an occasional bridge to give coherence, as she would have done if she were more articulate. But I have preserved her style: Mostly declarative sentences with occasional explosions of slang that erupt unexpectedly like a *crouton* in a *velouté*, turns of phrase which are exclusively hers, the intriguing contradictions that come from speaking in a language in which she will never be completely fluent.

I had long telephone conversations and exchanged letters with Nikolaiy before meeting him in person after his release. Nikolaiy's temperament is even more brittle than Svetlana's; his English is as bad, but he barrels into the language with masculine self-confidence. With him also, I have tried to leave his style intact.

I am indebted to Nadya Mathison, a serious *émigrée* from Leningrad, who played the role of wiser sister to Svetlana's often spacy self-destructiveness. Through the eyes of Mrs. Mathison, a fellow-Nordic, the writer was better able to understand the quasi-inevitability with which the histrionic, gaudy, soap opera-educated moth from Yefrimov was drawn mindlessly into the cold-war flame which destroyed her life.

From a lawyer's point of view, all three defendants were the sort of witness-stand nightmares that their former professors warned them about. Neither of the men were ever allowed to testify at all. (After all, in his nearly twenty-year career, Miller was only once permitted by the FBI to present evidence in court; once was enough.)

Miller's attorneys, however, were helpful in persuading him to let me interview him when he was free awaiting retrial.

The prosecuting attorneys also allowed themselves to be interviewed, at least until the retrial was ordered. From this, and from background interviews within the justice system in Washington, I was able to construct how and why the prosecution was put together with baling wire, and the desperation that attended the fears that it would collapse.

If the author has a grievance, it is with retired Special Agent John Hunt, who was Mrs. Ogorodnikova's handler as a swallow for much longer than Richard Miller, and whom she says she believed was going to marry her. It would have been extremely helpful if this employee and pensioner of the taxpayers would have agreed to talk to the rest of us, his employers, about this intriguingly human and professional relationship, but he refused to talk "unless you pay me."

The ethical guidelines about reporters engaging in what is called "checkbook journalism" are not straightforward, but the dangers that a bought informant will say only what he thinks a reporter will want to hear are evident. The risks of hype are enormous, and I admit that I had Svetlana's warnings ringing in my ears: "He's the most lying sonovabitch I ever met in my life."

Donald Spatny, a California jack-of-all-trades who has been of considerable assistance, including benign research aimed at helping to secure justice for Svetlana, quotes Hunt as saying to him: "There's a lot of money in this if it's done right. I know more about her than anyone else."

He apparently wanted to co-write a book with Spatny about the case. Spatny says that, when he turned Hunt down, the old G-man approached at least two other California writers, including a reporter on the *Los Angeles Times*.

The stories of the investigations and trials of Mata Hari and Iva Toguri were accounts of the sordid lengths to which prosecutors will go to "score"—to get promotion. *Sleeping With the FBI* has an unusual upbeat character, for an American book—Colonel Grishin. Here was a Babe Ruth or Joe Di Maggio of intelligence, the world's most demanding tourney of deceit, who was called to the mound against a stickball team—the Keystone Kops of the FBI office in Los Angeles, where 18 of the 19 members of the "Russian Squad" could neither speak nor read Russian, and were not even taking language classes; the pathetic figure of Miller; and Svetlana, a real-life *I Love Lucy* figure from a Russian village who was trying to stagger drunkenly through an exacting role more suited to Marthe Richard or Nur Khan. Above all, Grishin is a real-life spy hero whose memoirs may one day get a foreword from the real-life head of MI-5, MI-6 or the CIA. He had to turn a tragicomic target of opportunity into a minor crisis within the U.S. counter-intelligence bureaucracy—and to his own advantage.

Miller had wanted to be Bernard Samson—just once. But the role had already been assigned—to the other side.

# PART I

## The Principal Characters

# Chapter One

## The Sleuths

*Grayson pawed his beard thoughtfully. "R.W., you're playing with fire," he said. But it was the Russians, not Miller's colleagues, that he was thinking of.*

On Tuesday, August 14, 1984, Special Agent Richard William Miller of the FBI office in Los Angeles drove his Isuzu to Corona, a suburb of Riverside, and into the parking lot of the local Denny's, a chain of cafeterias. Minutes later, Lawrence Grayson, a small-time investigator and police informer, joined Miller in the cafeteria.

The two middle-aged men were old friends, going back to the time when Miller had been in the Riverside satellite office of the FBI.

Miller had just made a momentous, even outrageous, decision, and he needed help from someone in the law enforcement community, someone not employed in a disciplined service. Grayson lived in Riverside. Miller and his family lived on an avocado orchard at Bonsall in San Diego County, and Corona was just off the Santa Rosa Highway, which Miller regularly took to and from the L.A. office of the Bureau in downtown Westwood.

The two detectives could hardly have looked more different. Lawrence Grayson, despite his years, was slim and lithe, an aerobic version of the stocky, swarthy, brooding "godfather" in *The French Connection*, last seen disappearing from Gene Hackman's reach on the New York subway. Grayson had dark, intense eyes, a bushy, graying black mop of hair and a Van Dyck beard. His father, he would say, had been in the Irish Guards, before becoming a King's Messenger—a British diplomatic courier; but Dad had apparently come not from Galway or Cork but from Persia, and Grayson would describe himself as an Iranian. He would tell inquirers that his mother was "French, German and English," and that the gravel-voiced British comedienne Beatrice Lillie had been his godmother; but questions about his biography would soon get lost in a maze of apparent contradictions, garnished with phrases like "What I thought I said was...." He cultivated an aura of mystery and used aliases. His calling cards gave his name as Sears.

Denny's, with its stench of industrial ketchup, armpits and steam plates, its weak coffee and endless turnover of disposable waitresses, was an odd place to meet to plot to vanquish the KGB. It had no liquor license, not even for beer, but that did not worry either sleuth.

Miller was a non-drinking, non-smoking Mormon, with an appetite only for heavy food, especially candy bars, and what at Scotland Yard would be called crumpet. A colleague quotes him as saying once: "Show me a law-enforcement officer who hasn't humped a female informant, and I'll show you a fag." Grayson, perhaps as part of his image as the ayatollah of the San Bernardino Valley, drank mainly fruit juice. On this occasion, they took nothing from the steam plate line except plastic pints of pale, foul-smelling coffee. Miller was trying, once more, to slim, but when he didn't lunch, he snacked. At five feet nine and a half inches, he weighed over 250 pounds; despite his seniority—he was forty-eight—he had been threatened with dismissal from the Bureau for unacceptable obesity. The trim, athletic Grayson suppressed a smile, trying to imagine "R.W." giving chase to someone.

He heard Miller say: "Larry, d'you still have your equipment for a mobile surveillance?"

Did he ever! If physically he reminded people of the character in *The French Connection*, the film with which he would identify most easily would be *The Conversation*.

A waitress with uncombed peroxide hair and olive skin and what looked like basketballs for breasts was hovering close, and Grayson dropped his voice. "We talking audiovisual, R.W.? Sure. What's up? Who's the mark?"

"Me. Shake hands with James Bond," Miller said, holding out his free fingers and grinning through a mouthful of Mars. He was going to Mexico to meet "someone," he explained. He wanted to be photographed and monitored, including his hotel phone conversations. At first, he was hesitant to give further details, as though nervous about the assignment. Finally, he admitted that he was going across the border to talk to Russians. "What sort of Russians?" asked the man Miller wanted to bug their meetings. After the buxom Bolivian had replenished their ration of thin caffeine, Miller admitted that, yes, he was after the FBI's and the CIA's opposite number, the KGB. He wanted proof to show his superiors that he had hooked Soviet intelligence into a double-agent scam.

The bulky Miller looked down at the table, pensively. His chin disappeared into his neck. His hands trembled slightly. Like a compulsive smoker, he broke the wrapper on another Mars. The thoroughly startled Grayson suggested they move outside, to Miller's car, away from the ever-present waitress.

Once there, Grayson asked calmly: "Why don't you get your own people to do this?" He owed Miller a favor, for having once been allowed to buy bootleg copies of one of his clients' FBI files, at the bargain price of twenty-five dollars a page, but he was thinking that there were easier ways to earn a living than getting in Dutch with the KGB.

"My credibility's shot with the Bureau," Miller said, boyishly frank. "If they knew what I was up to, they'd say I was out of my depth, and pull me off. I want to be able to say to Christensen: 'This is Larry's video. These are his sound tapes. The hook is in.'"

"You mean Christensen doesn't know shit about this?"

They were talking of J. Bryce Christensen, the tall but mousy, crew-cut deputy special agent-in-charge of the great, sprawling Westwood office. A fellow Mormon, he was Miller's supervisor.

Grayson gave a little grunt of amazement. "What if your Russkie friends in Chicanoland are under surveillance by others—their own goons, the CIA, the Mexican police boys who caught the Falcon?"

"If you can, I'd like you to shoot them, too."

Could Miller be serious? Single-handedly taking on the KGB, doing a run in left field on his own...? "How do I get paid?" Grayson inquired.

Miller said Grayson would be compensated out of "authorized FBI funds." This made the private eye feel better. It implied, he thought, that Miller was in fact on a real op against the KGB, even if this particular move was one he had thought up on his own. "Authorized FBI funds" meant at least that there was a budget for the op itself. Miller, he knew, belonged to the nineteen-person "Russian Squad" in the FCI (Foreign Counter-Intelligence) unit in Westwood, even though his only foreign language was American-accented Spanish. Actually, only one of the nineteen spoke Russian; the rest of the sorry throng couldn't even read *Pravda* with a dictionary. Grayson fixed on the expression "double agent."

"What are you offering to do for the Russians?"

"An illusion. Playing the game," Miller said.

"Of course. But what illusion?"

"The illusion that I have access to important documents," said Miller, who was then on loan from the Russian Squad to "The Farm"—a lab where he transcribed boring audio surveillances of Mexican smugglers.

To Grayson, it sounded like yet another of the fat, incompetent agent's wild ideas, of which he had heard many in the past. It was, he thought, unlikely that R.W. would have the skill or the guts to go through with this charade. But he owed Miller one; he couldn't very well say no, so he said yes. Miller explained that he would pay one thousand dollars, plus expenses. It would take only about a day. So what, Grayson asked, was Miller going to ask for from the Russians?

"Fifty thousand bucks in Krugerrands in three different banks, to set up an evidentiary trail."

Grayson's dark, bottomless eyes looked into the fat man's shifty gaze. He saw the reason for Miller's only police skill: Informers trusted this roly-poly fellow, who looked no better than they were; he didn't intimidate like the real Hoover agents in their gray suits and frowns and their white spotless shirts. Miller, he decided, wasn't hoping only to hook himself a Russkie fish and save his career two years before retirement; he was also hoping to skim something off the top, perhaps the whole bucket. This made Grayson think of what he knew of the other side. He still wasn't enthusiastic about the assignment.

"You'd be slitting your throat, selling your soul for thirty pieces of silver," he said. Years later, he could still quote his biblical allusion. He had even gone back to his own car and noted down these remarks, to remind himself and others, should it be necessary, that he had entered this whole comic opera with reservations. "Why not ask for a million?" he said. "Either way, they'll never forgive you."

Miller said nothing. Grayson pawed his beard thoughtfully and uttered a final comment: "R.W., you're playing with fire." But it was the Russians, not Miller's colleagues, that he was thinking of.

# Chapter Two

# The Master:
# Lighting the Lantern

*If you laid all the Americans like Richard Miller end to end, Grishin thought, they would stay that way.*

Aleksandr Grishin looked from the window of his office on Green Street in San Francisco. The rain had stopped, and a sky of piercing Pacific blue was showing itself between the tall buildings opposite him. On the mezzanine floor of one of those buildings, he could see Linda Franusich of the FBI pretending to type a letter. Actually, he knew, she was one of the photographers who would take pictures through a zoom lens of everyone who came to the Soviet consulate-general for visas or whatever. Earlier that day, she had shot a famous Hollywood film star and his agent. He wondered why the FBI used such an antiquated method. What happened if Mrs. Franusich or one of the others wanted to go to the toilet? In Moscow, his people monitored callers at the U.S. Embassy by automatic videotape, keeping what they needed and recycling the rest of the tape. For this task, he reflected, both the KGB and the FBI were more or less blind at night.

He turned away from the window and walked slowly back to his desk, selecting a black cigarette from a silver box and lighting it. He saw his reflection in the box—the handsome, self-indulgent face, the "intellectual bald patches" revealing the widow's peak, but with his abundant dark hair combed and blow-dried over the right-hand patch. He had been ordered to go along with the initiative of an FBI special agent, John Hunt, who had passed the word that he was open to offers from the Komitat Gosudarstvennoe Bezopasnosti—the KGB.

The "dangle" had been transmitted more than a year before by an FBI swallow named Svetlana Ogorodnikova, who had told the cultural attaché, Boris Belyakov, that she wanted to marry Hunt. Hunt and Mrs. Ogorodnikova were married to others, but she had said that they were both planning to divorce. Why would a tall, fairly senior bureaucrat like Hunt want to marry a vulgar little tart like Svetlana, who seemed to put her makeup on with a palette knife and who had married a five-times convicted, divorced felon in Kiev because his grandparents had been Jewish and he could get a visa "for Israel"—meaning Hollywood?

Hunt's proposal, through her, had been an obvious scam; on Grishin's advice, Mrs. Ogorodnikova had been taken off the consul-general's invitation list. Belyakov had pretended, at first, to be annoyed with her. But the Ogorodnikovs had been allowed to go on showing Russian films both at the Episcopalian church in Silver Lake to which they belonged and commercially. And since she could never be of any use to the KGB, they had let her attract attention by continuing to visit her old mother in Russia every year.

It had been obvious what Hunt was after. Meetings. Monitored meetings. Eventually, Hunt would have handed over the Order of Battle of the U.S. Pacific Fleet, and then the feds would have moved in and arrested all the interlocutors, including him. *Personae non gratiae.* Expelled. Triumph for the FBI.

Fat chance! Yet now Anatoliy, in Moscow, was telling him to take the hook, or pretend to do so. And the idea no longer seemed so silly. For Grishin had found that Hunt was no longer Hunt. John and Svetlana had broken up. The marriage made in heaven, or the Hoover Building, or Svetlana's imagination, was not to be. Now, she was sleeping with another fed, a fat slob named Richard William Miller who was pretending to be Hunt for the purposes of the scam he wanted to set up himself—in Mexico.

So they had orders to tell Svetlana to work for the KGB–knowing she would pass this on. They had asked again for photographs of Svetlana and Hunt together, as though they disbelieved that he existed. They would pretend to be excited.

So he would set things up for Miller, alias Hunt. Or pretend to. And he would make sure that those dummies in Westwood knew everything. He would establish a pattern, always calling to Svetlana's bugged home telephone on the same day of the week, at the same time, instead of calling her at a pay phone, as he would do if she was really part of a KGB op. He would drive out to San Francisco International Airport and make the calls from an outdoor phone, so that he would be sure to be followed—and the bogies able to hear him without the competition of indoor airport sound. He would speak in a plain code so school-boyishly absurd that even the "Russian Squad" in Westwood would understand it, once those linguistic illiterates had had it translated.

If he didn't get overconfident, he told himself, he would bring it off. Miller would be caught—not by the KGB, but by the FBI, his own people, and Svetlana and her aging con of a husband might go to jail as well; more probably, he thought, the Americans would try to expel them back to the Ukraine. That would be another laugh, because they were no longer citizens, so it was unlikely that they could be sent anywhere. Then, to fix Miller for sure, there was another trick to play, taking advantage of the fact that the man to whom Ronald Reagan had granted an ex-equatur as Aleksandr Vasiliyevich Grishin, vice consul of the Union of Soviet Socialist Republics, was about to be promoted well over the consul-general's head. A deputy Rezident who would succeed Aleksandr Vasiliyevich was already in place. He was the man the Americans thought was actually Rezident. They thought Grishin was subordinate to the pseudonymous "Lev Zaydzev" (roughly, "Izzy Rabbit").

He stubbed out the black cigarette with the gold cork tip and looked at his wristwatch, a marvel of Soviet technology that could run for twenty years on a single cadmium battery. It was time to put the plan into action by going to the airport and making his first call—and to make it more suspicious by meeting no one on any flight.

Sometimes, he worried that it could not possibly be as easy as it appeared. Why did the FBI use inexperienced people whose specialty was illegal Mexican immigration or car theft, who spoke no Russian, who, like Hunt and Miller, were still employed at all only because the FBI was a government bureaucracy, not a profitable industry? Grishin's job was to be the Rezident for the western half of the United States, which contained three-quarters of America's defense industry. He had been trained for that. At thirty-six, he was what Americans called a *Wunderkind*. By their standards, he thought, they were probably right. Of course, he and all his staff, even the drivers and secretaries, spoke English.

He lifted his London Fog trench coat off the old-fashioned hanger stand in the corner of his office, in case it rained again, and slung it over his shoulder with a consciously debonair manner. He walked back to the window, hoping Mrs. Franusich would look up and see him and report that he was about to go out, that he had his raincoat on his shoulder. But Mrs. Franusich was focusing on the people from a catering service who were delivering Beluga caviar from Oregon for a reception that the cultural section was giving that night. He saw her snapping away with her Asahi Pentax at the youthful black van driver from Oakland and the Korean assistant manager from the caterer, who was politely but insistently complaining about a delay at the entrance. Grishin liked the Korean work ethic. He had heard it said in Vladivostok that when a Korean died, his family didn't put his ashes into a casket, but into an hourglass, so that he could go on working. Perhaps that was it, Grishin thought—why he was a *Wunderkind* by American standards. He liked to work. If you laid all the Americans like Richard Miller end to end, Grishin thought, they would stay that way.

# Chapter Three

# The "Researchers" I

*The KGB man's nom de théâtre meant Rabbit, but it did not mean that its owner was a John Updike fan. U.S. intelligence thought it implied "Catch me if you can."*

Thirty miles from Green Street, at the headquarters of Occidental Research in Emeryville, Alfred Merman and Malcolm Kitano were discussing the day's intercept "take" from the microwave horns embedded the previous year in the consulate-general's roof. It had been the work of a city repair crew that had included a "laborer" from Occidental.

"O.R." was officially an economic consultancy with a deep blue right-wing tint. Its putative owner, Mrs. Prudence Ayres, an affluent widow, had never suspected that Professor Alf Merman of M.I.T. was really a U.S. Signal Corps colonel; nor was she aware that "Killer" Kitano, whom she knew as Dr. Malcolm, was an honorary signals major born in the nearby Japantown of San Francisco—but whose heroes were George Patton, Ariel Sharon and the Shah of Iran. Mrs. Ayres' researchers, who all had sheepskins on the wall to prove that they were graduate students and the like, and who pirated their reports from the Heritage Foundation and the Hoover Institution, were really signal corpsmen and women from the local Army barracks in Oakland. "O.R." was in fact an "LP"—a listening post for military intelligence. (A few years later, it was to be abandoned by the Pentagon as ideologically fanciful.)

"This is a Valkyrie," Kitano said with intense conviction. The ultimate cold warrior, he tended to say most things with intense conviction.

A Valkyrie was a sexual trap, using a swallow—a female lure. It had originally been the name of a successful Cheka operation against Prussia in czarist times and had since become a generic for most Moscow Center operations of a similar stripe.

"Think so, Killer?" Merman's eyes lit up. Although older than Kitano, he had a similarly juvenile fascination with violence and death, even his own. When they had spoken of mortality one day over jiggers of gin, Merman had said that his dearest hope was to meet his end while "on an op."

Kitano looked at the unread library of economic treatises and IMF reports that formed the tapestry of "Professor" Merman's office walls. He said: "Well, Levchenko was the object of a V-13."

In intelligence jargon, a V-13 (victory for one side, bad luck for the other) is an assassination job. Levchenko, a Ukrainian defector from the Rezidentura in Tokyo, would have had to be lured out of the United States to be put to death. They had learned all that from the roofing bug. "That would be Major Zaydzev's task," Kitano said.

"Makes sense," Merman said encouragingly. "Why d'you think Myshkov has taken over from Chikvaidze as consul-general?"

"The Chik had finished his tour of duty."

"Maybe. You know, don't you, that Chikvaidze is a KGB cover name. There's another Chik in the embassy in Washington. Myshkov, I think, is not a cover name. Now, Grishin was the name of the KGB controller of the Falcon and the Snowman in Mexico City."

"So the Grishin here must be on Zaydzev's staff." Zaydzev was another KGB generic.

"Makes sense," Merman said again. "Lunch? We can talk in the car."

"Right on, Colonel!"

A corpsman drove. On the highway, by coincidence, they passed an FBI car. The San Francisco office of the FBI bought its cars from a Burlingame dealer who put his advertising tag holders on all his vehicles. This "flag" to every Russian spy and drug dealer in the Bay area was one of the FBI indiscretions and unprofessionalisms that "O.R." had mentioned to the Joint Intelligence Center at the Pentagon as a reason for not confiding totally in Special Agent-in-charge Bill Newman and his team. The "O.R." car, an anonymous Toyota, seemed to contain three friends, relaxing. It appeared to be Sergeant Johnson's car, and

Johnson, better dressed than the major and the colonel, seemed to be driving two of his employees into town.

Alf and Killer discussed Lev Zaydzev, whom they were determined to catch doing something incompatible with his diplomatic status. It was more a question of gamesmanship than high policy. The KGB man's *nom de théâtre* meant Rabbit, but it did not mean that its owner was a John Updike fan. U.S. intelligence thought it implied "Catch me if you can."

Johnson began to slow as he entered the city precincts. Merman said: "All Svetlana's messages to Zaydzev have been intercepted, yes?"

"We think so. A lot of them, anyway."

"Her task was to find the three Ukrainians, especially Levchenko, and she goofed—she let John Hunt have his will with her without getting him to give her a lead first. This is her chance to recoup? With Miller? Or go down."

"Reckon so," said Killer. "She's a major in the Komitat."

"But all she gets from them is films and other ways of making pin money. And Nikolaiy's her foot soldier."

"Support agent to the field agent, the penetration agent. But the other day, remember, we got something out of the burst—Zaydzev knocking Nik for saying they owe him back pay and expenses. That means the Rabbit's pissed off at him."

"You understand we're not giving all this to the local G-men anymore."

"Yes, I know—just innocuous stuff."

"What does the San Fran office pass on to L.A.?"

"Very little, I believe. The L.A. office of the Bureau is bigger and more prestigious, but San Fran has the Rezidentura and insists it's more important. It's got nearly fifty percent more people on its Russian Squad than L.A. and about six of them actually speak Russian."

Killer grinned. Both he and Alf spoke Russian, albeit with easily recognizable American accents.

"Plus," Kitano went on, "there are always FBI students doing Russian at the Army Language School in Monterey, and they're under the control of the San Francisco office, who can use them on standby duty. Slow down—turn left at the light!"

"Yes, sir," said the corpsman.

"So there's no love lost between Bill Newman and Bishop Bretzing," Kitano concluded. Richard Bretzing, the FBI special agent-in-charge in Los Angeles, was a Mormon bishop.

"So, if Miller comes here—" Merman began.

"Newman will split a gut over trespass on his territory."

The two spooks smiled at the thought of the FBI's internecine wars. Shortly afterward, they arrived at a French restaurant that they liked partly because it was frequented by their counterparts from Green Street.

As Alf and Killer entered, almost the first customer they noticed was Grishin, who was with his secretary, Ludmila. The Americans were sure that Grishin didn't know them by sight, so they made a point of walking boldly right past the Russians' table. Killer repressed a desire to ask Grishin if he had tried the *fricassée* of rabbit.

Grishin looked up, then exchanged glances with Ludmila.

# Chapter Four

# *The Loser*

*How far could he go in pretending to help them in order to win their confidence? How far had Pistone gone? Heaven only knew what he had had to do to appear to be a good soldier in the Mafia. Surely he had had to beat up some people, extort money, even screw some compliant chicks. Some people had all the luck.*

Richard William Miller continued the journey to Westwood. There, he was behind on transcribing the Hispanic tapes. He was always behind. He hated this work, but this time he worked on until well past nightfall. Finally, he went home to his father's old house in Lynwood, which he was using as a crash pad during the week; he would continue to crash there until his sister, Mary Ann—who had inherited it—found a buyer. He used only a bedroom and the kitchen.

Lynwood was a poor suburb of Los Angeles, and his father's house had not been cleaned for months. It had the smell of a house in which an old person had died. The bedroom was a pigsty. R.W. lay on the bed and opened another Mars wrapper with his teeth. He had stopped off at a 7-Eleven on the way and stolen three of them. He wasn't sure why he did these things. The FBI shrink had told him that Jung had said that people who stole unnecessarily were expressing insecurity. Well, that made sense.

He thought about the meeting with Larry Grayson. It seemed to have gone off well, and he still had time to change his mind if he didn't want to go through with his plan to hook the KGB. He recognized that his chances of success were fifty percent at best, that there were obvious risks involved. But if he brought it off—wow! That would put Christensen's prissy little smirk out of joint. It would impress Bretzing. It would mean he had succeeded where John Hunt had failed. All of those colleagues who tormented him because he was fat and said that the Mormon Mafia had protected him when he should have been fired—they would learn that, fat or not, Mormon or not, he was a law enforcement officer, a foreign counterintelligence specialist, to be reckoned with. A lot would depend on Svetlana. He remembered bringing her to this room and watching her undress and her saying: "How can you stand this place?" He remembered John saying Svetlana's own place in West Hollywood had looked like a pigsty to him. And he had said: "'Lana, I'm going to have to move, because my sis is selling up." And she had said never mind—if all went well with his scheme, he would soon have the money to live decently.

It had been a long struggle to achieve that. He had been born in Wilmington, a redneck district that was now a black slum, in 1936. Like Iva Toguri, who was convicted as "Tokyo Rose," he had gone to Compton Junior College. Then he had gone to work, finally earning enough to go back to school—the great Mormon university of Brigham Young in Utah. He had graduated only in 1964, when he was twenty-eight. You wouldn't guess it from his FBI reports, but he had majored in English, with a minor in Spanish. He had done his Mormon missionary work among Spanish-speaking people. Despite his poor college record, he had been recruited for the FBI while he was at Brigham Young. The Bureau had always welcomed Mormons, whose clean-cut life appealed to J. Edgar Hoover; and there had been a drive at the time to recruit Spanish-speaking agents—preferably non-Hispanics. Hoover didn't think much of Hispanics.

He had met his wife, Paula Gonzales, before college when he had been working in a bathroom appliance factory beside her mother. They had been making toilet seats. Paula had joined him at Brigham Young, and the couple had been married after graduation. Life had looked promising then to the new special agent of the FBI. But like good Mormons, they had not practiced family planning. Over the years, they had had eight children. The oldest, Paul, had been born in 1966. Drew, born two years later, had contracted spinal meningitis in Puerto Rico, and ever since had been deaf and partially retarded.

R.W. had served in San Antonio, in New York's Spanish Harlem, in Puerto Rico and in Tampa before coming to Los Angeles. In each place, he had been a Spanish specialist. For a while, he had been seconded to Riverside, which was where he had met Grayson, because there was a good school for the deaf in Santa Ana. He had asked to be named resident agent in Santa Ana, but that was turned down. He would never have his own shop, he was told.

He conceded to himself that he had a poor record. At Riverside, he had had problems with the office keys, his FBI car, the office fuel card. On each occasion, the local police had had to come to his aid. His paperwork was slow, sometimes nonexistent. Yes, he was lazy. He was lazy because he was fat. He was so fat he had been threatened with dismissal, many times. That lunatic Christensen had ordered him to jog. Miller feared that it might give him a heart attack. He had jogged for a few hundred yards, then gone to sleep in a park, where other agents had found him and reported the incident. In March this year, he'd been ordered to lose weight again. One day, he had logged in at 226 pounds. Six days later, there was an *unscheduled* weigh-in and he was at 247. He'd explained that he'd been taking diuretics before his scheduled weigh-ins. Christensen and Bretzing had ruled that that was cheating, and he had been suspended for two weeks without pay. That was about eighteen hundred dollars. With a family of ten!

Small wonder that he always had financial problems. At the time, he'd owed nearly three thousand dollars in property taxes. In the 1970s, he had cashed in an insurance policy and lost thirty thousand dollars in a business investment involving gold prospecting and condo conversion. FBI special agents, he knew, weren't supposed to be taken for suckers in scams like that. More recently, he had sold muscle relaxants made by an uncle and pocketed the proceeds. He had twice been behind on mortgage payments, and he was trying to sell an unsuccessful avocado orchard, which he and his family called the ranch. He operated this with his father-in-law in San Diego County. But in the end, his real debts were small, about six thousand dollars; nearly half of these were in credit cards. He didn't need money just to pay a few lousy debts that amounted to about two months' salary. He needed money to *get off the ground*.

Sure, he had screwed up his career. It was in tatters. As he'd told Larry, his credibility was shot. Mexico, with Larry and Svetlana, would save it, if only he could muscle up the courage to see it through. After all, it was the sort of thing he was meant to be doing. He was part of the Russian Squad, or Foreign Counter-Intelligence Unit I (FCI-I), run by Special Agent Gary Auer. He was in John Hunt's double-agent program within that squad—although he'd had no double-agent training. Anything would be better than working on the "Farm".

Penetrating the KGB just might be more his style. His best work had been with informants. He would probably get along with those pudgy Russians in their bad suits and dreadful haircuts. He had once cracked a pirate video racket through a network of Hispanic informers he had put together. Sure, he wasn't pretending that had made him a great agent. He bit open the wrapper of another Mars. Most of his problems came from compulsive eating, which came, he was convinced, from compulsive worrying. He felt very much alone in the Bureau. When an agent is suspended, as often happens in a disciplined service like the FBI, his comrades pass the hat to help out. But when he and his family of ten had been on their uppers for two weeks, not one of those pricks had raised a finger. Not one. Still, there were only two years to go. Then, he could take early retirement at age fifty, draw his pension, get a small job as a Spanish-language instructor at a local college, and hump a few female freshmen in return for A's. But first, he was going to go out in a blaze of glory. He was going to "join" the KGB in the way that Special Agent Joe Pistone had joined the Mafia.

He knew all about 'Lana—or Marie, to give her the code-name that was hers as an FBI associate. He had read John Hunt's reports on her dealings with the consulate-general, the things she had reported to John. They were in John's "134" on her. A 134 is a file on an asset. Miller knew that Bryce Christensen had met her and commended her. And he knew that both Bryce and John had concluded she wasn't good enough. Well, they'd see. After all, his talent was in bringing out the best in ostensibly below-average informants, people who saw him as a mirror image. And John had given him some wrinkles on how to handle her. She had potential, John had said. He had also said she could be trouble. Well, all women were trouble.

As well as recognizing that he was not a very good agent, Miller also conceded that he was a poor Mormon. In fact, he had been suspended from the church that year for adultery with another Mormon. The bishop of the eastern San Diego ward hadn't appreciated the FBI agent's boast to friends that the bishop's extrovert wife had made a pass at Miller. Paula had been ashamed—perhaps shamed would put it better. They had talked divorce. He had slept with many other women over the years. One of them, Marta York, the Hispanic widow of an informer, was hoping to marry him. Even Svetlana was talking marriage. So perhaps he wasn't so much of a disheveled, ill-dressed fatso as everybody said. One thing he was proud of—every time he'd humped another chick, he'd told his wife. As a federal agent, he had had to lie scores, even hundreds of times; but he'd tried never to lie about important things. And who knew what things wouldn't change if he brought off this dangle with the Russkies! John's dangle had come up with a great big zero. But as soon as 'Lana had passed on the word for him, there had been a positive reaction from this Anatoliy guy in Moscow.

Auer, however, had authorized only two meetings with 'Lana. He had told R.W. not to "develop" her further without his okay. When Miller had met her a couple of more times before she had gone to Moscow, it had been a breach of orders. Of course, he hadn't logged those unauthorized meetings. Well, John had logged only fifty-five meetings, or "substantive" meetings, in his first seven-month period. That was barely two or more meetings a week, and everyone had known that he had been seeing her almost every day. Maybe that was the trick: A night at Malibu was not a "substantive" meeting. Anyway, Miller had opened a file of his own, in the Lynwood bedroom, and titled it "Svetlana," and he was going to keep the paper-work of that up to date until he was ready to report the whole operation. Then, even if he had broken a few rules, this time they would forgive him because of the result. How many rules had Pistone broken to penetrate the Mafia?

He pulled open a drawer and selected between a Milky Way, a Kitkat and a Babe Ruth. Maybe a Kitkat would be less fattening. He lay back on the pillow and chewed like a contented dog, his dirty saddle boots resting on the unwashed coverlet. He pulled the knot of his tie free and slipped the noose over his grimy hair. Doing that made the tie look like a rag, but he couldn't be bothered to take a tie off differently. He chewed and looked at the paint peeling off the ceiling. What he was going to do with 'Lana wasn't easy, but it was simple. He was going to do what John Hunt had tried but failed to do—turn her into a double agent, use her to penetrate Soviet intelligence, either the KGB or the GRU. Apparently, it was more often the GRU that recruited Western moles. He had told her his plan, more or less.

In March, when she had called John to say she wanted to see him, John had sent two other agents to interview her. She had told them that the KGB wanted her to renew her relationship with John. This, she had said, would give John the opportunity he sought to penetrate Soviet intelligence. She had also told the agents that she was now in fear of the KGB because of her association with the FBI. It was then that John had brought her to see Bryce again, outside the office, and Bryce had again complimented her on her work and courage. Bryce had said that if she continued to work with John, the FBI would protect her. John had done the decent thing—he had put this commitment into the log. But in no time, he had given up on her again, apparently deciding that she was simply stringing him along. She was spacy. R.W. could see that, already.

Before she had gone to Moscow, 'Lana had also given him her own picture of John's operation. She had offered to get R.W. "information." But obviously her access to anything meaningful was far less than John had long pretended. R.W. needed her more as a key, a tool—a swallow. He had told her about his problems at home and at the office, his debts. If anything, he had exaggerated the situation. He had said quite frankly that he wanted to bring off a great coup and save his career. He had even told a friend who ran a local garage, that week, that he wanted to go out in a "blaze of glory." 'Lana had been sympathetic. She had said that she was on the outs with her husband because of her constant time with John, especially the nightlife, and that she needed continued FBI protection.

At their first meeting, at the filling station, in May, she had told him about the upcoming trip to Moscow. She had said that she would be meeting a senior GRU officer there. She was worried because he would ask her about her relations with the FBI. R.W. had taken all this with a grain of salt. After all, she had told Bryce that she was a major in the KGB. But, one way or another, it seemed to be a promising start, despite her rather distraught manner. She had said frankly that, because of the advances she had made to the consulate-general on Hunt's instructions, there were indications that the other side really did want her to work for them, against the United States. R.W. had been sympathetic; he had seen how such a development could be turned to the FBI's advantage. They had driven to Marina Del Rey, a rich residential area by the sea, for lunch.

After that first meeting, on May 24, he had left her in her car in a parking lot within view of the Westwood headquarters and had gone to see Auer about continuing the contact with her. Gary hadn't been enthusiastic. He had pointed out that John had been over this terrain before. At that time, Auer had authorized one more meeting, only. When R.W. had gone back to the parking lot, he had told Svetlana he'd be calling her soon.

Then he'd been busy on other things, and the second meeting hadn't taken place until a week later, May 30. They had become lovers. Svetlana had asked him if he knew the whereabouts of three defectors—Stanislav Levchenko, the KGB major who had crossed over in Tokyo, Anatoliy Shevchenko, who had been a deputy undersecretary of the United Nations, and the MiG pilot, Viktor Belyenko, who had landed his plane in Hokkaido. All, like her husband, were Ukrainians. She had been reading a book about Levchenko at the time. If he found out where any of them were, that would make him look good to the Russkies, wouldn't it?

At the office the next day, he had asked Auer if they could trace the three defectors through the CIA. Wouldn't it be a great idea to get them to lecture to the FCI unit?

As he invented this baroque reason for wanting to trace the men, his lip had trembled, and he had remembered a line from Spenser's "The Faerie Queene" that he had read at Brigham Young:

> *Oh what a tangled web we weave*
> *When first we practice to deceive*

People in police work and especially in intelligence were supposed to be able to lie glibly, but it was never quite as easy to lie to colleagues. In fiction, Len Deighton's Bernard Samson could deceive Bret Renssalaer, his superior, for the good of the cause, and be ultimately justified by his success, but it had been almost a relief when Gary had turned down Miller's suggestion.

There had been a final meeting with 'Lana, not authorized, on June 10, two weeks before her departure for Moscow. By then, he had been having doubts about her himself. Perhaps

Gary and John were right. Perhaps she was just a confidence artist after all.

She had left for Moscow on June 24 and returned exactly a month later. Unexpectedly, on August 2, she had called and asked for him at Westwood. He had been filling in for another agent at Santa Ana, so a colleague gave her that number. She had called Santa Ana, saying she wanted to see him again. He had agreed. Then he had conferred with Gary Auer, who'd said she'd been trying to get John Hunt since she returned, but Hunt had decided not to return her calls. Gary had authorized one more meeting to find out what she wanted, so R.W. had had dinner with her the following night.

It was then that she had told him that she had been debriefed in Moscow by an intelligence figure called Anatoliy, who had asked if her friend John Hunt still wanted to talk to someone in Soviet intelligence. Of course, he had said at once that he would take John's place; that was when he had decided again to proceed on his own. The two of them had discussed what sort of approach might stimulate her contacts in San Francisco. How far could he go in pretending to help them in order to win their confidence? How far had Pistone gone? Heaven only knew what Pistone had had to do to appear to be a good soldier in the Mafia. Surely he had had to beat up some people, extort money, even screw some compliant chicks. Some people had all the luck.

Svetlana had also suggested that he get her an FBI personnel list, with telephone numbers and assignments. Was the Rezidentura's out of date? he wondered. Or was this a test?

Or did they perhaps really not have one? Getting an FBI personnel list seemed like an excellent idea, he thought. There was probably one in every major newspaper office in the country, and he felt certain that the Soviet embassy in Washington had a recent copy. But if he stamped "Secret" on a copy and gave it to 'Lana for them, it would look like an offer in good faith. They had talked about other documents. So that she wouldn't ask for anything really sensitive, he had said that sort of stuff was kept in closed files, even in safes. She had asked him if he could break into Bretzing's safe! At the time, she had been as high as a kite, so he had said: "For a couple of million dollars, sure." But despite the badinage, he had been encouraged again. It really looked as though she was trying to recruit him for the Russkies! She had told him she would get twenty-five thousand dollars from the Russians for putting him into contact with them. John had said that he had been unable to decide where her first allegiance lay, and R.W. had come to the same conclusion. He would treat her, for all intents and purposes, as an enemy agent, and proceed accordingly. And he would have to try to be more romantic. More like John.

It had been during a dinner at the Charthouse in Malibu that the question of what the Russians might want—for him, what would be enough to get the gaffe in, without being swallowed by the shark—had come up again. It was August 5. She had been loaded once more. She had even repeated to him her boast to Bryce Christensen—that she had the rank of major in the KGB. He had taken this to be her hyped way of saying that she had been authorized by the Russians to make him proposals. Between the steak and the dessert, she had said: "Would you work for the Soviet Union?" Of course, he had played along, had said that he was interested. She had asked what sort of remuneration he would need. Obviously, he had had to ask for something, and it had to be neither too low nor too high to be unrealistic. He had hit on the figure of fifty thousand dollars, in Kruger-rands, in deposit boxes in three different banks, with receipts, making it clear who had deposited the gold. At first, he'd envisaged ingots, like golden Mars bars in a tray. The rands and especially the receipts would lay an evidentiary trail, if it was later decided to proceed against the Soviet agents who paid the gold. Two nights later, August 7, at another dinner, he had asked her if she could set up a meeting with a Russian official with whom he could discuss all this. She had been very inebriated by then, and had said that she would set up the meeting that very night. The agent, she had said, was waiting for him at her apartment.

In his Isuzu, he had followed her Mercury Lynx to 1155 Gardner Street. There, she had introduced him to a middle-aged man who had been sleeping, which was not surprising—it was nearly 1 a.m. She said his name was Nikolaiy Wolfson. He was drowsy but polite, dressed in a bathrobe. R.W. had made gestures to show that he knew the apartment was bugged by the FBI, and Wolfson had made gestures to show that he understood. They had gone downstairs to the garage underneath the building. He had told Wolfson he wanted to meet someone in

Soviet intelligence, but not in California. He had suggested Mexico. In Mexico, he knew, he would not need a passport. He could do everything in a day or so. He could speak the language. Grayson could track him. The man, Wolfson, had merely said: "Ya, ya," as though R.W. could call his own tune. R.W. had said that he would bring useful documents. Wolfson had seemed to be impressed. R.W. had repeated the figure of fifty thousand dollars in gold. He would probably have to hand over that, or most of it, to the FBI. He had also asked for fifteen thousand dollars in cash, to cover his and Svetlana's expenses in Mexico. And, of course, the Miller family debts. Wolfson seemed to agree to that as well, because he said: "Ya, ya." R.W. concluded that Wolfson already knew about everything, that he was an important figure who didn't waste time on details. It had certainly looked as though the hook was in.

It was 2 a.m. Wolfson had gone back upstairs, presumably to finish sleeping, and R.W. had driven straight back to Westwood, his head in a whirl of satisfaction. In the FBI office, he had put the name "Wolfson, Nikolaiy" into the computer to see what they knew about him.

When the computer answered, R.W. had smacked his brow with fury, feeling in his pocket for a Babe Ruth to still his nerves. John had recorded that "Wolfson, Nikolaiy" was the original family name of Ogorodnikov, Nikolaiy—Svetlana's husband. Ogorodnikov was the name of Nikolaiy's maternal aunt's husband, whose name Nikolaiy had been taken during the war so as not to become "Jewish labor" during the Nazi occupation. In two years, John had never reported on him. Nikolaiy's only known link with the Soviet consulate-general was that he was Svetlana's husband.

Once again, it looked as though 'Lana wasn't serious about trying to do for him what she had supposedly tried to do for John—that she only fantasized, when she was drunk, and her complaisant husband went along with her fantasies. In the morning, R.W. had called 'Lana up from Lynwood and bawled her out for deceiving him. He had said he wanted never to see her again.

Three days later, she had called him back; she had wanted him to escort her to a dinner at the house of friends. She had said she had news for him. He had relented.

(The hosts of the party turned out to be Vladimir Ratchikin and Ludmila Kondratjeva. The woman had come to the U.S. in 1979, and she and Ratchikin had been living together since 1981. Much later, when R.W. and Svetlana were both in prison, they were to learn that Ratchikin had choked the Kondratjeva woman to death and pushed her VW Dasher off the cliffs into the Pacific surf to simulate an accident. Unfortunately for him, however, he had left his murdered mistress on the back seat instead of the driver's seat. But on the night of the dinner, the lovers seemed happy, and Svetlana seemed pleased with what she had done.)

Her news was that she had passed on Miller's suggestions to the right places. Over the next day or so, they had had several meetings—on the *Queen Mary* at Long Beach, at restaurants in Monterey Park and Malibu, at her apartment, and at Lynwood. He had shown her a copy of part of a low-security briefing guide that FBI agents are given to teach them how to handle suspect foreigners. The 1984 issue had appeared that day. The guidance had been about as un-secret a document as he could think of, but it had the advantage of having "Secret" stamped on it because it was not intended for public circulation. However, 'Lana had not been impressed. Reading was not her forte, anyway. And so he had had the idea of The Letter, in Russian, to Belyakov. He would tell her what he wanted to say, and she would write it. For the boy from nowhere that he was, it was what you did—you made an application. It was what he had done when he had wanted to be made the resident agent in Santa Ana. It was probably, he thought rightly, something John Hunt hadn't thought of doing. His hopes up again, he had called Larry Grayson.

First, he had got Larry's message tape, imitating Stepin Fetchit telling his baass dat d'phone were ringing; should he take a message? Finally, he had got Larry in person, and they had set up the meeting at Denny's that had taken place that day.

He remembered how Larry, who was a pretty cool customer, had been staggered when he had told the private detective about the surveillance that he wanted. Well, he was still a bit staggered himself. Would he have the nerve to go through with it? What had Pistone had to have the nerve to go through with? He could see the headlines in the *Los Angeles Times*: FBI AGENT CRACKS. . . . He could see the commendation, perhaps a book, even a film. But he mustn't count his chickies before they hatched, he warned himself. That reminded him that there was still some fried chicken in the icebox downstairs.

# Chapter Five

## *The Feds*

*The Westwood office would have made an interior decorator cry, but it was not supposed to put a roof over such unseemly behavior by special agents.*

It was the following day. The windows of Special Agent-in-Charge Richard Bretzing's office on the sixteenth floor of the building that housed the FBI headquarters in Westwood looked out onto leafy Wilshire Boulevard. Up the street, he could see the University of California. A very tall, bespectacled man, his blond graying hair combed to the side like Grishin's to hide the same balding patch, Bretzing had the cold stare of a martinet; but he smiled and looked up as he heard the perfunctory knock and the simultaneous opening of the door. His deputy, J. Bryce Christensen, came in and sat in the chair on the opposite side of Bretzing's desk.

"It's about R.W.," he said. Christensen always came to the point at once.

Bretzing nodded. It was partly true, as so many of the other agents were always saying, that an agent as bad as Miller would not have been given so many second chances had Miller not been a Mormon like Bretzing and Christensen. On its face, to put someone of Miller's proclivity for goofing off into the Russian Squad was like carelessly leaving money on your bedside table in a cheap motel for the maids to find. But he and Bryce had put him there because they were in Mormon too. If that was favoritism, well, it was the favoritism that one extended toward a family member. But by the same token, Bretzing and Christensen had punished Miller like stern fathers—even though they were all about the same age—not spoiling the child by sparing the rod, but believing that with the help of God, they could carry this lost sheep to some valley where he could finally do justice to his talents, however limited they were, absolve his transgressions, and preserve his family in Mormon.

"Don't tell me he's selling circus tickets on commission again? Amway products? Has he at least got his weight down?"

Christensen shook his head negatively to all of this.

"He appears to be taking on a double-agent op that Hunt was ordered to drop."

"Svetlana Ogo-what's-her-face? We weren't sure if she was ours or theirs."

"Exactly. John figured he'd put her into an impossible situation where she'd be, well, vulnerable to their pressures. You'll recall she tried to resume her 'Marie' role with John and he gave her the pink slip. More than once. Well, at that point, it seems R.W. figured he'd see if he couldn't develop her himself."

Bretzing sighed; his eyes looked to the ceiling for guidance, then back at Christensen. The deputy went on: "It's true that he's better, or less bad, working with informants, especially flaky ones, because he makes them feel at home. Gary authorized one meeting, then a second, but we think there were probably others before she went to Moscow in June. Now, she's back, and he's at it again."

"Is she attractive?"

"Matter of taste, but I think that's probably part of the motivation. As you know, he's been largely taken off field work since three years ago, when he was moved from Riverside." He didn't say it, but both men knew he'd been moved from Riverside so that they could exercise some Mormon discipline on him, or try to. His supervisor at Riverside, Ronald Heller, had complained about Miller's paperwork. Then, there had been the less respectable mishaps: He had lost the satellite office's Mobil credit card, and for a week some happy hidalgo from the wetback community had been charging the diesel oil for his veggie truck to the FBI. Worse, he had left the alarm keys in the door when he went off one night, and the office had been unsecured until dawn. Thank God, the *Los Angeles Times* hadn't gotten wind of that.

"His weight?"

Bretzing remembered the caper with diuretics, of clipping the fat fool two weeks' pay.

Christensen raised his eyebrows to say: "No hope."

The phone buzzed quietly. Bretzing picked it up, listening briefly. "I'll see you in—" he looked at Christensen questioningly, and Christensen held up ten fingers for ten minutes—"five or six minutes." He put down the black receiver.

Christensen said: "His promotions are frozen. He's been threatened with dismissal many times for inadequate performance and, uh, unacceptable obesity. Basically, as you know, we've been trying to find a way for him to justify his existence for two more years, when he'll be fifty." That was the minimal age for a normal retirement with pension. Both men knew that Miller had a large family, that his moonlighting had been to pay debts or make ends meet.

The two agents' thoughts converged. "He has emotional problems," Bretzing said. He was a Mormon bishop, and he had a sacerdotal duty to comprehend human frailty, even if he were a cop. "I know that's a bureaucratic euphemism. Out on the street, they'd say he was a nut case. Well, FBI agents deal with those every week."

"It takes one to catch one," Christensen grinned.

Hoover would have twirled in his tomb, but today the FBI, like the CIA, had resident psychiatrists, people who could listen to your eyes-only phobias or classified dreams. In 1982, the in-house shrink had recommended that Miller be removed from all sensitive work. He had also said that R.W. might suffer a relapse, which was shrinkese for a mental breakdown, if he were continually pressed about his obesity. That was why Auer had agreed to take him onto the Russian Squad, the front line in the cold war between Westwood and Djerzhinsky Square, because he could keep him on "inside" work, which was usually not stressful.

Christensen went on: "That two-week suspension in April really got to him, apparently."

"Chapter Eleven?" Bretzing asked sardonically.

"Actually, his immediate financial problems are nothing much. According to our credit check, the computer says about five or six thousand bucks, nearly half of it credit card, which he can take years and years to pay. No, it was an emotional thing."

"That's what he said about his adultery! So if we really mess up a case, should we tell the director: 'My wife threw an ashtray at me?'"

"You know John Justice?" Christensen was naming one of the younger agents; it was impossible to expect Bretzing to remember all the names—there were two hundred sixty-two agents and over five hundred support staff in Westwood. But Bretzing nodded.

"Well, Justice says that the day you sent him up the yardarm for two weeks, he came into the squad room sobbing."

"Whaaat?"

The Westwood office would have made an interior decorator cry, but it was not supposed to put a roof over such unseemly behavior by special agents. Its endless corridors of offices, with internal partitions, could have belonged in any American bureaucracy, except that there was no relief anywhere to the impression that a staff member got—that he or she was a mouse or a guinea pig that had been captured and confined to the laboratories of the National Institutes of Health. The walls bore no posters of Abaco or the Grand Canyon, no cutesy cartoons taped up by secretaries. Even family photos were discouraged. And these offices were for the privileged, the samurai. For the ronin, there was the squad room to which Christensen had referred; but the term "squad room" suggests something more comradely than it was. It was just endless desks and telephones, a three-dimensional backdrop to some odd Menotti opera, with not even low-screen privacy. It wasn't the place for a 48-year-old SA who had just been disciplined by the special agent-in-charge to sniffle like a first-grader.

"He was quite bitter," said Christensen. "He talked of leaving the Bureau. He talked of leaving his family. He said he was always being nagged at work and at home."

Bretzing shook his head. In a quarter century of FBI service, he had occasionally heard of younger or female agents looking moist-eyed at a funeral, but never of an agent crying to other agents.

"Anyone else watch this performance?"

"Yep. Nancy Smith. She says he was shaking his head back and forth and saying: 'They didn't have to do this to me.' The 'they' of course was us. Rudy Valdez saw it too. He calls R.W. the Moping Mormon. Anyway, it wasn't for long. Then, Miller went back down to The Farm. But, apparently, he was still carrying on down there. He said he was bored with the transcribing work."

"Well, whose fault is that? Who was he blowing his mouth at, on The Farm?"

"One of the clerks, girl called Marianna Jones."

"I'm sure someone, somewhere, would say we should be more sensitive to him. But this is not the Salvation Army, this is the FBI! No one forced him to join!"

"Anyway, my point was that, in his present frame of mind, with his financial problems and the like, we think he's vulnerable, if he goes on seeing the Russian woman, especially as he's doing it without permission."

"Suspicious," Bretzing agreed.

"His marriage is on the rocks," Christensen said. "And who knows what the Russkies might not have picked up on our phones." It was accepted that the consulate-general in San Fran could hack into about a hundred lines per day, and that the Westwood office must be a popular place to fish. There were plenty of secure lines, of course, but an agent with personal problems would probably be discussing these on an open line with his wife or bookie.

"The Russian woman's husband was part of the Jewish Wave, no?" Bretzing said. "Lots of spies in that emigration."

"They'd tell them: 'Do a little work for us, we'll speed things along.' So, the more Jewish emigrants we insisted they send, the more spies they got to insert."

"A lot of real KGB inserts, some Jews, some pretending to be. The CIA says the Mossad is penetrated like a sieve."

"Ogorodnikovs, negative," Christensen said in jargon. The deputy special agent-in-charge looked serious. He really only smiled when Bretzing did, or was about to do so. Even outside the office, he still spoke in Bureau vocabulary. Bretzing had heard the office joke about Christensen: That his wife thought she was married to a prerecorded announcement. It was only with Bretzing, his brother in Mormon, that Bryce relaxed at all. He said of the Ogorodnikovs: "He's an old con. She's very spacy."

"Is R.W. having an affair with her?"

"Looks like it. He spends weeknights at his dad's old house in Lynwood."

Bretzing nodded. He remembered that one of Miller's problems was that he had recently lost his father.

"Bachelor pad?"

"You could call it that."

"What about her?"

"She wanted to marry John Hunt."

"Yeah. Heard about that. Not happy with the husband."

"Not happy, period. Homesick."

"All the Russians miss the cultural life." He looked over his shoulder, up the street, toward UCLA. Even Christensen thought it was an oddly sensitive remark for a man like Bretzing.

"They miss womb-to-tomb welfare—free medicine, good education, full employment. They feel insecure, as well as homesick," Christensen said.

"The paternalistic crucible of a socialist society."

"Come again?"

"Something I heard in a sermon once. So! Two malcontents, R.W. and Svetlana. Made for each other? But shouldn't lovers complement each other?"

"Well, he eats too much and she drinks too much. And I'd like to point out, to come back to where we started, that Zaydzev, our friendly neighborhood spymaster, has a past in controlling Jewish Russian spies. Mostly in the Middle East, of course."

"CIA say that?"

"Yes, but of course we're talking of two real noodles, here. However, they've often been outspokenly critical of the United States."

"Don't I recall they did some small stuff?"

"When I was in charge of FCI-1 myself, I remember that the husband took pictures of an anti-Soviet demonstration, outside a high school, apparently because San Fran wanted to see which *émigrés* were taking part. And they asked a few people if they knew of the whereabouts of Stanislav Levchenko, a fellow Ukrainian."

"The spook who defected."

"Right. KGB major. Tokyo."

"But you think San Fran might be running our swallow against us? They usually recruit people like that abroad, not here. Didn't she tell John pretty much everything about her escort work? That doesn't seem very naughty—the Russkies have this 25-mile limit, which makes it hard for them to leave

San Fran. I suppose they need some people here who speak Russian."

"The Ogorodnikovs get rewards—tourist visas to see their families, and their kid goes to a youth camp for little apparatchiks. Once, she went with some consuls to try to persuade an Armenian Russian, Karine Madevossian, not to ask for asylum here. The woman had run away from her husband, a Soviet official in Belgium. He wanted her back. She could return home without reprisals. It wasn't really a political case. And she drove a vice consul, Viktor Zenov, to Anaheim to bail out a Soviet student who had been arrested for shoplifting." Christensen paused, and went on. "Our intelligence colleagues in the East say neither of the Ogorodnikovs had any intelligence training, that they're not sleepers."

"Financial situation?"

"Small, shabby, rented home. Once, they spent all their savings—fifteen thou—on a Russian dumpling machine, but it broke down. They seem to be about as inept in business as our fellow."

Bretzing was tapping a pencil against his fingers. Back in the 1920s, Hoover had had this idea that every agent should have a tumblerful of sharpened pencils on his desk. Even with the invention of the ball-point pen and the mini-recorder, the forests of pencils remained, like little quivers of penises, reminding G-men of their duty. Tapping pencils was Bretzing's equivalent of lighting up a cigarette, like Miller's Milky Ways and the gum chewed by the Hispanic agents.

"Her handler was Hunt," he said.

"Yes, what I was getting around to was—"

"I've got someone due here in a moment. Find out if Hunt's free later today, and bring him in." What sounded like a request was, of course, an order in all but name. His voice had an air that said: "Class dismissed."

"Aye, aye, skipper," Christensen said without complaint.

Bretzing had wanted time to think. In the course of his career, he had known agents who had not "made out," who'd committed improprieties, been reprimanded, sent to Siberia, or even dismissed; but Miller's case was *sui generis*. Yes, and he had to take into account that, despite his suspension from the church for fornication, Miller was a child of Mormon, and he, Bretzing, was a bishop in Mormon. And now Miller was an agent who was not just stretching the limits to catch a pusher or a white slaver, but was presumably trying to outwit the KGB as a totally unauthorized double agent, with the prospect that—since he was always looking for some way to make an extra buck—he might actually get bought, and end up as theirs, not ours.

When Christensen brought Hunt in at the end of the day, Bretzing dropped the pally style and proceeded to run the meeting as a general would a staff session. He set the tone by not smiling, saying simply: "Hunt? Glad you could make it." When the two visitors were seated, he said briskly: "We're talking about Miller, that's *Richard* Miller, and Mrs. Ogorodnikova." He made a point of getting the Russian name right. "You first developed her two years ago, right?"

"Sir. I made a stab at her back in 1980," Hunt responded. "It was on June 18 that year." He was not reading notes. He was doing what an agent is supposed to do: Talking from the computer between his ears. He had prepped himself for this meeting. "Agent Robert Patton and I called on her after she had acted as driver for Vice Consul Zenov when he went to Anaheim."

Bretzing nodded. "The case of the Soviet student who got arrested."

"That is correct. We asked her if she would provide us with information from time to time. She asked for time to think. We gave her our cards. She never called. We just kept an eye on her and left it at that. In 1982, I tried again. She had just been to the Soviet Union. She acted as though she had never seen me before. She's spacy; she may well have forgotten the whole brief conversation with Patton and me."

"You approached her on your own?"

"I thought it might be less intimidating. I left my wing man in the car."

"When was this, exactly?"

"February 1982, sir."

"This time, you recruited her."

"Well, not at once. She had to be courted. She finally accepted to work for the Bureau on May 26, at a meeting where she and I talked alone in the parking lot of the Hollywood branch of Sears. She was fairly open about her work in chauffeuring Zenov. She admitted she had taken a Soviet consular official, Kurov, to see the Madevossian woman. You remember?"

"Yes."

"She said that she had given my card to the consulate-general."

"When?"

"Sir?"

"When had she given them your card—1980?"

"No, sir, it would be in February, I guess, February 1982, when I chatted with her at the building. But it might have been 1980. So, yes, the other side knew about my approach, and they'd had time to find out what they could about me, I guess."

"You guess." Bretzing's tone was gently sardonic. "How many people do they have up there?"

"A consul-general, five consuls, eleven vice consuls. Plus a staff of about thirty. That's about the size of the European Community delegation in Washington."

"Hmmm." Bretzing nodded. "Carry on."

"We had several meetings. I think you've seen the log. Her code name was Marie."

"As we understand it, Miller's relations with her go perhaps beyond the purely professional. What's her behavior?"

"Sir, I was coming to that. Shortly after we took her on, it was June 6, 1982, to be exact, I escorted her, at her request, to the Yesterdays Restaurant and then on to the Simply Blues nightclub at Sunset and Vine. When we came out, she threw her arms around my neck and said she loved me. She wanted me to take her to a hotel."

"Of course you'd done nothing to encourage this, right? Just asking questions and taking notes?"

Hunt flushed. "Sir, I'd danced with her. As I explained, when I'd asked where she would like to go, she'd said this club. I let her order what she wanted. When we came out, she was as high as a kite."

"How's your wife, Hunt?"

"Sir, I was coming to that. When I got home, I told Earlene what had happened."

"Did Mrs. Hunt know where you were?"

"I'd called her from the club and told her what I was doing, and that I'd be late."

"Carry on."

"Marie called the next day and apologized for her behavior outside the nightclub. She said she'd been drunk. At our next meeting, she brought me a gift. A tie. I was authorized to give her something in exchange, and Earlene selected for me a silk scarf and a pearl necklace."

Bretzing scowled, deliberately concealing the grin that had come to his lips at the thought of Hunt getting his wife to select the gifts for "Marie." Old John had certainly covered his ass, both at home and at the office! There had been reports from *émigré* informants that Hunt had made love to Mrs. Ogorodnikova in her apartment, but they had never been substantiated.

"You ran her as a tentative swallow, with Washington's approval, I recall."

"The Russkies knew I'd been seeing her. I told her what to say—that I was a playboy cop. They chastised her—some vice consul did. He told her to have nothing to do with me, that she was taking too big a risk. Then, they asked for proof that she really had a fed on a string, and they told her to tickle me along, after all. She told them I was pestering her for information. She reported back to me everything they said to her. They asked her to work for them. I'd expected that. I had more or less told her to accept any offer."

"You dropped her in 1983."

"Sir, I had determined that her loyalties were uncertain, her information often unreliable and inadequate. I had in fact merely used her to run some disinformation into the consulate-general."

"But a true double-agent operation was never authorized. That would have called for a decision as to what true pearls we could cast before them."

"I was just testing the weather."

"After you dropped her, it was she who tried to restore her link with the Bureau."

Christensen, with a glance at Hunt, said: "She called me on—uh—July 6, 1983. She behaved like a woman scorned. She was complaining about J—uh, Hunt."

"Complaining?"

"She said Mrs. Hunt was harassing her on the telephone because Hunt was in love with her."

"All this because you danced together in nightclubs?"

"Sir, I had to lead her along a bit," Hunt said, confidently. "I can assure you that I never—"

"Don't assure me of anything. You're not under investigation. The people under investigation are Mrs. Ogorodnikova and especially our gargantuan colleague. Anyway, she wanted to renew her association with you."

"Yes, sir. It was in 1983; she'd been to Russia again, and they'd checked on her 'seeing' me. Her husband had been back there, too. Eventually, I did meet her again for dinner in a restaurant. I was accompanied by another agent."

"I think I remember. Who was it?"

"Smith. Nancy Smith."

"Bringing along a woman agent was to dampen her ardor."

"And to enable her to speak to another woman. I thought it might help. She told Smith that, on my instructions, she had informed the consulate-general that I was her lover. What I'd actually suggested was that she let them think she had a boyfriend in the FBI."

"Well, in dictionary English, and I suppose in Russian, that's lover."

"Sir, this was a disinformation thing. I was trying to see what sort of reaction they would have."

"No problem. So, what happened?"

"Nancy told her she was a very pretty woman, and I agreed. We didn't want her as an enemy. I had been trying to develop her as our asset. Anyway, we decided not to proceed any further with her on these lines. We just urged her to call us if she had any information she thought we might like to have."

Christensen said: "She called often. We didn't know quite what to do about her. This year—March, I don't have the date in my head—I met with her and Hunt in a coffee shop. The idea was to keep her on our side, but no more. I thanked her for the risks she had taken on our behalf. But we decided—Auer, Hunt, myself, everyone—that there was uncertainty over her allegiance."

Hunt said: "Obviously, I'd put her in an invidious situation with the Rezidentura."

"And with her husband, one would suppose."

"Well, she said it was all over, there. Anyway, she kept calling. I decided not to return her calls. By May, I was having all calls from her to me routed to Auer as the head of the Russian unit. He sent Rudy Valdez and another agent to interview her. She told them that the KGB had finally responded to what you might call my 'boyfriend' approach. She told Rudy the KGB was now prepared to ask me to work with them. They wanted, she said, to invite me to a meeting abroad. Anyway, after a few days, she called Miller."

"Why would anyone call Miller? I thought he called her."

Christensen said: "Miller said she initiated the calls. We honestly don't know which came first, the chicken or the egg. I think he'd known about her since 1980. Probably, he called her. Perhaps he returned one of the calls she had made unsuccessfully to Hunt. Anyway, I think you know the sequence—the first meeting between Miller and her, which Auer authorized, and so on, before she went to Russia on what was virtually her annual visit."

Bretzing took off his glasses. The gesture in this stiff and rather formal man was not lost on his two underlings. It meant he did not want to see them, he wanted to think. They fell silent. Christensen and Hunt looked out of the window, purposely glancing away from Bretzing so as not to distract his thoughts. Two chicken hawks wheeled in the gloaming California sky as though looking for two victims.

Finally, Bretzing put his glasses back on, and went back to the subject of Svetlana's marital difficulties.

"She had fallen in love with you."

"I suppose that's what had happened."

"You suppose." Bretzing paused. "Why didn't you suggest that another agent be assigned to her?"

"I did. But she didn't want to be passed on from hand to hand. So I introduced her to my wife, even to my grandchildren."

Bretzing wondered what she had made of that. Cold douche? Concubine's approval by the senior wife?

Christensen said: "She was always complaining about you, right? And she hit the bottle."

"True," Hunt said. "After I closed her out. Last year. She would scream on the phone. I had to go twice to the home of a friend of hers to cool her down."

"Poor you. You said you had put her in an invidious position," Bretzing said.

"Sir? She was on the griddle, you might say. She wanted the visas, the films, the right for Matvei—that's her son—to go to this camp in the Crimea. As far as I was concerned, her file was closed."

"And Miller? You encouraged him to take her over."

"Not really, sir. Frankly—I have said it before—I don't think Miller should be on the squad at all."

Bretzing said: "Last month, she made another stab at resuming relations with you, Hunt, and—no, don't read anything into my word 'relations'—and started a series of assignations with Miller, right? Which were unauthorized so far as he was concerned. So now it looks as though Miller is having his last hurrah with the Bureau by trying to re-launch your 'boyfriend' ploy with the Rezidentura, and I have some picture of Mrs. Ogorodnikova. I'm just wondering whether she isn't supremely indifferent as to whether you, Hunt, or Miller 'penetrate' the KGB, or whether you or he are 'turned' by that organization." He paused. "What do you think of that?"

Christensen nodded. "She told us she was a major in the KGB, so obviously she wasn't. She even said she had slept with Yuri Andropov when he was head of the KGB. She's, well—spacy." Hunt seemed to be agreeing with Bretzing, too; Bretzing hoped they weren't being sycophantic.

Hunt said: "She's a loose cannon."

"And Miller's a loose cannon," said Christensen. "The question is, given his background: Can he be bought?"

"Or, if he can't be bought, can he be hired for the afternoon?" asked Bretzing, authorizing himself to smile briefly. There would have to be a surveillance of Miller, his goings and comings, his telephone calls. And that would require a court order. It had never been done before, so far as he knew: the FBI asking for permission to bug its own offices. He thought to himself: In a simpler world, a movie, I'd set up an audiovisual surveillance of Miller meeting the Reds.

He didn't know that Miller had had exactly the same idea— and had just done something about it.

# Chapter Six

# The "Researchers" II

*Lipset had swept the boat for them so that "even God cannot overhear." Kitano had wondered, when that was said, whether Lipset had been archly referring to himself.*

Killer and Alf were looking from the deck at the choppy water, and remembering the tunnel they had tried to dig under the consulate-general. Both of them still half-believed in the tunnel plan. However, Hal Lipset, the veteran bugging specialist in Oakland–whose name had become a household one in America because of the myth that he had bugged a martini olive and used the toothpick as an antenna–had been against the tunnel idea. Both Merman and Kitano had admired Lipset so much—Kitano used to address him as "Hi, God!"—that they had gone along, eventually, with his advice to bug the roof instead. Lipset had said that the microwave horns had a better chance of transmitting from there. Neither Alf nor Killer could know that Lipset would tell his friends: "Those Occidental people were looking for a communist under every bed, so naturally they preferred to be under, not above!" In his cups, nonetheless, Kitano would say things like: "I still have the Green Street dirt under my fingernails! It's there forever!"

Alf and Killer would be in their cups quite often. One of the things they detested about the FBI was how they arranged meetings: A tradition that the old whiskey-scoffing hypocrite J. Edgar Hoover had created was the Bureau's predilection for weak, industrial coffee in places like Wendy's or Colonel Sander's. Alf Merman would say: "Suppose you dropped down dead in Harry's Bar in Venice? You would always be remembered well. But imagine it being recounted that you had collapsed in a Wendy's cafeteria!"

The "researchers" still hadn't told Justice or its FBI subsidiary about Svetlana's *spravka*, her "bursts" in a KGB file. Merman and Kitano were convinced that she really was a field or penetration agent and that Nikolaiy, like those little male spiders which live on the body of the mother insect until she eats them, was her support agent. This scenario had not come from the Rezidentura microwave traffic, but from some of the cousins in Europe with whom Occidental Research was linked. These cousins had even produced Svetlana's alleged earlier *spravka*. They said that she had been selected while in high school, that her marriage to Nikolaiy had been arranged by the KGB. The cousins even claimed that Nikolaiy had originally been chosen as a field agent, too, but had succumbed to "sting" temptations while in training and had been defrocked. As a consequence, the story went, he was condemned to be an eternal private, serving as dogsbody to his spouse.

Now, Killer and Alf were sitting on Alf's boat, off Alcatraz. Lipset had swept the boat for them, so that "even God cannot overhear." Kitano had wondered, when that was said, whether Lipset had been archly referring to himself.

He heard Merman say: "D'you think Hunt knows that we've milked the 'Lana-Zaydzev traffic?"

"Only if Newman has told Bretzing, which wouldn't be likely even if Newman knew. And how could Newman know?"

"So that dumb flatfoot in L.A. doesn't know he's been to bed with a KGB major?"

"How could he? She wouldn't tell him, would she!" Kitano said.

"Or that she's been balled by Andropov!"

"It's enough to put you off sex for life," smiled Kitano, showing all of his teeth.

# Chapter Seven

# *The Swallow*

*What was it that Marx had said? That God was the aspirin of the mob?*

She was a little drunk, as usual, and Nikolaiy would complain when he came home from the wholesale butchery. But so what? He was becoming more American. He didn't beat her as much as he had done, back in Kiev. And even her mother had said that she was the sort of girl who needed a beating from time to time.

She had called John Hunt to report on what she was doing with Miller. She was really John's swallow, not Richard's. She would always be John's swallow. He had told her she was his Mata Hari and that he would give her Mata Hari's code identification of H21; but her real FBI code-name was Marie. She wasn't sure why the FBI was spying on the FBI, but John had told her to report to him on all her meetings with Richard. Yet Richard had said he was taking over John's work. Were they not friends? It seemed that policemen, like crooks, did not trust each other. And they would never really tell her what they were doing.

Truth to tell, Svetlana Ogorodnikova was tired of working for, and sleeping with, the FBI. Now, she was going to have just one more drink at Mischa's, and then she would go home to Nikolaiy and Matvei, their thirteen-year-old son. Nikolaiy always said that she was not a good mother, that she went out with too many people and stayed out too late; but really she loved Matvei.

She did not believe that Nikolaiy would ever succeed in America. And she would never succeed if she stayed with Nikolaiy. But even if she never succeeded, Matvei would succeed. If only John was not slipping away from her! Had slipped.

Could she do anything with Richard? She would be seeing Richard the following evening. Belyakov had repeated the offer of twenty-five thousand dollars if a link with Miller was established. And Nikolaiy said Miller had told him that he wanted sixty-five thousand dollars in all. All those zeros appealed to her.

Back at the apartment, she found Nikolaiy and Matvei waiting, talking. There was less trouble than she had expected. She heated up some food and served them in the living room, then went to eat in the kitchen, the way Nikolaiy's mother had taught her to do in Kiev. In the kitchen, she would hear Matvei talking, Nikolaiy's urgent, piping answers. She wouldn't sleep with him tonight. He was always complaining that she drank too much, just like her father, and that she smoked. Strangely for a Ukrainian, Nikolaiy had never smoked. She would sleep on the couch in the living room, and let Matvei share his father's bed.

By midnight, all was quiet in the apartment. Nikolaiy, poor man, was always tired from his mindless job, chopping up animals, and he slept well. Both her "menfolk" were now asleep in the bedroom of the shabby little apartment on Gardner Street. She watched a little television, staring at the commercials as though they were entertainment, too, and now she was drinking and smoking herself to sleep. Outside, it was as quiet as it would ever be. The sounds of cars, buses and uncouth shouts were more spaced out than they had been earlier. It was quiet enough for her to think. She thought of Yefrimov.

Yefrimov was a sprawling village—a town by American standards—in Tula province, south of Moscow. She had been born there on May 10, 1950. She could not remember her father. She was told that one day he had gone off to work and had not returned. And then her mother was told that he had died. At the time, Svetlana had been only two years old. Whenever she asked about her father, people would always preface their response by saying that he drank too much. But what did that mean? What man in Russia did not drink too much? People like Khrushchev and Brezhnev were always stumbling drunk, and no one minded. Her mother had been left to raise the little girl and her elder brother. To share the task, she had taken up with a German prisoner-of-war, one of those whom Stalin had forced to stay in Russia and rebuild what the Germans had destroyed. Svetlana didn't remember much about the German, either, but his association with her mother must have been a good idea. He must have been very lonely, this man who had been forced to stay away from his home, not for any fault of his own, but because of where he had been born. And there was such a shortage of Russian men, after the war, that no able-bodied Russian male was going to offer the gift of himself to a country widow with two children. But the other children had teased her about her German "daddy."

Then, eventually, he had been allowed to return home to Germany. By then, she had been about five. Her mother had had to work hard to raise the children alone. Of course, her mother's parents had helped. She had spent a lot of her childhood with her grandmother.

There hadn't seemed much to look forward to in Yefrimov. In 1967, when she had been seventeen, she had set off for Kiev, the biggest city of the south and the capital of the Ukraine, to study for a certificate in cardiac technology. She had always thought that would be a nice job, medical technician. You wore a white uniform and people treated you with respect. She had wanted a life better than her mother's. Her mother had been only forty-four when Svetlana had gone to Kiev, but Svetlana had known that her mother's life was already over. Svetlana had wanted to be somebody. She had not wanted to go back to Yefrimov. She had made up her mind that she would stay in Kiev, or perhaps go to Moscow. Emigration was virtually forbidden in Russia, so that was even more attractive. If she had been able to select where to live, the first choice would have been Hollywood. Hollywood!

And here she was, in Hollywood, on Gardner Street, sleeping on the couch, and drinking, and homesick, not just for Kiev, but for Yefrimov. How she had dreamed of emigrating! But single women did not get exit visas. Almost the only people who ever got exit visas were Jews, because the Americans made a fuss about them. She often wondered why the Americans were not concerned about Christians. Her poor mother was a Christian. But so what?

It was in 1969 that she had met Nikolaiy Ogorodnikov. Now, she could hear him in the next room. He was sleeping on his back, to give Matvei more room, and so of course he was snoring, and catching his spittle in his throat, and in the morning there would be spittle at the edges of his lips. But back then, in 1969, he had been different. And he had been in love. Svetlana knew that she was not beautiful, but the few men in her life—the young kids before Nikolaiy, then Nikolaiy, then John—had said that she was pretty. Nikolaiy had liked the fact that she was very short, only five feet, because he was not much taller himself. Ever since they had been in America, they had had difficulty finding each other in crowded places.

In Kiev, she had been attracted to him at once—a handsome little man who drank in moderation, played the piano, sang, and laughed a lot. He had been a taxi driver, so he had even had a car to take Svetlana around in. No one she had ever known in Yefrimov had had a car. He had asked her to marry him. He had been thirty-seven, a real man, not just a jerk-off kid. His grandparents had been Jewish, and his parents had been brought up that way when they were very young, before the revolution. That was why she ate in the kitchen and served Nikolaiy in the living room. That was their custom, his mother had said, and she had made Svetlana follow it. Nikolaiy, like most Russians, had no religion, but because he was of Jewish descent, he was allowed to consider himself a Jew. So she had been sure that, if he tried, he could get a visa. And they could go to Hollywood! So she had said yes.

She got up from the couch and refilled her glass. Before lying down again, she turned the television on once more, but without the sound. It was an old film. Because it was in black and white, it reminded her of home. Nikolaiy stirred and coughed again. Matvei was sleeping like a baby, although with adolescents, who knew what dreams he had? At adolescence, she had had dreams that she would not recount to anyone.

She was only nineteen when she had said yes to Nikolaiy, yet her mother had seemed glad that she was going to have the security of a husband and a home. But not all her friends at the technical institute had thought much of Nikolaiy. He had been divorced. He had been to prison. Five times: robbery, burglary, and a sort of drunken seduction exaggerated into rape. It was even said that he had been involved with an American vice consul. There was a rumor that the American had been a queer, but she couldn't believe it when people said that Nikolaiy had—well. Then again, would a man who had spent most of his adult life—fourteen years—in prisons hesitate about that? She didn't want to think about it. As she lay there in the lamplight coming through the slats from Gardner Street, she felt sorry for Nikolaiy. Whatever it was that he had done, it was not his fault. At eleven, he had had to leave school, because of the war.

She sipped the cheap American brandy and thought about being forced to live with Nikolaiy's mother and his aunt. Nikolaiy might no longer be a Jew, but his mother had still been a Jewish mother, and especially a Jewish mother-in-law to her son's young wife. It was obvious that she didn't think that a medical technician from a small town, whose own mother had been an enemy prisoner's companion, was good enough for her Nikolaiy. Svetlana thought bitterly: What did she expect for a man with five prison terms and a divorce—a doctor? They had all treated her as a maid.

Out in the street, a man shouted something in rough black tones. Someone shouted back. A car revved noisily, with supreme unconcern for the hour. Svetlana sipped more brandy, feeling more and more angry at her impotence to solve life's problems.

She had had two abortions in Kiev. She had not wanted to have children until she had qualified at the institute. Nikolaiy had had other women. He had always had other women. People said that he would chase after anything that was female and still breathing. After all, he had been a taxi driver; that gave him reasons to be out at all hours. But it also gave everyone in the household a certain protection. All authoritarian regimes, of the right and the left, are corrupt, it was said. They have to be. The Kiev police relied on taxi drivers for some of their information, and they had looked the other way when he bought his young bride blue jeans and cosmetics on the black market.

She had qualified. She had been sent to a job. *Ai*! Finding a job is difficult in America, she thought. She had never found a real job in America. Perhaps she had not tried hard enough. But finding a job is not difficult in the Soviet Union. On the contrary—you could be punished for not working. But now, she had wanted a child, and in 1971, when she was twenty-one, she had had Matvei. She had told Nikolaiy that, now that they had a son, they should also have a home of their own. And Nikolaiy had said, sarcastically, how could they have that? For if finding a job was easy in the Soviet Union, finding an apartment was like looking for an honest policeman. But she had had the answer: "Let us go to America," she had said. "So far as the government is concerned, you are a Jew, so it is easy!" Later, it had become more difficult, when something in America called the Jackson-Vanik Law had provoked Moscow into stopping Jewish emigration for a while. But when Nikolaiy had applied, they had not had to wait very long. She remembered how happy she had been—for herself, for Matvei. No more mother-in-law, no more Kiev. Hollywood!

In 1973, they had flown to Vienna. From there, they were supposed to go to Israel, but of course almost nobody in the plane had wanted to do that. Nearly all of their group had flown on to Rome, where they had been lodged at a special center. An organization called the Jewish Family Service had given Svetlana and Nikolaiy tickets for New York, where they had stayed with Nikolaiy's Aunt Lisa for a few days. The organization had lent them money to get to Los Angeles and for food until Nikolaiy could find work in spite of his poor English. But there had been a setback. Uncle Sam had died.

Sam Wolfson had been Nikolaiy's father's brother. In America, he had called himself Sam Wolf. He had had a business. He had come to Kiev on a visit, and he had said that if Nikolaiy and Svetlana got to America, he would help them. But when they had come to his house in Los Angeles, his wife had answered the door and had said that Sam had died, the week before. They had known at once that they were not welcome, the gnarled convict and his young wife. The widow had barely invited them into the house. After two days, she had given them a hundred dollars, and wished them luck. They had not seen her again.

Fortunately, the Jewish Family Service had found jobs for Nikolaiy. Soon, a Jewish butcher from Hungary, Joseph Russo, had made Nikolaiy a "meat cutter" with his company, Hoffman Brothers. It was a situation such as they had never known before, quite unlike Russia. Nikolaiy's foreman, Adam Uribe, was Jewish also. They didn't seem to employ people from other religions, except for a few blacks in the totally unskilled jobs. It had all been new to Nikolaiy and Svetlana. Mr. Russo had found it odd when she and Nikolaiy had joined the Episcopal church in Silver Lake. The Jewish Family Service had found them an apartment, too. In Hollywood. Well, West Hollywood. The first thing they had learned was that nearly everyone else in the building was also Russian.

Something on the screen caught her eye. Vivien Leigh was kissing a man in officer's uniform. An American officer. Both the actress and the actor were sad, so this must be goodbye. In some ways, television was much better without the sound. You could make up your own stories. She could see that this was Europe. They were on a bridge over a river. Was someone going to commit suicide? It was foggy, so it must be London. It must also be World War II, when Russia and America had been allies. She watched the scene and the film to the end, then got up, switched the set off, and refilled her drink. In the light from the window slats, the couch looked rumpled from all the getting up and going back, the shifting around, the drinking. Perhaps she should have slept with Nikolaiy after all. She could hear him snoring, the spittle in his throat. He was fifty-two now. He was never going to get anywhere in America. Perhaps they should have stayed in Kiev.

*Ai!* What a shock everything had been in America. She thought life would be easier. But Nikolaiy had had to work harder, much harder, just to pay the rent and the bills. She had stayed at home and looked after Matvei, learning English along with him. There were child nurseries for working mothers, but they were not free, as they were in Russia. In America, it was as though everything was on the black market! And when Matvei had become old enough to go out to play, she had felt that she had to go out with him, because the streets were full of black and brown children, screaming and shouting and running wild, and she had feared for Matvei's safety. The other children would hear his accent and say that he was Russian. And they would play World War III and break his little head.

But she knew she could not go back to Russia. She was condemned to live in America, where everything seemed so much harder. Even medicine was not free. In Europe, even in Canada, she knew, medicine was paid by taxes. Not in America. The state schools did not guarantee that your child would be educated enough to go on to university; to be educated as well as in Europe, you had to pay for private schools. But how could a cutter working for a wholesale butcher pay for private schools? And there was no full employment in Western countries, except for Sweden. But the worst thing in America, she thought, was the crime, the criminals. In Russia, the people in prison were mostly wretches, but here in America they were animals. If she ever had to go to prison, she would die.

She drank some more brandy. She closed her eyes. She was beginning to feel slightly dizzy. It was said that when people were as short as she, they got drunk easily—that she was lucky, that it cost her less to get high.

When she had first seen Gardner Street, it had looked nice. There were trees. Some of the houses were pretty. They had been told that the houses and the pretty roofs were in the Spanish style. And everybody had seemed to have a car. But soon she had realized that appearance was not reality. They were still poor. And now it was worse, because they were homesick, too. Nikolaiy had said that they should not have come. He had blamed Svetlana. It had been her foolish idea to come to America, and now they could not go back. They were no longer Soviet citizens. It was not true that it was all her idea. He had wanted it, too. He had been excited. No one would know that he was an old con, in America. And Nikolaiy had said that Uncle Sam Wolfson would help them. But Uncle Sam had died, and now they had only the other Uncle Sam, the one in the silly drawings who did fuck-all for anyone.

In the apartment above, she could hear someone moving around slowly, probably going to the toilet. The other Russians in the building were not always friendly. Many had come to America years before, when getting out of Russia was more difficult. These people did not like the new wave of emigrants like Nikolaiy, who got out by the tens of thousands just by pretending they were pious Jews who wanted to make *aliya* to the Holy Land. And she knew that they also looked down on Nikolaiy because he had left school at age eleven and yet naively expected to be able to make a life in America, and to give as much money to his mother as he had done in Kiev, all with his broken English. And she knew they thought of her as a flighty girl from a village in Tula who had married a Jew because, they said, a Jew is an airplane ticket in trousers. So what was wrong with that? She sipped more brandy.

Mostly, the other Russians had wanted to tell them how disappointed *they* were in America. They had come to find a future, a new life, as she and Nikolaiy had done, and all they had found was *exile*. They had not been able to find good jobs, those who were living on Gardner Street. They resented paying for medicine and paying taxes—something they had never heard about before. They complained that it was harder to be poor in America—because so many Americans were rich. There was Hollywood just up the street! And it was hardest of all to be poor and old in America, and many of them were growing old. In exile.

A police cruiser went down the street, its siren blaring despite the hour. The lights from its roof twinkled through the blinds on the window that looked out onto the concrete corridor that overlooked Gardner Street.

From the start, Nikolaiy had always worked long hours. They had saved up and bought a car, a little Mercury. Being a butcher in a factory had been a come-down from driving a taxi; but with the car, at least he had wheels under his bottom again. Svetlana had learned to drive. She had sent her mother in Yefrimov a photo of herself at the wheel. They had bought a second-hand, upright piano. Nikolaiy could play and sing. But he had not been happy. He had worried about his mother, who was in bad health. He had not been able to visit her. They had known, when they had flown to Vienna, that this would be the case. When emigrants claiming to be Jews left Russia, they pretended that they were going to Israel, where they would become Israeli citizens right away; so the Russian government took away their Soviet nationality and forbade them ever to return. Of course, there were exceptions, but it wasn't easy. So they had not been happy. He had worked long hours, cutting up meat, and he would come home tired, and because they were not happy, they would quarrel. And when they quarreled, he would hit her. But that was not so important, she told herself. In his heart, she knew, he was a good man, a kind man, and he loved her. Was there a taxi driver in Kiev who didn't beat his wife? And she still had hope. She had watched television and she had told herself, over and over again, that America was full of people like her, simple immigrants, and some of them did very well.

A car went up the street, toward Hollywood. It was probably a convertible, she thought, because she could hear young voices raised, and laughing. She remembered how she had wanted to get out of the house. But Nikolaiy had always been tired, too tired to go out after dinner, and for a long time he had not allowed her to go out alone after dark. They had been living in

Hollywood, but in some ways they had still been in Kiev. Why would a man who insisted that his wife eat in the kitchen, Asian-style, allow her to go out alone at night? And she had to admit that, probably, he had been right. All their Russian neighbors had said that it was dangerous for a young woman to walk around in West Hollywood, alone, after dark. So she had watched a lot of television. Everybody, or almost everybody, in the shows seemed to have a much nicer home than she and Nikolaiy did. They were *American*. And she held to the thought that, even if it was too late for Nikolaiy, it was not too late for her, or for her little son, to become *American*. They would be different from the sour old Russians of Gardner Street. They would get away from this street of lost hope.

Some of the older Russian *émigrés* had turned to God. What was it that Marx had said? That God was the aspirin of the mob? There was a Russian Orthodox church in the neighborhood. But because the Russian community was so divided, many did not go there. Instead, they had joined some of the strange American so-called churches that existed in all the poor districts. She had seen some of this funny Christianity on television. *Ai*! She remembered saying to Nikolaiy: "This is religion?" There was always a lot of clapping and singing, and the priests were dressed up like pimps. Voodoo! America was very different from Europe. But she had always known that there was another America, not so poor, not so silly, where the ethnic groups didn't each stick together like flocks of Astrakhan sheep. That was the America she had come to America to find. But she wasn't going to find it with poor Nikolaiy, or lying drinking cheap brandy in a one-bedroom apartment facing onto an open-air corridor on Gardner Street.

After they had been there three years, Matvei had been five years old—old enough to go to school. They had been worried about this, and Nikolaiy had made inquiries to see if Matvei couldn't perhaps go back to Russia and attend a more serious school than the jungle schools in West Hollywood. Meanwhile, Matvei had gone to school anyway, and she had had a little more time to herself. And that was when she had thought, since she was in the cinema capital of the world, what would be more natural than to go into the film business?

*

All those homesick Russians liked seeing Russian films. So she had found out how to rent a theater or a hall, and how to rent films, and print and sell tickets. For a time, Nikolaiy and Svetlana had had a partner, Viktor Nachaev, an ice-hockey player who had defected and married an American woman. The main source of the films had been Sovexportfilm, and the main contact had been the cultural officer of the Soviet consulate-general in San Francisco, Boris Belyakov. Belyakov was a pleasant fellow, with a sense of humor. She had liked him. She thought of him as a friend, even though he would never let her have the most recent films. She had competitors, of course. They had more experience, and Belyakov favored them. But he had pointed her toward other film sources.

Svetlana still wasn't feeling very sleepy. She was inebriated, but her nerves were playing tricks again. She got up to pour more brandy. She was trying to think through what she had done, what she was going to do. She thought back to when she had started showing Russian films; that had been intended as the first step out of Gardner Street. She had become what Americans called an exhibitor, a sort of part-time movie-theater manager, an impresario *volant*. And from that time on, some of the Russians in West Hollywood had begun to show respect for her. There had been parties after the shows. She had started to make new friends. It had become a rather different life. She would attend local film festivals with people from the consulate. There had been invitations to official parties given by the consul-general. He would even murmur a word of thanks to her for helping to propagate Russian culture, because naturally not all the people who came to see the films were *émigrés*. Some were American students, learning the language. There had been intellectuals and people from the show-business world. She met Shirley Maclaine, Diana Ross, directors.

The consul-general had asked if she was prepared to be an escort for Russian visitors in southern California. Of course she had said yes. There was no pay for the work, but the visitors would pay for the meals and the drinks in nice restaurants. She would take them to beautiful places in beach resorts like Marina del Rey, where she could not have afforded to go with Nikolaiy, and where Nikolaiy would have felt out of place.

She remembered the time when, after an American peace delegation had visited the Soviet Union, a Russian delegation had come to America in return. When they had arrived in California, she had been one of the escorts. Another time, a cruise ship had arrived from Vladivostok. There had been four escorts: an American couple who spoke Russian, Svetlana, and another *émigrée* woman. They had all been invited aboard to a captain's party. Svetlana sipped brandy and remembered how much she had enjoyed the party, how different it had been from the dull existence on Gardner Street.

Because she was doing these chores for the consulate-general for nothing, she had asked Boris Belyakov if he could get a visa for her, and perhaps for Nikolaiy and Matvei, too, so that they could all visit Matvei's grandmothers in Kiev and Yefrimov. Ostensibly, she had asked for a visa for herself to visit Sovexportfilm and attend the annual film festival in Moscow. Above all, what she had wanted to do was to visit her old school friends and show off a little. She would bring back American luxuries such as toasters and electric pencil sharpeners. She would be the girl from Yefrimov who had succeeded in America. The film exhibitor.

Belyakov had said that the problem was that she didn't have a passport valid for the Soviet Union. She had only one of those little blue things that Americans call green cards and a United States Reentry Permit that said she had been born in Russia. Because Nikolaiy had claimed treatment as a Jew, she had also been treated as a Jew in order to be authorized to emigrate to Israel. So officially, she was regarded as an Israeli who had renounced the right to go back to Russia. But Belyakov had sent her to a travel agency in Beverly Hills, Beverly International Travel, which also distributed Russian films; and the owner of the agency, Diana Baskevitch, had had a copy of Svetlana's reentry permit made; and this copy had said that she had been born in Czechoslovakia. This meant that she could go to Russia because she had never been Russian! *Ai*! Mrs. Baskevitch had also changed her date of entry to America, so that the Soviet embassy in Washington could more easily grant a visa, because the new date didn't coincide with the dates of the massive Jewish emigration. Her birthday had also been altered a little, so that she could keep the same name without being the same person. She found out later that the FBI knew all about the Baskevitch permits and didn't mind. After all, they weren't meant to deceive the Americans—only to make it possible for the Russians to fool themselves with a clear conscience.

Another police car, its colored roof lights dancing on the window blinds, went down Gardner Street. She thought of how quiet and inactive the streets of Kiev would be at this hour, and even more so the streets of Yefrimov. She had just been back to Russia for the third visit. This time, there had been problems, because of John Hunt. The visits in previous years had been nicer. Nikolaiy had been back to visit his sick mother three times, and Belyakov had twice arranged for Matvei to attend the Artek youth camp in the Crimea, along with the sons of all sorts of *apparatchiki*. Nikolaiy had been very proud of that; it was as though the old felon's slate had been wiped clear—white as snow. What Svetlana had liked most of all had been the film festivals. At one of them, she had been presented to Secretary-General Brezhnev, and he had winked at her! If she could have put a wink into a frame and hung it on the wall, that is what she would have done. But this last time, they had been rough with her, physically rough. A KGB man had called her a CIA whore. He had meant an FBI whore, of course.

She put the brandy glass down and lit another cigarette. She heard Nikolaiy's throat clearing itself with a throttling noise while he continued to sleep. Nikolaiy, she remembered, had been a little jealous of her success. He was still chopping up meat for ten hours a day and trying to stay ahead of the bills. But he was becoming more American. One day, a car had hit the back of theirs and dented their bumper, and she had told Nikolaiy not to worry, that insurance would pay for the repair. And he had said: "Better! Whiplash!"

He had explained that when Americans are bumped from behind by another car, they complain that they suddenly have a great pain in the neck. Pain, he had said, could not be measured; you had to take people's word for it. The pain was called whiplash. You went to the court and the court ordered the other driver to pay you money. Svetlana had been dubious, because the American girl driving the other car had looked at least as poor as they were, but Nikolaiy had said the girl's insurance company would pay. Just like that? Well, they would need a lawyer, but the lawyer would pay himself out of the insurance company money. Nikolaiy had been told about this at work. And he had been right! The insurance company had agreed to pay $22,500. That had been more than Nikolaiy earned in a year! She couldn't remember how much their lawyer had kept for himself, but it had been a beautiful ending to what had seemed like a bad thing, an accident. Of course, they had needed a doctor who would say that they had whiplashes in their necks, but that had been easy: There was this nice physician from Russia, Dr. Matthew Jeikov. It was a pity that all the money they got had been eaten by that dumpling machine. But they had got a smaller sum after another little accident, and even something from Svetlana's dentist for what Americans called malpractice. Imagine complaining about a loose bridge in Kiev! She had begun to learn that the way you made money in America was not always the same as the way you earned a living in Europe. It was the lawyers who had shocked her the most. *Ai*, the rascals! What parasites! And they all had big cars and houses.

She picked up the brandy glass again and it nearly slipped from her hand. She was quite drunk now. Her thoughts were becoming a whirl. She took a heavy sip, then put down the glass again, to grope for another cigarette. She had reached that point in the night when she chain-smoked herself to sleep. Groping between the glass and her purse for the cigarettes, she knocked the purse to the floor. Something fell out. She picked it up. In the dim light through the blinds, she could see it was the passport photo of John that she always carried. This made her think of being with John at Malibu, of his arm around her, of his deep reassuring voice.

*Ai*, John! They had begun going out in 1982. By then, she and Nikolaiy had been in America for nine years. She had been in the "film business" for six of them. She had acquired a few nice clothes, but still they could not afford a house, she and Nikolaiy. They were always paying off something else. Nikolaiy was still working long hours. With the meat and the movies, they were earning a little more each year; but everything was costing a little more each year, too. They had not known this constant inflation, back in Kiev. But in Russia, there was so little to buy that the cost didn't make so much difference. In America, there was everything to buy, but who could afford it? And that was when she had started going out with John Hunt.

It had been a very American meeting, like something out of television. She had been taking out the garbage, one morning, and the first words he had spoken to her had been a lie. She had found this tall American looking at the names on the mailboxes. He had been behaving as though he were looking for someone, not as though he had found whom he was looking for. She knew he had been pretending, because he had telephoned earlier. But he had said, guilefully, that he was looking for Mrs. Ogorodnikov, omitting the -*a* suffix that belongs to a married woman.

She had said: "I am Ogorodnikova." He must have seen the name on their box, of course. He had been sizing them up, how they lived, and so on, and doing it in that indiscreet and obvious way that seemed to be the trademark of the FBI. He had shown her his badge and had said that he was from the Bureau. He had given his name. He had reminded her that they had talked briefly two years before. He had said now that he wanted to talk to her again. Was her husband home? She had said that Nikolaiy was at work and Matvei was at school. She had let him come into the apartment, and she had made him tea. Then he and another detective had taken her out.

John and his partner had said that they knew that she had just finally returned to Russia on a visit. They knew that she had made many visits to the consulate-general in San Francisco. Later, John had told her that the FBI had a room in an office building across the street and that they took pictures of everyone as they entered or left the consulate-general. He had asked her about the film work, and her visit home. He had been courteous and smooth, and she had found herself talking to him more freely than perhaps was wise. She had heard herself saying that her visit had disillusioned her about her homeland, had made her feel more American. He had asked her about helping that Soviet consul set up the Olympic display at the university, about looking for the silly Madevossian woman who had left her husband. Then, John had sent his partner back to the car and had told her not to be worried about his call. They might want to ask her some questions from time to time, that was all, he had said. It was routine. He had held her hand for longer than was necessary and tried to look sincere with his eyes. So this was America's KGB! She had asked him to leave her alone. He had asked her to call him.

Fat chance! Why would Nikolaiy allow her to call another man? She hadn't called John, so he had called her. She had told him at the apartment that one reason she had become involved in showing films was that she liked the parties in nice restaurants, and so he had invited her to go out with him for dinner.

She had hesitated. At the time, she had been taking a night course to qualify as a medical technician—the same sort of course that she had passed in Kiev, but with differences required for an American license. She had wanted to pass the course and get a full-time job.

On the night when they had received their diplomas, there had been a party for the students and instructors. Everyone had brought wine and food, and gifts for the teachers. She had brought some wooden Russian dolls. And while the party had been going on at the school, John Hunt had appeared. She had been nervous. It was relatively late. But he was FBI. She had felt she had to be nice to him. So she had gone with him to a bar for more drinks, and then to a restaurant, and she had given him one of the Russian dolls.

At the restaurant, he had told her she could order anything she liked; the FBI would pay. So she had ordered expensive dishes and champagne. John had asked her more questions about the consulate-general people. What did they do outside the office? He had said that if she could provide him with answers to questions like that, it would demonstrate her loyalty to America. *Ai!* Even through the champagne, he had sounded like the security people back home. And how would she ever get answers to questions about the life of the Soviet consuls? Did he think she could get information like that just because she spoke Russian? She hadn't realized then that the FBI had a Russian squad that didn't speak Russian. She hadn't really been sure what John had wanted to know, anyway, but for the moment she had pretended that she understood. It had been a nice dinner, and it looked very much as though John wasn't interested only in information. Surely, she had thought, if that was what he had wanted most, he would have gone to someone else. With his words, he seemed to be squeezing her for information, but with his hands he was squeezing something else. *Ai!* The rascal! She had decided that she had better not see him again.

But John kept calling. He had told her that he wanted to see her every day, and in order to justify this with his boss, she had to find him some information. After the first two visits, she had insisted he stop coming to the apartment. The neighbors had begun to notice and to ask who the gentleman caller was. So she had had to agree, in exchange, to meet him somewhere away from Gardner Street. And then, for the rest of the year, and for some of the year following, it seemed, in recollection, as though they had met every day. John would set a place and time to meet for drinks, and she would go.

On the outside, John could be almost gentlemanly. Despite his curt, American policeman manner, he could even be respectful. But when you knew him better, to a woman he seemed just like a little boy. He certainly seemed to be in love. She had been worried about what Nikolaiy and Matvei would say. She had confided in a neighbor, an old Russian lady, and the old lady had shrugged and said it was just like the KGB—you had to accept it.

For a while, she had resisted the notion that she was really in love with John. She loved the thought that he loved her, and the prospect of what he seemed to offer—a life better than being a sort of married housemaid in Kiev or on Gardner Street. She didn't think John would ever hit her, as Nikolaiy did. John was a real television American. He had told her he was risking his job just to be with her. That had made her care for him even more. She was beginning to feel like a new woman.

Outside, a motorcycle went noisily by. She leaned over to pick up her glass. Her vision, in the half-light from the window slats, was becoming blurred, but that was at least partly because she was crying now. Had John ever really loved her, after all? They had been meeting sometimes twice a day. He had told her about his job, his family, his life. She had been out so often that Nikolaiy had known there was something going on. Their quarrels had grown worse. John had liked dancing, and she had liked dancing too. She had taken him to Mischa's, the Russian nightclub, in Hollywood. She had been back there today, thinking of John.

Uncertainly, Svetlana raised herself from the couch. She went to a drawer where she kept personal things. Under a pile of old letters, she drew out a photo and walked over to the window. She eased open a couple of slats on the blinds and looked at the picture taken in Mischa's of a group of people at a table. You could see that she had been a little tight at the time. John attracted more attention than anyone else in the picture because he had a hand in front of his face. His excuse for being there with her was that she was introducing him to other Russians. *Ai!* He was supposed to be keeping an eye on the Russian community in Los Angeles, and he spoke no Russian! The only Russian he had his eye on, it seemed, was Svetlana.

He had told her he especially wanted to meet Armenians, because some of these were terrorists, and they had even done mad things in California. He would look good, he had said, if he caught a terrorist. He had made it sound like catching a big fish. He had always been saying that he had to have something to report to his superiors, so that he could go on seeing Svetlana. Once, she remembered, a friend of hers said that if she had no intelligence to give him, she could always cook up something, and she had said: "You mean blinis?" and her friend had laughed. John had gone on seeing her anyway. They would dance and hug, and go for long walks on the beach in the moonlight. The way people did in Russian films, and on American television. Yes, he had seemed to be in love with her, and she had thought: *Ai!* Am I in love also? Is this possible?

She had always done whatever he had asked. She had told him what little she knew about the people at the consulate-general, what restaurants they frequented, the latest visitors, and what they had said when she had driven them around. So far as she could remember, she'd always told him the truth, because he'd said he must have something to report every day, or almost every day, or he would not be allowed to go on seeing her. In particular, he'd asked her to pass on whatever people said at parties. Obviously, he thought there were spies in the *émigré* community, although he had never told her what they would be spying on. Her best friend, Nadya Mathison, worked for Frederick's of Hollywood as a catalogue illustrator. Were the Russians thought to be spying on the latest designs in sexy nightwear? She had never quite understood how John justified spending so much time with her, especially in the evenings. And she didn't go to many parties anymore because she was usually with him. Sometimes she had gone to parties and actually taken John—but not often, because she was afraid that someone would tell Nikolaiy. But whenever John had picked up what he called information, he would tell his supervisors that it was thanks to her, or that it actually came from her. And if that made his boss happy, and saved him from having to do real work at his age, and they could go on being together, why not? One

Russian woman had let them use her apartment in the after-
noons, so that they could be together in more privacy. Always,
Svetlana had had to be home in time to make dinner for the men,
Nikolaiy and Matvei. Then, sometimes, she would make an
excuse to Nikolaiy as to why she had to go out again, something
to do with the films, and she would say that she knew that he
was too tired to come with her. And she would meet John again.
She had decided that being in the FBI must be rather like being
a taxi driver in Kiev.

They had even met on weekends. Once, she recalled, John had
brought his grandchild, Amy. He had said he had told his wife
that he was taking the little girl for a walk—which was true, but
he had also been meeting Svetlana. She had told him she wanted
to get divorced, and he had said he would like to live in northern
California.

They had been making plans. Or at least *she* had, and she had
thought that he had been making them, too. As she had understood it, he was going to take retirement at fifty-five in a couple
of years, divorce his wife, marry Svetlana, and go to live with
her in Marin County, or perhaps in some foreign country. She
had not told Nikolaiy then that she wanted a divorce or that she
was going to marry an American. But she had gone off, and
taken Matvei, and lived on her own with the boy for a few weeks
on welfare money.

As she remembered it, it was just before this time that John
had taken her to meet Bryce Christensen, the No. 2 apparatchik
at the big Westwood office of the FBI. Christensen was John's
supervisor. The three of them had met at a simple cafeteria near
the FBI office. To a European, it seemed an odd place for such
an encounter. Christensen looked like a bank clerk, but serious
and intelligent. Courteous. The meeting was because John had
started asking her to do something more, and he had wanted to
show her that his boss had wished her to do it, too. The consular
people had learned that she was spending a lot of time with
someone in the FBI, and John had asked her to tell Boris
Belyakov that she had an FBI lover, but that they weren't having
much fun because the lover was short of cash. Actually, he
hadn't said lover, he had said "boyfriend". But John was over
fifty, so clearly she could not attempt to translate an absurd
expression like "boyfriend", as though they were both still in

high school. John had said that she should tell them he was always asking her questions about the consulate-general. He had told her that he wanted to see what they would say when they heard this news about the relationship. He didn't offer to spy; he didn't ask for money to pay off debts. He had left it to them to drawn their own conclusions. But she had said: "How can I do this?" And John had told her that if she couldn't do that, his supervisors would say that he was wasting too much time with her, and then they would make it hard for him to be with her. So she had said, well, she couldn't promise, but she would see if it was possible. She had never been more scared in her life than at what John was asking her to do. To Russians like Belyakov, the FBI was what the KGB was to Americans like John.

The fact that John wouldn't spell out what exactly it was that he wanted had only made it harder. When she had tried to get him to explain, he had told her she wouldn't understand, that she shouldn't ask what he was doing. It seemed obvious to her that he was hoping that someone from the consulate-general would get in touch with him—through her. But all he had told her was that he would like to know what they *said* when she told them that she was going around with someone in the FBI and was thinking about a divorce. Of course, John had known that she was in love with him, that she would do anything he asked. And he had got Mr. Christensen to talk to her, to say it would be good for John's career before he retired if he brought this off.

She got up slowly, weaving a little, lit another cigarette, and walked over to the furniture where the brandy was. She poured herself another shot, a little bit larger than before. She was so angry with John now, she wanted to scream; but if he had been there, she would have thrown herself into his arms. Had he no idea how much of an embarrassment it had been to tell Boris Belyakov, a Soviet official, that she had a "boyfriend", which meant a lover, in the FBI? But John had pleaded with her, and Mr. Christensen had said how much they appreciated her work for the Bureau, and what he called the risks that she had been taking for them. And John had offered to buy her the ticket for San Francisco, and she had gone. She had needed some films, and Belyakov was expecting her. But because the FBI had offered to pay for the ticket, she had felt she had to do something for them as well. And she and Belyakov had been joking around, as they often did, and then suddenly she had blurted out to Boris that yes, it was true, she had met a man in the FBI, and they were becoming very close. She remembered how nervously she had expressed herself. John, she had said, was an apparatchik who pestered her with questions about the Soviet Union and the consulate to have an excuse for seeing her. Really, their relationship was emotional. That was what John had instructed her to say. And Belyakov had told her she was playing with fire.

John had met her at the airport when she had returned from San Francisco. He had asked her what had happened. She had told him that Mr. Belyakov had been annoyed and that she was afraid that she would lose the film business. But she had done everything that John had asked her to do. And John had seemed pleased and had called her "my Mata Hari"; and then she had had her picture taken at one of those costume photo studios as Mata Hari and had signed a copy for John, "From Your Mata Hari With Love."

It was then that she had told Nikolaiy for the first time about wanting a divorce. After all, if the consulate-general knew she had kicked over the traces, then Nikolaiy had a right to know, too. It seemed that somebody—probably that tart Nina Thomas who had blabbed on her to the consulate—had already arranged for Nikolaiy to learn that his little Svetlana had a cold from getting out of a warm bed and going home. Or perhaps he just *knew*, anyway. They had been together a long time, and because they had lived together in California, sharing the bitter bread of exile, they *knew* each other. So she she told him boldly that she was planning to marry an American man. And Nikolaiy had seemed more sad than angry. He hadn't even busted her across the mouth, as she had expected and deserved. Then later, on the phone, Belyakov had contradicted himself, in that way that civil servants did so easily, and said that she should not break off her relationship with John. She should work for her own people; henceforth, Belyakov had said, she was a major in the KGB. She should say that she had met Andropov, and slept with him—"He sleeps with every girl in the office." And now he was secretary general! So she had become a cat's-paw, with no choice but to take orders from the two apparatchiks, the Russian and the American.

Svetlana lit another cigarette; she closed her eyes. There would be ash all over the couch in the morning, but so what! She tried to put herself in John's skin. He must have been hoping that he would be contacted by someone in the consulate-general. Someone in the KGB. But nothing had happened. John mentioned at one point about their perhaps wanting proof that her "boyfriend" was in the FBI. When nothing had happened, John had said something about his not having told her to say enough. All that had really happened was that there were no more invitations from the consulate-general. As the Americans would say, she had been shitlisted, in spite of Belyakov's request that she go on "seeing" John. She had worried about what that would do to her film business. And then John had said that Christensen had told him that perhaps she was not really effective. But how could Christensen say that? she had wondered. Hadn't she told him she was a major in the KGB and had been Andropov's mistress? And Christensen's eyes had glazed over. And John, the sonovabitch, hadn't seemed jealous at all. Christensen had looked at her with those little-boy American eyes of his and had told her how much he appreciated the risks she was taking for America—those were the words the little prick had used—and now he was saying that she was not effective! And John had said that he had been ordered to drop her as an FBI asset. That was when she had hit rock bottom and begun to drink heavily.

She had been worried all along about her affair with John, about the gifts she had given him. About the accident they had had together. About going to the doctor with him. She had felt guilty. She had felt badly about Nikolaiy slaving away in that awful factory, making chops out of pigs, scraping the brains from the skulls of calves. She had worried about little, innocent Matvei.

She had never told Nikolaiy John's name, but John's existence had never been a secret from her son. Matvei had seen John at the apartment, anointing the shabby dwelling with his smug, towering arrogance, even taking them all out to dinner once. Matvei had told her: "Mama, I don't like this man." Matvei had been even more troubled when she had confirmed the boy's fears: She had said that she planned to marry John. She had told Matvei to be patient, that it was right that he should love his father, but that John would be a good father to him, too. But it was the day after she had told John that she had asked Nikolaiy for a divorce that John had told her that he had been ordered not to see her anymore. And when she had asked him: "John, why?" he had said that, well, it was because she was not productive enough for the FBI. But he had gone on meeting her or, talking to her on the phone. And they had quarreled bitterly. But he had introduced her to his wife, which obviously implied, she thought, that there could be a troika.

When John had said that he had been told to drop her, she had become a wreck. She had tried to understand. Before John, she had not liked America; but because of John, she had been making plans for a real life in the United States. Now, she had asked herself: What will become of me? She still couldn't face the facts. She had told her serious, respectable friend Nadya what had happened, and Nadya—wise, educated Nadya—had said: "I don't believe it! Don't you see this man just used you?" But Svetlana had refused to believe that that was the answer. A woman always thinks she knows when a man is in love, and John had seemed to be in love, this tall, confident police officer who conducted himself like a little boy.

A truck rolled up the street outside, shifting gears, then shifting again. Now, of course, she realized that John had never loved her. He had only encouraged her love for him. He was never going to leave his wife, and when she had spoken about divorce he must have panicked. He could see trouble ahead. *Ai!* The rascal. But she had been very hurt, very lonely, and she had welcomed the brief opportunities to talk with him again.

On May 23, she had gone to the consulate-general. Belyakov had asked about John. The next day, she had called the FBI office and had left a message for him. Another man had called her back. He had said his name was Miller. He had told Svetlana that he wanted to meet her. She had said no. He had called again, and she had said no again. John had asked her to tell him if anyone else called from the FBI, and so she had called John and told him about the calls. John had asked for the name, and she had told him. John had said there were two Millers in the Westwood office. She had said that she thought the first name was Richard, and John had said: "He's right here. I'll pass you on to him." Just like that. The bastard! He had set her up with Richard, knowing what would happen.

The memories of meeting Richard were all confused. The first time had been at a West Hollywood filling station. He had taken her to a restaurant in Marina del Rey for dinner. Then, they had walked along the beach in Malibu, and she had tried to recover the magic she had known there with John. But Richard was different. He was fat. He wore terrible clothes. He was shorter than John, about five feet ten, but he weighed about two hundred fifty pounds. In the restaurant, he would drink Cokes, like a child. He didn't smoke. He chewed candy bars. Later, he had admitted to her that he had often been in trouble because of his weight and appearance. She had asked him: "Richard, where do you get your suits—the Salvation Army?" And she had asked herself, after two "dates" with him: How can I be seen with a man like this?

But he was a nice man, really, she had decided. She had felt sorry for him. He was rather like a puppy dog. He was a real American, but he was a loser, just like her.

From the first meeting, he had wanted to make love to her. But he had that smell of fat people who don't change their clothes every day, and the idea had been repulsive to her. She still belonged to John, and because John had asked her to report to him everything that happened during her meetings with Richard. . . . Why was the FBI spying on itself? Now, when she called John to report on her meetings with Richard, John was nervous. His behavior was, well, suspicious. She had asked him what was the matter, and John had said, as he always did, that she wouldn't understand. And he had said: "Do whatever I tell you, otherwise you will be in danger, from the FBI and the KGB." And she had said: "Why, John? Will someone kill me?" And he had said: "No. The CIA kills. The FBI and the KGB only hurt." Or something like that. He had told her that in order to be safe from the KGB, she must do whatever the FBI told her to do—which meant whatever John told her to do.

John had taught her how to know if she was being followed. It was much easier than she would have thought. And he had said constantly: "Before you go out with Miller, always tell me. Tell me everything before and everything afterward." And he had also said again: "Do what I tell you, because the FBI are crazy people, and they can hurt you." He had said that she would not always understand, and that she should trust him, and tell him everything. And she had asked many times: "Why are they going to hurt me?" And he wouldn't explain. And she had asked again: "Could I be killed?" And he had said again no, that the CIA killed, but that the FBI only hurt people.

By now, she had realized that she was not only an informant. She was an FBI swallow. And John had told her to do whatever Richard asked her to do, and then report back. And so on the second date, she had allowed Richard to hump her on the seat of the car. John, she thought bitterly, had become her pimp. But by then her time was consumed with plans for her annual trip. On June 12, she had gone to the consulate-general. Two weeks later, she had left for Moscow.

Svetlana got up slowly and carefully, and poured the last of the brandy into her heavily fingerprinted glass. From the feel, she knew there were only two cigarettes left in the pack. She should try to sleep. She put down the glass, and lit another cigarette. She closed her eyes in thought again.

As John's swallow, if that is what she had been, she had gone out with Richard about four times in the three weeks before she had gone to Moscow. They had gone to the same sort of restaurants and hotels as she had visited with John. Sometimes, Richard let her pay. But then, John had done that sometimes, too. And on each occasion, Richard had insisted on sex—which, like most fat men, he had no talent for.

She had come back from her trip to Moscow, Kiev and Yefrimov on July 23—or was it 24? The journey had been planned many months before, but John had said that, now that she had told the consulate-general that he was her lover, and that he was in the FBI, perhaps she shouldn't go to Moscow anymore. At one point, he had seemed to be joking, saying that they might force her to join the KGB or the GRU. Then, turning serious, he had said it might be dangerous for her in Moscow. But she had wanted to see her mother, and she had already told Nikolaiy that she was going. It would have been hard to explain to her husband, suddenly, that she didn't want to go to Russia. He would have asked her why, and what would she have said? She had to go, because Mama was sick. And her grandmother, who had brought her up, was sick. And she had films to buy from Sovexportfilm, and this time they were offering her a very good price. And Nikolaiy had been already, and Matvei was going later. And she had felt that, thanks to John, somehow even in Moscow she would have some FBI protection from the KGB. But it looked as though John had been right to worry her; she had been beaten up in Yefrimov.

It had been late at night, and she had been going back to her mother's home with her aunt's husband. She had been drinking, and when security people stopped her she had thought it was because she was making too much noise. The police didn't allow people to bark in the streets like dogs, the way they are allowed to do in America. They had taken her to a police station. And she had asked: "For what? Were we making too much noise?"

Inside the station, they had pushed her into a badly lit cell, and she had cried: "I am from the United States! You must let me go!"

They had thrown her onto the bed. She had tried to struggle, so one policeman had held her hands and sat on her. The other had used her hair to swing her head against the wall, until she could taste her blood.

And John had been right, because they had called her a CIA whore. And she had said it wasn't true, that she hadn't worked for the CIA and she didn't want to work for the KGB. She was a film exhibitor!

They had let her go home. The next week, she had gone on to Moscow. One day, she had been called to a security headquarters there. That was normal. All Russians living abroad were debriefed when they went home. The security officer who had debriefed her was a Ukrainian, like Nikolaiy, and he was calm, at least to begin with. He had said his name was Anatoliy. He had known about her life, and about John Hunt. He had said: "I know all about your love affair." He had reminded her of what she had told Boris Belyakov, long before. Anatoliy had asked her if she still had a relationship with John Hunt. She had said yes. He hadn't apparently known anything about Richard Miller. If they had known that she had had two FBI lovers, how could they not have been certain that she was an American spy?

Anatoliy had said: "Svetlana, what do you think? Could you invite your friend Mr. Hunt for a trip abroad?" He had seemed to be testing her, to see if she could do something for them. She remembered Boris Belyakov, back in May, asking her about

John. Anatoliy had said that she could communicate with him through her letters to her mother. Any news she gave for "the acquaintances" she had met in Moscow last summer would be for him. John, Anatoliy reminded her, had talked of going to Vienna with her. Did he still want to go to Vienna? She had said that she would ask him. Was this what John wanted? That she would make him a star with his supervisors?

But apparently Anatoliy, the wily old professional, had sensed that she really was bonded to this FBI man, that she was his swallow, that she was just saying what she thought Anatoliy wanted to hear. Because when she had refused to be more definitive, the Ukrainian had become irritable, even threatening; at one point, he had said that perhaps it would be wiser for her if she never tried to return to the Soviet Union.

# Chapter Eight

# The Master: Self-Portrait

*"The end result of the American intelligence system is not as bad as one would be entitled to expect. . . . But mistakes are, of course, common. I like to think they keep the peace."*

Grishin tore off a page on the note-block calendar on his desk. At the head of the new sheet it said Thursday, August 16. Beneath that was a scribble in very abbreviated Cyrillic to remind him that he had to brief the visiting delegation from the Supreme Soviet of the USSR—a response to the countless congressional junkets to Russia. Moscow Center had said he could tell them virtually everything he could tell the special commission of the Soviet. The delegation of nine people spending eleven days in the United States had been very carefully selected, so the instructions from Center had not surprised him. What it really meant was that he could tell them everything that the *Americans* knew already. The question was: What did the *delegates* know already? Well, they knew his name. They knew he was the Rezident in San Francisco. Just as the Americans thought Lev Zaydzev was the Rezident; just as Center knew that Charlie Kozlowsky was the CIA station chief in Leningrad.

Ludmila, Grishin's secretary, brought in the morning traffic. She was a woman of forty or so, the wife of one of his subordinates, quite tall, with what the French would call an appetizing figure. Her long hair was swept back and piled up in a tortoiseshell comb. She said: "The delegation from the Supreme Soviet—" He interrupted her with a nod. "Yes. Nine-fifteen."

The tiny auditorium had no windows. There was a slightly raised dais that was sometimes used as a stage, with a polished, American-style lectern. Behind where the speaker would stand hung one of the old profile shots of Lenin, alongside an avuncular portrait of the secretary-general. This, too, was in black and white in order not to upstage Vladimir Ilyich himself. As Grishin walked in with the consul-general, Anatoliy Georgiyevich Myshkov, the nine visitors looked up expectantly. Two of them were women. The group was of varying ages and was entirely European, except for the ruddy figure from Kazakstan with his dark brown eyes like elliptical marbles. With them were two interpreters from Moscow, a man and a woman, and, sitting at the back, three members of the staff of the consulate who were acting as dogsbodies for the visitors. One of these, of course, was Grishin's man.

Grishin and the consul-general came to the lectern. Myshkov uttered the usual amenities and introduced "your speaker." He didn't say the name because they knew that Occidental Research might get the speech on one of the bursts, and Myshkov and Grishin wanted "O.R." to believe it was Zaydzev speaking. Grishin noticed how the two women from the Supreme Soviet were watching him intently; he was not ashamed of being handsome or, since he was divorced, of being seen as available. He heard Myshkov winding down, saw the diplomat gesturing to him to approach the lectern.

He said confidently: "Comrade deputies, I know you have a busy program. I will be concise, but if anything I say is not clear to you, please do not hesitate to interrupt me with questions."

Now, he knew, he must discreetly inform them that he was important, too. He went on: "I have the honor to be in charge of the Rezidentura of the western half of the United States. That's an area the size of all of Europe except for the Soviet Union, from Poland to Portugal, from Lapland to Malta. More than half of the military industry of America lies in this region, more than half of the productive threat to our country. Our consulate-general is in San Francisco and not in Los Angeles, which as you know is a more important city, because of Washington's insistence."

He looked at his notes, on tiny sheets, for the first time. One of the deputies took advantage of the pause to clear his throat. Grishin looked up, wondering if this meant a question. No one spoke.

Spreading his eloquent fingers across the lectern rim, he continued his lesson: "San Francisco is a major port, but barely of city size—less than one million people, about the size of Alma Ata in Kazakstan."

He glanced in the right direction, and the Kazak deputy smiled with his somber eyes. Knowing he had the man's attention, he went on: "Thirty-eight percent of the population of this town is of Asian origin." He made a brief but meaningful pause because he knew that what came next would draw a gasp. "Approximately half of the adult male population is homosexual." When the gasp was over, he went on: "Since the former favor large families, and the latter none at all, San Francisco will eventually be more Japanese and Chinese than New York is Russian."

Came the anticipated laugh. He had them in his hand. He hoped Myshkov, a dull speaker, wasn't jealous. Grishin's mien became serious. "San Francisco is the outport for what is called Silicon Valley, a high-technology industrial area. However, as I've indicated, neither as a port nor as an industrial region is it as important or as threatening as Los Angeles; southern California is arguably the single most important center of America's military industries."

He turned over a page of notes and said: "So much for this little office in this huge and hostile area. What of *them*?"

He let the rhetorical question hang in the blue air for a moment; most of the deputies were smoking as they listened intently. "As some of you may know already, American espionage is conducted by several different agencies. The most important is the National Security Agency, which deals with communications. This is much larger and more secretive than the better-known Central Intelligence Agency; but the secretary-general of the CIA, who is known as the Director of Central Intelligence, has oversight powers on the NSA as well."

He sipped from a glass of water, felt the desire for a cigarette, but decided to continue without one.

"As in all countries where there is a division of duties of this sort, relations between the agencies tend to be competitive and prickly." His audience nodded contentedly. "In addition, the defense ministry, usually called the Pentagon, has the Defense Intelligence Agency, comparable to our GRU, and each of the three armed services—the Navy, which includes the Marines, the Army, and the Air Force—has its own intelligence arm as well." He cleared his throat. "About eighty percent of all

America's intelligence budget is spent by the military agencies. Just keeping seven Blackbird spy planes in the air costs a quarter-billion dollars a year. And more than half of the twenty percent that remains is spent by the NSA. In addition, I should mention, the State Department has an Intelligence and Research Bureau. But the CIA isn't poor. It has proprietary companies, even banks, which earn it income. The Committee for State Security, the KGB, does not have that option."

He looked across the room. Some of his listeners were actually taking notes. He said: "The National Security Council, which is part of the 'White House'—the president's palace—has oversight over all intelligence; and the National Security Adviser, who directs it, and who is for all intents and purposes a cabinet minister, is what Americans call a traffic manager, coordinating information for the president and senior cabinet members."

He turned another tiny page of brief notes typed in big Cyrillic letters.

"Of course, as I've indicated, these various agencies that report to the NSC often disagree. Within each organization, the leaders of sections tend to select information that supports their own analyses or opinions, and that reinforces the policies that they recommend. The overall directors again exercise a similar right to fashion the shape of the final product."

He paused while the deputy from Byelorussia cleared his gritty throat again. The man blew smoke and picked tobacco from his tongue. Then Grishin went on: "The end result of the American intelligence system is not as bad as one would be entitled to expect. It reminds me of my childhood, when we played football in heavy, inflexible boots, yet managed to play as well as our children do today in reinforced running shoes. But mistakes are, of course, common. I like to think they keep the peace."

He stopped again for a little hiss of not-quite-laughter, once again worrying about Myshkov's reaction. Shifting his hands on the lectern, he looked stern once more: "Because the various American intelligence agencies are all projected toward the exterior, there is no directorate of the CIA, for instance, that guards internal security. Of course, the law that theoretically forbids Americans to spy on Americans is bent like a pretzel every day, in particular through the existence of CIA branch offices in places like Miami and Honolulu. But broad responsibility for the counterintelligence function lies with the Federal Bureau of Investigation, a sort of federal police force whose members are more noted for marksmanship than introspection. We should be thankful for this."

The self-satisfaction he imparted to his listeners was palpable. He went on: "The FBI has a large office with a large unit known as a 'Russian Squad' in San Francisco. When you entered the building just now, they took pictures of you with a recent-model Asahi Pentax camera with a Takumar 4/200 zoom lens. In Los Angeles, the FBI has a larger office but with a smaller 'Russian Squad,' because of our official non-presence there. Yes?"

It was the woman from one of the Moscow districts. She said: "We had to bring our own interpreters. You people who are here permanently—"

"Yes, we are restricted in our travel to about forty kilometers from the epicenter of the city. The Americans in their consulate-general in Leningrad are restricted in the same way. To go further, we need authorization from the State Department. Of course, we always welcome a chance to see more of California." He tried to make it sound innocent, or humorous. "For instance, if a seaman on one of our ships falls sick and has to go into the hospital, say, at Long Beach, which is just south of Los Angeles, then somebody from this consulate can go down there. Once, one of our exchange students was arrested for—it was claimed—shoplifting in Sacramento, which is where the soviet of California is situated, and one of us had to go there and get him out of prison!"

He thought briefly of the local driver, Svetlana Ogorodnikova, who had chauffeured the man from the Rezidentura. He wondered if all of his audience realized the opportunities such journeys offered to talk to the little network of informants they had built up further south. He said: "Of course, wherever we go, we assume we are watched, by the FBI, by the Russian Squad. There are, I believe, nineteen in the squad in Los Angeles, for instance."

"So this is the CIA by another name?" asked one man in the delegation.

"Yes and no," Grishin said. "To be fair, these are usually just ordinary policemen. They are called special agents, but all policemen in the FBI are called special agents. Some of them may be specialists in car theft, or prostitution, or illegal immigration. Counterintelligence is largely a white-collar job. There are no risks of violence, so some of the agents chosen are simply too old or unhealthy for normal field work."

"How good is their Russian?" the same deputy asked.

"Not always very good." He didn't want to say that only one member of the Los Angeles unit, Michael DiPretorio, could speak the language. He did not want to say that some of the people in the unit had been put there because they were not considered good enough for more serious FBI work. It would make his own task seem too easy. He added: "You must understand: Down there, there are nineteen of them and none of us."

"What about the telephone lines?" It was the pushy Moscow woman. Oh well, Grishin thought, the Americans knew all about their electronic surveillance work, out of Washington and New York and Chicago and here. He had learned about the American guesswork figure, which was a slight underestimate, so he used it.

"We can tap about a hundred lines on a given day. I can't tell you which are our favorites!"

There was a little chuckling hiss again. He assumed the Americans knew that it was more logical for the Rezidentura to tap the lines of the many FBI offices and homes across the state, using the satellite, than those of almost anyone else except the defense industry. He did not want to speculate on what lines were tapped by the FBI. His informants usually called from pay phones, not from their homes.

The man from Alma Ata said: "Tell us what you know about the non-European Americans, the ethnicities."

This was a sensitive subject. On the whole, Grishin conceded to himself, the United States had done a rather better job of amalgamating its peoples, despite the recentness of many of the immigrations, and of forcing everyone to speak the national language. But there were soft spots in the picture that he could pick on, and he knew that what they really wanted to know about was the Russians in America. He moved his pianist hands on the lectern again, distracting the gaze of one of the women deputies. He said: "America is not so much an amalgam of different peoples as a communal farm of mutually suspicious human ingredients." He decided, because of the man from Alma Ata, not to use again the term Asian, but instead to list some specific peoples.

"It isn't just the exclusivistic groups like the Chinese, the Koreans, the Iranians, or the Armenians," he went on. "Almost every part of America has its ethnic pockets, barricaded within their insularity." He saw his audience nodding; they were pleased that America shared the USSR's problem. "But to be fair, many of these people are successful, particularly if they break away from the barricade and join what Americans call the mainstream. A river flows faster in the middle."

He shuffled his notes together. He wouldn't need them any more. He saw one of the interpreters looking at his watch. He must leave a little time for questions. He gave a half-smile.

"I know you want me to tell you about the people who have come to America from our own country. They are mostly from Russia, Byelorussia and the Ukraine. The Americans, of course, call them all Russians, because of the language and because, like Poles, they were all Russians under the czars. The principal Russian communities in America are in the two most populous states of the federation, New York and California. In the Los Angeles area, we estimate that there are about thirty thousand persons who come from our country, if we include their children born here, but I have seen some estimates of fifty thousand for all of southern California."

This was a sensitive subject, too, because he was talking of people who had abandoned the USSR. He continued: "The oldest members of this community are people who rejected the Revolution, or their parents did. The more recent members are those who have taken advantage of easier emigration rules, especially people whose families were Jews before the Revolution."

He cleared his throat. Pre-Revolution statistics, especially about religion, were not even taught in school, because it had been decided that they could be too easily misinterpreted. Of course, you had to learn them when you joined the Committee for State Security. The issue of Jews was touchy, even though they had played a disproportionately important role in propagating the message of Marx and bringing about the Revolution. Stalin, like Hitler and the Zionists, had believed that once a Jew, always a Jew, but this derogatory doctrine no longer enjoyed currency with the audience in front of him.

He went on: "Before the Revolution, about eighty percent of the people in what the Czar called 'all the Russias' were Christian, and about one percent were Hebrews. Of course, eighty percent of us do not look to the archimandrite for guidance today, and one percent are not Israelites. I mention these figures because it means that, as I think you know, about two and a half million of our citizens can point to Jewish ancestors if they wish to do so, and therefore demand permission to make a permanent pilgrimage to Palestine. I think you are aware that of the people who leave the homeland in this way, only about eight percent go to where they say they're going. Most of the others come to America.

"There is some friction between the older *émigrés* and the new ones. What they have in common is homesickness." He saw heads nodding again approvingly. "It is the truth," he went on. "We Russians do not expatriate as easily as, perhaps, Nordic Europeans. The more recent immigrants are habituated to our social system and find the American system harsh—unemployment, having to pay for medical treatment, being neglected in old age, and so on. The drug problem, crime. There are two and a half times as many murders in Los Angeles each month as in the whole of the Soviet Union. Good education is for the bourgeoisie only. And the so-called economic opportunities are a lottery."

He himself had been surprised that some of what he had been taught about America was truer than he had dared believe. But enough with the preamble; time was short. He said: "These are, after all, people who, how shall I say, exploited an ancestral religious link in order to emigrate for economic reasons, non-dialectical materialism; and they are economically frustrated here, most of them. We who represent our government find relations to be easier with the new emigrants than with the old reactionary *émigrés*.

"There is more that I could say, but I think I have used up your time."

"Just one last question, comrade Rezident."

It was the youngest member of the delegation, a man with intelligent eyes and the accent of the Ukraine. "If it's at all possible, can you tell us something about your function? You said that the American authorities know that you are the Rezident. Of course, say only what you know is already within the knowledge of the other side."

"Well, you know I can't tell you more than that!" He had thought they might smile at the remark. Instead, they looked serious. He said: "I belong to the First Chief Directorate of the Committee for State Security, which is solely concerned with activities in foreign countries. Mostly, the First Chief Directorate is organized like our ministry of foreign affairs, divided into geographic departments. Each controls security officers like myself who work abroad as diplomats, what we call members of the PR section. Here, I am a PR officer, fulfilling a consular function in order to carry on my security task.

"Prior to coming to America, I was in S division of the First Chief Directorate. I think some of you know what that is. S controls those brave people who work for our security overseas without the benefit of diplomatic protection and immunity. Of course, although we cannot give these people the same protection that those with diplomatic credentials receive, we do our best to shield them. If they are citizens of the USSR, and they are arrested by the host government, we invariably arrange for them to be exchanged for captured spies from the other country. This arrangement works particularly well with the United States."

"What if the agent is a citizen of the host country?" It was the woman from Moscow.

"Well, naturally, we try to help them to escape. There have been some spectacular successes. But not here in California!"

The young member of the delegation said: "So you have a dual—uh—"

"I am, as the Americans say, wearing two hats in San Francisco—or three, if you include my official consular task. So you can see why I am losing my hair! I am PR, but it is no secret to the Americans that I'm also in charge of S people in the western provinces of America, both citizens of the USSR and others. I think you must understand that that's about as far as I can go."

He saw Anatoliy Georgiyevich walking up from the back of the room to his rescue. "The curtain is coming down," he said. There were appreciative nods from the audience, no applause.

After the delegation had left for their photo opportunity at the Golden Gate, Myshkov and Grishin went back to their offices. Ludmila reminded Grishin that he had wanted to speak to Zaydzev and Menshikov. Valeriy Nikolaiyevich Menshikov was the latest addition to Grishin's staff, the new No. 3, the man who would inherit Zaydzev's post, when Zaydzev inherited Grishin's. Menshikov had arrived only three days before. Grishin asked Ludmila to call both men in.

# Chapter Nine

# The Swallow's Husband

*There were more criminal gangs in the city of Los Angeles than there were football teams in the whole of the Ukrainian Soviet Socialist Republic.*

They had been on since seven-thirty. It was time for the mid-morning break. Nikolaiy Ogorodnikov got a lemon drink from a machine and walked out into the warm sun. He sat on a packing case on the loading dock, away from the others, sipped the drink, peered at the cumulus. He was fifty-two, and he was beginning to find the work tiring, cutting up the carcasses. He would pass his product to a young woman who would weigh it on a digital machine that related weight to price and printed an appropriate label, with a black computer code for the checkout counters. She would wrap the Styrofoam tray and its contents in transparent polyethylene and throw it carelessly onto a conveyor belt.

Driving a taxi had been better. The weather here was an improvement on Kiev. But wherever you were, life was hard. He had been back to Kiev again, and he could make the comparison; and Svetlana had been, and Matvei was going. Svetlana had had a bad experience there, had been beaten up in Yefrimov. It was all because of this involvement with the FBI. He had been in two minds about it from the start. And now she was talking about perhaps having to go back to Europe again, with this fat American equivalent of a KGB officer.

He took another swig from the bottle neck. Spiked with vodka, it would have done something more for his spirits. Life was hard, he thought again.

Like Svetlana, he had been without a father to direct him since an early age. He had been six, in 1938, when his father had gone off to work and had not returned. In this case, it was not a heart attack. His father had been arrested. One of the purges, his mother had told him later. He had never really understood. It was Stalin's time.

He was only nine when the Germans had invaded. An only child, he had fled with his mother to Kazakstan. Two years later, they had been able to move back to Kiev. Instead of returning to school, he had joined the army: dispatch carrier with Red Army guerrillas operating behind the German advance. He had even been wounded twice.

In 1945, he and some other members of his unit had been captured by the retreating Germans. He had given his name as Ogorodnikov, the patronymic of an uncle, his father's sister's husband, because his true German name would make Germans suspect that his was a family of Jewish descent, which it was. A Gestapo officer questioned the prisoners, and it was rumored that he was sending the Jewish captives off to labor camps.

The Germans had to take their prisoners with them as they retreated. They couldn't really afford to keep prisoners. He had been afraid that he would be shot. So, at age thirteen, he had taken his chance, and "jumped." Perhaps they had simply let the skimpy youth escape.

At the victory that year, he had been commended. He had received a medal for bravery. And the officer who had decorated him had also given him what he had treasured most—a gun, the same as adult soldiers had.

He had gone home to find Kiev destroyed. He had been placed in a special school for juvenile ex-servicemen. And not long after that, Marshal Stalin, who was always worrying about plots and rebellions, had ordered that all old soldiers should hand back their weapons. Nikolaiy had disobeyed, as many did. He had wanted to keep his pistol and show it to the son whom he would have one day, and say: "This is the gun they gave me for fighting in the Great Patriotic War." A neighbor had informed on him—that he had been showing the pistol to other children.

"Nick!"

It was one of the other butchers, or meat cutters as they were fancily called, signaling to him that the break was over. Nikolaiy nodded, gulped down most of what remained of the lemon drink, eased himself off the packing case. He walked with bowed shoulders back into the factory, pausing at the trash container to finish the lemonade and to dump the bottle. He wiped his mouth with the back of his hand and resumed his station; soon, he was splitting the side of a calf with powerful, deft strokes. Through the mindless task, he went on thinking of Russia.

He had soon found himself in prison. Not because of the pistol, but because he had been part of a street gang of boys scrabbling to make a living. The gang had stolen clothes, one day, from a hospital; he had been the lookout. Two years.

He had gone into jail a fatherless ragamuffin and come out an antisocial adult. Prison was like that. And so, soon, he had been back in prison again, for robbery. He had been released in the amnesty of 1952. Then, he had been to prison three times more. Twice for robbery, once for rape. In reality, he had never really raped the woman. He thought of her angrily, lifting the cleaver and splitting the T-bone of the calf in one blow. At the time, he was being questioned as a possible "American spy" because he had acquired an American friend, a consul named Adams; he had wanted Adams to help him get into the United States. It was 1966, and this girl had accused Nikolaiy of taking her against her will.

It hadn't been true. Was it rape to get a girl drunk, so that she didn't know what she was doing? Everyone knew you had to get them drunk, the first time; after that, it was easier. It wasn't as though he had emptied the bottle down her throat, or that she had been drinking against her will. But in prison, before the trial, he had been called into the KGB office and questioned about Adams. They had told Nikolaiy that Adams was homosexual and that if he, Nikolaiy, could seduce Adams as successfully as he had seduced the girl, he could get him to talk about many things. Blackmail. If he could do that, the rape charge would be dismissed. So they had let him out, but Adams had refused to be drawn. As a consequence, they had given Nikolaiy eight months for rape.

He pulled over the calf's head and began separating the brain from the bone; he was remembering the face of the judge who had sentenced him. His co-worker, the girl who weighed and packed the meat, was saying something, but he ignored her. Everyone in the plant knew that Nick the Russian had taciturn days, and she did not repeat what she had said.

In all, he had spent fourteen years in prison in the Soviet Union. He should have done things differently; he knew that now. But after being a soldier, it had been impossible to go back to school. Others like him had become good citizens, but he had not. He wished his father hadn't died.

He passed the brains to the packer. Now, he set his aim at the ribs, the chops, the escallops. But in his mind, he was back in 1967. Ex-convict, freshly released, and freshly divorced, with a daughter living with her mother. Taxi driver. Living with his widowed mother and her widowed sister. Because of the war, theirs was a generation of widows. But being a cabbie was fine. He was not shut up in a factory, which was like a prison.

Nikolaiy could feel the walls of Hoffman Brothers, meat packing plant, closing around him like a vice. Driving a taxi in Kiev had given him a means of transport—a great way to meet girls in Russia. It was in late 1967 that he had met Svetlana Malutina, who was studying at a medical institute while working as a cleaner in an apartment building. Seventeen. Nice-looking little woman. She had told him that she wanted to go to America. He had confided that he had had similarly subversive thoughts. He had even made a few inquiries. You had to pretend that you were going to Israel.

They had fallen in love. She had come to live with him in his mother's house. They had made love there. He thought about it, tearing out the kidneys and passing them along to the girl, then returning to the ribs. In 1969, Svetlana had become pregnant. They had agreed on both abortion and marriage. Svetlana had finished her courses and had been given a job at the Heart Institute of Kiev.

His mother had not approved of her. She had learned that the Malutina family had a history of heroic drinking, and learned about the father's death. But to Nikolaiy, Svetlana had been like a young fruit in spring; the down was still on the peach. She had been all the hope he had. But she was always reminding him of what he had said: Did he still want to go to America? She reminded him that he was Jewish—more privileged than any other Russian to get an exit visa. Of course he still wanted to go, he had said. Even his father, he remembered, had talked of going there. His father had had a brother in California. And by 1971, there was an added reason for him and Svetlana to go to the United States. The joy of Nikolaiy's life, Matvei, had been born. Because of Matvei, he would have given Svetlana the jewels in the Romanoff crown. Instead, he would give her California.

Nikolaiy wiped calf blood from his arms. He had split his plastic gloves, which he had always found a crazy thing to wear with cleavers; he tore them off and pulled a new pair from the dispenser. He scraped the fleshy scraps from his chopping table, thinking for an instant of the first Red Army ambulance he had ever seen, and pulled over another half of young ox.

He hadn't been as confident as Svetlana that he could build a new life in a new country. At the same time that he agreed to set the plan in motion, he had been seized with terror. There was his age. There was the language problem. But everyone said that America was a paradise for Jews and that Jewish Russians were kings of the heap. They ran Hollywood, where Svetlana wanted to go, the way the old boyars had run the peasants in the Ukraine. His father's brother, Samuel Wolfson, who had called himself Sam Wolf in Los Angeles, had visited them in Kiev. He had said that he had a shoe factory. If they came to California, he would help them. But still Nikolaiy didn't want to leave his mother; Svetlana, however, had wanted nothing better.

He had finally applied to emigrate in 1972. He had had to pretend that he was still a Jew, like his grandparents, and that he wanted to go to Palestine, where he would be a citizen of Israel, and that he therefore consented to give up his citizenship in the USSR. He had chuckled to Svetlana and said:

"California, here we come!"

In the early 1970s, scores of thousands of Russians with Jewish family backgrounds had been allowed to leave like lemmings for the United States, in response to political pressure from Washington. Many, like Nikolaiy, had had criminal records. They didn't have much future in Russia. Nikolaiy noted that, when you thought about it, the authorities must have been getting rid of criminals, the way Castro did. Perhaps Castro got the idea from Moscow; after all, didn't he get all his ideas from Moscow?

Nikolaiy separated what remained of the calf's front leg, and began slicing through the osso buco in big chunks. He remembered another taxi driver in Kiev who had said to him angrily:

"America loves Jews! Why don't you go? We don't need criminals here. America is the best place in the world for criminals. Here, the hooligans steal car tires—there, you can rob a bank!"

And the cabbie laughed, and the other drivers had laughed. And even Nikolaiy had laughed at the thought of robbing a bank.

When he had applied for an exit visa, there had been questions from a KGB officer. The man had seemed to be sounding him out about doing some work overseas, but what the apparatchik had principally wanted to know was if he really was going to Israel. The Mossad wanted Russian-speaking agents, and the KGB would be glad to supply them.

They had had to wait only six months. Nikolaiy, Svetlana, and Matvei had been authorized to leave for Israel on January 23, 1973. They had flown to Vienna, where they had spent two weeks in the prettily named refugee center at Schönau. Now, he remembered, Svetlana was saying that perhaps she would be going to Vienna again. With Mr. Something.

At Schönau, an American Jewish organization had given them tickets for Rome, where the U.S. embassy had stamped visas on their papers. They had been told that they were political refugees. To achieve that status, they had had to write statements, which some of the "intellectuals" at Schönau had written for people like Nikolaiy. They had to write them in English, because the Americans at the Rome embassy who dealt with the Russian emigrants didn't speak Russian.

In his application for a U.S. visa, Nikolaiy had had written for him:

"I wish to be free and to live in a free country. One of the main aims of my leaving the Soviet Union is the desire to get rid of the Soviet authorities, which do whatever they want. During the epoch of Stalin, they killed my father." There hadn't been very much that he could add to this, so the Schönau scribe had concluded for him:

"I beg you not to make me recall all these tragical events. I ask you very much to give the opportunity to go to the U.S.A., one of the most democratic countries in the world."

Svetlana had had to make an application, too. She had said:

"I wish to be free to bring up my son in freedom and democracy." She had thought that sounded nice.

He pulled suet from a heart and kidneys and threw it into the trash bin under the chopping table. It was astonishing how much he was instructed to waste. You could make wonderful Russian dumplings from suet.

He thought about flying to New York and staying for a few days with his aunt. Aunt Lisa had also spent time in prison, because she had lived with an S.S. officer during the occupation.

Then they had flown to Los Angeles. Most of the expense for all this had come from the Jewish Family Service. They had been put in a modest hotel for the night; the next day they had gone to Uncle Sam's house; and there, they had found that he had just died. His widow had taken them in for two days, then the Family Service people had found them the apartment on Gardner Street and a job for Nikolaiy as a night watchman at a supermarket. Then, there had been jobs on construction sites, jobs that didn't require much English, and finally the job at Hoffman's. Now his weekly pay, before tax, was about four hundred dollars, with overtime. Tax had been a shock. It wasn't only the government in Washington, but the state government, and the county government, and something called Social Security. Four taxes. He had preferred the Soviet system.

Adam Uribe, the foreman, was walking past the cutting stations, so Nikolaiy put on a display of working quickly, making deft little movements as he sliced the fat off the chops, throwing it away. Adam nodded to him and he nodded back, respectfully. At first, he had welcomed the fact that nearly everyone at the plant was Jewish. It had made him feel a part of a club. And he had been excited by America. Kiev had suddenly seemed drab, and California seemed to have a monopoly on the sun. But he had always missed the real, solid furniture of his mother's apartment. The things they had in West Hollywood— he could have broken the chairs and table apart with his hands—didn't make a home. And neither he nor Svetlana had felt comfortable living so close to so many noisy black and Spanish people. They were frightening. He had bought a pistol. One of the other *émigrés* had told him that there were more criminal gangs in the city of Los Angeles than there were football teams in the whole of the Ukrainian Soviet Socialist Republic. He had never thought that he, Nikolaiy Wolfson-Ogorodnikov, would live to praise the Soviet penal system until he saw the extent of the drug trade and hooliganism in America!

He reached for yet another long side of veal. He wondered what they would give Matvei for lunch at school. As he worked away with the cleaver, he worried about his son. He had wanted him to have the education he had never had. But now he realized that a factory butcher, even with the fancy name of meat cutter, would never be able to live in those parts of America where public education was as good as or better than in Kiev. He was an ex-convict who had always lived on his wits, but he wanted Matvei to be disciplined enough to be able to stand on his own feet and have a career. If they had stayed at home, he would have hoped to see him go into the Army. Not as a dispatch carrier, but as an officer.

He had learned that in America, there was an élite that looked after its own, and that to enter the élite from the outside you had to be above average. Matvei needed direction, and if he grew up in a poor quarter of Los Angeles, he wouldn't look to his uneducated father for that, and he wouldn't get it from the environment. He wouldn't get it from Svetlana, either. His little flower was a wild flower. She was not much more than half his age and had more hope, but her hopes were not very practical. That was how she had become involved with the FBI. And in America, it was harder to discipline your wife. Of course, he still had to hit her sometimes—but only because he cared for her, and because he cared for his son.

The girl next to him who was doing the packing had given up trying to draw him into conversation and had started talking to another girl two stations away. He listened to the loud, scratchy voices with displeasure. He continued chopping, methodically. He missed Russia, his family, his friends, his language. He missed being sure of always having a job; he missed free medical care, especially now that he could see old age just down the street of time. They had never managed to save enough to make the down payment on a house. They were foreigners, with no credit rating, so they would have to pay fifty percent in cash. He remembered the cabbie in Kiev saying: "In America, you can rob a bank!"

He knew for sure that he never intended to break the law again, however poor he was. He was determined to do no more prison. Not just for his own good, but for his son. He had read in the papers about the Mafia started in New York by Jewish *émigrés* from Russia. They were repeating the crimes that had put them into prison in Russia, except that now it was things like diamonds. There were Jewish Russian gangs in Los Angeles, too. You could see them meeting in parks, talking Russian, playing cards so as not to look suspicious. Svetlana had told the FBI about them.

He scraped surplus into the trash again and reached for another side of veal. He had labored hard in America, and he hadn't broken the law. True, he had worked a few wrinkles, like bringing that lawsuit after he had backed his car into someone else's. But that was all right; the money had come from a rich insurance company's profits. Litigation was just a lottery in this country. They had had three hits. The money had gone to buy the dumpling machine, some new things for the apartment, the piano, new clothes—mostly for Svetlana and Matvei.

Adam Uribe walked past again, looking at no one. Nikolaiy felt self-conscious about pretending to be Jewish, even though it was a sort of birthright. Hitler and Stalin thought that people like himself were Jews, by inheritance. Once a Jew. . . . That was prejudice. Stalin had got the idea from the czars, who had kept Jews in ghettos long after they had been assimilated in the rest of Europe. What did Stalin think Karl Marx was—Greek Orthodox? Was Svetlana a Christian? They had joined the church in Silver Lake because it was what you did in America. But if they hadn't received a visa for the United States, he still would not have gone to Palestine. He would have asked for Australia, or Europe. If they would have taken him, with his record.

But among many of the Russians in West Hollywood, homesickness for Russia had revived religion. One of the reasons they had joined the church in Silver Lake was because it had a Russian atmosphere and a Sunday school for Matvei. At the church, they could share their problems with other Russian families. One of the children in a Russian family with six kids had been shot dead by American street kids. They had wanted to go back to the Soviet Union, and Nikolaiy and Svetlana had advised them to do so. So had others. "Better red than dead," one of them had quipped. But others in the congregation had been angry with them because those people desperately wanted to prove to themselves that they had been right to emigrate in the first place. But almost everybody liked Russian films, and the church had a hall and two projectors. That was really what had given Svetlana the idea of being an exhibitor.

He wiped his brow with the back of a plastic glove. In spite of the air conditioning, the work was making him perspire. Perhaps it was middle age that caused that. He was trimming chops again, and thinking of those film evenings. He had agreed with Svetlana that it was a good idea. It was part-time work that wouldn't interfere with her duties as a housewife and mother. It would give them a little extra cash. And, as Svetlana had pointed out, it would give them more respect in the community. He had always liked films, himself. And films were Svetlana's dream world.

It meant contacting the Soviet consulate-general in San Francisco. A Russian friend, Viktor Nachaev, had introduced them to the cultural attaché. Eventually, Nikolaiy had summoned up the courage to ask if they could send Matvei to a school in the Soviet Union—even though Nikolaiy and Svetlana had surrendered their citizenship—in the way some other immigrants sent their children back to France or Britain for their education. The man had said that since Svetlana was performing a cultural service for the USSR, and if Nikolaiy could perform some little services, too, then he would see what he could do for Matvei. If not boarding school, then perhaps summer camp.

Services?

The vague word had troubled him. But they surely couldn't expect him to spy on American defense and high technology from a butchery plant, especially since he had finished schooling at eleven. There had been demonstrations outside a local high school because some Russian dancers were performing there. Some of the demonstrators had been *émigrés*. Since he had no sympathy for silly demonstrations against ballet, he had accepted the consulate-general's request to take photos of the demonstrators. Aleksandr Polovets, who edited a local anti-Soviet weekly in Russian, *Almanac Panorama*, had also taken photographs. Nikolaiy supposed that if there were anti-American demonstrations in Kiev, the American consulate-general in Moscow would want some pictures. I am not anti-anything, Nikolaiy thought, as he deftly cut away some neck of veal for stuffing.

He had begun to develop a headache, and it was because he was worrying. He was worrying about Svetlana and the FBI and the talk of a trip to Europe. It had begun with the film work. That had changed her social life. Svetlana had developed from a pretty girl into an attractive woman. She attracted attention. And because of that, she had ceased to be satisfied with life at home, cooking, looking after Matvei and the apartment. Sometimes, Nikolaiy would return from a hard day's work, and she would not be there. But when that had first happened, he had had a weekly mistress, so he hadn't pushed Svetlana too hard.

But the truth, he felt, was that she was not a very good mother or housekeeper, and the two of them were not as close as they had been. It was only their love of Matvei that kept them together. Two years before, in 1982, they had separated. Legally. Svetlana had come back, but they had remained legally separated. They were no longer really lovers. But they were friends.

He reached for a new side of meat and straightened it up in front of him. Sometimes, he varied the pattern with which he dissected the beast, to relieve the boredom, but now he was so preoccupied that he was doing each side of veal in exactly the same manner. He was more homesick than Svetlana. He had been past forty when he had arrived. He worried about his old mother in Kiev. Because of the films, he had been allowed to visit Russia, for which he was grateful; but sometimes he wanted to go back for good. However, Svetlana didn't want that, and she would never let him take Matvei back permanently. Svetlana still had her American dreams. She still liked meeting American actors and actresses, and talking about it. She enjoyed the escort jobs. That was work for a pretty woman, not a middle-aged butcher! But they had been together to Mischa Makarian's, the nightclub run by a man from Soviet Armenia.

Svetlana. He supposed she was an American spy on the *émigré* community. He was nervous about that, and about her relationship with the Soviet consulate-general. She thought it was all romantic, respectable. He could see how it might be dangerous. But he was glad that Matvei had been allowed to go to Artek. That was the best of the camps—the one that had foreign children from Europe, America and elsewhere. There were ten or fifteen kids from America each time, Matvei said; many were children of *émigrés*, but not *émigrés* classified as Jews, because those had surrendered their citizenship in order, theoretically, to become Israelis. So he and Svetlana had been privileged. Certainly, Matvei would never have been admitted to Artek if they had remained in Kiev, where they had been very unimportant people. Now, they were "friends of the consulate-general," and able to visit Russia, although this was hard on their savings. And this was also a guarantee that they would never be asked to work for the KGB, he thought, because no one who did work like that would be allowed to attract attention by going back every year to Russia. Now, all the consulate-general asked him to do was to spot people who wanted to go home for good, because there was a new program: Someone would call on them and say that they could go home; they would have an apartment and a job. But now what was the FBI getting Svetlana to do?

Svetlana's little services for the consulate-general had been simple enough. She had been a chauffeur, or rather a chauffeuse. Once, there had been trouble aboard a Russian freighter, and she had driven a Soviet consul there. That was the most political task she had ever performed. Nikolaiy cut a leg in three parts and passed the top two to the packer. The only truly political work that she had been asked to do was by the FBI. Recently, she had been told to fly to San Francisco and deliver a package to a man whom she would meet in a restaurant. They had both been nervous. Nikolaiy had worried that the job might be dangerous, and had said that he would do it himself. But before leaving the airport at Los Angeles, he had opened the package. It contained character reports on some of the Russians in the Los Angeles area. He supposed it was something which that man John Hunt had given to Svetlana to excite the consulate's interest. And Nikolaiy had flown to San Francisco, and gone to the restaurant, and met the man, and silently given him the package.

Russians who lived abroad were always debriefed when they returned home. Once, in Moscow, he and Svetlana had been asked if they knew the whereabouts of Stanislav Levchenko, a KGB defector who was thought to be in California. Nikolaiy had suggested that they employ a lawyer, Donald Levinson, who could perhaps find a private investigator. He was authorized to tell Levinson that he would receive ten thousand dollars if he traced Levchenko; Levinson had told him that he had gone to the FBI and asked if it was okay to proceed.

The important thing was to stay on the right side of the law. They possessed doctored reentry permits that said they had been born in Czechoslovakia, but that was all right because the FBI knew all about them, and so did the Soviet authorities.

He supposed Svetlana was on the right side of the law, as well. But since she had taken up with the FBI, she had started to drink much more than before. And he didn't approve of all her other friends, either. There was Nina Thomas, a Russian interpreter who had persuaded an American posted to Russia to marry her so that she could come to America, where they divorced. He didn't approve of Nina. But the main problem was that not all of Svetlana's friends were women. She received some gifts, and it wouldn't be a woman giving her jewelry or a *négligée*. And she gave gifts, also, and obviously they were to men. And she had brought that fat FBI man home that night, recently. Nikolaiy hadn't caught his name. Nikolaiy's English wasn't as good as hers, and he had been asleep when they had arrived. For some reason, she had told Mr. Something that he was Nikolaiy Wolfson.

Back at Gardner Street, Svetlana was already nearly halfway through her first cigarette pack of the day. Was Richard getting cold feet? He had put off meeting her that night, which was unusual. Normally, he was bound to her by the promise of sex. He had asked her to do what John had asked her to do, and she had done it. He was talking about being the first FBI agent to penetrate the KGB. He was even talking about getting fifty thousand dollars and more from the consulate, and also saving his career; and she remembered that they had told her in San Francisco that if she "recruited" Richard, there would be twenty-five thousand dollars for her. She didn't completely understand who was doing what, but she certainly understood the dollars. Yet Richard was now saying things like "maybe". The fool had done nothing yet about getting a passport, or a clearance from Christensen. And even if he didn't need a passport for Mexico, wouldn't she need a visa, and wouldn't Richard have to see to that as well? Had the consulate-general people made up their minds? Was Richard ever serious? About anything but sex. John had probably told Richard that she was good in bed, in the way men talked about these things, and perhaps that had been the only reason that Richard had called her in the first place. He had had an excuse: Both he and John were in the counterespionage squad, and in the double-agent program. She thought she knew what that meant, but she wasn't sure. The only thing sure about Richard was that he had the hots for her. Yet sex with Richard wasn't good. It was just her duty. He was the FBI. You had to sleep with the FBI if they told you to. But she did feel sorry for him, with his puppy-dog ways. Although she didn't like going to bed with him, she was beginning to like having him around.

She got up from the armchair and fixed herself the first brandy and margarita mix of the day. She lit another cigarette and went back to the television.

# PART II

## The Action

# Chapter Ten

# The Master: Turning Up the Wick

*"What she wanted was for Belyakov to upgrade her—to give her first-release films. But of course it was John Hunt who wanted to be upgraded."*

Lev Zaydzev had awakened with a sense of optimism that he rarely felt when living in enemy territory. The new op seemed to be progressing very well. And if Colonel Grishin's plan worked, Zaydzev in turn would be promoted.

Zaydzev had had his usual breakfast: a wine glass of vodka with a great hunk of the black bread that he bought from an *émigré* grocery, while listening on his Walkman to a frivolous waltz by Nikolaiy Rimski-Korsakov and reading a sensitive chapter of Aleksandr Sergeyevich Pushkin, his favorite writer. With few variations, these were his matinal rites.

The only thing that nagged at Zaydzev's nervous mind was that, so far, everything had seemed to be too easy. There had been this team of American workers on the roof, and of course it had been assumed that they had planted electronic gear—and they had. So, of course, the Rezidentura had left it there and had used it to make the Americans think—among other things—that Zaydzev was the Rezident.

Now, if need be, they could use this facility as a disinformation channel on the Svetlana caper. He thought about the little woman from Yefrimov. They had tested her to see where her loyalties lay. They had given her a task to perform and she had not performed it—to trace Levchenko and the others, through Hunt. She had sold her sex to Hunt for *nothing*.

She is trying to infiltrate *us,* the Rabbit thought with disgust. So they would try to trap everybody—the FBI, Svetlana, and Nikolaiy Sergeivich. No violence—the FBI would do it themselves, Grishin had said. Good riddance! Grishin would go home to his great promotion, and Zaydzev would inherit the Rezidentura and become a colonel.

Hunt had been an easy catch at first. Informants in the Russian community had said, in their own words, that he matched a profile for Svetlana—that he had a taste for diminutive, blonde women. Svetlana Malutina was what the Komitat called his female body type. So it was Zaydzev who had arranged through Nina Thomas for Hunt to learn that Ogorodnikova had been to the Soviet Union, with the suggestion that he ask what she'd been doing there. Nina had told Hunt that both the Ogorodnikovs spoke well of the Soviet Union and critically of the United States.

When Grishin had talked about the apparent romance between Svetlana and Hunt, Zaydzev had said: "There must be scores of small, pretty blondes in the secretarial ranks of the FBI." And Grishin had said yes, of course—but that Hunt had been tempted by the chance to troll his rod in forbidden waters.

That had been in 1982, when Hunt had used Svetlana to make his amateurish dangle. And Grishin had played coy at first, and now Hunt had been replaced by Miller, which made the FBI scam more obvious. The enemy was riding for a fall!

That morning, after talking to the parliamentary delegation, Grishin asked Zaydzev to join him in one of the "quiet" rooms— the jargon for the bug-proof ones—and to bring Menshikov, Zaydzev's newly arrived assistant, who was destined to become the deputy Rezident.

When they were seated, Grishin addressed himself to Menshikov: "I want to tell you about an arrangement which is coming up with an FBI counterintelligence agent called Richard William Miller. He has indicated that he might be prepared to work for us."

As he spoke, Grishin smiled inwardly at the rapt and puzzled expression on Menshikov's face. The new arrival was a few years older than Grishin, about the same age as Zaydzev, a wafer-like man with worried features. He had seemed an odd choice for the laid-back atmosphere of northern California; but he had an exceptional career record, and his American English was even more correct than Grishin's.

"Is he serious?"

"No." Grishin enjoyed watching the expression change in Menshikov's eyes. He went on: "Let me explain about his cut-out, if that's a suitable expression under the circumstances. But no, let me tell you about her husband, Nikolaiy Sergeivich, originally born Wolfson. A notorious hooligan. He has a criminal record so long—and absolutely, totally, nothing to do with politics—that he would never have received an American visa if he had been, say, a Frenchman or an Englishman. He got it because he is of Jewish descent and could pretend to our authorities that he wanted to go to Israel. He and his wife live in Hollywood, but very poorly by American standards. He works in a butchery factory. He has done some small services for the consulate-general, and we have allowed him to go home on visits. And his son has gone to Artek."

Menshikov nodded. "They are S?"

Grishin laughed. "Perish the thought! No. 'Friends of the consulate-general.' They show Sovexport films, at their church and in cinemas. But that's mostly his wife's work. She's the one who will be coming here a week from today, next Thursday. She may be bringing Mr. Miller. Her name is Svetlana, Svetlana Malutina. She's from Yefrimov." Grishin gave an urbane smile as he mentioned the rural origins.

"Just a moment. Church?"

"She is not of Jewish descent, and Nikolaiy Sergeivich's only Jewish connection is that a Jewish organization helped him find a job and an apartment. As you know, Lev, Svetlana told us last year that she was having an affair with an FBI agent called John Hunt. She said Hunt wanted to marry her."

"Was that true?"

"Probably not. He was obviously trying to hint to us some sort of collaboration. Anyway, now she's bringing Miller, who is Hunt's replacement, and perhaps a letter from Miller."

"Replacement? How do you replace a fiancé? Does she want to marry both of them? That's not possible." Menshikov managed to say this in all seriousness, without a smile.

"Exactly. It's an obvious scam. Boris Belyakov in the cultural section, who deals with films, can show you his file on her, and we have some stuff here which you can read. But let me quickly give you a bit more background on the two of them, on her and her husband."

Grishin offered cigarettes to Zaydzev and Menshikov, then lit for both of them and himself. He blew smoke and said: "They arrived in 1973 with a two-year-old son, Matvei. Nikolaiy had been in prison five times, I forget for how long in all, more than ten years. He'd been a truck driver, but at the time he left, he was driving a taxi in Kiev and doing small services for the police. Unreliable. Anyway, they come here with poor knowledge of English, and this Jewish organization finds him jobs. He's been chopping up meat for eight years."

"He's from Yefrimov also?"

"No. Kiev. Anyway, it's a classical story. They are cast ashore here, as on a desert island. He's forty; she's twenty-three, a silly girl, perhaps a bit more adaptable to America. But they're both homesick. They have mothers—widows, in poor health—back home. So, after some years, they wanted visitors' visas to go and see their mothers, since they didn't have citizenship any more. They were told that if they did some small services, well, maybe. Nikolaiy Sergeivich even wanted to send his son to school in Kiev, because the schools are so bad here; but of course we said no."

Grishin recalled the minor services, mostly chauffeuring, which the Ogorodnikovs had performed, and the rewards—the visas, Artek for Matvei. The phone buzzed and he took a call from the consul-general. He put down the receiver and looked at Menshikov again.

He said: "Svetlana was clearly flattered by—and probably exaggerated—her ability to do services for the consulate-general. To continue to get her visas, and her films, she was prepared, I think, to do anything legitimate. In 1980, before my time, after she drove one of the vice-consuls to Anaheim, she informed us that two FBI agents had called on her and asked her to keep them informed of anything we asked her to do. She gave us their calling cards, as they must have known that she would do. Their names were John Hunt and Robert Patton. We asked her to keep us informed of any approaches or harassment by the FBI; but since she was of limited intellect, we didn't anticipate anything useful coming from these reports."

"As you know, we have such people everywhere."

"Of course; so do the Americans—'friends of the embassy' who tell their favorite commercial secretary what they hear in the American colonies in Moscow or Leningrad. It's precisely because these two misfits aren't S people that I think we may have an opportunity to pay the FBI back in kind."

Menshikov leaned forward. Grishin told him more about John Hunt's initial approach, through Svetlana, to Belyakov, the year before. They had recognized his name from the calling card and used Nina Thomas to bring him along.

"We knew he was in the 'Russian Squad.' We concluded from his approach that he must be in charge of their double-agent program. Like us, they work through informers, but they obviously hoped to make this stupid girl from Tula a sort of double agent. She was frightened, but we told her to go out with him. We would give her some tidbits on the consulate, so that she could sustain the relationship. She told Belyakov that she had become Hunt's mistress."

"He must have told her to do that, to see how we would respond."

"Of course. Belyakov had pretended to be annoyed at her, at first, so we told him not to frighten her. We pretended to have some doubts—we asked for photographs or other proof that she had this relationship. Belyakov told her not to be ashamed, after all, about having an affair with this American cop. She claimed he was talking of divorcing his wife and of marrying her."

"You think he told her to say that, or she made it up?"

"Your guess is as good as mine. You know her type—what Dostoyevsky made Karamazov call the barefoot peasant. She was very bashful when she explained the relationship, so perhaps she was trying to look respectable—to pretend that she wasn't being unfaithful to Nikolaiy Sergeivich just to make money, or to go to nice restaurants. She was hinting to Belyakov that she could get information from Hunt, that Hunt wanted to help. Of course, we feigned excitement—to encourage Hunt. Once, Hunt sent us some reports on the *émigrés*. Nikolaiy brought them. Nothing we didn't know, of course."

"So Svetlana—"

"—wanted Belyakov to upgrade her—to give her first-release films. But of course it was John Hunt who wanted to be upgraded."

"He wanted you to set up a meeting with him."

"Of course. Taped and photographed. Probably more than one meeting. Then we'd be denounced for conduct incompatible with our diplomatic status."

"He'd get a medal."

"I think they call it a commendation. Anyway, promotion."

"So what's her loyalty?"

"So far as I can judge, until very recently it was primarily Hunt. Nikolaiy Sergeivich had been her passport to Hollywood. Hunt would be her passport to bourgeois prosperity—then she wouldn't need our films. What could we offer her in competition to him? The visas. Artek for the boy. But it was Nikolaiy Sergeivich who wanted those most."

"She thought Hunt was serious about her?"

"That was and is my impression. But now that she's bringing Miller here instead, who knows where her allegiance lies? Anyway, that's what I've instructed her to do—bring Miller, I mean, so that we can see him, on the twenty-fourth. I've said that if we recruit him, she'll get twenty-five thousand dollars."

"Twenty-five thousand from us for following the instructions of her FBI supervisor? It's an offer she can't refuse."

"Exactly," Zaydzev put in.

For once, the dour, skinny Menshikov smiled.

Grishin went on: "Number one: No FBI man would ever have become involved with Ogorodnikova except on his own initiative, right? Hunt's in the Russian Squad. He's probably, as I've said, their top so-called double agent. He knew about her contacts with the consulate-general. And she, poor simple soul, was trying to lure him into marriage! There's no way the Ogorodnikovs could have thought of this, to ingratiate themselves with us. Now, it's Miller who's initiating, which doesn't make sense if Hunt really was a potential mole. Miller's already asked for money, so he's simply taken on a scam. Do you agree?"

"Of course. But what's our advantage, comrade? First Hunt, and now Miller, wants us to set up meetings and invite him to work for us. Ogorodnikova, with an excuse for calling here for films, would be the cut-out. Then, one day, they still jump on us."

"Exactly. My surprise was not only that Miller's approach could be so naive, but that either Hunt or Miller would think that a vodka-head like Ogorodnikova would be able to play such a double role, or that *we* would assess her as suitable for such a role."

The telephone buzzed. It was Ludmila. There was an incoming call from an S person in Mill Valley. He passed the call to a subordinate. He put the receiver down and looked into Menshikov's eyes.

"I toyed with the idea of suggesting to Center that I offer to be one of 'theirs'. I was going to say: 'Look, Mr. Hunt, I know you're a loyal American, and I'm glad you are, because you're just the contact I'm looking for.' Would he not see promotion staring him in the face? But then I decided that they would probably have found someone more serious than Hunt to handle me. In the final analysis, I couldn't see any safe advantage in pursuing Hunt's initiative, so in 1983 we never really responded. And given her relationship with Hunt, and her apparently romantic feelings for him, I had her taken off the consulate-general invitation list. But we allowed her to go on renting films. After all, love doesn't last forever!"

Menshikov said: "I've never been anywhere else where there were so many *émigrés* pining for Russian films. It sounds like a useful factor, but it's so obvious that—"

"That even the FBI must notice!" Zaydzev chipped in. "Of course."

Grishin said: "And of course Ogorodnikova isn't our only outlet in Los Angeles. There are other capitalists! There's a travel agent, Diana Baskevitch, in Hollywood. It was she who made it possible for us to give them their visas. She produced U.S. re-entry permits that said that they were born in Czecho-slovakia!"

Menshikov stared in amazement. Grishin went on: "Oh, the FBI knows! It makes no difference to them. It's for our bureaucrats, not the Americans!"

"So, do people like Ogorodnikova depend on the good graces of people like Hunt to get those things?"

"Well, we could hardly expect to control that ourselves," Zaydzev said.

"What was Center's response to all this, Aleksandr Vasilievich? I wasn't in Moscow last year."

"Center told us to leave Hunt in the wind for a while," Grishin said. "Then, Anatoliy Parshenko suggested that I invite him to Europe. That was this year. Parshenko interviewed Ogorodnikova in Moscow in July. I was in Moscow myself at the time. The interview didn't go very well. Like us, he saw that he couldn't trust her at all. But he said the GRU would like to invite her and her American lover to come to Warsaw."

Menshikov nodded. Bringing in the GRU had become the way of deflecting some of the heat from the KGB offices in the embassies and consulates.

Grishin said: "Some months before, she appeared to have broken off contact with Hunt. But in May it seemed to be on again. At least, that's what she was telling us on, let's see, May 23. I think that was why Moscow acted."

Grishin toyed with the ash on his black cigarette, and went on: "Belyakov saw her not long after she came back last month, and she seemed frightened—which of course made us wonder whether Hunt might not, after all, be a serious defector, and whether she was worried about where that would put her, in the United States. She passed on Parshenko's invitation to Hunt, and almost at once two different FBI men arrived at her apartment and questioned her. They gave her their calling cards— both members of the Russian Squad, of course, and naturally neither could speak a word of Russian! She told them about her debriefing by Parshenko, but she pretended that it took place in her Moscow hotel, because she thought they might find it suspicious if they knew she'd been taken to a safe house."

The phone buzzed again. Ludmila told him that a visitor whom he had been expecting had arrived. Grishin said he would be free in a few minutes. He heard Menshikov saying: "So, you were right to keep Hunt at arm's length!"

"I was right. But Center decided last month that I should go along. They thought he might just possibly be a real defector, so we should sound him out—do nothing about him here, but say that if he would like an appointment to talk things over in Europe, and was traveling at his own expense, not ours, well, of course we were interested in freedom of travel! But now Miller has taken his place. What are we supposed to believe— that when one mole goes sick, or is too busy to leave the office, the FBI finds us a substitute?"

Menshikov jerked an index finger toward the ceiling. "Then he could be a *genuine* defector—unlike Hunt."

"He doesn't fit any profile for that. He's in the double-agent program. He wants to be a double agent—for America, I presume. And now she says he wants her to write us a letter, in Russian, for him, making his offer."

"In writing? Extraordinary! He's hoping for an incriminating letter in response."

Grishin nodded. "If we do this right, the FBI will not arrest us—they will arrest him!"

"You mean?"

"I'll explain later. And after they come here—just in case this Miller fellow might be sincere—Svetlana will be informed that we've followed them and photographed them together."

"Could we do that—here?"

"It would be very difficult. I wouldn't even try—we might run into the rest of the FBI!" He smiled. "Now, I have another appointment. Ask Ludmila to give you the file."

# Chapter Eleven

# Moths to the Flame

*He said a little prayer that everything would be all right. That was asking a lot, he knew; nothing had been all right for a long, long time.*

She waited in the Sears parking lot in West Hollywood for Miller to appear. The FBI seemed to like meeting in parking lots. It made everything seem shifty. Drug dealers, she knew, met each other in parking lots.

It was August 23, 1984, and they needed to get started soon. The air was crisp at that early time of the day, before the streets filled with traffic. They would stop for breakfast somewhere on the highway. She wasn't hungry, but Richard was always hungry.

Would Richard come? Was he serious? She was out on a limb, or at least two limbs at once, like a squirrel being chased by a cat from one tree to another. John's initiative last year had only got her into trouble with the consulate-general. The normally humorous Belyakov had been critical; obviously, they all were suspicious of her. She had noticed that she was not receiving any more invitations to official events. Now, however, the consulate-general seemed enthusiastic. And so did Richard. Yet somehow this combination of enthusiasms didn't make sense. Her main concern was to keep the film distribution arrangement, partly so as to be able to return to Yefrimov each year and see her mother. The film business was important to her socially, too.

Why had John said she was not effective, after what Bryce Christensen had told her? She still didn't really know where she stood with John. At least he had paid the doctor's bill. That must surely have been his own money, not the FBI's, and it must have been about a week's salary before deductions. She knew all about deductions; Nikolaiy was always complaining about them. There had never been deductions, back in Kiev.

She looked at her watch. Richard was late. Of course. She thought about John. He had been better about keeping time, about everything. She thought of Nikolaiy. She had never told Nikolaiy John's name, but she was sure he knew. Matvei had seen John so many times at the apartment, and the boy and his father were very close. And now she had introduced Richard to Nikolaiy. So there was Richard, and the consulate-general, and Nikolaiy. She was out on three limbs, not two. She was a squirrel with two cats coming after her from two different trees. She looked at her watch again. She wanted to be in San Francisco before nightfall.

Miller ambled up, swinging sideways from limb to limb the way fat people do. He had parked his Isuzu in the wrong parking lot, then realized his mistake and decided to walk up the empty sidewalk in the soft sun, find the right lot, and walk Svetlana back to his car. He dragged his feet, uncertainly. He had never been so nervous in his entire life. He felt as though he was walking onto the high-dive board. There was still time to draw back. Could he really cheat the Russians, both of money and in intelligence? Could he trust Svetlana? She was so spacy. But she was Russian, so she knew them, and she was his ally. Or was she? Would he have taken on this mission impossible if John's Russian informant had been a man? Had he been drawn into this because he needed love? He had always needed love. He had told 'Lana he loved her. Well, you had to say that. Sometimes, he felt it. He had told Marta York up in Oregon that he loved her, too. Marta wanted to marry him. But there were her children and, above all, his. Would they ever understand? Best of all, he knew, would be if he and Paula could somehow make a go of it, if she would somehow stop screeching at him.

The Sears parking lot came into view. Come on, R.W., he told himself, no time to back out now. The two things he absolutely had to do were to save his career and make some money. Could he really emulate Bernard Samson? Could anyone?

Deighton had written in one of his novels that Miller had read that, at certain times, a double agent becomes uncertain which side he's on. That made sense, Miller thought. You begin to build a bridge on the Kwai River *for the enemy*, not because the enemy insists on it. Surely, he thought, 'Lana must be even more confused than he.

He entered the lot. It was almost empty at that hour, before people came to work. His shortsighted eyes came into focus on the tiny figure waiting there; he saw 'Lana's smile. She seemed pleased to see him, or at least relieved. At her request, he was wearing a freshly cleaned suit, a clean shirt, and tie. He didn't plan to go into the consulate-general unless he had to, but he supposed that he might have to do that. How would he handle their questions? He thought of Special Agent Joe Pistone joining the Mafia. He said a little prayer that everything would be all right. That was asking a lot, he knew; nothing had been all right for a long, long time.

They walked back to Miller's FBI car, and he gave her the keys to drive. Perhaps because of the time of day, they said little at first, as she headed out on 405. The big Dodge was a mess, as always. Junk on the back seat was now held down by the canisters of films, the reason for 'Lana's journey. They pulled off the highway near Sepulveda and had breakfast at a truck stop. 'Lana had coffee and toast. He had ham and pancakes and syrup. That made him feel better and more talkative. Back in the car, he slid his arm around her shoulder. She cozied up to him, looked at her watch again, and accelerated. He closed his eyes.

Mid-morning, out on Route 5 in the Tulare Lake area, he said he wanted a sandwich, so she pulled over into a highway rest facility, where he ordered a triple club on white toast. Svetlana was still conscious of time, but she welcomed the short rest, and she needed a drink. Now, the drama of what they were about to do was getting to her as well. In the parking lot, she went into her big woven bag for a bottle of brandy and a bottle of margarita mix. She found two Styrofoam cups in the glove compartment.

When he had swallowed his Coke, she said: "Relax, Richard. Have a drink for once."

And for once, he did. And twice. And as the late morning wore on, and the sun stood in judgment over the highway, a few more times.

"Haven't been to San Fran for five years, about."

"Really? You were on a case?"

"Looking for Patricia Hearst," he remembered. His memory was off by about four years.

She had been surprised when he had accepted a drink. Even more surprised at the second. And the others. As the signs began to say so many miles to San Francisco, he was beginning to giggle a little and mix up words. Richard, she knew, was a Mormon, and Mormons didn't drink.

Drinking, stopping, she got only as far as Lost Hills, where they stayed at a hotel in the Economy chain. Richard continued drinking at dinner. They would have to start early again, because her appointment with Belyakov was for nine o'clock. But the pair of them were so pie-eyed by the time they finally got to bed that nine o'clock was the time at which they woke up. It was Saturday, and the mission would close at the end of the morning.

When the skyline of San Francisco came into view, Richard said: "Will they want to see identification, to prove I'm in the FBI?" John had asked her that, she remembered, but Belyakov, after some appearance of hesitation, had seemed to take her word for it—that John was FBI. Had Richard got the idea from John? Surely the consulate-general had its own means of checking out who people were. Or was Richard just lightheaded? He had been drinking again, since leaving the hotel.

"You must be joking! Your badge and stuff? Suppose they didn't give it back?" She had said much the same thing to John before. Then, she added a lie: "Besides, they think you're John Hunt. Because that's what you told me to tell them. If I show them you're someone else, what will they think of me? How will they believe that you are my boyfriend, when they think my boyfriend's name is Hunt?"

"You're right, 'Lana. Good girl. When we get back to L.A., we'll do that letter anyway. I don't think I want to go into the consulate today."

"It's nearly two already." Now, she wasn't sorry about being late. Richard was virtually drunk again. She couldn't take him into the consulate-general in that condition.

Miller hiccoughed, shook his head. He had never been like this before. Something bothered him: Why, since he had introduced himself to Nikolaiy Wolfson, did they still think he was John? He said: "They—they know what ol' John looks like?"

"I don't think so. They don't know what you look like, either."

"John told you to tell them he wanted to go to Vienna, right?"

"No, he told me to tell them that I wanted to go to Vienna for my health and that I wanted to take him along for a vacation."

So John had never proposed meeting any Russians in Austria, Richard thought. And they hadn't responded. He would have to be more direct, in his letter. Mexico. Grayson. Gosh, so this was what it felt like when you were drunk?

Actually, it was only 1:04 p.m., according to Linda Franusich's log, when Svetlana stepped out of the FBI sedan in Green Street; but at the Saturday lunch hour there was no sign of life. Miller got out to stretch his legs. Mrs. Franusich shot them both, five times. She knew Mrs. Ogorodnikova by sight, but the man was new. He looked American. There was a Weight Watchers program at the San Francisco office of the FBI, and the man looked uncommonly like "Before" in the advertisement on the bulletin board. She was trying to read their lips. They seemed to be talking in English.

"Just wait for me somewhere, away from here, while I take these in," Svetlana was saying, clutching the canisters. "It won't be a long time. I don't know exactly how long." She wasn't sure if Boris would still be there.

He looked up the street. It had been three hours now since the breakfast at the hotel. He needed lunch, and he knew that when you had been drinking, you should eat to help you sober up. He felt like a big steak with plenty of fries. But there was another hotel bill coming up that night for sure, so he'd better stick with chicken. He said: "I'll go to a restaurant. I'll meet you back here in half an hour."

She knew he meant a cafeteria. Richard always called cafeterias restaurants. If he was going to be back in half an hour, he could only mean a self-serve place.

"Fine."

He found a fried chicken outlet, ate, walked back, got into the car. Mrs. Franusich shot him again. Svetlana kept him waiting for nearly an hour. On a whim, he started to drink her cognac and margarita mix once more. Afterwards, he could never remember exactly what he had done. Had he given her his badge to show them? Had he given her the reporting guidance to bait the line? He hoped he had not. He had certainly not intended to. But by the time he awoke the next morning in Livermore, he was unable to remember much.

When Svetlana came out of the consulate-general, she didn't ask him how long he had been waiting.

"Everything okay?" he queried, mechanically.

"Sure. Okay." She could see he couldn't replace her for the drive back to Los Angeles, as they had planned. He was nodding off to sleep. "Can we spend the night here?"

Miller nodded. "Let's go out of town somewhere."

And "somewhere" was where they went. She wanted to be more than twenty-five miles away, so that nobody from the consulate could follow them to talk to Miller. Not in that parlous state. "Somewhere" turned out to be Livermore. The Holiday Inn. Ironically, almost walking distance from where Svetlana was to be sentenced to spend eighteen years.

Miller, like most people in the condition in which he finally went to bed that night, blind drunk, had a total short-memory loss. Ever afterward, he could remember absolutely nothing of what had transpired in his life between arriving at Green Street that fateful afternoon and waking up in the morning to see the sunlight dancing crystally on a swimming pool.

His first words were: "Where the heck is this? It looks nice, but I've got a very thick head."

She muttered something, hiding her concerns. She had still not spoken to Belyakov at the consulate, only on the phone to another man, who had asked her many searching questions. But now she called Belyakov at home, to ask about films.

The FBI's tap on the Belyakov house, near the Presidio, heard a preliminary discussion about "first-release films"; then, the monitors heard Belyakov say: "We followed you last night and photographed you together." The woman's voice answered noncommittally. Who was "you"? the monitors wondered. The woman was calling from Livermore. How could the Russkies follow a couple to Livermore, outside the twenty-five-mile limit? The risk would be foolish. It sounded more like a menacing bluff than the truth.

By then, although it was Sunday, Christensen was in Bretzing's office down in Los Angeles. San Francisco had called—an emergency.

"San Fran says that Miller was at the Soviet consulate-general yesterday afternoon," Christensen confirmed. "Someone there identified him from the surveillance shots. He was with the Ogorodnikova woman. She went inside, carrying film canisters."

"Containing whatever they might have put in them," Bretzing said.

"Right. He went down the street, out of focus, then came back again and waited for her in her car. R.W. wasn't identified at once, so they logged him as 'Before.'"

"I don't follow. How was he logged before?"

"I mean as 'Mr. Before.' Get it? Anyway, they were followed, and they spent the night at a hotel at Livermore. This morning, the monitors heard a call from Livermore to one of the Russian vice-consuls at home. When this was reported, two and two were put together."

"R.W. called a Russkie?"

"No, our little Ninotchka did."

"Okay. When is our Mr. Before due back on duty?"

"Tomorrow."

"Well, I guess this is it. We really will have to go to court and get an order. Operation Whipworm, against our internal parasite."

Bretzing had held off for a few days. Now, he was furious with Miller, even with himself.

Their counterparts of the opposite persuasion in Green Street, San Francisco, were also in a quandary. Especially consul-general Myshkov. If anything went wrong, he was the one who would feel the heat of official American displeasure, the stories in the papers.

Grishin wished he had had a chance to meet Ogorodnikova and size her up. When she had not arrived by eleven o'clock the previous day, he had concluded that she wasn't coming, that one or both of them had had cold feet. He had gone home and put a pizza in the oven. When she had come, at one, she had wanted to leave the canisters with the guard and go, but the guard had reminded her that she had been expected to come earlier, and said someone wanted to talk to her on the phone. The guard had called Grishin, and there had been a long conversation—over an hour. She had seemed comfortable, if pixilated, on the phone, and it meant that he had not needed to give her a name. Or a face.

He had encouraged her to talk about her life, her marriage, her family, her problems in America, the films. He was trying to make an analysis. Belyakov had said that he had the impression that she had been sincerely unhappy when Hunt had dropped her as his swallow and had implied that he was dropping her from his life. Grishin had bemusedly reminded himself that all this was perhaps his fault—that he had lukewarmly responded to the dangle of her Lothario. But since May, Belyakov had said, she had seemed to be in better spirits and was saying that she still had her lover in the FBI. She wasn't playing both sides, she had said. She was bringing both of them together, if that was what both of them wanted. After that, it was up to them. But she hadn't told Belyakov, in May, that it wasn't Hunt anymore. It was only after her return from Moscow, and her session with Parshenko, that she had owned up to deceiving them. She had told Belyakov in explanation that Miller had told her not to give his name, but to pretend that he was Hunt. And yesterday, she had said that she had done what Miller had asked because she was embarrassed. Going from one man to the other, just like that, and having a husband, well. . . . Grishin had been inclined to believe her. She obviously wasn't at all sophisticated. It was difficult to get more on the phone. He couldn't look into her eyes as she spoke. He could tell that she was nervous, of course.

"This man is on the Russian Squad, like the other," Grishin said.

"That's right."

"Speak any Russian?"

"No. Spanish."

"That's why he likes Mexico."

"I think so."

He had heard the fluttering, inebriated, butterfly voice. She would never be America's great spy on the Soviet Union, Grishin had decided. He certainly wouldn't want her in S. The only quality she had as a swallow, he thought to himself cynically, was the prerequisite for the job: She was broadminded about adultery.

"He wants you to write a letter," Grishin said.

"Yes. His letter. I will write."

"I understand."

One thing was nagging at his consciousness. It was key to his analysis.

"Is he following orders? FBI orders?"

"What do you mean?"

She knew quite well what he meant, of course. She was giving herself time to think, the minx. Unknown to Grishin, she was thinking of how John had told her to report to him everything that she did with Richard. Was she going to report to John on San Francisco?

Then, Grishin had said impatiently: "I mean, is he acting under orders or on his own?" Or pretending to be acting on his own initiative, Grishin had added in his mind.

"I think he is going a little bit on his own."

Grishin had thought: A little bit? Miller was trying to scam the Soviet Union on his own? At least, to begin with, perhaps.

Now, the following day, Grishin wondered how well Ogorodnikova had told the truth. For the purposes of his own dangle, this was the bottom line, as Americans would say. If they got Miller overseas, they could strip him of any listening devices and talk to him in a completely sanitized environment. What could he hope to achieve, this Miller? That we accept him as our double agent, our FBI mole?

The fact that he had got out of the car in front of the consulate-general, in full view of the FBI photo-surveillance, could only mean that this was a scam. Why was he not more sophisticated? Grishin had been appalled—well, amused—at the man's girth. He would make the late secretary-general, Nikita Sergeivich, look like a ballerina! Anyway, back to basics. If he reacted negatively to going to eastern Europe for the meeting, that would mean he doesn't feel safe with us, Grishin thought— additional indications of a scam.

But in spite of his posing, as it were, for the Green Street cameras, could he be working on his own initiative? If he succeeded, what difference would it make, for the FBI, how he succeeded? Had Miller thought this through? He was in debt, Ogorodnikova had said. Perhaps he could be bought. Had that been Parshenko's conclusion? That we could turn him? But for that, Miller would need great skill and courage. Obviously, his skills were small. So we must use him against his own people in a different way.

Myshkov had said: "This is a rum affair, Aleksandr Vasiliyevich. I'm not sure I completely understand."

And Grishin had said cryptically: "The adversary has a strange sense of priorities. I am trying to think as they think in Westwood."

In another part of the city, Bill Newman, Richard Bretzing's opposite number, decided he had fulfilled his duty by telling Bretzing about the latter's wayward agent, Richard Miller—whom Newman's men had followed by car to Livermore. At this point, Newman was mostly concerned with a turf question. Manifestly, this was a *Rezidentura case*, therefore a case for the San Francisco office of the FBI—which had made the initial discovery in any event.

But when Newman had spoken to Christensen that morning, Bretzing had called back to say he didn't see it that way: It was a *Miller case*, therefore a case for and within the L.A. office. Bretzing had asked for the pictures that Newman's agents had taken of Miller and Mrs. Ogorodnikova together.

"No way!" Newman said. "This is my territory."

"But we have more agents and more resources to follow this," Bretzing insisted, speaking more quietly than his counterpart.

"Not on FCI, you haven't!" Newman snapped.

"Well, keep your precious photos," the bishop said icily. "Even without them, there's ample proof that Miller and this woman were together and that they spent the night at a hotel in Livermore."

Newman put the phone down. He could see another in the unending series of rows between San Fran and Westwood coming up again. That evening, he called his legendary predecessor, Charlie Bates, who had retired seven years before, to tell him about it. Bates was a pro; he had served in London, as the FBI liaison with MI-5. Bates still had his ear to the ground, and of course he knew who Miller was. Miller, after all, was also a legend of sorts in the FBI. "Miller stories" had been going the rounds of the FBI for years; they were like Polish jokes.

"There's a lot of things wrong with that L.A. office, 'specially in counterintelligence," Bates drawled in his good-ol'-boy Southern accent. "If Miller'd ever worked for me, no way he'd have been in FCI! No way he'd have stayed in the Bureau this long! It's that damn Mormon Mafia! How could that dummy let that KGB woman drive him to the goddamn Russkie consulate in his own FBI car an' not know we'd be watching? And that his FBI car would be identified in two shakes of a possum's tail! Makes me wanna throw up!"

Newman gave a laughing grunt. "There's no law in these United States against being stupid, Charlie!"

"Well, damn well oughtta be one," Bates parried.

# Chapter Twelve

# *Puppets on a String*

*i*

*Bretzing had bought the DeFlores theory, in part because to reject it would have reinforced the Mormon Mafia theory—that he was protecting Miller.*

In the letter to Belyakov, who was the only known contact they had, Miller reaffirmed his willingness to go to Mexico, to begin work for Soviet intelligence, that he had expressed to Nikolaiy. Svetlana, an unlikely choice for secretary, put Miller's informal English into awkward Russian. She was puzzled that he didn't just write the letter in English; perhaps he thought that the Russians in San Francisco were at the same linguistic level as the counterintelligence unit in Westwood.

Svetlana repeated her side of the bargain: "It's enough that I put you together. Then, it's your business."

"But you'll come with me to Mexico."

"Of course." Of course. Mexico was a vacation!

Bretzing, Christensen and Auer, the head of the Russian Squad, were worried about what might have been inside Svetlana's canisters in San Francisco on the twenty-fourth. What documents might Miller have tried to spirit away, if he was going to deal with the Russians?

Gary Auer recalled Miller mentioning to him the names of the three Ukrainian defectors and asking him if their whereabouts could be discovered.

"Was he serious?" Christensen looked startled. "What did you say?"

"I said we had no means of knowing."

Bretzing obtained the court-authorized wiretap on the two Miller homes, and on Miller's and Svetlana's cars. Miller and Svetlana had returned on Sunday, August 26. They had written The Letter together. Miller had returned to work the next day.

The Ogorodnikovs' apartment had been bugged since more than a year before. While awaiting the new authorization, Bretzing had eight videocameras installed in the Westwood office, at locations where Miller might often be. Like a nurse monitoring a heart patient in intensive care, an agent was already watching the console of little screens to follow Miller's movements, especially when he went to a photocopying machine. Under normal conditions, he would not have access to especially sensitive materials, but who knew what he might be copying now?

One of the surveillance cameras was placed in a light generator box which was installed in Miller's workspace. When he first saw it, Miller stared at it for a long moment and asked a colleague a few paces away what it was.

"It's a light generator box, R.W."

"You boys wouldn't be spying on me, would you?"

Miller thus established early that he was aware that he was under surveillance—although he naturally denied this to Svetlana and everyone else (and denied it in court, when it was used to give a false interpretation of why he had reported his operation to Christensen). Initially, he thought that if they were keeping an eye on what he was doing with Svetlana, that might help ensure that they knew how much of a scam it was. But he was never to detect the audio surveillance of his car, and so went on making love to Svetlana in it.

For sixteen days, Miller heard nothing from Svetlana. He concluded that, since the Russians had not reacted to The Letter, his plan had failed, just as John Hunt's had failed. He decided to drop the whole effort; failure was a conclusion with which he felt at home.

However, a week or so after Svetlana's return from San Francisco, Matvei, who was then thirteen, noticed that strange cars were constantly stopping outside or very near the apartment building on Gardner Street. The cars contained men in white shirts, dark suits and ties, looking just like the FBI agents you saw on television. All they needed was a flag!

Nikolaiy nodded at Svetlana and looked at the door. She put down a magazine and followed him out. They said nothing until they reached the privacy of the street. Long before that fat FBI man had reminded them that night in August, Nikolaiy had known that his home was bugged. In the street, he said: "We're under some sort of police surveillance."

"Yes, I know."

"They don't seem to be hiding it," Nikolaiy said. "They want us to know."

"Don't ask questions," said Svetlana, nervously. "I'm under FBI protection."

But Nikolaiy was worried, and he could see that she was worried, too. So they quarreled. They usually went outside to quarrel, because Matvei was very upset to see his parents fight. Sometimes, Matvei would lie awake all night after they had quarreled.

Svetlana admitted that she wished she had not become involved with the FBI. But she didn't see how she could get out of it, and neither did her husband, nor did they see how they could drop their friendly links with the consulate-general that the FBI wanted Svetlana to maintain. So Nikolaiy told his wife to do whatever the FBI man asked her to do. He had thus, he was to learn later, committed a felony.

Tuesday, September 11. At 7:54 p.m., the female agent monitoring the phone taps heard a man with a Russian accent calling the Ogorodnikov apartment. Svetlana had answered the call in English and he had responded in that language for the amenities, before switching to Russian.

The Westwood counterspooks had to wait until the following day to find out, from DiPretorio, what had been said. The conversation had been as tendentious and awkward as Grishin could make it.

"I am calling you on behalf of [the] acquaintances whom you met this summer."

"Yes."

"Do you still want to take a journey for your health?"

"Yes—uh—in principle."

"Does your friend still want to go with you for a vacation?"

"Yes, I think so." They had Richard's letter by now, she thought, so everyone knew it wasn't Hunt.

"Your friends would like to propose that you, as well as your friend, go by the means that you know to see them. All expenses will be reimbursed. And your friend should bring everything he can, as the acquaintances discussed with you in the special house. Tell him to bring all his luggage for the vacation."

At the trials, defense attorneys were to point out that Grishin did not say "the rest of the luggage," which would have indicated that Miller had already passed information.

Grishin paused. "Do you understand?"

"No. I mean, yes. A little."

What a peasant! Grishin felt irritated. "Now, listen!" he said. "You must travel south."

"You mean, where we came last time?"

Grishin fought to contain his impatience.

"No! Where your friend wants to go."

"San Francisco?"

"No! South!" He was using a prearranged code which she had forgotten, and which would sound suitably deceptive to the monitors. South meant East. Then, memory stirred—and she broke the code.

"Moscow?"

"No. The second place. Do you understand?"

"No. I don't understand." She had been drinking when he called. Now, she had no recollection of what this man was referring to. Second place?

"Warsaw," Grishin said.

"Oh!"

After putting down the phone, Svetlana wondered about the voice. It was not Belyakov's, of course. Was it the man who had spoken to her from his home when she had been with the consular guard on Green Street? Now she had to talk to Richard. She decided that it might be better to go to Richard's place than to try to pin him down on the phone.

Nikolaiy's cousin John, the son of Nikolaiy's Aunt Lisa in New York, had just arrived to stay with them, and she called his name. He was snoozing in the bedroom. She asked the young man to go with her and help her find Miller's place in Lynwood.

She soon noticed that she was being followed, but she continued. Driving around and around, in the gathering dusk, she never found the house. She became more and more exasperated with herself and with the innocent John, who knew nothing of Los Angeles. At one point, she thought of asking the perplexed FBI agent who was following her if he could help her find Special Agent Miller's house. Special Agent Ronald Durkin saw her stop, get out of the car, walk a few paces toward him, then change her mind. She got back into the Lynx, drove home, and called Miller from West Hollywood. By then, according to the FBI log, it was 11:12 p.m. The first words the monitor heard Miller say were: "I never expected to hear from you again."

They made a date for the following evening.

The FBI was there. Special Agent Allen Robinson watched Miller park his car on a lot on Sepulveda Boulevard, then look through the contents of a briefcase. At 5:57 p.m., Svetlana drove up. Miller got out and joined her in the Lynx, carrying a slim office envelope. Robinson reported that night that Miller had given the envelope to Svetlana. But in court he was to say that he had forgotten whether Miller still had the envelope with him when he went back to his own car. Miller was to testify that he carried the envelope with him both ways to remind himself to mail it. It was, he would say, an application for a bank loan— which the bank would testify to receiving.

Richard and Svetlana spent *four hours* in her car in the parking lot, with Miller finally driving off alone at 10:09 p.m. She had passed on Grishin's message. Miller said that he didn't want to go to Warsaw. It would have to be somewhere else. Mostly, the recordings showed that they spent almost the entire four hours in the groans and sighs and little endearments that musicalize copulation. The best exchange of remarks was a post-orgasmic Miller saying: "You know what you've done, 'Lana? You've stolen my heart!" and Svetlana responding: "I know. I was trained in cardiology, in Kiev."

From the moment Operation Whipworm started, Svetlana was to notice that they were being followed every time they met. John had taught her how to know if she was being shadowed; but actually, it didn't require much skill to see a car locked in behind them on the highway, a single grim-faced man at the wheel who would never overtake, even if you slowed, and who would always park his car near theirs in the parking lot of a restaurant and still be at the wheel when they came out, two hours later. If they went for a walk on the moonlit beach, you could look back and be sure that their guardian angel, still dressed for the office, would be ambling through the sands as well.

John had told her that her telephone was tapped on a selective basis and that she might be followed now that she was dealing with Miller. She had heard about how the FBI could put wiretaps around a home. John had said that she shouldn't worry.

Richard said the same.

"He's not following us."

"Richard, he is! I think that's an FBI car."

"Forget it, 'Lana. Relax."

"I'm sure that's an FBI car, Richard."

"Okay, take the tag number down. I'll check it out."

He did, the next day. Of course, it was an FBI car. That night, he told Svetlana: "That car that was following us—it must have been Russian."

"Oh, my God."

"It wasn't an FBI car, 'Lana."

Beyond FBI headquarters, most of the rest of Los Angeles was concerned with only one thing that month: the Olympics. Just as the Moscow Games had been spoiled by the absence of the United States, so the results in California would be skewed by Moscow's decision not to send a team. America's disappointment was shared by Grishin: Putting several hundred Russian athletes, with their coaches and other staff and security men, into L.A. would have been a great opportunity.

In Westwood, Operation Whipworm continued. In reports, Svetlana was referred to as Whip, while Miller became Worm. The day the Games began, Special Agent Ronald Foster, who was in charge of security precautions in the huge office, reported getting a strange request from Worm: Miller wanted a copy of the FBI personnel list. The list wasn't classified; it was something every agent consulted when he wanted a transfer, and it couldn't be withheld from Miller. Now, if he photocopied it before returning it. . . .

John Martin, the director of national security at the Justice Department, a trim, athletic man in his forties, had flown in from Washington to oversee Operation Whipworm. He was puzzled. If Miller was planning to be a mole, he would have to come up with something much sexier than a telephone book. Was there another motive in wanting the book? A plan to subvert others? But the answer was the simple one: Miller was putting together a trove of minor baubles in the hope of selling them for fifty thousand dollars worth of Krugerrands to the KGB or the GRU.

From the surveillance:

September 13. Miller and Svetlana met at the Café Casino again. She was sick, but she came anyway. They went on to the Palm Motel for sex. Back home, she went for a walk with Nikolaiy under the palms of Gardner Street.

September 18. Another Tuesday. For Alex Grishin, another duty call to Ogorodnikova and the FBI listeners-in between 7:30 and 8:00. He drove out to the airport, parked his car with its privileged consular-corps plates in a spot for discharging passengers, and walked to an open pay phone. He saw the FBI trail car pull past and stop in a similar spot about fifty yards away. They would, he presumed, be shooting him by video through the back window. A young man with serious mien had left the car and was approaching to listen in to his chat with Svetlana and, presumably, corroborate whatever they heard at the FBI office. Grishin paused cockily, a black cigarette dangling from the corner of his mouth, to give the young fed time to get closer. Then, using his telephone credit card, he made the call.

He resumed the high school version of "clear code."

"Have you reached an agreement with your friend?"

Ogorodnikova gave the same cautious answer as before: "Yes, in principle."

There was more talk of the "second place." She said her friend preferred that she go for her treatment in Mexico. Grishin made a noise of demurral. If Miller was scared of communist Poland, perhaps they should compromise on Vienna, he thought. They still did not know what goodies he was bringing, for bait.

"Have him bring all the baggage," he reminded her. "That will help with his vacation."

"I understand," said Svetlana in a little voice.

Afterwards, once again, the odd couple from Kiev walked up and down their palm-lined street, many times. For two hours, they talked in the soft light of the September evening, away from the ears but always within the sight of Operation Whipworm's eyes.

These walking discussions in the privacy of the street, away from the monitored environment of their home, were being noted as suspicious circumstantial evidence by FCI-1, and were to be cited by the prosecution four times in the chronology of the main charge against them and Miller.

In Riverside, Larry Grayson was getting impatient. It was time for Miller to stop cutting bait and fish. That is, if he was ever going to fish at all. Why was he talking of waiting until the next month, October? The days were getting shorter. Grayson would be shooting without lights, of course, and at some distance. He had been thinking about the difficulties of the video part. He was worried about the whole thing. Why didn't R.W. tell his supervisors what he was doing? He had never heard of a rogue operation like this, outside of Len Deighton and the movies and television. Was Operation Mother still on? That had been the agreed code word. He called Miller.

"R.W.?"

"Larry? Hi!"

"So—how's Mother?"

Miller hesitated for only a second, thinking of Warsaw. Now, there was some talk of perhaps making it Vienna. Either place, it was curtains for Larry.

"Just disregard everything," he said.

"You've changed your mind?"

"Uh-huh."

After he put down the phone, Grayson felt neither surprised nor too disappointed. He had never truly believed that R.W. would have the nerve to go through with "Mother."

At the console in Westwood, someone was tracing the origin of the call to Lynwood, while the agent who recorded the conversation pondered the reference to Mother. She was sure that Miller's mother was dead.

The Whipworm file grew. There were more recordings of sex. The romance between "R.W." and "'Lana" seemed to be a matter of "your car or mine?" The FBI also learned that Svetlana had told Miller that she had been informed that arrangements would be made for him to meet a Soviet official in Vienna instead of Warsaw. Special Agent Patricia Peyton reported that she had shadowed the couple walking together on Redondo

Beach pier: "He had his arm around her shoulder. I believe she had her arm around his waist, but I couldn't see clearly."

On Thursday, September 20, Miller called Svetlana on his bugged office phone to arrange to meet her that night at the Café Casino in Santa Monica, not far from her home. The archetypical yuppie hangout, heavy on light salads, is decorated in a contemporary equivalent of *art déco*. They soon went back to the car and off to a local motel for yet another erotic encounter. At Westwood, someone said that if they couldn't get R.W. for espionage, they could sell the file to Paula for use in divorce proceedings. Back at Gardner Street later, Svetlana and Nikolaiy went for another half-hour walk under the lofty palms. Later, jurors would have to decide: Were they discussing the Vienna trip, or Matvei's grades, or having one of their regular marital disputes away from the boy's hearing?

The next day, Miller went downstairs in the building housing the FBI headquarters, where there was a passport office. He collected an application for a passport. Because people in a hurry are given priority, there is a question about "date of departure" from the United States. Miller wrote in that he planned to leave on October 10.

The file contains a recording of a call that day by Miller to Gardner Street. Svetlana was not in. The call was taken either by Nikolaiy or, more probably, John or Matvei. Miller spoke in what was apparently meant to be a Russian accent, gave his name as Boris, and left a message: "Tell her I'll be bringing the rest of the stuff from my father's house. Also tell her I went downstairs this morning and got an application for that item."

Miller was obviously still hesitating. He had filled in the passport application form, but had not yet turned it in. Later in the day, he called Gardner Street again. She was still not there. Not wishing to appear too anxious, he tried to hide the fact that this was a repeat call by "Boris"; instead, he adopted a Spanish accent, which came off better. He said: "Tell her Pedro called." What Svetlana ever made of that, we do not know.

That night, Miller had a date with Marta York—who, like Svetlana, had no difficulty spotting that they were under surveillance.

The reason Svetlana had been absent, she was to recall later, was that she had been meeting John Hunt, who had asked her to tell him everything about her meetings with Miller. "Tell me everything before [the meetings] and everything after," he had said.

Hunt seemed astonished that things had proceeded so far.

He heard her saying, in cooing tones: "I asked Richard: 'Why does your boss want you to do this?' And he said I shouldn't ask questions, that I wouldn't understand. And in reality, that's right. I still don't understand."

"You mean you're going to Vienna with R.W., to meet with someone from the GRU? That's crazy!" Hunt exclaimed.

"It seems crazy to me, too, John."

At first, she recalls today, he advised her not to go. Svetlana, for her part, was beginning to put two and two together. Miller was being shadowed, she knew, by agents in cars. She was certain her phone was bugged. Probably, Miller's too. John was against the Vienna journey. Miller must be acting on his own. She didn't know Miller very well. They had met only four months before, and for a month of that time she had been in Russia. When she had returned from Moscow, she remembered, she had been met at Los Angeles airport by John—not her husband and son, not Richard, but John. And John had told her, afterwards, to do anything that Richard asked her to do, but to tell John everything they did. John had said that any double-agent operation would belong to him, even if Richard helped to set it up.

"John, tell me. What should I do?"

Hunt knew that if Miller really was planning something very illegal, he should say nothing to warn him off and spoil Operation Whipworm. If Svetlana backed out, so might Miller.

"Just keep me informed, 'Lana. Keep me informed, okay?"

"If you say so, John."

"This is a very odd case," Zaydzev agreed. "There are so many possible interpretations." Menshikov nodded too.

"Exactly." Grishin came back from the window and sat down at his desk. "The appearance of amateurishness could be professional. Everyone is supposed to know that there's a surveillance. Which means we're supposed to get the message that Miller is suspect to his own people as a potential defector. He himself can hardly be unaware of the surveillance, which would explain why, when Ogorodnikova told him about it, he told her she was mistaken. Which means it's just a repeat of the Hunt dangle."

"I'm still confused," Menshikov said, rubbing his thin chin. "To want us to pick up the surveillance is one thing, but why are they making it so obvious? Again, if the disinformation message they are sending us is that Miller is a genuine turncoat, but one who has already been surfaced by the FBI, what use would he be for us? Why invite him to Vienna and take him on? We couldn't even use him to pass disinformation, because they would know that *we* know that he's a phony."

Grishin lit a black cigarette. "Not necessarily. Listen: There are two main possibilities. One is that the FBI scam is exactly what it appears to be, and the show of suspicion of Miller is meant to induce us to believe that he's a true defector. The other is that he is genuinely trying to mount a scam of his own, and his colleagues genuinely suspect him of disloyalty. The farcical sloppiness of the surveillance would then be just that—a sloppy farce."

"It's dangerous to underestimate one's rivals."

"Dangerous to overestimate them, too," Grishin retorted.

"Sure, but I've never heard, either from experience or in the literature, of anyone trying to be a double agent against his enemies *without telling his own people*. Mr. Miller would be unique."

"The whole thing is unique to all of us. Either way, I think our game plan must be the same. We must do what we can to delude the FBI into thinking that their man is in fact a traitor, to try to get them to embarrass themselves publicly and punish one of their own."

"You're the boss," Menshikov said, shrugging.

Grishin smiled and stubbed out his cigarette.

"As you know, I've made arrangements for Ogorodnikova to bring Miller to Vienna for the meeting, which he has requested in writing, with a representative of our security services. Instead of meeting with the woman, which might have evaded scrutiny, I am, as you know, calling her on the telephone, on the same day and at the same time every week, to make sure that the calls are intercepted and recorded, even if their monitoring operation is not very good. I am making the conversations as suspicious as possible, using guarded language that *sounds* guarded, plain code that a child could interpret, and so on. I wish to give the impression that Miller has convinced me of his *bona fides*, and that we are inviting him to Vienna in the expectation that he will be bringing substantial secret information."

Zaydzev was shaking his head. "Put yourself in their place," he said.

"I did. Let us assume that the other side is more professional than it appears to be. Let us imagine that you or I are an FBI bureau director who has concluded that Miller either wants to betray his country or could be persuaded to do so; what would we do? We would let him depart for Vienna and watch him like a hawk when he got back. We at the FBI would ensure that he got disinformation, which he would pass on, and then we, the Americans, would watch to see what the USSR did in reaction. We would perhaps, as FBI men, also pass on a little true information for him to pass to us—I mean the real us—and watch to see how we would change our working habits, our programs, and so on. He could, for instance, tell me that the FBI knows what route I drive every day to work, and watch to see if I change my route. Do you agree?"

"Yes. We fool them. But to what advantage?"

"Of course, we would not be idle. I mean the real *we*. We would test his allegiance in the obvious ways, for instance by asking him for documents which we already have."

"We've done that. We've asked him for the FBI personnel list."

"But that doesn't prove he's deceiving us. How does he know for sure that we already have it? I was thinking of something more elaborate, something that would deceive the other side as to the extent of our knowledge. If we compared what we got with what we already possessed, and found that the data he produced was doctored, we would then try to deceive them into thinking that we had been deceived by how we reacted."

Menshikov nodded. "We would, in fact, use Miller as a channel for our own disinformation, whatever the ways."

Grishin almost reflexively lowered his voice.

Speaking of Pelton, Howard and Walker—all about to be surfaced—he said: "For instance, if other moles in NSA, the CIA, or naval intelligence came up with something very precious, we would try to disguise our possession of it by asking Miller if he could get it, even if we knew that this was beyond his limited access. And if he came back with a doctored version supplied by his FBI or CIA masters, we would pretend to accept it as genuine, perhaps by paying him a bonus. They, of course, would be getting stuff from us, some of which would be doctored, and we would have to determine how much of this was accepted and how much not."

Menshikov leaned forward. The Rezident was lighting another cigarette. Grishin blew smoke and said: "As you know, Miller wanted a rendezvous in Mexico. He speaks Spanish. At the time, he was still pretending to us that he was Hunt. Mexico City has more spooks than a rat has fleas. It's a city we've learned not to use. Anyway, he didn't want Warsaw. Why not, if it's *our* protection he needs? So, we've compromised on Vienna. As you know, I've told Ogorodnikova to bring Miller there and said he'll meet a GRU general, whom we've called Mikhail. Whom he's going to meet, I have no idea."

Zaydzev closed his eyes briefly in thought, then said: "We still don't know why he took over Mr. Hunt's role as Ogorodnikova's FBI handler. What is Hunt's role, now? For a job like this, he seems to be more impressive than Miller."

"You mean Miller's not impressive at all. Nor is Ogorodnikova! Nor is her husband. He was here today, returning films. He says they're under intense FBI surveillance."

Menshikov smiled.

Miller was so nervous that he had slept badly. He had munched until two that Monday morning, then dozed fitfully. In a way, in spite of the prospects of being a star in the counterespionage firmament, he was sorry San Fran had responded on September 11. He had been ready to throw it up. He knew when he was way in, over his head. He had told Larry Grayson to forget about Mother. He wasn't sure why the squad had mounted its intensified surveillance of Svetlana at that time, especially without telling him—well, perhaps that wasn't surprising, considering how incapable they thought he was. It meant they were following him as well—and therefore it meant his having to lie to 'Lana about there being no surveillance. They might well be suspicious of him for meeting with 'Lana and not reporting it. Yes, indeed, they might well. In Green Street, he must have been photographed by the regular surveillance across from the consulate entrance, but surely no one there would find it abnormal for a member of the LA Russian Squad to be driving around with one of the FBI's informants. Would they?

He thought about Hunt. Hunt had a better record with the Bureau, but he had grossly overestimated 'Lana's capabilities, Miller thought. Hunt had been her handler for so long. Some of his reports made no sense. She had obviously never been more than a spacy, low-grade informant under some degree of FBI protection. John had claimed that 'Lana and he had never been lovers; so why the long relationship? John had told them in the squad room about 'Lana flinging her arms around his neck in the street and suggesting they go to a hotel. Well, Miller reflected, she had never tried to seduce *him*. Or he, her. He had told her at times that he was "in love" with her, but she was still too wrapped up in John to respond. 'Lana, Miller thought, was really his mistress only in a technical sense, not in the sense that she had any mastery over him, or that he had any control over her. She would go back to John in a flash, if she had the chance. Really, she had become very Californian in some ways. After eleven years in Hollywood, she seemed to regard sex as being as normal a dessert as a baked Alaska after a hearty meal.

He thought with trepidation about going to Vienna. If he had really wanted to go over the wall, as the Russians presumably believed that he was doing, Warsaw would have been safer; but the thought of being an FBI special agent alone in a communist capital was terrifying. Would the man at the consulate-general be suspicious of his unwillingness to go to Warsaw? Hadn't that been a giveaway, on his part? He had made it clear that he had a plausible reason for preferring Mexico City, apart from the proximity: He spoke Spanish. The only Polish he knew was about putting in a light bulb.

As Grishin had said, Nikolaiy had flown to San Francisco that morning with the canisters. His FBI guardian angel at the Los Angeles airport had called the San Francisco office, and they had had someone ready to track him when he landed. Nikolaiy and his tracker took the airport bus into town, then walked and bused from the downtown terminal to Green Street, reaching there at 10:20. Miller was to say at his trial that Nikolaiy wasn't carrying papers from him in the canisters. Nikolaiy was to say that it was just the monthly run up the coast that either he or his wife took to exchange films. The prosecution was to say that they could offer no contrary evidence.

Nikolaiy emerged fifteen minutes after he had gone in. The Asahi Pentax across the street clicked. He was empty-handed. Then, he turned and went back inside for another fifteen minutes, coming out this time with a large green book.

He returned at once to Los Angeles, where he was met at the airport by Svetlana and Matvei. Both mother and son had spotted an FBI trail car on the way from West Hollywood, and Matvei had jotted down its tag number. The FBI report says Nikolaiy was wearing a black leather jacket, black trousers, a black cap—and brown shoes. The family drove home, with Nikolaiy at the wheel. Matvei, sitting in the back of the Lynx, looked through the rear window and spotted the tailgater again.

"We're still being followed, Mama!" It was just like television.

Svetlana looked over her shoulder. John had told her: "If you think you're being followed, slow down and see if the other car overtakes; if it slows down too, be suspicious." Nikolaiy was looking in his driving mirror.

"Slow down," his wife said.

Sure enough, the other car slowed also. Matvei had outwitted the FBI! Now, the thirteen-year-old had another idea.

"Pull off the road, Dad."

Nikolaiy pulled onto the shoulder. The FBI car went past. Nikolaiy drew back onto the highway and began tracking the FBI car. Matvei loved it, but Nikolaiy and Svetlana looked grim. What was going on?

Matvei had said there was surveillance on their apartment building around the clock, men in conspicuous white shirts and dark ties walking up and down beneath the palms, standing out like a bevy of commissars at a gypsy camp, or women sauntering up and down the sidewalk endlessly, but who never made eye contact with cruising males.

Nevertheless, she met Richard again that night. As usual, they were followed into the restaurant parking lot by a car whose grim male driver did not emerge. In the restaurant, Miller told her to go ahead and book passage for Vienna for the two of them. He was bothered by the obvious surveillance; but he would deal with that later.

*

The next day, Tuesday, August 25, Svetlana called Diana Baskevitch.

"Beverly International Travel," said Mrs. Baskevitch's switchboard woman.

Svetlana asked for Diana herself so that they could speak in their own language. She told Mrs. Baskevitch she wanted discount fares to Vienna, where she and a companion wanted to spend three nights.

"It's cheaper if you stay seven days or more."

"My friend has to be back at work."

"What a shame. It's also cheaper if you travel on weekdays."

"Well, we're leaving on a Wednesday."

"Yes, but you want to come back on a Sunday. Can your friend return on Monday?"

"No, he has to be back at work on Monday."

"Can he leave earlier?"

"No, he can leave only on the tenth of October."

Mrs. Baskevitch tapped away at her terminal. She took Miller's name and initial. When a passenger has tight requirements about dates, he loses the bucket-shop fares that are the underpinning of agency work. He might have to use more than one airline. Either way, the price goes up, as does the agency's commission. Obviously, Mrs. Ogorodnikova wasn't paying; it would be the man. If he'd asked her to make the booking, he must not be concerned about money. She couldn't think of any other reason why the man would leave that sort of thing to Svetlana Ogorodnikova.

"You want business class?"

"I suppose so."

Mrs. Baskevitch went on tapping.

"All right. October 10. I've got you on Capitol Air from L.A. to Frankfurt, arriving next morning, and straight on by Lufthansa to Vienna. Return, October 14, by Alia to Geneva, then TWA to Los Angeles. That will be about four thousand dollars for the two of you."

That was more than twice what Miller had expected from reading the bucket-shop ads in the Sunday *Los Angeles Times*. Svetlana said: "Alia?"

"That's the airline of Jordan. They look after you better than any American line."

"We get back here the same day?"

"Yes, you gain nine hours, on your watch, between Vienna and L.A."

Since it was a Tuesday, Grishin called that night shortly after 7:30. Special Agent Robert Otstott watched him place the call from a San Francisco airport booth, later checking with the telephone company to find that the call had been to 213-876-3148, the number of the Ogorodnikov apartment. (The number was to remain unchanged for six years, until Nikolaiy came out of prison. Then, he discovered that his young cousin had recently run up bills totaling over two hundred dollars, whereupon, as the family elder, he had the line cut off. He now has a different number.)

Grishin continued to sound as much like a bolshie Hollywood plotter as possible. Svetlana reported that she would leave with her friend on October 10 for her health treatment, and arrive at 11:40 a.m.

Svetlana had been instructed by Anatoliy to pass messages to "the acquaintances" through her mother in Yefrimov, so Grishin asked: "Have you made arrangements with the acquaintances?"

"Yes."

"Good. They will be waiting for you on the tenth to set up your vacation and everything." Then, he realized that his dates were not the same as hers. "You are flying out on the ninth, right?"

"No. The tenth."

Grishin contained his impatience. Their arriving on the eleventh, a day later than planned, didn't really matter, so long as the "acquaintances" were informed. He said cordially: "I think everything will work out as it should, and you will definitely be able to have a good rest and recover your health."

"Fine. Yes."

"And your friend, also. Is he still keen on going? Is everything else satisfactory?" He was concerned about how much luggage her friend would bring—the more, the better.

Svetlana, aware that she was not very good at this sort of stuff, but clinging to the analogy of traveling for her health, said: "I think so. I won't really know until—you know—I am in the operating theater."

This was irritating, but otherwise Grishin was delighted; by now, he knew from Nikolaiy that everyone was being trailed and bugged.

DiPretorio reported the conversation as having been in "plain language code."

Miller spent the evening with Marta York. Again, she spotted a surveillance.

On Wednesday, September 26, Miller finally ordered his passport. Now, Svetlana had to do something about making Richard presentable. She didn't pretend to know much about how people, like the voice on the phone, or Richard or John went about their work, but she did know that you didn't meet a Soviet apparatchik, perhaps in the Soviet embassy in Vienna, in a torn rugby shirt and scuffed chinos that were too tight around the waist.

The next day, she had to go shopping for Matvei, so she brought Richard along. At Ness Shoes, a salesgirl named Tali Harahman sold Miller a pair of burgundy loafers that Svetlana selected and paid for. At the At Ease Men's Shop in Westwood, Miller liked the look of a Burberry raincoat from London. The price tag of six hundred and fifty dollars staggered him, as it presumably would most men looking for a raincoat. But he remembered her saying: "Richard, can you please change your clothes when you are with me? Because you look terrible."

He said: " 'Lana, what does this look like?" To Miller, it looked like Bernard Samson.

"Would you like to try one on?"

The words came out of salesman Mark White's mouth as reflexively as the bark of a guard-dog that has been challenged. Miller was thinking that even if he never went to Vienna, he still had to go to Washington soon on a Mexican drug case, and he would need something decent to wear for that. To White, he wasn't saying no.

"Size 50-long," White murmured. At five feet nine and a half, Miller wasn't long, but regular, but White was thinking that if he wore a long version it would de-emphasize his size-fifty girth.

Miller tried it on, looked in the mirror, and liked what he saw. But he had only a few dollars on him. Svetlana had paid for the burgundy shoes. She said she would make a down payment and gave White twenty-five dollars.

Out in the street, Svetlana noticed that they were being followed by two men. She pointed this out to Miller.

Miller was wondering why his colleagues made what they were doing so obvious. (Why weren't they wearing his sort of scuffed clothes, as the L.A. police would do?) He made his routine remark: "You're crazy."

Svetlana said: "Look, Richard, over there! Two men are making a movie of us with a camera!"

"Horse shit, 'Lana."

Both of them had their cars. They got into hers. She gave him the flight details.

Then, sensing his hesitations, she lied: "I paid for the tickets."

"You did what?" The listener-in heard the fierce shout. "You're crazy! I told you to make reservations, that's all. I don't yet have permission!"

"The friends in San Francisco will pay us back." She was still using Grishin's "clear code."

"That's not the point."

She calmed him. It was all arranged, she said. "You will be meeting with a GRU general called Mikhail. Aren't you pleased? Your career—your debts."

"I guess so," Miller said unhappily.

"Do you have your passport?"

"I've applied for it. I'll have to go downtown and pick it up." He tried to sound in control. "We'll have to go to the Austrian consulate and get visas, or at least you will. I don't think Americans need visas." He was thinking: Either I tell Christensen now what I'm doing, or I have to ask for a few days' vacation time. One way or another, it seemed that he was now committed, like Joe Pistone. Was he a man or a mouse?

He lowered his tone, sorry to have berated Svetlana, who had only been doing what he had asked her to do.

"You know what? I'm worried about doing this. I don't know what to—what should I say to this, uh—if he is a very important man, then I—I need to tell him—you know what I need to? See, you know the type of Russian better than I do. Is he a typical Russian? You're gonna have to teach me what to say."

He thought: That briefing guideline didn't say how to handle GRU generals on their own terrain. Holy smoke!

She said: "I teach you. You do very good, you know?"

The listener at the console then heard Special Agent Richard William Miller try to explain to Svetlana Ogorodnikova about the elocution lessons in the musical comedy *My Fair Lady*. He got into a convoluted explanation about the action of George Bernard Shaw's original play, *Pygmalion*. Svetlana, never strong on socialist literature despite her Soviet origins, was having problems following him. Finally, he said he would have to get back to his own car, and the drive to Lynwood. He mentioned again that he wouldn't be able to use the house much longer. His sister had put it up for sale.

Svetlana said, as she had said before: "You're not tired of living like that?"

"Yes, I'm tired—of living like that. But right now, I don't have any choice."

"Well, after you come to work, you know, you can rent a good apartment."

"Well, we'll see."

Much was to be made at the trial of her response: "Please!"

Once again, she had noted an FBI car parked near her own. She pointed this out to Miller. Once again, she nursed suspicions that Miller was acting outside orders. She said: "Richard, is something going to happen to us?"

"Don't worry."

She wrote down the tag number and gave it to him. "Check and see."

"Sure."

She drove her car back to the parking lot near the FBI building where Miller's own car was parked. Fifteen yards behind, Special Agent Paul DeFlores recognized Miller. The Hispanic agent was not on the Miller surveillance; he was on a murder, and was sitting at the wheel of his car writing up notes. At one point, he thought he saw Miller, who was necking with Svetlana, look back and spot his colleague. Then Miller got out, saying he was going home, and walked to his Isuzu.

But he did not go home. First things first. He drove to Ness Shoes. There was no way he could go to Washington on the Mexican drug case in burgundy shoes. The style was okay; it was the color that was unthinkable for an FBI agent; even he knew that. He didn't want to choose a totally different pair of shoes, because they had been a gift from 'Lana, and she would notice; but she probably wouldn't notice if he got a more respectable shade of brown. But in his size, it turned out, the only other color was blue. He tried to imagine J. Edgar Hoover, in his tomb, viewing a middle-aged fed, or any fed, in blue shoes, like Elvis Presley. He stayed with burgundy.

By now, he had made up his mind about something else. He wasn't going to Lynwood. He might not even have time to go there, anyway, before his date, that night, with Marta York. She had come down from Oregon for a two-week vacation, with an obvious program in mind: to persuade Miller to divorce Paula and marry her. But what he had decided, most important of all, was that the moment of truth in his whole double-agent operation had arrived: He had to report to Christensen the next day. And right now, on the way to his date with Marta, he would pick up an application blank for a health club, to show Christensen that he was serious about slimming.

Svetlana was sure something was amiss. The little woman from Kiev consulted her husband. They went for another walk under the towering palms of Gardner Street. She confided that she was worried that Miller might be a real defector, that his operation wasn't authorized.

"Why did he want you to buy the tickets?" Nikolaiy asked, rhetorically. "One of the secretaries where he works could have done that for him."

"I asked him. He said it was too top-secret to bring in the clerks. But how can it be top-secret if we're always being followed? He says all this is good for his career, and that the FBI will give me a bonus."

"And what happens if they decide, in Vienna, that it's all a trick?"

"I'm only doing what San Francisco asked me to do, just as I've only done what Richard asked me to do, and he asked me to get San Francisco to tell us what they wanted. But suppose he really is a defector? John Hunt, the other agent, speaks badly of Richard."

"But why does San Francisco call you on *our* telephone? They know as well as we do that the FBI listens in. They could call you anywhere—a public phone. Why do they call here?"

"That I don't know, Nikolaiy." She shook her head.

"And why is the FBI making its watch on us so obvious?" Ogorodnikov asked her again, scratching his skull for an idea. It was odd, he thought, that the Russian *apparachiki* in San Francisco actually wanted the FBI in Los Angeles to know what they were planning with Svetlana, while the FBI in Los Angeles seemed to want him and his wife—and therefore the Russians in San Francisco—to know what the FBI was doing. "Why so obvious?" he said again, as they passed a man in a gray suit and a white shirt, going by in the opposite direction, accompanied by a hawk-eyed young woman in a navy-blue two-piece with a high-neck blouse.

"That I don't know, also," Svetlana said. "Maybe the FBI doesn't know we can see them."

Nikolaiy threw up his hands in a helpless gesture. "They are playing with you, both of them," he said. "Certainly, the consulate-general is playing with you."

"That I know," said his wife.

Nikolaiy felt tired. Ah, life! If it wasn't one thing, it was another. He had seen a student wearing a T-shirt that day; the T-shirt said: "Life's a bitch, and then you die." He said in his squeaky but firm, husbandly voice: "You must go to the police."

He too was thinking: First things first. If Svetlana had got herself into a mess because of her working for these FBI people, the main danger came not from Moscow but here in Los Angeles. If she suspected that Miller was not a true American patriot, she should tell the police.

At Nikolaiy's urging, she called the emergency number for the L.A.P.D. from their apartment.

A harsh woman's voice said: "Can I help you?" She didn't sound as though she wanted to help anyone.

Svetlana said in her nervous, accented voice: "I want to talk to an officer about someone I think may be a spy for the Soviet Union."

"Oh, sister, gimme a break, will you?"

The line went dead.

She called John. He wasn't in. He never returned her call.

## *ii*

The next morning, Miller went to the office on Wilshire Boulevard and called Christensen, saying that he would like to speak to him urgently. Miller's supervisor and fellow Mormon told him to come in right away.

He took a chair by Christensen's desk and came to the point at once. He explained that he thought he had successfully set up, through Svetlana Ogorodnikova, a meeting with a Soviet intelligence officer in Vienna. The Russian, he believed, expected to recruit him.

"I have taken this as far as I can, on my own," he said. "Now, I obviously need authorization to go to Vienna. I also need guidance and help as to how to handle this Russian, this General Mikhail."

Christensen seemed stunned. How did all this check out with what they knew already from their own surveillance? He would not only have to report to Bretzing. He would also have to talk to Hunt and Auer, and to John Martin from Justice.

"Why Vienna?" he heard himself say.

"They wanted Warsaw, but that was too much their territory. In Vienna, I assume I can be covered." He explained how his real preference had been for Mexico, and how he had arranged to be shadowed by Larry Grayson. Christensen's brows went up at the notion of a special agent on such a mission relying on a private eye rather than FBI resources.

"Why didn't you come to me before?" To Miller, Christensen seemed to be in two minds as to whether what Miller had done had been useful or not.

"To be honest, I was afraid you'd nix it as unlikely to succeed, or else put somebody else on it."

Christensen's brows went up again. "Who are you talking to, at the consulate-general?"

"Well, I've never spoken to anyone directly. 'Lana's dealing with this guy Boris Belakov, Byela—"

"I think I know whom you mean. But whom do you think you have the hook into, and who do you think *thinks* he has the hook into you?"

"I don't know."

"You *don't* KNOW!" Christensen closed his eyes. "R.W., you're something else!"

"You're right. But I'll get the name. And now I would need to take some stuff to Vienna to bait the hook for General Mikhail."

"Did they offer you money?"

"No."

"You were expecting them to believe you'd do this for nothing?"

"Oh, no, of course not. You asked me if they *offered* me money. I told them I'd need fifty G's in gold. My idea is that they place it in three different banks' deposit boxes, to set up a cast-iron evidentiary trail based on receipts."

Christensen's mouth hung open. "Really?" The deputy special agent-in-charge's mind was thinking in several directions at once. He was thinking of Operation Whipworm, of all those surveillances of restaurants and nightspots, those recordings of sex in cars.

Miller was watching Christensen's face. What Christensen was thinking, he felt almost sure, was: "R.W., you're in over your head."

"Auer never authorized this."

"I admit that I exceeded instructions."

"Well, that's for sure!"

"What d'you think Washington will say? D'you think they'll let me go ahead?"

"I don't know what Washington will say. R.W., what got you into this in the first place? You were never Svetlana Whatsername's handler."

"Well, I've been on The Farm, as you know. I was bored to death. I'm forty-eight. My career—well, I was hoping this would—uh—redeem my career. I know I haven't been the best agent—"

"Sure," said Christensen noncommittally. Did Miller know anything of Operation Whipworm? Had he not spotted any of the surveillance? Christensen thought again of that porno show on the sound tapes. Was Miller leveling with him now, or just trying to outsmart their own investigation? His thin features looked reproving. He said: "You and Mrs. O are, well, having an affair, yes?"

Miller nodded. "Could that be left out of the report?"

"Perhaps. I suppose so. I'll have to ask Bretzing."

Christensen picked up the phone and told his secretary he didn't want to be interrupted. The two men talked for over an hour longer, going over what Miller had done in chronological order, while Christensen typed what became Miller's Statement. It stretched for six pages, single-spaced. Miller insisted that he had never been specific about what sort of information he could get for the Russians. In answer to a direct question from Christensen, he said he had told Svetlana to tell her contact at the consulate-general that he could not give them any information on FBI "investigations or procedures." That wasn't strictly true, of course, but it was not unusual to clean up a report before it went to the Hoover building, leaving out data that would only raise problems for the reporting agent. What had Joe Pistone had to leave out about his life in the Mafia?

Christensen typed in FBI jargon. Miller had never told anyone anything; he had always "indicated." Svetlana had never informed him of anything, only "advised that. . ." or sometimes, ungrammatically, "advised," without the "that." Miller had so far given the Russians no classified materials "whatsoever"— the late J. Edgar's favorite word.

Miller read it through and signed. Christensen said he'd show it to Bretzing and Hunt and Auer. He didn't mention Martin. Miller should come back in the morning and see him again.

This was the only FBI interview with Miller taken down verbatim. Except for a brief addendum the following morning, he was not asked to type anything, and he was not recorded. Christensen said Miller's initiative with the swallow "Marie" and his request to go to Vienna would be "evaluated." He did not mention Whipworm. When told the next day of a surveillance, Miller said he did not know of it.

Miller walked out of Christensen's office that evening feeling intensely relieved. For the first time in a couple of months, he no longer bore the burden and the tension of his clandestine operation alone. Now that he had given a full report, he was no longer exceeding orders. Like Bernard Samson, he was back in the fold. Christensen had shown some exasperation, which was understandable; but for the most part, he had been friendly. He had agreed to try to keep his sexual liaison with 'Lana out of the report. Miller was especially relieved about that, because the sex part aggravated his misconduct in acting without orders. They might have taken the operation away from him because he couldn't keep his pecker in his pants. What would Bretzing say? Would the bishop dock him another half-month's pay for fornication? Surely Bretzing would be able to see that hooking the KGB or the GRU was a lot more important than just slavishly obeying Gary Auer's orders.

He looked at his watch. He could just make it on time for his next date with Marta York. Over the previous week, he had spent more time with the Ecuadorian than he had spent with 'Lana. They had been to movies together, and the county fair. Her husband had been an FBI informer on the Latino community. Miller had known the Yorks since 1970. Marta and Paula had been on friendly terms. York himself had just died, in June. Now, Marta seemed to be shopping for a new breadwinner for herself and her fatherless children. But Miller had made up his mind that he was going to try to make his marriage work, after all.

Before going to Christensen, Miller had been half-decided to break his date with Marta. Burdened with his worries about Vienna, he had not relished the thought of having to tell Marta, who had come down from Oregon solely to spend her vacation with him, that he was going back to Paula. He anticipated tears, perhaps a Latin display of temper. That morning, edging nervously out further onto the diving board by buying his "wardrobe" for Vienna, he had felt that he was too strung out to go through an emotional scene with Marta on top of everything else.

Now, as he left the building, the fat man's step was springier. Going to Christensen had been like a Catholic going to confession. Even if they didn't let him go to Vienna, surely they would now give him more sophisticated counterintelligence work. Surely they would see that he had initiative, that he wasn't as poor an agent as they had always told him he was. If anyone took his dangle any further—even if it wasn't him—surely he, Miller, would qualify for a commendation, or at least a nice letter in his file. Back with Paula, he could also make his peace with Mormon and be readmitted. Paula had kept up his tithing payments, bless her.

Chewing a Milky Way and swilling a Coke, Miller drove off to his date with Marta York with that almost inebriated confidence that he needed to say to her, with a smile: "Well, it's been great knowing you, Marta, babe, but. . . ."

\*

When Special Agent Richard William Miller came to work in the morning, he was a little less jaunty than he had been when he had left after his session with Christensen. The evening with Marta York had been more demanding than the session with his supervisor. She seemed to feel she had been jilted. She had cried. But they had parted friends, at least he thought so. Now, he supposed, he would have to face Bretzing and Auer as well as Christensen. Thinking of this reminded him that Marta had said once more, the previous evening: "We're being followed." Following Svetlana, or Svetlana and him together, was something that would be almost understandable, he had thought; but why would anyone be following him on "dates" that had nothing to do with his professional work?

Christensen was waiting for him, looking even more thin-lipped than usual. He wanted Miller to type an addendum to what had been agreed the day before, stipulating that he believed he had been the target of a Soviet intelligence recruitment effort. Since he had offered the Russkies a dangle, that didn't make much sense, except in the measure that he believed that they had taken the hook; it implied that 'Lana had approached *him* and that he had pretended to go along, in order to be a double agent. But they all knew that John Hunt had made the dangle, and that he, Miller, had repeated it. . . . Oh, well. But first, Christensen said, he wanted to ask a few more questions, so that the addendum would make the statement complete.

After Miller had gone off on his date, it had been a busy evening at Westwood, involving calls to FBI residences in Washington, three time zones away, where the working day was already over. The reason Christensen had looked severe when Miller came in the next morning was that they were trying to reconcile what they knew, or thought they knew—from Operation Whipworm—with what Miller had said in his report.

But the decision had been taken to wind up Whipworm. Overall direction of the brief surveillance operation had been in the hands of Assistant FBI Director Edward O'Malley and particularly those of the supervisor of Foreign Counter-Intelligence, Don Stukey II, both in Washington. Justice had sent John Martin, its top man for counterespionage, to San Francisco to ride herd on the operation. Now, after Martin had read

Miller's statement through twice, he concluded that "there's no case against R.W."—regardless of what in-house action the FBI might see fit to take because one of its subalterns had gone over the top without instructions. Miller had apparently not broken the law of the country. Stukey in Washington, noting that Martin was checking out from Los Angeles, had sent a message that morning, handing over direction of Whipworm to a local Los Angeles agent, Larry Torrence—to bring it to a conclusion and recommend what sanctions, if any, should be meted out to Miller. Stukey also wanted a file opened on Hunt's handling of Svetlana as his associate.

Miller, in his statement, had never admitted that he had spotted the surveillance, since this would have raised the question: "Why didn't you report what you were doing earlier, since you knew you were being watched?" Now, the only reason for doubting Miller's story, and his innocence of treasonous intent, was a report by Paul DeFlores, who said he had spotted Miller and Svetlana in her car in a parking lot the previous day—the day of the burgundy shoes and the Burberry coat. DeFlores had been about to go off duty, and apparently had happened to park behind Svetlana's Lynx by coincidence. He claimed that he had seen Miller look in Svetlana's driving mirror, then over his shoulder, and recognize his colleague. Miller had "raised his eyebrows and his eyes had "gone wide with surprise." DeFlores knew about Whipworm, even though he was not involved with it. Had Miller seen DeFlores draw in behind, wrongly suspected that DeFlores was doing a surveillance of him, and gone in to see Christensen to head the investigation off at the pass?

No love was lost between the Hispanic agents like DeFlores (who believed they were discriminated against within the Bureau for promotion and attractive assignments) and the "Mormon Mafia" that the Hispanics detested—and that they believed had shielded and protected the incompetent Miller for years. Bretzing knew that. Yet the DeFlores testimony was to breathe new life into Whipworm even before John Martin's plane had landed back at National Airport in Washington; and this comedy of errors was even staged for the juries at Miller's trials, with DeFlores unable to remember if Miller was wearing his glasses or not (he usually took them off to neck or copulate with Svetlana). His lawyers insisted that, if he had had his glasses on, DeFlores would not have been able to see any movement of Miller's eyebrows or any "widening" of his eyes (presumably meaning staring); if he had had them off, Miller would not have been able to recognize DeFlores, who would simply have been a blur behind a sunlit windshield.

At first, before writing the addendum, he had faced more questions from Christensen. But Miller had been relieved not to be facing Bretzing, nor the agent he had specifically disobeyed, Gary Auer.

Yet, as Christensen's questioning developed, Miller could see uncomfortably where the deputy special agent-in-charge was heading. He was turning the story upside down, as though the Rezidentura, through 'Lana, had made the approach. On its face, this was better than Miller making his own unauthorized approach, but what Christensen was doing was questioning whether Grishin had not in fact succeeded in luring Miller—not disloyal or ideological, only in need of money—into his web.

In this second round of questioning, Miller agreed that Svetlana was unreliable as an informant. He said he had spotted this earlier than Hunt, who had taken a year. But like Hunt, he had tried his dangle. He had concluded, as Hunt had done, that the situation in which the FBI had placed her had meant that her allegiances were confused. There had been no immediate response to his dangle, just as had been the case with Hunt's, but then—he conceded under Christensen's relentless barrage—Svetlana had returned from Moscow with a new agenda. She appeared to have been asked by someone in Soviet intelligence to recruit him—even if, he thought to himself, they thought that he was Hunt!

He said: "But that was what I *wanted* them to do. Wasn't that what John Hunt had wanted them to do?"

"I'll ask the questions," said Christensen, now tired and testy. And as so frequently happens in such cases, the questions became the answers. If Miller said "yes" to anything, Christensen's entire sentence became Miller's.

He typed up and signed the addendum that Christensen wanted. Then, that same day, he consented to a house search at Lynwood. He had foolishly said that there were no FBI documents in the house at all; but like most untidy people, he was a pack rat, and there were papers all over the place. And there was the folder marked SVETLANA, containing a photocopy of the eleven pages on the Soviet Union in the 1984 Positive Intelligence Reporting Guide. He was asked why it was in the house.

"I don't know."

Then came the foolish lie: "It [bringing it home] must have been an accident."

In a more sophisticated intelligence service than the FBI, Miller might have been simply encouraged to resign, to spare the service the public revelation of R.W.'s childish endeavor. But the probe into the fat, unpopular agent had acquired a momentum of its own. On the next day, the twenty-ninth, Miller was called in by Bretzing, the special agent-in-charge, the bishop.

Bretzing's steely gaze moved from Miller's report and addendum and focused itself on the flabby features of Westwood's worst agent and, in Bretzing's view, worst Mormon. He began to talk to Miller of "adultery." Christensen later remembered the dialogue.

"This whole thing has moral dimensions," Bretzing said. "There are spiritual ramifications."

"There are?" Miller asked.

Bretzing had bought the DeFlores theory, in part because to reject it would have reinforced the Mormon Mafia theory—that he was protecting Miller. Miller had sold Amway products from the tailboard of his FBI car; he had sold circus tickets, muscle relaxants, on FBI time. Why not secrets? As a bishop, Bretzing could appeal to the discipline of the church that Miller had known all his life. Any man who, even though broke, was paying his tithe of ten percent of his salary to Mormon each month, despite being suspended from membership, was still under its command, Bretzing felt. If Miller could be brought to repent of adultery to save his soul, he could be brought to confess to espionage by the same obedience and save Operation Whipworm. The bishop was going to make an example of Miller that no one would ever forget.

Miller heard himself say: "Sure, I was having an—uh—committing adultery with Mrs. Ogorodnikova." He was beginning to shake like a child who had been caught masturbating by a church elder. "But I, sincerely, never worked for the Russians."

"Be silent!" Bretzing roared, rising to his feet like a gangling prophet. "Be silent, and repent!"

Miller was too distraught to laugh. He was beginning to cry. That night, he went home to Bonsall, and Paula.

Despite the garage meeting, Nikolaiy still didn't know Miller's full name, only that Svetlana was due to leave with him on October 9 or 10 for Vienna, and return on October 14, when the FBI man had to be back at work. He had got this information from her on Friday, September 28, when she had tried to call Miller a dozen times in the afternoon and evening. She had tried again in the morning. She didn't know that he was being questioned, and driven back by one of his supervisors to his main home near San Diego; but she had guessed that he had gone home for the weekend. She, too, was worried. There had been no word from Richard for two days, since the shopping expedition.

When she called him at Lynwood that night, there was no response. Had Miller decided to back out? She needed to know if they were going to Vienna or not. What would she tell the voice from the consulate-general when next he called? What would she say to Mrs. Baskevitch? Svetlana convinced herself that Miller was at Lynwood, but was simply avoiding the phone, avoiding her. Where else could he be? She felt he was afraid to go to Vienna, and afraid to tell her that he was afraid. She had to have it out with him. Again, she took John, Nikolaiy's cousin, with her, and went looking for the Lynwood house. Again, she was followed. Again, she got lost, but her anxious search for Miller only strengthened the belief of those who suspected that the Vienna trip was more of a Russian than an FBI enterprise.

That day, the twenty-ninth, an FBI polygrapher named James Murphy had tested Miller. Asked if he had given the reporting guidance to Svetlana in San Francisco, he had said he was "not sure." His credentials? He gave the same answer. Because of his unaccustomed drunkenness that Saturday, the facts were just not in his cerebral computer. Murphy announced that he had failed on some questions. Miller complained that Murphy, who was not a special agent but a technician, was hostile to him, and demanded a second test by someone else.

After the emotional auto-da-fé with Bishop Bretzing, and the polygraph test, Miller was exhausted. Christensen offered to drive him home to Bonsall, a three-hour journey. He was on the road while Svetlana was searching for him, by phone and car, in Lynwood.

"I failed the lie-detector test," he said.

"Yes, I know," said Christensen.

"I think I know why." Christensen waited for him to continue. "He asked me if I'd ever done anything dishonest, and I told him the things I'd done—stealing candy from stores, keeping money that belonged to my uncle. Then he asked me if I'd ever been dishonest with the Bureau, and I told him about moonlight work on Bureau time. He asked me if I had ever sold Bureau information, and I said no. I think that was what did it. Because I have sold Bureau information."

Christensen almost held his breath. "Go on."

"Couple of years ago, Larry Grayson, in Riverside, asked me for Department of Motor Vehicle rap sheets on one of his clients. I ran off copies and gave them to him."

"How much did you charge him?"

"Twenty-five dollars a page."

"How many pages?"

"About forty."

That meant Miller had made about a thousand dollars. "You think Murphy—"

"—will probably have noticed that when I said that, I started reacting, you know, sweating and stuff, and he must have decided that I sold something to the Russkies in San Fran. Of course, I was so nervous, and what with my weight, I was probably sweating anyway."

"Why didn't you just admit to the Grayson thing?"

"Heck, I seem to be in enough trouble already. I don't want to be dismissed from the FBI."

Now Torrence, leading Whipworm on Stukey's instructions, was doing most of the questioning, along with another agent called Graham Van Note, and it was getting uglier. To make things worse, by the thirtieth, three days after he had reported to Christensen, and Martin's decision to return to the Justice Department in Washington, Paul Minor arrived from FBI headquarters. He was the Bureau's head of polygraphy.

Minor said he must question him first, before wiring him up. Had Miller copied the reporting guidance at the office? Miller foolishly said he doubted it. So why was there a copy of part of it at Lynwood? The agents asked themselves if there had been more than one copy, which could mean that one had been given to the consulate-general. But then, *why* would he make more than one copy?

The whole day, a Sunday, Minor neither taped nor polygraphed him.

The next day was more of the same. Miller asked why he was not testing him. Minor said: "Did you give them the reporting guidance? If it's yes, say so. If it's no, say so. Then I can test if you are telling the truth."

Sure by now that he would fail the test, whatever he said, because of this state of nerves, Miller said: "I'll say yes." If he said that, and Minor said he was lying, they would let him go. Still Minor did not wire him up.

Now Miller knew, or thought he knew, what the intentions of his colleagues were. They were trying to get him to admit that he had given *something*—the telephone book, the guideline on how to question foreigners—to the Russians, and then they were going to try to fire him. It would mean that he would be out of not only a job, but a pension!

Miller had steadfastly refused his right to a lawyer. He didn't want the questioning to be a total I-versus-them thing. He wanted it to remain in-house, a family dispute. After all, they were all on the same side. Weren't they? He had consented to the search of his father's house and, embarrassing though it was, to a search of the farm at Bonsall, in front of his kids.

At both places, they had found papers that should never have left the Westwood office—mostly older ones at Bonsall. None were high-security. The most interesting discovery was the eleven pages on the USSR in the reporting guidance—the papers that the Whipworm investigators suspected had been carried into the consulate-general inside one of Svetlana's film canisters. The reporting guidance was becoming the Pumpkin Papers of the inquiry.

Miller thought that it might even be a good thing that the eleven pages had turned up at Lynwood—still in his own possession; but he realized that they might think that he had made more than one copy. He had freely admitted to brandishing the papers in front of Svetlana, as evidence of the sort of goodies he would have to offer in his dangle.

"Did she read it?"

"No, she didn't seem very interested." Sure enough, the only fingerprints found on the copy were Miller's. Perhaps, Miller thought, one reason she had not taken it was that she feared that he *wanted* her prints on it.

Miller explained where he had been standing when he showed her the thing. He mimicked doing it again.

Back in bed at Bonsall that night, Miller was reasonably satisfied. He had, he felt, done the right thing in not bringing in a lawyer and appearing hostile—and therefore suspect—and in consenting to searches without making them go to court for a warrant. The material turned up had been innocuous. It could still cost him his career, though, if they chose to make a mountain out of a molehill.

But Minor had been creepy. Minor hadn't hooked him up to the machine or tested him at all. It is normal for polygraphers to go over the field of questioning first before hooking a subject up, but Minor had just sat there with Torrence or van Note, or occasionally without them, a malevolent presence who asked endless questions. Minor, Miller thought, believed in the cops' motto: All truth is relative, but all confessions sound good in court.

The next day, Christensen took over the questioning again, then was relieved by Minor, who was still refusing to hook Miller up. Miller wondered if Minor was afraid of what the result would be. Could there be any other explanation? Larry Torrence and Graham van Note came back. Now, he drew them a diagram of where he and Svetlana had been standing when he had shown her the guidance pages at Lynwood. He said again that he had never given it to her in San Francisco. Miller, on the griddle for the fifth day, with no lawyer, no friendly face, was beginning to lose control of his memory, to have difficulty distinguishing between what he remembered doing and what others said he must have done. In a climate of hostility and tension, if two versions of events—what you know and what the questioner implies—are constantly played against each other, the tired mind begins to forget which is which. Under incessant or hostile questioning, people forget how old they are, their mother's names, the alphabet. They try to eat soup with a fork or greet an arrival with "Good-bye!" His tormentors were, Miller knew, using on him, their colleague, the techniques they used on the bad guys they arrested. That meant they believed that he was guilty and felt they needed a confession at any price. That was why they were ensuring that he no longer knew clearly what were his own recollections and what were simply the memories of recently repeated questions—*their* version of what had happened or might have happened. He remembered a book he had read in college about Cardinal Mindzenty. When the cardinal had confessed, there hadn't been a bruise on him, either.

At one point, he heard himself saying: "I'm not sure any more what I remember and what I remember you guys saying."

Then, later, he said: "If all you want is some excuse to fire me, after eighteen years of service, then I'm prepared to say that I gave 'Lana my I.D. and a copy of the reporting guidance to take into the consulate." Raising his voice, he went on: "Yes, I'll confess to anything you say! Yes, I was sleeping with 'Lana and it's against FBI rules to have sex with an informant, although if you took that rule seriously you'd have to fire half the FBI!"

He heard a voice saying: "You'll sign that you actually gave—"

"That I made the dangle real, if that's what you're getting at."

Christensen left Miller with Minor and went to see Bretzing. He told him of Miller's decision.

"He thinks he's going to be fired. He doesn't realize he might even be arrested," Christensen said.

"We'll have to interrogate Hunt, too," Bretzing retorted in episcopal tones. "I think he's reached the end of his usefulness, also." He was nodding, noncommittally. "Okay. Ask Mr. Minor to come in here."

Christensen and Minor exchanged seats in front of Miller, who was now sobbing, his huge frame shaking like a great jellyfish. He had his glasses in his hand but, having no handkerchief, he was wiping his eyes with the sleeves of his jacket.

In Bretzing's office, Minor was confirming what Christensen had said.

"He says he's prepared to sign anything."

"I don't want him to sign *anything*. I want him to sign to the truth, whatever it is. Does he not realize he could be arrested?"

"I don't see how he can't have realized that—but he's a simple guy."

The questioning went on. The same ground was covered, in the hope of turning up a contradiction. Westwood was going at Miller as though he were Walker or even Pelton. With an occasional break for coffee and snacks, the questioning went on until late into the night. Miller was given a cot in the overnight room. Despite his exhaustion, he was awake shortly after first light. It was 6:30.

"I'd like to call my wife." He had told her that he would be very late, that he might sleep over, that she shouldn't worry. But she would still be worried.

Miller lay on the army-style camp bed and picked up the phone on the bedside table. At the console, they were listening in. As Paula sleepily answered, Miller began to cry again.

They spoke for about thirty minutes. He and Paula had had their ups and downs, and more downs than ups in the last few years, but they had had a lifetime together, and she was the only person he could talk to.

"You're being dismissed? Just like that?"

"Yeah. And maybe arrested."

"Because of your operation with the Russians?"

"Yeah."

"But Richard, what did you do?" As always, when she was excited, her voice rose. It sounded like more interrogation.

"I don't think I did what I'm accused of doing, but I can't tell, anymore, what happened from what they say happened."

"Why don't you call in a lawyer? You know how bad you are in court. You shouldn't try to defend yourself alone."

"I know this is going to sound silly, Paula, but I didn't call a lawyer because I felt it would look uncooperative, and lead to my being fired." He began to blubber uncontrollably now.

When he had composed himself a little, he said: "I'm lying here in bed, remembering this over and over again and I draw a blank."

"The trip to the consulate."

"Yeah. The trouble is, I was drinking and I'm not a drinker. In the critical area of—uh—documents, I draw a blank. I had a hangover in the morning, and I never clearly remembered what had happened the evening before. But they apparently have, you know, data and communications that indicate that I gave them some documents."

"You say 'they' have. The Bureau?"

"Yeah."

"And you gave 'them.' The Russians?" Her voice was rising again.

"Yeah."

"*What* documents?" She was beginning to sound like Torrence.

"I don't know what they would be or anything like that," he said weakly. He knew about the reporting guidance, of course, but Christensen had said there were other papers, too. At least, he thought it was Christensen. He was beginning to feel very tired.

"Oh, Richard, this is awful. I'm so sorry," Paula said.

Crying like a child once more, Miller said: "I've come to the conclusion that I've been led down the primrose path." He shook, and paused. "I'm suffering from a tragic case of naiveté." There was another pause for crying. "During the night, I was ready to sign and say: 'All right, I did everything you guys think I did, but I don't remember.' "

He couldn't bring himself to admit that he had already signed. He said: "I'm sure these guys think I'm the best bullshit artist this side of the Atlantic Ocean, but it ain't true."

"Are you coming home?"

"Yeah. I'll be home soon. Don't tell the kids anything of this."

Now, it was past seven. He wanted to call Marta York before she went off to her waitress job. He needed to prepare her for the fact that she would be visited by FBI agents.

The call was brief. He made it from a pay phone. He explained that he was suspected of passing documents to the Russians in the course of his FBI work. Marta had sounded upset at his call, still angry at being "jilted," but her voice softened when she realized that R.W. was in trouble.

"Did you [give anything to the Russians]?"

"I'm not sure. I might have given them one document as a 'dangle,' nothing much." This friendly "confession" to Mrs. York was to help trigger Miller's arrest.

But Marta York remained a woman scorned, with a Latin temper, and later she was telling reporters that Miller had given the Russian spymaster not only "documents" but also his FBI badge and his *gun*.

While Miller rested, his colleagues in the Westwood office yawned. Torrence was telling Bretzing: "He said: 'Just give me a confession. I'll sign anything.' "

"I know. But what did he admit?"

"First, he admitted giving Svetlana a photocopy of one document, then he made it 'documents.' "

"The reporting guidance."

"Yes, sir."

"What were the others?"

"Sir, he couldn't remember."

"Dear Lord, give me patience."

"Well, he said he knew he was out of line, that he had deluded himself, that he had lied to himself about this, and to other people about his conduct."

"But the crux of the case—he can only remember one picayune document?"

"Sir, he said he had been considering giving them a real classified document, something that would be 'not damning'— that was his phrase. He said he ran off a copy of the reporting guidance, or part of it, in the office here."

"Just one? But we found one in the Lynwood house."

"Sir, he admitted that he thought he had passed it to the consulate."

The Mormon bishop was left to wonder to himself: If Miller had been Hispanic or black, wouldn't we simply have sanctioned him, docked his pay?

Bretzing ordered Miller aroused, and brought in. Now, the fat man looked like a zombie. Trying to sound reasonably crisp and matter-of-fact, Bretzing formally dismissed him from the FBI. The director, William Webster, had earlier authorized this momentous step. Incongruously, although in civilian clothes, and with nothing on his head, Miller saluted his chief and bishop, wheeled ponderously around, went downstairs in silence, and drove home to Bonsall. At least, he had not been arrested. That was a relief.

Bretzing waved everyone away except a secretary, and began to dictate a report for Webster. He recommended that, unless more damning evidence should come to light, no further action should be taken. Bretzing buttressed his dispatch with the relevant FD/302s and the more sensitive FD/92 field reports on the investigation.

It was Tuesday, and that evening Grishin made his regular call. He did not yet know that the puppets he had set in motion were about to carry out his will to the final act. This time, the conversation lasted less than three minutes.

Svetlana, the cardiologist's assistant from Kiev, trying to imagine going to Vienna for her health, had still not heard from Richard. She could base what she said only on his last instructions to her, about the airline reservations, and on the shoes and the Burberry for the trip.

She said, firmly: "The doctor is agreeable to the operation."

Grishin asked about the date of the trip again. She hedged, saying her companion still didn't have his passport and "various papers." Once again mixing her metaphors, she approximately repeated something she had said the week before: "I won't know the exact time of departure until just before I lie on the operating table." A moment later, however, she said: "So tell the relatives not to worry, everything is fine."

Grishin said: "I understand. Other than that, you don't have any problems?"

This was not the time, she felt, to say that Richard seemed to have disappeared. She said: "No problems. No problems. Everything has been settled." Then, contradictorily, she added: "I am trying to do everything possible."

"It's unfortunate that you can't give me a date." They were supposed to leave eight days later. "I'll call you in one week's time."

At no point did Svetlana reveal that she had tried, unsuccessfully, to call Miller six times over the past few days.

But the trap was sprung. Grishin felt confident that she and Miller would soon be arrested, probably just after their return from the Austrian capital.

While Miller did chores on the farm and relaxed, trying to recover from the five days of interrogation, and to adjust to the fact that he, whose badge had been law for eighteen years, must now register for the dole, even more drastic events were afoot back in Washington and Los Angeles. William Webster had decided to overrule Richard Bretzing and John Martin: Miller was to be arrested and charged. Gary Auer's Russian Squad was to be disbanded, its duties handed over to the Chinese Squad—*none* of whom spoke Russian.

In Los Angeles, there was a scramble to put together the documentation for an arrest warrant. Work went on into the night. At 10:30 p.m., assistant U.S. Attorney Russell Hayman went to a magistrate's residence in Manhattan Beach and waited while the papers were read. At about midnight, the warrant was issued. Hayman called Bretzing, who was parked just down the street from the Miller farm, staring at his cellular phone. Because he had not anticipated that there would be a case, he had allowed Miller to go home to a different jurisdiction.

Bretzing heard Hayman's message, grunted, rolled down his window and told two local troopers who were lounging by their cruiser: "That's it!"

Moments earlier, two FBI agents had turned up at the house of Larry Grayson. They were checking on Miller's acknowledgment that he had asked Grayson to cover him audiovisually in Mexico.

After the initial questions, Grayson stroked his beard and said: "You mean this is not just a song and dance? I never thought he'd have the nerve to go through with it."

One of the agents said with a saturnine frown: "This is a national security matter. This man is in a lot of trouble."

"Well, if I can be of any help," said Grayson, slightly shaken. "I used to be a deputy sheriff around here."

"Yes, we know your background and we know about your relationships with Miller," the other agent said icily.

Grayson thought at once of the rap sheets he had bought from Miller. He thought about the Mexico trip. If Miller was in trouble because of that, what could they throw at Miller's friend in Riverside—conspiracy, the catch-all in any limping prosecution? What, he wondered, was the "max" for conspiracy in a national security case—twenty-five years?

After they had left, Grayson pondered what he should do. His father, the King's Messenger, had told him that the difference between a man and an animal on two legs was loyalty. He should at least make a try—tell R.W. that the feds had been to his place, asking questions about the Mexico caper. His wife, he knew, would tell him to leave well enough alone.

*

In most democracies, arrests cannot be made at night except *in flagrante delicto*. Unless something illegal is believed to be going on inside, a citizen's home is inviolate during the hours of darkness. In France, every cop-film buff, every Maigret aficionado knows the scene when the inspector waits wearily in his car outside the serial murderer's apartment building for the sun to rise. Dawn is similarly the hour of executions. In 1989, when the Ceaucescus of Rumania became the Louis XVI and Marie-Antoinette of Bucharest, Europeans who had no sympathy with the convicts were shocked, not that it took place on Christmas Day but on Christmas *night*.

Curiously, nothing in the U.S. Constitution protects the homes of sleeping Americans from the knock on the door in the hours of least resistance.

It was after midnight. The exhausted former special agent was fast asleep in bed with Paula when the knock came. He went downstairs in pajamas, thinking that perhaps police had spotted a prowler stealing avocados from the trees.

It was the local police all right. The fat man in sleepwear stared, blinking, as the uniformed officer said: "Richard William Miller? I have a warrant for your arrest." And he read him his Miranda rights.

Paula had followed him downstairs and heard the Miranda part.

"I'll get dressed," Miller said.

"Could you all keep your voices down?" commanded the woman who for eighteen years had been the wife of a fed. "There are eight children sleeping here." The two Bonsall cops looked sheepish, accommodating. "Would you all like some coffee?" Paula went on. "It's only instant."

"Gee, yes," said one of the Bonsall cops.

Ten minutes later, Miller was dressed, the coffee drunk. He looked more exhausted than ever. At the door, he embraced Paula. They were both crying. The two rural cops stood back. They had never arrested an FBI agent before; they were unlikely ever to do so again.

"They didn't have to do this to me," Miller said.

The phone rang. Who could be calling at this hour of the night?

"They surely didn't," said Paula.

"Better see who that is," Miller said. As Paula went to the kitchen to take the call, he announced: "Okay, gentlemen."

It never occurred to the provincial troopers that this could be the Rezidentura calling. Perhaps the Kremlin. Out of deference to the fed, even in disgrace, one of them was saying: "We're not using the cuffs."

"I never was a fast runner," the fat man said.

Back in the kitchen, Paula took Grayson's call. He had made the professional guess that, if Miller's line was bugged, the surveillance would probably cease at midnight, when everyone would be asleep. Even in the FBI, there's a limit to what the taxpayer can be made to pay for, and telephone surveillance of a sleeping residence rarely makes the budget.

"Is R.W. there?"

"No." It was true. She had just heard Richard close the front door behind him.

"Could you give him a message?"

Could she? How? "Yes," she said, automatically.

"Tell him two people were inquiring about putting flowers on his mother's grave."

"That's the message?"

"Yeah."

"All right, Larry, I'll tell him when I see him."

"Sorry to wake you up. Good night."

Outside in the car, Bretzing and another agent had been waiting to drive Miller to the FBI office in San Diego. On the way, Bretzing asked: "What other documents beside the reporting guidance did you give them? Did you give Svetlana your credentials?"

Miller, Bretzing reported later, sighed and "hung his head." He said: "I'll tell you the rest of the story before we get to San Diego." Then, he went back to sleep.

Miller was taken from the FBI office to the metropolitan detention center, a "holding facility" aboom with the roars of drunks and junkies going cold turkey in their cages. Miller, being a career policeman, was given a cell to himself.

A little earlier, at 2 a.m., the Ogorodnikovs had been taken away under the startled eyes of Matvei and cousin John. Nikolaiy, suspecting a thief, had come to the door with a gun and had been lucky not to be blown away by the police. With all the drama of the Walker, Pelton, Pollard and Howard cases, the judicial investigation as to what had really happened to a minor FBI reporting guidance was on.

By 7 a.m., a red-eyed Hayman was clambering into an FBI helicopter to fly to San Diego and have Miller arraigned and returned to Los Angeles.

Why the arrests were made at the witching hours remains unclear. It meant the news wires got a beat over broadcasting and the papers. The first Grishin knew of the success of his plan was when the *San Francisco Examiner* called the public affairs officer of the consulate-general. In the indictment, Aleksandr Vasiliyevich Grishin was to be named as an unindicted co-conspirator. But, long before that, every editor in the region knew that the consulate-general housed the KGB's West Coast headquarters.

Grishin didn't speak to any reporters, of course. His name was still not known to the press. He smoked his black cigarettes and enjoyed his last lunch at the good French restaurant that Occidental Research favored, with Zaydzev as his guest. They raised their glasses, so that whoever was standing in the rain and peering through the window from across the street could see their good humor. Because Moscow was half a day ahead, Grishin waited until the evening before calling S. A few days before, he had been appointed director of one whole division of the S directorate. It had not come as a surprise, but no one is ever totally sure of a promised promotion until it happens. He was leaving San Francisco not only on a success, but on the sort of anecdotal success that would be a postprandial story for years back home.

Back at the office, chain-smoking the good Turkish tobacco, he went back in his mind over the whole, brief operation. Nothing seemed to have gone wrong. They had fallen for his calls to Ogorodnikova, as a trout snapping for a worm. And he seemed to have been right about Miller: He was doing a solo operation that he would reveal only when it was on the road—and that he didn't know his ass from a hole in the wall where intelligence matters were concerned. He thought of The Letter, and nearly laughed out loud.

Ludmila came in. She had been to his apartment with some of the consulate-general labor, all scruffy security men, and done his packing. Now, she was bringing him his tickets for Tokyo and Moscow.

"Not Vienna?" he complained. He and Ludmila laughed. Zaydzev came in.

"Want to try the throne?" Grishin asked, pointing to the seat on which he was sitting. Everyone laughed again.

"You were right, colonel," Zaydzev said, breaking the rules by giving Grishin his correct KGB rank title. "The scoundrel was taking a ship to sea without his admiral's permission!"

"I feel a little sorry for our compatriots." Grishin paused. He knew they had to go down with Miller. There could be no question of rescuing them in a swap, because they weren't members of the Soviet intelligence family. His people had offered to put the girl into play, and she'd shown which side she was on—unforgivable. "The Americans really are bastards," he said to Zaydzev. "They put on this big act about helping political refugees, but they never give them a passport as all other countries do. Officially, they leave them in limbo for five years, but in fact it's longer than that.

"But then again, have you noticed that the Ogorodnikovs have been here eleven years now, and they've never asked for naturalization? With American passports, they wouldn't have needed those spurious re-entry permits. You know what that means?"

"One or both of them wanted to keep the option of going home, eventually."

"If the prosecution notices that," Grishin said: "it'll be further circumstantial 'proof' that their loyalties were to the USSR. Let's just hope, for the sake of Nikolaiy and Svetlana, that our American colleagues are as incompetent on that as on the rest."

He lit another cigarette. He said: "I think the girl from Tula was torn in her loyalties. If that fellow Hunt had married her.... But again, I don't think she really enjoyed sleeping with the FBI."

"I don't understand why they didn't let him go to Vienna, then arrest him afterward," Zaydzev said. "The case would surely have been stronger. After all, this is an open court, with the press."

"Just as well they didn't, I think," Grishin said. "I had a feeling he would back out. I think he would only have had the courage to take us on if his directors had ordered him to do so.

"But you're right—if they'd had one kopek's worth of sense, they would never have arrested the boob at all. They would have played him on the line, or tried to, after he returned from Vienna. It was a case of premature arrest."

"That's their problem," Menshikov said.

"As you say. My concern was to turn the situation to our advantage, to play those clowns Hunt and Miller for whatever we could get. And, in all vanity, comrade, I did it! It won't make any difference in the Cold War, or anything much, but victory is always sweet. Alas, someday, some bastard will put all this in a book. But I think I'll still come out looking intelligent. That's better than being a pleasant fool."

"You've made up your mind to leave tonight, without being declared *persona non grata*?"

"Yes. Of course, that way, we lose the chance to deport one of theirs, but we can always do that later. I think the important thing is to direct the attention of the inquisitors to the manifest guilt of Richard Miller and his conspirators in West Hollywood! It will be announced tomorrow that I have gone on leave. The United States establishment will bend to my will and say that this indicates that I was the controller of Richard Miller the spy! And the establishment press will sit up and beg for the privilege of echoing the government's propaganda."

"You should write a novel, colonel."

"Why? Reality is so much more fun! I will be an unindicted co-conspirator, and I will exchange Christmas cards with Richard Nixon!"

They began to laugh again. The wine from the lunch was still in their systems.

"Seriously," Grishin said. "This should discourage these people from trying to do double-agent operations against us again, and teach Nikolaiy Sergeivich and Svetlana Malutina to know where their sole loyalties should lie."

Ludmila came back. "The consul-general would like you to come to his office. I don't think I'm supposed to tell you, but everyone is there to toast you, so I think you should comb your hair." Ludmila grinned and added: "Comrade."

"Wipe that grin from your face, my lovely," Grishin said. "I'm having you sent to Siberia."

Now, they were all laughing like children.

*

At Occidental Research, Alf and Killer agreed with their nemesis, Aleksandr Grishin.

"Their arrest is very premature, very premature," Merman said.

"Can't the FBI do anything right?" Kitano asked.

Also in agreement was Bill Newman, the special agent-in-charge in San Francisco, and his legendary predecessor, Charlie Bates.

"Don't really know whether to laff or baff," was Bates's comment.

*Richard William Miller at age 26 in a Brigham Young University yearbook in 1963, the year that he graduated. Despite his poor academic record, the FBI recruited him while he was still in school. (Courtesy UPI/Bettmann.)*

*Richard William Miller in 1989, after five years in prison. (Courtesy UPI/Bettmann.)*

*Svetlana Ogorodnikova in 1987, after three years in prison.*

*FBI surveillance photograph of Aleksandr Grishin, the KGB Rezident in San Francisco.*

*FBI surveillance photograph of Miller and Ogorodnikova in Santa Monica on September 20, 1984. (Courtesy UPI/Bettmann.)*

*FBI Special Agent Richard Bretzing making an official statement to the media on October 3, 1984, following the announcement of Miller's arrest. (Courtesy UPI/Bettmann.)*

# PART III

## Trials and Witnesses

# Chapter Thirteen

# *First Trial: Hung Jury*

*By labeling Grishin's stilted conversation as "plain code," the prosecution was admitting that Grishin knew or suspected that the conversations were being tapped.*

Svetlana couldn't believe it was happening. All those police. The drawn weapons. The melodramatic use of handcuffs, so startling to Europeans. The middle-of-the-night arraignment, as in a film. She and Nikolaiy were being treated as though they were major criminals. After the arraignment, spending what remained of the night in the notorious Sybil Brand "facility"— the sheriff's holding jail for women in Los Angeles—soon had her crying like a child. She needed a drink. One of the whores in her cell gave her a cigarette.

"First time, honey?"

At the arraignment, they had been promised lawyers. In the morning, she found she had two of the species, on *pro bono publico* loan from a firm that was well-known in the local big-bucks litigation mart. Even to Svetlana's unpracticed eye, Brad Brian and Gregory P. Stone seemed young and innocent, a couple of rich kids out on a lark, defending Ninotchka. She didn't know they had never tried a major criminal case before.

One of the first things they asked was if it was true that she had recently returned from a visit to the Soviet Union. She latched on to that as the beginning of her explanation of why she was *not* a Russian spy. If she and Nikolaiy had been spies, would the KGB have allowed them to travel back and forth, year after year, to Kiev and to send their child to a privileged youth camp in the Crimea? She had been *working for the FBI.*

She urged them to speak to John Hunt.

"I worked for him, in the FBI. Everything I did, I did because of him."

"He was your boss?"

"And my man."

How, she asked herself, had John allowed all this to happen to her?

By the time of the second meeting, Brian and Stone had a picture of how Svetlana had been drawn into the outer fringes of intelligence.

"So you say he was meeting you every day, officially because you were his informer, but mostly for, well, sex?" one of the young men with the buttoned-down collars asked.

"I try to keep him away from the apartment building. So sometimes, we, you know, use his car, sometimes mine, or hotel rooms."

"Little motels? D'you remember the names?"

"Well, there was the suite in the Ambassador that the FBI always has."

Suddenly, she began to cry.

"Why did he drop you?"

"His boss say I not so good."

"Did he say he didn't know which side you were on, America or Russia?"

"I don't know. Maybe. How he not know? I never did anything in all this except what John make me do."

"But John's boss, let's see, that's Christensen? You say he told John to drop you. But you were still his informer?"

"It was always the same line: He say he must have something to report to his superiors, so that he can go on seeing me. He know I want to see him."

"But, Mrs. Ogorodnikova, was he really in love, d'you think?"

It was a question that touched a raw nerve, and she didn't respond directly to it.

"We would dance, and he would hug me and kiss me, and we would go for walks on the beach in the moonshine, no? He seem very much in love. And I think: *Ai*! Am I really in love, also? Is this possible? So I always do whatever he say."

"How long did this relationship go on?"

"Two years."

Stone and Brian looked at each other. That seemed at least a slight exaggeration. But she was distraught. They would have to put an investigator onto Hunt. They would need one who was a former FBI agent, like Hunt, as many of the private investigators were. It was to be assumed that Hunt would deny that he was getting his informer to sleep with him.

"If the FBI hears that this John couldn't keep his pecker in his pants, they'll shove him over the side for sure," Brian said to Stone. A week or so later, they were to learn that Hunt had been persuaded to take immediate retirement. To Svetlana, Brian said: "Can you remember some particular incident that shows that he was your lover?"

"We were in an accident together."

"Yes?"

"In my car. We were both drinking. The police came."

"This was in L.A.? The L.A.P.D.?"

"Yes. John was worried about being in the car with me when it happened."

"It would be on the police blotter, yeah. Look, I'm not doubting your words, Mrs. Ogorodnikova, but his being in the car with you at the time, and your both having been drinking, doesn't prove he was your lover."

"If I was not his mistress, why did he pay for my abortion?"

"When was this?"

"Last year. We went to Dr. Jeikov's clinic. John paid eight hundred dollars."

"A check?"

"Uh-huh."

The investigator would have to get the doctor's records. The lawyers asked for Jeikov's address.

"There's another doctor there, now," she told them.

"Where is Dr. Jeikov?"

"He died."

Brian hoped that wouldn't make the investigator's task difficult.

"Was there anyone else in the doctor's office when John took you there for the abortion?"

"His secretary. Yes—and she's still there."

That might help, especially if the secretary still had her copy of the bill, and if it said what procedure it was for.

"And the child was John's, not your husband's?"

In truth, she didn't really know. In arithmetic, the odds were that it was John's, she thought, because she rarely slept with Nikolaiy any more.

"Why would John pay for an abortion if it not his baby?"

"Well, maybe he wasn't sure who was the father, but he paid because it might have been he."

"He paid because he was my man," Svetlana said, her peasant pride stirring.

That morning, Nikolaiy also met his public defender, Randi Sue Pollock, who also hired an investigator, another retired cop. She brought him along to the first substantive meeting with the excitable butcher. The gumshoe's first question was: "How long have you been a Russian spy?"

"A what? I am not," said Nikolaiy.

Later, Miss Pollock and the private eye were to agree that their client was convincing.

Nikolaiy had little to tell. He knew his wife worked for the FBI, which was interested in her contacts with the consulate-general, where she got most of her films. Because of the film work, and driving visitors around, he and she had been allowed to visit their mothers in the Ukraine and Russia, and Matvei had gone to the Artek camp. He knew that the FBI man wanted Svetlana to accompany him to Vienna on some sort of scam. He had met the man, but he claimed he didn't know the details.

He was in Terminal Island Prison, worrying about Matvei, who remained in the apartment with Aunt Lisa's son, John. Most days, if he could get to a phone despite the interminable lines, he would call Matvei, but he didn't know what to say. It wasn't just that he knew that all calls must be monitored. What could you tell your only child except that you were innocent? Matvei knew that already.

"Are you all right, Matvei?"

"Yes, Father, don't worry about me."

"Don't cry, boy. Your mother and I will be home soon."

He had heard that Svetlana was having a rough time in that hellhole, Sybil Brand. Once it was known that she was a "Russian spy," patriotic American female felons had begun picking on her, assaulting her. Svetlana, he knew, had a temper; she would strike back, however hopelessly outnumbered. He was more worried about her, and about Matvei, than about himself.

*

Miller had been assigned two good lawyers, Joel Levine and Stanley Greenberg. Levine, a jurist's jurist, had helped prosecute Christopher Boyce and Andrew Lee, the "Falcon and the Snowman." Greenberg was an exuberant "jury" lawyer. Because Miller had been in the FBI for two decades, he knew what to expect from a trial, but Levine and Greenberg noticed at once that he was the least likely FBI special agent they had ever known.

Miller explained about the FCI-1, the "Russian Squad," his own role. John Hunt had tried to develop 'Lana as an FBI asset, he said, but Hunt had finally given up on her. He had tried to succeed where John had failed, and the fact was that he had! He had hooked Grishin! And now Bretzing and Christensen were trying to make it out to be the other way around. At the same time, Miller was claiming that 'Lana had turned her oar—that she had been turned by the Rezidentura.

"Look, Richard, so that we can help you, you're going to have to tell us the truth, the whole truth," Levine said.

Miller was bothered by these strangers calling him Richard. Only Paula and Svetlana had called him that. Everyone else, even Marta, called him "R.W."

But he said: "I know. As a Fed, I've been obliged to lie I don't know how many times, a thousand times. But I've tried never to lie about the big things. I can say in truth that at no time did I ever remotely consider becoming a Soviet spy, so help me God."

Levine and Greenberg wanted to know who, out of Miller and Svetlana, had seduced whom. They would get around to John Hunt later. Miller dodged the question; he said he didn't think sex had been his undoing. He had started having sex with Svetlana on the second time they had met, about a week after the first meeting, in May 1984. It had been in her car, beside the beach at Malibu. He had made love to her, he said, because she appeared to be expecting it, and because he had decided to do everything he could to encourage her to bring him into contact with the KGB. John had done the dangle first, and the Russkies had responded with silence. But when he, Miller, had cast out the hook again, they had begun to bite at the line, even though they had thought, until near the end, that he was actually John Hunt. He had never concealed his original plan from his superiors, he contended; after all, he had reported to Gary Auer, the head of FCI-1's Russian Squad, on those first two meetings.

During the week, Miller described his life and career and his brief attempt at double-agentry to Levine and Greenberg. He was frank about his dismal FBI record, a discussion that led him in turn to admit to his shoplifting at 7-11, his petty dishonesties with his uncle. He readily agreed that he had broken in-house rules by continuing to frequent "'Lana," and by not reporting what he was doing to his supervisor. But John Hunt, he pointed out, had done the same: He had not reported the visit to Dr. Jeikov, for instance. Would anyone, in Hunt's or Miller's position, have done so, Miller implied?

It was 'Lana who had described John's "dangle" operation to him, and who had seeded in his imagination the desire to leave the Bureau in a blaze of glory, Miller said. She had told him that, on her visit to Moscow that summer, she would be meeting with a senior GRU officer. He had taken this with a grain of salt, because she had told Christensen that she was a KGB major. Later, she had made the same boast to Miller, at the Charthouse. She had even claimed to have been Andropov's mistress. But was that so absurd? Was there anyone female and under thirty in the Kennedy White House who hadn't accommodated the president's *penis erectus continuus*? He had accepted her claim as meaning that she had *access.*

He told of her asking him if he would work for the Soviet Union, of his asking for fifty thousand dollars, of his meeting with Nikolaiy. By then, word was filtering back to Levine and Greenberg that the confused "'Lana" was denying that she had ever set up that meeting—which Nikolaiy nevertheless confirmed had taken place. Then, Svetlana would place it closer to their date of departure. Miller told his lawyers of looking up Wolfson in the FBI computer and of deciding then and there that "'Lana" wasn't serious. He told how he had relented on seeing her again, and had accompanied her to the dinner with the Russian couple.

Miller recounted the San Francisco trip.

"Did you meet any Russian officials? Remember, you were photographed."

"No. I was too pissed, in any event."

"Did you speak to Grishin or anyone over the phone, from Livermore perhaps? Remember—"

"I know what you're going to say about monitoring—I'm an FBI agent, you know. No. I went straight to sleep. I was pissed."

"No one came to see you there?"

"I think the reason we chose Livermore must have been that it's outside their twenty-five-mile limit. No, no one came."

"Did you take any documents with you to San Fran?"

"I took eleven pages of a reporting guidance in case I wanted to use that as a dangle. It was the thing I had already flashed under Wolfson's eyes, and 'Lana's. I wasn't going to give it to them, only flash it."

"Did you take it into the consulate?"

"I never went into the consulate. The photos will show that."

"Did you give it to 'Lana to take in?"

"I'm almost sure I didn't, but I don't remember everything. The eleven pages were still in my dad's place at Lynwood when the Bureau did it over. When they were questioning me, they made me think that's what I'd done—given them to 'Lana to dangle—but I don't think I did. They were just sort of hypnotizing me into thinking I did. I had very little memory of anything, the next day, and maybe less still now."

"Did you give her any ID to show the Russians, to prove you were FBI?"

"I'm almost sure I didn't. What good would it have served?"

"They could have photographed it, to blackmail you later."

"Well, yes, I guess. But no, I honestly have no recollection of giving her anything."

"But you'd talked about producing ID. So did John Hunt, you say."

"Yes, that's true. I guess we were both playing her along, 'Lana, I mean." He paused. "I'm sure there were no prints on that guidance except mine."

"You could have wiped them off, they might say."

"Without wiping off my own, or smudging them? C'mon, gimme a break!"

"Relax, Richard, we're your friends. Now, would you ever have given them that guidance, which after all doesn't sound too cosmic, in order to bring off the dangle?"

Miller paused again, then looked Levine in the eye. "Sure."

"Without clearance from your supervisors?"

"Probably not. I had specifically told 'Lana not to promise the Russkies anything in particular because, as I explained to her, I couldn't actually give her any documents at all without talking to Auer or Christensen." He paused again; he fancied a Milky Way. "It would have been difficult to find a more—uh—"

"Innocuous. Yeah, I know," said Greenberg. "A more innocuous document. And you could have given it to the Russkies fairly safely by passing it to some reporter or columnist."

"Exactly!"

"Relax, Richard," said Levine, a skinny marathon runner whose manner changed easily from legal eagle to mini-Kojak.

To the defense, the government's case didn't look very strong, unless there was more in the video and sound surveillance than Miller was telling them. But Miller would be a terrible witness, as the FBI had decided long ago. One of the strongest proofs of Richard's loyal intention was his engagement of Grayson; but Grayson wouldn't talk to Levine or Greenberg. Eventually, through Al Sayers, a retired former FBI special agent who had once been Miller's supervisor and who was now his investigator, a meeting was set up in Riverside between Grayson and Levine and Sayers; but Grayson never turned up.

However, Miller appeared to have done nothing that implied that his operation was unlawful—only irregular. He had applied for his passport at the office in the FBI building in Westwood. He had spotted a surveillance in his workspace, and yet had taken no apparent precautions. He had, he insisted, never suspected Operation Whipworm itself. True, he had given his occupation as "translator" in his passport application, but he was hardly going to put "special agent of the FBI" when he was going to Vienna on a double-agent operation.

But if Svetlana, Nikolaiy and Matvei all knew they were being trailed by the FBI, why did he tell 'Lana that it wasn't so? Because, said Miller, he thought that it wasn't so, or that they were trailing her, not him.

This was one weak spot in Miller's defense, his lawyers thought. The government was saying that he had gone to Christensen only because he thought that he was about to be arrested, that he had just spotted a surveillance. Miller was saying, on the one hand, that he had spotted the workspace surveillance well before, that he knew he must have been photographed on Green

Street, but that this was routine—he thought if a car was trailing them, it was only for 'Lana.

"I don't get it. You're in the car with her. You haven't asked for a tail. Why would they tail just her, when you're already with her?"

"I didn't really think they were tailing either of us. I thought she was paranoid. Well, she was!"

Greenberg and Levine had done criminal law long enough to know that the innocent often lie as part of their own misjudged defense. But juries could hardly be expected to have the sophistication to savor that.

They came back to Svetlana's credibility, why John had recruited her.

"She was his swallow, although officially she was just an informant under some degree of FBI protection," Miller said.

"He found her physically attractive. So did you."

"He'll say that whatever he said about her charms was not based on personal experience," Greenberg warned.

"Well, he's got Earlene Hunt to answer to!" said Miller.

"The Russians were doing what you were doing—running 'Lana against the other side, meaning you."

"For sure."

"She seduced you."

"No. And I didn't seduce her. John did, maybe; he's more attractive."

"You apparently told her—it's on tape—that you were in love with her."

"Well, sure."

Levine wasn't sure whether he would ever call Miller as his own witness; but he had to prepare for that.

"Why did you agree to go to Vienna? Why not insist on Mexico City?"

"I said no to Warsaw. If I'd really wanted to 'go over,' a communist capital would have been ideal. Maybe by insisting on somewhere else, like Vienna, I gave my game away to the Russians."

There was one other weak spot in the defense, the worst of all, whether in terms of law with the judge, or in terms of theater with the jury. Miller had confessed to giving the consulate-general The Guidance.

Greenberg asked him why he had done it.

"You guys weren't there. I made a silly decision, to get them off my back."

"Forget about us not being there. We know they read you your Miranda stuff."

"They were pressuring me. I couldn't take any more."

"Richard, these were your colleagues. They weren't going to hit you. At any moment, you could have said: 'Look, enough is enough, I want to talk to a lawyer.'"

"That's what I should have done."

"But you didn't. But that still doesn't explain why you gave them the confession they wanted if it wasn't true. Was it true?"

"I don't think so."

"You have no recollection of giving 'Lana or any Russian anything at all?"

"No. I figured they were going to fire me, anyway. It wasn't as though I'd never been threatened. I'll admit it, I was crying. I told them I'd sign anything."

"You didn't know they were planning to charge you with treason?"

"Espionage," said Levine.

"Espionage," Greenberg corrected.

"Never in a million years."

"You didn't know about Operation Whipworm, that you were suspected of being a traitor?"

"Of course not."

The trial of Richard William Miller opened in Los Angeles nearly a year after the trio's arrest, in a blaze of press and television publicity. Surrounded by marshals, looking a little dazed as he stared with his myopic eyes through spectacles, the burly Miller pushed through the sidewalk crush to enter the court and take his seat beside Levine. Together, they looked like Jackie Gleason with a Dustin Hoffman in high-lift shoes standing in for Art Carney.

There were the usual alarms and excursions that start a trial, when the defense tries a few hundred-to-one motions that are not expected to work—but that may serve a subsidiary purpose, even so, if there is an appeal. It was a jury trial, and Judge David Kenyon looked grim-faced at the prospect of all the theater that goes with that, the attempts to slip ideas into the jury's hydra-headed mind, regardless of sustained objections. This is not only tiresome but also testing for any judge because it enlarges the judge's opportunity to make appealable mistakes. Anyone who has read the late John D. MacDonald's masterpiece, *No Deadly Drug*, perhaps the best account of a murder trial ever written, knows that a trial is as much a prizefight between lawyers as a search for truth.

John Hunt, an early witness, was to appear as a model of circumspection, a folksy man with years of experience on the witness stand. His relationship with Svetlana had been strictly that of FBI handler (the FBI doesn't say "controller," but prefers the old circus lion tamer's term) and informant. The prosecution, of course, did not want to call Svetlana, and the defense decided against calling her or her husband. They were not to call Miller, either. So Hunt's version of his operation with Svetlana was challenged only in cross-examination of himself. He was to spar carefully and diligently, and charm the judge—a professional witness performance.

Hunt's own lawyer, Jim McDaniel, a former FBI special agent himself, was to be cited in the press as quoting his client as saying that Hunt was "just stringing Svetlana along" in the matter of personal relations.

"A lot of cops tend to do that with informants, particularly female informants," the ex-cop lawyer told reporters. "They've got to do that to get them to give any worthwhile information. They've got to charm them, impress them."

The bench had sustained the government's objections whenever the defense attorneys, as part of their efforts to discredit the witness, had sought to show that Hunt had seduced Svetlana with promises or hints of a lasting relationship.

The prosecution had to establish that Svetlana had been dropped as an associate of Hunt's because her allegiance had either shifted to the other side or had always been pro-Moscow. Occidental Research had accepted the European intelligence report—which the Rezidentura had half-encouraged—that Svetlana was a KGB major and field agent, and that Nikolaiy was a support agent who had been married to her for convenience. But FBI Special Agent-in-Charge Bill Newman, in San Francisco, had either not believed this, or had spitefully decided not to pass it on to Los Angeles for other reasons; Newman knew that if Miller was acquitted or got a hung jury, this would further discredit Bretzing. So Robert Bonner, the leading U.S.

attorney, followed the acceptance by FCI-1 in Los Angeles that Svetlana had not been an enemy operative *before* "Miller time," and that Hunt had therefore been justified in "courting" her. Bonner had to try to prove that Hunt's long, day-after-day frequenting of Mrs. Ogorodnikova had been necessary in order to test her usefulness—that it was plausible that it had taken Hunt more than a year to make up his mind, finally, about whether she was an asset or not. Hunt said he had dropped her in 1983, having determined that she was unreliable, her information inadequate. He had, he said, used her mainly—in the double-agent sense—to run disinformation into the consulate-general. He denied that he had ever used her to stage a true double-agent operation, in which he would have pretended to supply information to the KGB.

Levine asked him: "Did you hope to lead the Russians to think that they could use you through Mrs. Ogorodnikova?"

Hunt fell back on what Washington humor calls John Boren's First Law for Bureaucrats: When in doubt, mumble.

He said: "It was an effort to get a response we could measure. It didn't mean that we were going to set up a scenario and allow it to happen. We were interested in how they might take a first step in implementing such a desire."

Investigator Dale Kelley, himself an ex-FBI agent, chuckled later that "all that was missing was 'at this point in time.'"

Hunt testified that Svetlana had been upfront with him about how she had traced Karine Matevossian and tried to persuade her to return home to Soviet Armenia.

Both Hunt and Miller—in his pre-trial briefings of his attorneys—agreed that Svetlana had never asked them anything about the work of the FBI.

Christensen testified about Svetlana's calls to him, her complaint that she was being harassed by Mrs. Hunt because Hunt was in love with her. The court heard about Svetlana's attempts to renew her links with Hunt, interpreted as being part of her instructions from the Rezidentura; both Christensen and Hunt played down her romantic attachment to the tall G-man. Christensen told about his own meetings with her, his encouragement of her, now seen as failed attempts to bring her onto the American team.

This set the scene for the strongest part of the government's argument: that Miller had acted without orders and had concealed what he was doing from his superiors. The trip to the consulate-general on August 24, 1984, was not something that an agent should do without telling his superiors where he was going.

The defense was not denying that. Greenberg and Levine were to portray their client as "Inspector Clouseau played by Jackie Gleason," an agent with a poor record trying to make a run in left field on his own that his superiors would have deemed beyond his limited prowess. But, they were to insist, although he broke the Bureau's rules, his aim was to hook a KGB officer. So, he had charged without waiting for orders, and captured the enemy position! For Miller, remembering both his first two trials later, the best moment came when Greenberg, expatiating on this theme, flourished a blow-up of the FBI surveillance picture of Grishin looking around him at the airport before making one of his monitored calls to Svetlana from a pay phone. Greenberg, with no reticence about court theatrics, shouted: "The fish was on the hook! This was the fish!"

The hole in the defense's fishing net was still that the blubbering Miller had admitted to having given Svetlana the eleven-page Soviet section of the 1984 *Positive Intelligence Reporting Guidance: Foreign Intelligence Information*. The prosecution also claimed that he had given her his FBI credentials to establish his *bona fides* with the consulate-general. It was the prosecutor's belief, the jury was told, that she took the eleven pages, or a photocopy thereof, and the credentials, into the Soviet mission that day inside a film canister. This hypothesis, unsupported by any verifiable evidence, or so far by any admission by Svetlana, could carry weight with a judge—and even more with a jury— because of Miller's "confession," even though he had recanted it. And although a judge enjoins a jury to approach a trial with open minds, there is a supposition in most minds—therefore in most jurors' minds—that if the FBI says that a shifty-looking Russian and his promiscuous spouse are Soviet spies, then surely they are.

The court was told about Operation Whipworm, about the videocameras at Westwood, about the audio buggings at West Hollywood and Lynwood and in Miller's and Svetlana's cars. They were told of the calls from San Francisco—with the caller now being identified as "Grishin"—to Mrs. Ogorodnikova. By labeling Grishin's stilted conversation as "plain code," the prosecution was admitting that Grishin knew or suspected that the conversations were being tapped. It did not explain why he had not therefore devised some safer form of communication with Svetlana, such as pay phone to pay phone; nor did they allege that he had done so, but implied instead that the calls to her bugged apartment were the only ones. The defense did not point to this as showing that Grishin was trying to draw attention to Svetlana and Miller, to get them arrested—because it was their intention to try to prove that it was Miller who had hooked Grishin, not the other way around.

The jury heard about the meeting between Miller and Svetlana on September 12, on Sepulveda Boulevard, with Miller carrying a letter when he left his car to join the Russian woman in hers. The surveillance agent, Allen Robinson, admitted under cross-examination that he had never actually seen Miller hand her the envelope, nor did he remember whether Miller still had it with him when he returned to his Isuzu. The defense pointed out that the business envelope that Robinson saw would have been a tight fit for the guidance, which was the same size and roughly the thickness of a slim issue of *Time*. Miller insisted that it was a bank loan application, and his bank sent an employee to testify that it had received it two days later.

Jury and press listened entranced to all the surveillance evidence of sexual congress in cars, and to the breathy dialogue between the lovers. These tapes also testified to the decision to go to Vienna, but they also showed that Miller, when told (untruthfully) by Svetlana that she had already purchased tickets, had reacted with irritation, reminding her sharply that he still had to have permission from his superiors to make the trip.

Building the case against Miller involved building a case against the Ogorodnikovs. It was obvious that the case against Nikolaiy was weak. He had walked up and down Gardner Street with his wife in earnest conversation at least three times. If this was to avoid bugging, as the prosecutors hypothesized, why had she taken Grishin's calls inside the apartment? Nikolaiy had flown to San Francisco on September 24 with a film canister, and had emerged from the consulate-general with a green book. He had noticed that he was being followed by another car, on his return to Los Angeles, and had driven off the road (on his teenage son's advice) to shake the tailgater.

There was evidence from Mrs. Baskevitch about the tickets, an FBI agent's evidence about the shopping trip during which Miller and Svetlana bought burgundy shoes and nearly bought a Burberry. Then, Miller had gone to Christensen to recount what he had done and to ask for instructions.

Christensen said on the stand: "He said he had carried this operation as far as he could carry it on his own."

Levine picked up on this in cross-examination. "And he said, did he not, that to carry it further, he needed the approval of the FBI?"

Said Christensen: "Yes. He indicated [sic] that he felt this would be an opportunity to redeem what he termed an otherwise poor career in the FBI." Miller, Christensen contended, had shown no sign that he was aware of Operation Whipworm. This strengthened Miller's insistence that he knew nothing of it.

Miller's six-page statement to Christensen was admitted into evidence. In it, he said that he had resisted "blandishments" of money. He testified that he had "told the Russians he would not give them any information on FBI investigations and procedures." This left an obvious hole into which the prosecution could dig. How could he pretend to be willing to be an agent for the Russians if he had told them he could not give them any information?

Also admitted was the addendum that Miller had signed the following day in which he had said that he had been the "subject" [sic—presumably, Christensen meant "object"] of a Soviet recruitment effort.

The defense strategy was to exculpate Miller partly by stressing his attempt to be a double agent and "hook" Grishin; the defense did this partly by "loading" Svetlana and portraying her as a Russian swallow with whom Miller had pretended to be in love—but whom he simply, James Bond-style, had violated and deceived.

Miller's lawyers insisted that his admission to giving pages from the guidance to Svetlana had been made under harsh duress, after the man had been reduced to a nervous wreck by relays of questioners seeking exactly that objective, and that the admission had since been recanted. Miller had given the Russians nothing, and would never have given anything until after he had permission to go to Vienna and instructions as to what to give.

They called Larry Grayson to give evidence about the plan to have Grayson shadow Miller in Mexico.

Grayson was not a cooperative witness. He made it obvious, without saying so, that he was testifying only because of a subpoena from the defense.

Levine was to tell this writer later: "They [the prosecution] obviously [had] hosed him down. They must have made it clear that, if Miller was convicted, they could go after Grayson for conspiracy. Conspiracy to spying for Moscow!"

Levine then recounted his efforts to speak to Grayson, and how Grayson had failed to turn up for a meeting with the lawyer and Sayers. When this writer first spoke to Sayers, this rather conservative man could not contain his fury at Larry Grayson's desertion of Miller, which helped the other side.

"He's a prostitute!" Sayers blared.

Five years later, when Miller's retrial was ordered, Grayson was still refusing to cooperate with the defense. But by then, the rather engaging Riverside private eye had agreed to meet this writer at Ontario Airport, take him to a nearby hotel, and explain what had happened. Levine had asked that Grayson be reminded, at this meeting, that he now need fear nothing from the FBI, because a five-year statute of limitations on "conspiracy" had passed. But Grayson remained cautious.

"One thing that always surprised me," Grayson had said earlier, on the phone, "was that, in court, neither side asked me if I thought R.W. was telling me the truth about trying to scam the Russians."

When this comment had been passed on to the lawyer, Levine had exclaimed: "Of course we didn't ask him if he had any doubts! He wouldn't talk to us before, so we had to put him on cold! We had no idea what he might say in answer to a question like that."

If the prosecution didn't ask it either—after having interrogated Grayson—it must surely have been that they did not want Grayson's answer. If he had told them that he had entertained doubts about Miller's good faith, a charge of conspiracy would have loomed more starkly. In the phone conversation, this writer asked Grayson how he would have responded to such a question.

Said Grayson: "If I'd thought for one moment that R.W. was going to stiff the nation, I'd have squawked to Christensen at once!"

But Grayson's apparent fear of speaking frankly, at the trial, had left a cloud of suspicion in the jury's mind about Miller's intentions.

Despite the surveillance evidence that showed that Svetlana had complained to Miller about their being followed by FBI cars, the prosecution and the defense both claimed that Miller had not known about this, or any other aspect of Operation Whipworm, with one exception: The prosecution insisted that Miller had spotted Special Agent Paul DeFlores parked forty-four feet behind him on the day before he revealed his operation to Christensen. It was this, the prosecution contended, that had suddenly convinced Miller that the FBI were on to him; it was this, they said, that had decided him to go to Christensen with a cock-and-bull story, to head off action.

DeFlores testified that he was not part of Whipworm, and that he had found himself parked behind Miller's and Svetlana's trystmobile by coincidence. Miller, he repeated, had looked in his driving mirror and recognized his colleague, whereupon Miller's eyes had "gone wide." DeFlores said he couldn't remember whether Miller had his glasses on or not. Miller, his lawyers retorted, never spotted DeFlores at all, and had therefore not raised his eyebrows at him.

The jury was taken to the parking lot in question to do a test. Another agent, Fred Scott, impersonated DeFlores. Each juror took his place in turn. Miller sat in Svetlana's car and turned his head each time. The prosecution complained that the light was not as bright as on the day in question, but the defense was able to establish that if Miller had been wearing glasses, as he normally did all day, DeFlores would not have been able to see what the burly Fed did with his eyebrows. If he had taken his glasses off to get them out of the way while kissing Svetlana, Miller's optical prescription showed that R.W. was so shortsighted that DeFlores and his unmarked car would have been no more than a blur on the Westwood landscape, especially with the sun shining on DeFlores' windshield.

Miller's contention, presented by his lawyers, was that, as a policeman, he would always have known when he was under surveillance; and that, as a law enforcement officer, he had no reason to fear a police surveillance, anyway. He had known about the routine camera surveillance on the consulate-general in San Francisco, but he had not thought that anyone would find it remiss that a member of the Los Angeles "Russian Squad" should be driving around with one of the Bureau's known informers.

The defense insisted that Miller had expected, when going to Christensen, that the deputy special agent-in-charge would be surprised, even shocked. He had anticipated that he might not be allowed to continue with his enterprise. He had, however, *hoped* that he would be allowed to continue and redeem his career. At worst, he feared in-house sanctions of the sort that he had suffered before.

No document of any significance had been found in Miller's room in the Lynwood house, the defense noted. But when Levine asked for a list of the documents and their contents to be admitted into evidence, the prosecution objected that the documents were "classified." The judge sustained the objection. (Apart from the guidance, the documents were a one-page affair entitled *Development of Counterintelligence Awareness*, the restricted but not classified FBI telephone directory, with agents' assignments, and forty-eight other "official papers," some classified, some not. These included memoranda on Soviet intelligence, on the handling of "assets"—informants— and on the role of double agents.)

The defense had earlier been prevented from getting an expert witness to describe the contents of the briefing guidance, to show that it was innocuous. Greenberg had tried another tack: He had asked the witness if he read *Time* or *Newsweek*. The witness said he did. Was there anything in the guidance that a diligent reader could not have learned by reading a newsmagazine for a year? Objection. Again, Kenyon refused to allow the witness to answer. The defense tried and failed to get a synopsis of the document admitted. In their summation, however, the prosecution conceded that most of the Lynwood and Bonsall documents were old, and that none was of a "highly sensitive nature."

Miller's attorneys were also not allowed to introduce into evidence the transcript of Miller's telephone conversation with Paula on the morning preceding his arrest. They had wanted, of course, to show what a malleable, weeping wreck the bulky G-man had become. The bench agreed with the prosecution that the conversation was irrelevant. However, his subsequent telephone conversation with Marta York, in which she had asked him if he had actually given anything to the Russians— and in which he had responded that he didn't think so, but that he might have given them one document as a "dangle"—*was* admitted.

As an expert security witness, the government called a *Reader's Digest* editor, John Barron, who insisted that the United States did not engage in double-agent operations. On the other hand, Barron testified, Miller fit the profile of the sort of person whom the KGB would set out to recruit. The Russians were looking for a "person with financial difficulties, poor judgment, sexual promiscuity, social isolation, and career frustration." It seemed that the profile was tailored to fit Miller, rather than the other way around. Miller fumed at the defense table, reminding Levine and Greenberg that the Russians had never initially set out to recruit him at all: He had offered himself, through Svetlana, as Hunt had done, and the Russians had *responded* with a recruitment offer—thinking he was Hunt.

Barron said the Russians would use a sexual relationship to "change political thinking," but this point was not to be pursued—the prosecution was not to allege that Miller's political thinking had been changed, or even that it existed. David Major, who had left the FBI to become the head of intelligence and counterintelligence at the National Security Council, agreed that special agents should not get involved sexually with informants, but he said it would have been "unthinkable" for the KGB to have used Svetlana as a "honey trap."

"It is well-known that the KGB does not set sexual traps in the United States," Major said. Questioned further, he insisted that "the KGB is not going to entrap sexually, and subsequently blackmail, Americans in the United States, whether they be FBI agents or not."

Honey traps, he said, were set only in Russia itself, just as the U.S. set them only in America. He admitted that the FBI had subverted Arkadi Shevchenko of the United Nations with a "honey trap," stressing once more that "it's not a KGB technique here. It's something intelligence services sometimes do on their home turf."

Major also rejected the prosecution term "utility agents" for Svetlana and Nikolaiy, saying it did "not exist in the FBI lexicon." He further threw down another prosecution theory—that a Western "asset" like Svetlana was in danger of being killed by the KGB if uncovered and not "turned." Of course, she had told Miller that she believed that they were both at risk from a bullet, Major conceded, but he said the KGB had never killed Western assets in the United States. She might, he agreed, still have been in danger whenever she visited the Soviet Union, if the KGB regarded her as Hunt and Miller had done—as an FBI informant on Russian officials.

Part of Miller's defense was that, even when extending the guidance as a "carrot," he had deliberately chosen one of the least sensitive of all classified documents. The government produced a retired major general named Richard Larkin, who had been chief military attaché in Moscow; he said the loss of the eleven pages would "betray the game plan for collecting information." The guidance was America's "play book," which "relates directly to the national security . . . and would enable [the Russians] to take countermeasures." It would "betray our ignorance" and "provide them with a beautiful opportunity for disinformation: They could provide false answers to questions." It could help the Russians to discover U.S. sources and "endanger their lives."

Greenberg asked Larkin if he had noticed any changes in Soviet tactics that would imply that Miller had given them the "game plan". Larkin said he had not.

Judge Kenyon wouldn't let Paul Minor of the FBI answer the question as to whether there was anything in the guidance that wouldn't appear in *Time* over the course of a year. So Greenberg got Minor to agree that he was "informed" about "problems of geography, fuel conservation, Third World emergence, things like that." But when Greenberg asked Minor if that was the sort of material in the guidance, once again Kenyon wouldn't let him answer.

Guided by Miller and others, the defense attorneys were to emphasize later that a double agent, choosing which initial documents to offer to establish his *bona fides*, would either choose those he knew the other side already had, or hand over a doctored version—then watch to see what unnecessary changes in tactics Moscow made. But it was Barron's earlier contention that the FBI didn't do double-agent operations—soon to be contested by FBI Director William Webster himself—that gave the defense its best target, since Barron had implied that John Hunt's double-agent unit, to which Auer and Miller and most of the rest of the "Russian Squad" belonged, didn't exist.

David Major testified that all double-agent operations had to be approved in advance, including which classified documents could be passed to foreign intelligence to give the American double agent his credibility. This also refuted Barron and rationalized Miller's approach to Christensen.

The court refused to allow Miller to call his own intelligence expert, Colonel William Kennedy, to refute Barron further, but some help was to come from Director Webster. Later in the trial, he told the Scripps-Howard papers that FBI double agents had been effective in leading the Bureau to Soviet spies. He said:

"I think by maintaining a substantial counterintelligence campaign against known Soviet intelligence operations through the use of double agents, we're identifying and compromising their principal intelligence agents over here, intelligence agents who will work with us. We're also causing them to be suspicious of people who are offering information, because they don't know whether that's a *bona fide* traitor or an FBI agent."

Judge Kenyon forbade Miller to subpoena Webster, then refused to allow the jurors to read what Webster had already said publicly in his interview. Miller's only minor relief on this aspect came when Christensen testified, over the prosecution's objections, that Miller was part of an ongoing double-agent program in the Los Angeles office.

Grishin's old office staff in San Francisco was, of course, more fortunate than the Miller jury, and read Webster with interest. The Scripps-Howard interview was circulated to the Rezidentura staff and sent back to Moscow. The San Francisco "consuls" were advised to be alert to scams, and particularly to scams of a more threatening nature than the rather insignificant one that Miller had tried to mount.

After three months of hearings, Judge Kenyon sent the case to the jury, which remained divided for fourteen days. A compromise was discussed, as the jurors, anxious to get home, realized that a genuine verdict could probably not be reached. The compromise would have been that those who believed Miller innocent should agree to find him guilty on a minor count, for which he would be expected to get a light sentence. Those who believed him guilty would "settle for that." In the end, the two groups agreed to differ, and Kenyon declared a mistrial.

After Miller's arrest, the Russian Squad had been broken up. Its chief, Gary Auer, had been posted to a "Siberia"—a small satellite office of the Bureau. Richard Bretzing, the agent-in-charge at Westwood, soon took early retirement and became security manager of the Mormon Church. His deputy, Christensen, was given a dead-end job at FBI headquarters in Washington—ironically, arranging language classes. As mentioned earlier, Hunt had been persuaded to take early retirement less than a month after R.W.'s final fall from grace.

# Chapter Fourteen

## Second Trial: Hung Out to Dry

*"We do not believe we have to prove an intent to betray or injure the United States, because that is not charged in any of the counts."*

W. Somerset Maugham, whose brother was a lord justice of the High Court, and whose low opinions of lawyers roughly equaled that of the citizens of Washington (where attorneys outnumber cab drivers six to one), once noted how trials bring out the worst traits in prosecution witnesses. The defendant expects his or her friends to rally, not by lying, but by emphasizing the positive. But like dogs when one of their number bleeds, the pack instinct is to fall on the victim. In the Miller case, in lawyers' parlance, many government witnesses appeared also to have been "hosed down"—scared into obedience toward government counsel.

Miller's second trial was preceded by that of the Ogorodnikovs. Several of their "friends" testified to the fact that the longer the couple stayed in America, the more they looked back with nostalgia on their mother country. In the loaded language of the trial, these witnesses testified to the defendants' "pro-Soviet feelings."

Aleksandr Palovets, publisher of a small Russian-language weekly, was one such voice, even though the *raison d'être* of his paper was the nostalgia and homesickness of the *émigrés*. Mikhail Makarian, the Armenian *émigré* who had opened the Hollywood restaurant-nightclub Mischa's in 1977, told the court that Nikolaiy and Svetlana came often, and that they had shared with him their disillusionment with America. They had brought

Soviet officials in as customers, and Svetlana had left Soviet periodicals around for future guests to read.

Makarian said: "She spoke of the USSR as a crime-free society. She always thought up the negatives about the United States—crime, drug abuse, whatever." Makarian also testified to her fecklessness. She had told him, he said, that she remained with her husband only for the sake of their son.

Gregoriy Shenderovsky, who had known Nikolaiy in Kiev, testified that he had met his old friend at the Oriental Theater on Sunset Boulevard when Svetlana was exhibiting a Russian film. Shenderovsky said Nikolaiy told him that he thought Shenderovsky had made a mistake in coming to the United States; he would find that it was difficult to get a job, and "you could be killed for a dollar in this country." Shenderovsky said he had asked Nikolaiy why he didn't go home, and Nikolaiy had answered: "I'm working on it." The consulate-general had told him, Nikolaiy had said, that he had to earn his right to return. Showing films was part of the effort, and it enabled the Ogorodnikovs to pay home visits and to send Matvei to the Crimean camp.

The Ogorodnikovs' criticisms of the United States appear to have matched those of most immigrants, and even those of the *Los Angeles Times*. But the prosecution was clearly setting the scene to show how animosity toward America had given the consulate-general a hold on the couple, who had thus become more or less willing chattels of the KGB.

Svetlana wanted to give evidence on her own behalf. To her lawyers, she seemed a rambling and often incoherent person who disliked speaking through an interpreter; they persuaded her against testifying. She was, however, to get her chance on the stand at the upcoming second Miller trial.

Her lawyers presented her as an associate of the FBI, recruited by Hunt and passed on to Miller. They made much of her relationship with Hunt, and of Hunt's dubious downplaying of it. There was the disappearance of the L.A.P.D. records of her accident on the evening when Hunt was in her car, and of the late doctor's records for the day Hunt had taken her to him—despite the presence of Dr. Jeikov's other files on her, including records of two other abortions. Fortunately, Dr. Jeikov's secretary, Doris Schantra, told the court that she remembered Svetlana being treated that day, and she recognized John Hunt as the man who had paid her eight hundred dollars. She said she did not know what sort of operation Mrs. Ogorodnikova had undergone, but that if patients did not want their husbands to know that they had had an abortion, "Doctor would try to hide it." Hunt testified that he thought he had paid for some blood tests. Had the case continued to the end, Svetlana's lawyers would presumably have challenged the notion that blood tests could cost so much.

Christensen agreed on the stand that he had congratulated her on her efforts for the FBI, that he had said that the Bureau was grateful for the risks she was taking on its behalf. He conceded that he had said that the FBI would do its best to protect her. He agreed that there was a double-agent program in the Los Angeles office, with a routine meeting every week or so to discuss results. John Hunt, Richard Miller and Gary Auer had all been present at those meetings, and Auer, despite the fact that he spoke no Russian, had taken over the Russian Squad from Christensen. Hunt was the coordinator of the whole double-agent program.

Miller testified against her. She had, he said, ultimately tried to recruit him for Soviet intelligence, and he had "played ball" as part of his own double-agent project. To establish that he was a natural target for Soviet recruitment, the prosecution questioned him about his poor record with the FBI, the various peccadilloes he had committed and the in-house sanctions he had received. Much was made of his five or six thousand dollars of debts.

Randi Sue Pollock was convinced of Nikolaiy's innocence, but she too had a tiresome client on her hands. His broken English was sometimes worse than Svetlana's, and in his attorney's presence he had tended to talk incessantly. Nikolaiy was principally worried about Svetlana. To protect her from the violence at Sybil Brand, the judge had ordered that she be transferred to a prison in San Diego, but this meant that she had to rise at three a.m. each day, to be in court on time. One day, the judge ordered that both prisoners must always have a hot meal on their return from court—a necessary measure because prison staffs go off at five p.m. and therefore serve "dinner" at four. Nikolaiy laughed at the judge's order, and said afterward to his lawyer: "With all this, you think I know whether food is hot or cold?"

Because Nikolaiy had not been interrogated very much by the FBI, it was only at the trial that his suspicions of his wife's sex life with that institution were confirmed. He had known that she was often at parties, that she drank like her father, that she worked for the FBI, but he seemed honestly surprised to learn that this branch of American intelligence slept with its own swallows.

The court showed a videotape of Miller and Svetlana in the Ogorodnikov family car. It was filmed through the back window, from another car several yards away. Miller seemed to be moving around a lot, but the sound track from the bug in the car showed only grunts and no articulate conversation.

Randi Pollock recalls Nikolaiy asking her in a whisper what was going on.

She responded: "They're doing it, Nikolaiy, can't you see?"

"Doing what?" asked the startled Ukrainian. Then, suddenly he realized how naive his question had been, and the attorney heard him exclaim: "Svetlana? I don' believe! *Ai!*" He looked at his wife at the next table and swore at her under his breath. Svetlana swore back.

Randi Pollock felt fairly confident about Nikolaiy's case. All the prosecution had were those evening strolls together in the September dusk. One of the prosecutors, Merritt, was to tell reporters later: "If it had not been for all the walks that Nikolaiy took with Svetlana, they probably wouldn't have arrested him at all." Randi Pollock argued that European couples had a tradition of evening walks before dinner, passing friends whom they would acknowledge as they went back and forth.

At one point, she told Nikolaiy that she thought the government would accept her suggestion that he plead *nolo contendere*—no contest, which means that the defendant neither admits guilt nor asserts innocence. He would, she hoped, get only a small sentence, probably "time served"—by then, more than a year—and he could go home to Matvei. It would mean that he had been convicted of knowing or suspecting what his wife was doing.

But it was because the prosecutors were not much interested in Nikolaiy that his position was to prove less easy. The objective was to ensure that Miller's guilt stood up at the retrial, and nothing would ensure this better than guilty pleas by those accused of conspiring with him. This would mean a longer sentence for Nikolaiy, and a still longer one for Svetlana.

Brian and Stone were civil litigators. For them, if a client was sued for a million dollars and, although innocent, was ordered to pay one hundred thousand dollars, that would be, not a bungled defense, but a nine hundred thousand dollar victory. Criminal lawyers, both for the prosecution and the defense, expect to lose some cases, and criminal *defense* lawyers know that *most* persons tried for a crime are convicted. But the notion of total defeat was unacceptable to Svetlana's lawyers, who needed only to avoid life sentences to feel victorious. They urged Svetlana to agree to plead guilty. She would get eighteen years, under an agreement, they said, and be eligible for parole in six years. If she did not plead guilty, but was found guilty anyway, the government would ask for several consecutive life terms, and she would remain in an American penitentiary—as foreign to her as a Russian penitentiary would be to an American—for the rest of her life. Svetlana was a Russian accused of being a Soviet spy by the FBI; she went back and forth to the Soviet consulate-general, back and forth to Russia; she was on record as saying that life had been better in Kiev than in Hollywood. Would any jury find her innocent? Svetlana, a weeping, neurotic, hysterical wreck, when she heard all this, eventually agreed.

Both Nikolaiy and Miss Pollock were harder nuts to crack. They turned the offer down. The prosecutors, in what was later contested as being an unethical procedure, talked to Nikolaiy outside of his counsel's presence. They told him that if he didn't plead guilty also, the deal with his wife was off. Matvei would never see his mother again. If Nikolaiy also was convicted, the child would be a virtual orphan. (A former U.S. Attorney who is still in government legal service told the author recently: "Such a 'wired plea'—refusing to honor a plea bargain unless all the defendants in a case agree to one—is strictly forbidden under Justice guidelines.") But Nikolaiy, the old con, scented a judicial scam and remained reticent. Then, by suspicious chance, he could suddenly hear Svetlana weeping her heart out in the next room in the courthouse. Nikolaiy then made up his mind to give in.

To his lawyer, shortly after, he said: "They afraid that if I go free I talk to the papers and tell everyone what really happen!

Everyone know Svetlana is idiot, and now I know FBI make her prostitute, but she not spy. They don' even want me on witness stand. Okay. Tell me what I do. What I must say?"

"Just a minute, Nikolaiy," Randi Pollock said. "I'm not going to let you plead guilty unless you tell me what you think you are guilty of."

Nikolaiy ruminated.

"Well, I give her advice, about the trip to Vienna."

The attorney shrugged her shoulders. "Okay."

In chambers, Judge Kenyon said that wasn't enough. Miss Pollock asked if she could ask her client some questions, and the judge agreed.

Nikolaiy was asked if he had ever told Svetlana not to go to Vienna. He said no, that he didn't think he had that much influence on his wife. He had simply told her that he didn't think her work for the FBI was worth it, that it would get them both into trouble with the Russians eventually, that they might lose their visiting privileges. What advice had he given her about the trip? Well, she had told him that the FBI man was taking some documents, so he had told her to make sure that he carried them, not her, in case he was doing something he should not be doing.

"I told her that because she is the mother of our child," he said plaintively, and he began to shake.

The judge asked quietly if Svetlana had told him that they were going to be met in Vienna by a Russian official.

"Sure," said Nikolaiy.

"Did she mention money?"

"Of course."

He said he had told her where to buy shoes for the FBI man, because she didn't think the fellow looked elegant enough for Europe. She had said she was going to buy him a raincoat. He had advised her to get cheap tickets from the Baskevitch agency.

The judge asked Nikolaiy why he had stopped on the shoulder when he was driving back from the San Francisco airport on September 24. Nikolaiy said it had been because Matvei had said that they were being followed by an FBI car.

He agreed that he had tried to call a number that Svetlana had given him on October 1. She had asked him to get the number and pass her the phone. Was it Miller's number? He supposed it had been, although she had not told him that, and he had not known Miller's name at the time.

Kendall, one of the prosecutors, told Kenyon that he accepted that Nikolaiy's visit to the consulate-general on September 24 had been solely for the purpose of exchanging films. That cleared Nikolaiy of any possible involvement with Miller. The Ukrainian recalled later that he had racked his brains to try to think of how he was guilty of something. Should he have *forbidden* his wife to go to Vienna, or to act any longer as a go-between between the FBI and the consulate-general?

"What I'm saying now," Nikolaiy told Kenyon, "is that I didn't plan any actions. I didn't perform any actions. I just said everything so as to help her."

Randi Pollock suggested a sentence of five years with a judge's recommendation of parole after two years. The prosecution wanted eight years. Miss Pollock said that was acceptable, providing there would still be a recommendation of parole in two years. Nikolaiy was surprised at the rug-trading, and even more surprised when his lawyer told him later: "If the judge says so, you can get parole in a month."

The judge said he couldn't promise Nikolaiy early parole. The old cabbie raised his squeaky voice. He had pleaded guilty only to help his wife, he said, because the prosecutors had said she would go to prison for life if he didn't.

"I not guilty of anything! I being used as sacrifice! I only 'gree to plead guilty to save the mother of my son from going to jail for life!"

Nikolaiy said he had been given to understand that the worst that could happen to him would be completing two years in prison before parole, which would put him out the following year. If he had not pled guilty, he said, he would never have been found guilty. He had only pled guilty because he had heard Svetlana crying.

Judge Kenyon asked him if he wanted to take back his plea.

"Maybe I guilty of something by your understanding, Judge," Nikolaiy said, "but I didn't do no espionage. What I say to Svetlana, I say only to help her, to keep her from danger."

Kenyon again offered him the chance to retract his plea and stand trial. Nikolaiy said: "Guilty? I don't know. I explain everything about what I remember. This time, you got decision whether I'm guilty or not." In other words, the judge would have to decide whether he had done something wrong, because Nikolaiy didn't know. But on the question of a sentence,

Nikolaiy began to raise his voice again. The prosecution was being "cheap" by not agreeing to two years, after he had done what he could to help them, and Svetlana had also done what she could, so that the government could win its case against Mr. Miller.

The man who had been a soldier at eleven, and a bitter loser ever since, began to sob. He said: "I have lost my son. I have lost my wife. She was raped by FBI agents, but they are safe under American flag. They take my wife and use her as prostitute and leave me outside like dog." His gimlet eyes stared at Richard Kendall: "And now you being cheap about the two years, about my parole. You making me serve the sentence twice."

But Nikolaiy did not retract his plea of guilty. Technically, under the law, he felt, he had probably done something wrong, although he wasn't sure what it was, and he didn't see how a spouse could have done anything but what he had done. He had been opposed to her acting as a go-between for the FBI and the consulate-general, but perhaps, he thought, as a husband, he should have forbidden her, not just advised her.

Kenyon asked Kendall what he thought Nikolaiy had admitted.

Kendall said: "The primary admissions would be that the defendant was aware that Mrs. Ogorodnikova was to travel to Europe, and that he was aware that the caller from the consulate had requested that they go to Warsaw; that he knew that Mrs. Ogorodnikova and Mr. Miller, whom he did not know by name, but whom he knew was an FBI agent, were at least going to Vienna; that the purpose of the trip was for Mr. Miller and Mrs. Ogorodnikova to meet Soviet representatives, and for Mr. Miller to deliver documents to these representatives in return for being paid sums of money; that he knew that this proposed trip was illegal [sic] and that he gave Mrs. Ogorodnikova advice on how to accomplish the trip successfully." By "illegal," Kendall presumably meant that the journey had a felonious intent.

Kenyon said he would give Nikolaiy eight years, as Kendall had asked, and he would make no recommendation about early parole.

Randi Pollock wasn't happy, but she said to Nikolaiy after they had left the chambers: "Nobody has ever been acquitted in an espionage trial in this country, so maybe this sentence is the best you could have hoped for." Kenyon gave Svetlana eighteen years. With no parole recommendation, this meant she would probably have to serve twelve years.

Now that every juror in the Miller retrial knew that the Ogorodnikovs had pled guilty to conspiracy, exculpating the man with whom they had supposedly conspired was nearly impossible. Sure, Miller's attorneys were saying, Svetlana had set out to recruit Miller for the KGB, with some advice from her husband, but Miller had had his own agenda. But to Miller, the thread of events looked uncomfortably clear. Once Bretzing had decided to make sure Hunt ]was exonerated and go after the *brébis galeux* of the Mormon flock, the whole thing had acquired a relentless momentum of its own. Investigators usually start at the end of an affair, not at the beginning, and they can lead juries that way as well, so that the onus of the trial is reversed—it is innocence, or absence of incontrovertible guilt (which is different) that has to be proved, not guilt itself, which is inadmissibly assumed.

As Randi Pollock had told Nikolaiy, there had never been an acquittal in a spy case in the United States. It's not only juries that assume that such a case would never be brought if the defendant wasn't guilty, but judges have a similar mindset. Who would put trust in those two flaky Russians—Nikolaiy with his squeaky, unitesticular whine, 'Lana with her spacy manner and alcoholic memory. Once the prosecution had convinced the sorry duo that they didn't have a prayer with a red-blooded American jury, and that they would go to jail until they were old and white unless they bought that monstrous plea bargain, even a cautious punter would have bet heavily on Miller's conviction. Only the memory of that first hung jury held out any hope. A jury is not the bench, but a spin of the coin. One quirkie could save his bacon. They should have tried to get one really fat juror, Miller thought.

Technically, Miller decided, poor 'Lana was guilty of something, though she didn't deserve the sort of sentence they handed out for serial armed assault. Even though he and John had used her to try to penetrate the KGB, she had inevitably ended up hitting the ball from both sides of the net. Indeed, she was more like the table tennis ball itself. She had done only what he and John had asked her to do, and so she had had to do what Grishin or whoever it was asked her to do, much as an FBI drug informer might sell a little crack on the side to keep up appearances. Don't shoot the messenger, they said; but people did. And he had admitted, before recanting, to passing that one low-classification document. And she had got eighteen years—and that was in a "bargain," a discount sale just to get *him*. So what would they give *him*? Life, for sure. Two life sentences? When he had testified against 'Lana and Nik, the prossies had treated him as a hostile witness, asking irrelevant questions about his poor past in the FBI. They were setting him up.

The principal difference between Miller's first and second trials was that Svetlana Ogorodnikova testified—for three weeks. She was brought to the stand in prison garb—what the reporters called a jumpsuit, as though she were going 'chuting or skiing. As she entered the courtroom, her eyes fell on Tres, Miller's fifteen-year-old son. He reminded her of Matvei. He was sitting next to his grandmother, Verna Gonzales, Paula's mother, who had come to give her soon-to-be ex-son-in-law moral support. Svetlana was to say later: "I knew I couldn't help to send his father to prison by lying."

Svetlana retracted her own confession, as Nikolaiy was to do. "Neither Richard nor I ever spied for Russia. He never gave me any document at all."

The judge pointed out that if this was true, the confession on which her sentence was based was perjury. Each false statement could be a separate count. She could get up to twenty-five years for each. And if she had not perjured herself in Kenyon's chambers, she was perjuring herself now. But Svetlana stuck to her guns and went on to try to exculpate her husband. "He only say he guilty for me."

Svetlana confirmed that Miller had been trying to infiltrate Soviet intelligence; that because of her nationality "nobody" would believe her; and that the price of a plea bargain had been that she had to "confirm" that Miller gave her classified documents for the Russians, but that this was not true. She had said that only to head off the threat of a life sentence.

She testified that Miller had never spoken to Grishin, or met him, either in San Francisco or Livermore, which was outside Grishin's 25-mile limit anyway. The only telephone call had been hers, from Livermore to Belyakov's home the next morning, to ask him what films she would be getting next. Then, Belyakov had questioned her about Miller.

If she had not taken the guidance or other classified documents, what about Miller's identification? Svetlana asserted that John, when telling her to tell Belyakov that she had an FBI lover, had offered to lend her his badge; but that had not been necessary. The people at the consulate-general were not fools. They knew who John was from his card. Richard had made the same offer; perhaps he had got the idea from John, she didn't know.

"But I said: 'You joking, Richard! Your badge and stuff? Suppose they don' give back? And they will know you not John, then, so what they think of me? How they gonna believe you my boyfrien', when they know his name is Hunt? Huh?'"

The FBI agent had absorbed this lesson in how to handle counterintelligence and had decided to write a letter instead, applying for the post of mole.

John, she said, had told her to go on seeing Richard, but to tell John everything he said, everything they did. She had been worried and puzzled because the FBI was thus spying on the FBI, but she thought that maybe all secret services did that. (Spy novelists would agree.) Had she suspected that Richard did not have permission to do what he was doing? Yes, but John had said that she should do everything Richard asked her to do, then report to him (John). What had she told her husband? Only that she was rendering some services to the FBI. And toward the end, she had told Nikolaiy that she was worried, that things were going on that she did not understand, and that no one would explain to her. What had Nikolaiy said? He had said that she should just do whatever the FBI told her to do; that it was just like the KGB in Kiev.

Money? Well, Richard had talked about fifty thousand dollars. In gold, she thought. And fifteen thousand in cash, she thought. And Richard had said that the FBI would pay her a reward for setting up the meeting with a Russian official.

She had made the reservations for Vienna, and that night she and Miller had gone to another restaurant, and she had pointed out to Richard that they were being followed—a car in the restaurant parking lot that pulled out with them. Yes, she had been puzzled, and worried, but Richard always said, like John: "'Lana, you wouldn't understand."

And did she understand now?

"No."

Gary Auer, head of the Russian Squad, testified to Hunt's long association with Svetlana. He had read all of Hunt's reports.

Auer said Svetlana "had a history of making unsubstantiated and wild allegations." She had said she was a KGB major, that she had slept with KGB Director Yuri Andropov. Yes, she drank a lot, and fabulated when she drank. By 1984, "It was my policy that no special agent should ever meet with her alone." Agents usually operated in pairs, anyway. Auer had told Miller "that she had been determined to be unreliable and undirectable." He went on: "That was the bottom-line summary—that the problem we had with Svetlana [was that] *she* could never determine with whom her loyalties lay. I advised [*sic*] him [Miller] that in view of the series of difficulties the squad [had] had with her [he should] have no further contacts with Svetlana Ogorodnikova." (Obviously, this was not just advice, with the judgment being left to Miller, but an order; Auer had fallen victim to police pidgin.)

Auer said that he had called in Hunt, to help explain things to Miller. Auer said he had told Miller that he was "not to initiate any contacts, but if she called him he was to accept whatever information she had and relate that directly to me." Auer said he had authorized the May 24 meeting, and one other. From then on, Miller didn't bring up Mrs. Ogorodnikova's name in the office again. Miller, from the defense table, could see the trap closing: He had deceived his own people!

Bonner, the leading U.S. attorney (now director of the Drug Enforcement Agency), asked Auer: "Did you have reason to question Mrs. Ogorodnikova's loyalties to the United States?" Auer said yes. Miller knew the word "loyalties" was wrong; Svetlana was not a U.S. citizen. Levine and Greenberg let it pass; Bonner, they felt, meant "loyalties" in the company sense—but the phrase was loaded, suggestive of treason. Svetlana had no citizenship, only a U.S. re-entry permit. International society had deprived her of the ability to commit treason. In the measure that she was a spy, then, like most spies in fiction, she had been working only for herself. It was who was in control of her that counted—at any particular time. That was what Bonner had meant. She was either devoted to one player or she was the table-tennis ball.

The prosecution, of course, was determined to portray her as a Russian swallow. The junior member of the government team, Russell Hayman, was to say of Miller: "He was infatuated with Svetlana. He developed emotional ties to her. Sex was an important part of their relationship."

This was in Hayman's address to the jury, in which he asserted: "You should remember that some, if not all, Soviet *émigrés* in this country are KGB agents." Svetlana had "clearly" been an "agent" with "the assignment of recruiting Miller to the Soviet cause, and obtaining classified information from him." Later, he said: "She's an admitted liar under oath, [so] you are entitled to reject her testimony entirely, and the government urges you to do so." He threw out a wild card: Svetlana had tailored her testimony to "please the KGB and enhance her prospects of figuring in an exchange."

What may have reinforced her image with the jury, as a Soviet swallow, was her physical distaste for Miller himself—the image that she had continual sex with him because it was her KGB job to do so. One of her "friends," the late Mrs. Ludmila Kondratjeva, had testified to the FBI that Svetlana had brought Miller to a dinner party at her house in August, 1984. She had introduced him as "Richard" and described him as a "business partner." When Mrs. Kondratjeva had quietly asked her about the relationship, Svetlana had denied that Miller was her lover, explaining that he was "too fat" and even—although the agent was only a decade older than she—"too old." Because of Auer's instructions to Miller to avoid single contact with her, Miller recalled that he had asked her to be discreet in this way.

To reinforce further her image as a KGB agent, there had been evidence about the search of the Ogorodnikov apartment, which had turned up two advertisements from the *Los Angeles Times*, one offering jobs in the Tomahawk cruise missile program, the other jobs on a Hughes air radar system. There had been a newsletter on U.S. defense capabilities.

On Miller, one of his lawyers told the jury: "He's done a lot of stupid and dumb things in his life, but he's not on trial for any of those. What he's accused of is espionage."

Bonner was to counter: "We do not believe we have to prove an intent to betray or injure the United States, because that is not charged in any of the counts." Miller's acts were sufficient for a conviction, "whether or not he intended to be a spy. . . .

"The evidence shows that there was never a double agent in this case. In the late spring of 1984, Mr. Miller was a man in dire need of money and obsessed with getting it. That was not his only obsession. The evidence [shows that] Mr. Miller was also extremely interested in women—in women who were not his wife. [He was] the classic target for KGB recruitment. He was sexually vulnerable. He needed money, and he was unhappy in his work."

Certainly, Miller was far from the classic FBI agent. His oldest son had been quoted in the press as calling him a "teddy bear." He was a rather soft fellow who dreamed of leaving law enforcement and becoming a Spanish-language teacher. His hobo taste in dress betrayed his lack of self-discipline.

His wife was divorcing him ("I know this will look awful," she said of her appearance of abandoning him at such a moment) but she also complained bitterly to the press that he had not had a fair trial. The financial aspects of his troubles had been exaggerated, she said. The avocado garden was a "white elephant," but they had been planning to sell it anyway and move to a smaller place with less expenses. Although managing a family of ten on an agent's salary could sometimes be "overwhelming," she had, she said, always managed to tithe ten percent of Richard's salary to the Mormon church.

Marta York, the "other woman," was less helpful. She testified that he was "obsessed" with money problems. Miller reflected that he had emphasized these to soften the blow for Marta of his decision not to leave his wife. Mrs. York even claimed that he had told her that he had given Mrs. Ogorodnikova "his badge and his gun," then admitted that perhaps she had not remembered clearly what he had said. Did she believe that his money problems were a factor that had driven him to contact the Russians? Yes, she said.

Although the polygraph evidence was not admitted, Judge Kenyon admitted the verbal hearsay evidence of polygrapher Paul Minor, who said Miller had admitted to keeping a stash of low-classification documents at Lynwood, and that he had intended to use these as bait for the consulate-general.

The biggest defense hurdle was still Miller's confession about the guidance document.

Greenberg emphasized to the jury that Special Agent-in-Charge Bretzing had "falsified the situation" by using his rank as a Mormon bishop to "urge Miller to confess for the salvation of his soul."

Under Greenberg's grilling, Bretzing had said: "I believed he had done things he knew to be unlawful and a betrayal of the country. I believed from his teachings in the FBI and as a youngster in the Mormon Church he had every reason to feel guilt."

Said Greenberg: "And you were trying to appeal to that guilt?"

"Yes."

He had actually re-confessed to Bretzing in the car, between Bonsall and San Diego, Bretzing noted. It had been at that point that Miller had admitted again that he had given Svetlana the 1984 positive intelligence reporting guide.

Levine had tackled Christensen about Bretzing's religious approach to getting a confession. Christensen said Bretzing, at the Bretzing-Miller encounter of September 29, 1984, had urged Miller to consider the "moral and spiritual consequences" of committing espionage.

"Mr. Bretzing talked about the process of repentance and the necessity of restitution," Christensen explained.

Levine asked: "By 'process of repentance,' you mean a type of action within the Mormon religion?"

Christensen considered the awkwardly phrased question, then said yes. A little later, he said: "Next day, Mr. Bretzing asked Mr. Miller if he had thought over their conversation. At that time, Mr. Miller came forward voluntarily about his association with Mrs. Ogorodnikova, and Mr. Bretzing said that if he had done what the allegations said he had done, then he should consider telling the government, so that a damage assessment could be made."

Agent James Nelson, who had been driving the car from the Miller farm after the arrest, confirmed the admission to Bretzing, saying he thought that Miller had agreed to having given Svetlana both the guidance and his FBI credentials as well.

Special Agent Larry Torrence, who had taken over from Martin and had been involved in the Lynwood search, testified that Miller showed Torrence exactly where he had been standing, in his bedroom, between a dresser and a door, when he had shown Svetlana the reporting guide. Torrence said Miller had "advised [sic] that she seemed to be disinterested." Since her fingerprints were not on it, it could be presumed that Miller had refused to give it to her, Torrence agreed, but showing it to her implied that he had been willing to give it to someone else. Torrence said Miller had admitted taking two documents, one of them being the excerpt from the briefing guide, to San Francisco—but the FBI had no transcript of this admission. He said Miller had told him that Svetlana had offered him money "on more than a dozen occasions," and Miller had mentioned the figure of two million dollars. Miller had also told Torrence that he had never been blackmailed by Svetlana or Nikolaiy or anyone else. These admissions, the prosecution was to say, were not the random outpourings of a man undergoing a mental breakdown. At the defense table, Miller remembered 'Lana saying: "Richard, if anyone know, one day, what you trying to do to the KGB, you get the first bullet, you know!"

The first bullet! 'Lana loved to exaggerate. But even his colleagues seemed to want to put him on a par with Kim Philby or John Walker. They'd even dragged up all that old irrelevant stuff about skimming informant funds and selling MVD poop to Larry Grayson, things for which he'd mostly been already reprimanded or fined. The tackiest thing about the whole experience was how his colleagues had let him down, Miller thought. They had never had the decency or the common sense to balance whatever doubts they had about him with reason. The name of the operation, Whipworm, said it all, especially as they had referred to him as Worm and 'Lana as Whip. Tacky, he thought.

He remembered Allen Robinson testifying about that meeting with 'Lana, him tapping the savings-bank envelope on the steering wheel. Robinson had implied that it had been some ultra-secret document, and then he'd said that, well, no, he hadn't seen that, that "I lost track of the envelope." Tacky.

Then there was Paul DeFlores, who was outside the loop but who was, like all Hispanics, prejudiced about the Mormons, talking about seeing him with 'Lana in the parking lot and how Miller had spotted him and he'd seen Miller's eyes go wide. And he'd gotten the time wrong, and the clothes Miller and Svetlana were wearing wrong. And they'd built the whole case around a hypothesis that he'd gone to Bryce just after because he'd seen that he was under surveillance, Miller thought. Tacky, tacky. Then, there was that other colleague, Dave van Bockern, who said Svetlana and Miller had spotted van Bockern tailing them on September 24, and that Svetlana, who had been driving, had tried to elude the pursuer. Well, it was true she thought that they had a tail, and it's true that she had noted the tag number of the car, and it was probably true when it was said that an old envelope had been found in her car after her arrest that had the number of Dave's FBI car written on it. But that would imply that she'd told him about the surveillance two days before they now said he'd noticed it. They couldn't have it both ways! It was true she had noticed a trail car, but it was also true that he had told her she was crazy. Tacky, tacky, tacky.

Jim Murphy, the polygrapher, had been hostile from the start. But he had said, correctly, that the reason Miller didn't insist on having a lawyer with him was that he didn't want to cut off lines of communication with his colleagues—that he still trusted them. Paul Minor said that Miller told him that the choice of a "dangle" document for the Russians had to be made carefully, that it would have to be "an item of interest to the Soviets." That was true. But he also pretended that Miller had volunteered to him that he'd actually passed on such a document. That was untrue, Miller thought to himself.

He remembered that, after the all-night session, he had said that he'd sign anything, and he had signed off on the document. But he had never said it to Paul Minor. Larry Torrence had said that Miller had told him that he was looking for an innocuous document, something "not damning," but Minor had made it sound as though Miller had committed a felony by simply wondering what to suggest to Bryce as a tempting "carrot."

The four-month, second courtroom ordeal was nearly over. The Associated Press' Linda Deutsch had said percipiently on May 3 that the jury's decision on Miller would probably be based on its image of Svetlana: "Was she a naive Soviet *émigrée* or the sexual bait of international intrigue?. . . Did [she] work for the KGB, the FBI, neither, or both?"

On July 14, 1985, after being out for three weeks, the jury found Richard William Miller guilty on six counts, and exculpated him on one (accepting the Burberry coat). The would-be Bernard Samson of Westwood had become the first special agent of the FBI to be convicted of espionage. Kenyon sentenced him to two consecutive life terms, plus fifty years. He had been condemned for passing classified documents to a foreign government for possible use against the United States, of conspiracy, and soliciting payment. Jonathan Pollard, who sold tens of thousands of ultrasecret documents for hundreds of thousands of dollars, received only one life sentence. The Falcon and the Snowman had been given forty years apiece. Michael Walker and Jerry Whitworth each got twenty-five years. As he was led out, Miller's only comment to the press was: "Thank God for the appeal process."

In Moscow, Grishin read the news on Tass. He was shocked by the harshness of the sentence, even though the American news agencies said it really meant twenty years, with parole. Even under Stalin, if you weren't shot, no one received more than fifteen years for anything. Eighteen years and eight, for Svetlana and Nikolaiy, also seemed incongruous for a couple of bumbling extras. But Nikolaiy, Grishin reflected, had been jail fodder all his life, and he'd rather Ogorodnikov be lodged and fed at American expense than by the Soviet Union. He felt more sorry for Svetlana, because she was a woman. But any girl from Tula who would sleep with not one but two middle-aged American counterespionage individuals surely deserved a salutary period of re-education. They had never been S people. Had they been, he would have brought them home, in exchange for two Americans.

Grishin tapped a black cigarette on his desk, slipped it in cupped fingers between his lips, lit it, inhaled deeply, removed it from his mouth and blew out smoke reflectively.

The FBI people had said they were unsure where Ogorodnikova's "loyalties" lay. He shared their uncertainty. Perhaps Ogorodnikova did, too, he thought. Where he felt less in common with his counterparts in Los Angeles was in the massiveness of their incompetence, their naiveté. There was the notion of using a bottle-doll like Ogorodnikova to begin with. There was the clumsiness of the dangle, like hanging a rusty mousetrap on your fishing line; the preposterous idea of two people pretending to be one defector; above all, there was the bizarre failure to try to exploit Miller's invitation to Vienna, especially if they were convinced of his guilt. Wouldn't he have been the only S spy in California who was surfaced before he started?

# Chapter Fifteen

# *Witnesses: Svetlana, John, Nikolaiy & Nadya*

*"He wanted money from the Russians and glory from America....
She was like a mosquito, always bothering them, asking them to give
her something to do."*

America no longer has convicts in penitentiaries guarded by
wardens. It has inmates in correctional institutions monitored
by correctional officers. Eventually no doubt they will get a
union minimum for the license plates they make so that they
cease to be slave labor in competition with their honest compatriots outside, and they will then be charged a condo fee for
their board, lodging, recreational opportunities and administra-
tion.

The federal correctional institution called Pleasanton is on the
grounds of a former Air Force base, Camp Parks, just outside
Dublin, California, about fifteen minutes' drive from the great
federal nuclear weapons research center at Livermore. The
"streets" in the camp have names and a prisoner—pardon,
inmate—can use a street number and a street as his or her
address, providing his or her correspondent also adds the
famous "number" given the tenant by the Federal Bureau of
Prisons.

His or her? Until very recently Pleasanton was a co-correc-
tional (as in co-educational) prison—pardon, institution—
grouping minimum-security men, such as first-offender
scoutmasters who had embezzled some of the Christmas fund
or law-abiding drivers who hit a wobbly cyclist, with maximum-security women who had been armed-assault recidivists

or husband poisoners, or (in one case) had taken a potshot at President Ford. (After nineteen years, this white-haired old con is a great-grandmother, but Mr. Ford has still not gotten around to asking that she be given parole.)

Now, the two hundred men for whose attention the five hundred women vied have been moved to a separate "facility" on the same old airfield, or elsewhere. No longer do convicted-felon couples walk, like male and female choristers at a church picnic, hand-in-hand, occasionally ducking into a corridor to have instant sex—while a fellow-inmate plays lookout and earns a pack of generic cigarettes. One to five pregnancies a month helped to end all these idylls of incarceration. Says a former male inmate: "Now when it happens, they'll know the father is on the *staff*!"

The forlorn battalion of fallen women are allowed to wear make-up, "do their hair" and wear their own clothes. It's no secret that incarceration is harder on women than men, although judges don't always take that into account, and these encouragements to self-esteem may certainly help correct the lack of self-discipline that puts people into penitentiaries in the first place.

Svetlana Ogorodnikova may well be the most fashionable felon in the federal jail system. A male prisoner who bred expensive dogs on the outside called her the "pick of the litter" at Pleasanton, and she in turn seems to have enjoyed the pick of the minimum-security men for as long as bi-sex warehousing lasted. But she is also a tragic figure, as disculturated as Tammie Bakker would be in Lefortovo, turn by turn optimistic and nihilistic about her chances of reversing the fate into which she naively walked, and filled with petulant hatred for the way John Hunt handled her.

She sits at a picnic table in the prison grounds, under the occasional desultory eye of the prison psychologist in his nearby office; but he knows her Slavonic temperament, and when she screams at the approach of a wasp, the psychologist doesn't bother to look up from his desk.

She chain-smokes. She trusts no one. The only person apart from her (now dead) mother and her son and, to some degree, her husband for whom she expresses a certain cautious affection is her friend, the illustrator, Nadya Mathison from Leningrad.

"Nadya was right when she said that John had been using me. Today I don't know how I could have been so stupid! But everything was pressing me emotionally. I wanted to get out of the home. Today, I'm surprised that a normal person could do this without thinking. But I was interested in romantics. I wasn't really interested in anything else.

"Now Nadya tells me that John has been to visit her and the warden says he has made a request to be put on my visitors' list. But I have said no. How can I trust him again? I think he just wants to write a book and make some money out of me.

"In court, the sonovabitch said that he never made love to me, not one time! I said to my lawyers: 'Is this possible?' And they said: 'Yes, it's possible. This is the FBI.' He even said he would sue my lawyers for saying [outside the court] that he was my lover. He even said he was not sure if I was true to him or to Russia."

She goes back over the old grievances. Why are the L.A.P.D. traffic records missing for the day she and John had a night-time accident together? Why are Dr. Jeikov's 1983 records about the apparent abortion, which she and the doctor's secretary say Hunt paid for, missing?

If she sees Hunt as a scoundrel, she sees Miller as a figure of pity, a fat scarecrow with a childlike yen for candy bars.

"I asked myself: How can I be seen with a man like that? But he was a nice man really. I felt sorry for him. He was like a puppy dog. Even his wife, who has divorced him, says he's a nice guy. His children love him.

"Richard wanted to make love to me. I didn't want to make love. In spite of what John said in court, I was still seeing him, because he was asking me to report on all my meetings with Richard. I was seeing John all through 1984, even after my trip to Moscow. I still loved John. But Richard forced himself on me. Even at the trial, he admitted that he forced me. Apparently, he made love to as many women as possible! He was a man who needed love. All the time he was making love to me he was talking to another woman [Marta York] about marriage! Poor Richard!

"But he was a big liar. He said he was divorced, or separated, I forget which, from his wife. He betrayed his wife! He lied to his children. He has eight children! Once, when I told him he was a liar, he said he had lied for the government a thousand times. But I think even that was a lie, because they had never let him testify in court. His lawyers wouldn't let him testify at his own trial. Nobody would believe him, even if he told the truth. But he testified against me. He told the court a completely different story from the truth. If he gets a new trial, I don't know if I'll testify, because I hate him so much now. But I feel sorry for him. It is John Hunt who should be in prison. He's the biggest sonovabitch I ever met in my life."

She has a fit of sobbing, recovers, lights another cigarette.

"How naive I was! And now everyone in Moscow knows I worked for the FBI. Mr. Russell, I didn't know that helping the FBI is dangerous work, and that everyone in America hates the FBI. I know my willingness to work for John is hard to explain to most people."

She talks in a stream-of-consciousness style. This, taken with the absence of nuances in her limited vocabulary, could be interpreted by an unfriendly court as contradiction.

"In reality, when I was working for John, and Richard, I wasn't working for the FBI seriously. It's true that John told me he would make me America's Mata Hari. I suppose John was using my love for him to make *me* the double agent. And the Russians knew I loved him so they must have thought he loved me, because that was what I thought; so I suppose it is also possible that the Russians tried to use me. But I told John everything I did, and everything that anybody said to me, even what I had done in Moscow."

The eyes grow moist again but she keeps her composure.

"And then John said he couldn't see me anymore. I couldn't believe it. John had used me! For what? To look good at the office! And I think of him taking me to Dr. Jeikov and paying for the abortion. I am a married woman, so I don't know if the father was John or Nikolaiy. John said in court that he couldn't make a woman pregnant, that he had had an operation. But when? If it had been true when we were together, wouldn't he have told me, so that I wouldn't worry about becoming pregnant? And if it was true, why did he pay for the abortion? I think the FBI is covering up for him. In my heart, I feel sure John was the father. I slept with Nikolaiy only about once in three months—I would close my eyes!"

She tries to brush John Hunt from her mind and comes back to the subject of Miller.

"Richard said he was taking over John's work. He asked me to do the same thing that John had asked—to make a connection for him with the people at the consulate-general. He was going to be the first FBI agent to penetrate the KGB!"

She pauses to smirk as everyone seems to do when they think of Miller.

"At the trial the government said Richard was one of the worst agents the FBI had ever had, but they also said he was the sort of person the KGB would try to recruit! What a circus! Sometimes, they had suspended him without pay, demoted him, and so on, and yet they thought the Russians would be after him like some baseball star! And anyway, the consulate people didn't know it was Richard—they thought it was still John Hunt!"

She draws on her cigarette and looks at freedom beyond the wire.

What exactly had Miller told her, to explain his plans?

"Well, I asked him: You are going to meet a Russian [in Mexico] for what? And he said: 'To play the game!' It would make his career better. It would prove he was not a crazy guy. But I was scared. I suppose perhaps I didn't really want to know everything. In reality, I wanted to forget all this life. So I asked my husband what I should do, and he said I should do whatever the FBI was asking. So I felt I had no choice, and Richard and John both said the FBI was going to protect me. But then, when he got scared, even Richard lied about me.

"Yes, it's true I agreed to go to Vienna with Richard. It's true someone called me from the Russian consulate-general. It wasn't any voice I knew. It sounded like the voice of that FBI agent in Los Angeles who speaks Russian. After I was arrested, they told me the caller was Aleksandr Grishin. I had never heard of him before."

True or untrue? Does it make any difference which consular names she knew?

She shakes her blonde hair and takes another draw on the cigarette.

"John had told me my telephone line would probably be tapped by the FBI. And of course, when Richard and I went to San Francisco, I knew that the consulate-general was always watched by the FBI, because when John first came to Gardner Street, he said he had records of my visits there. And of course

Richard must have known, too—that we would be watched, there.

"At the trial, when the prosecution threatened me with prison for the rest of my life if I didn't plead guilty, they said I must say that Richard had given me a paper to take into the consulate. You understand? I couldn't plead guilty unless I said I was guilty of *something*. Of course, they wanted to get Richard. But it wasn't true—about the paper, I mean. I took nothing, only the film. I lied. The government made me lie."

Svetlana Ogorodnikova picks up the pack of generic cigarettes again, then changes her mind and puts it down. This taut woman is beginning to relax. It is thinking of Hunt that makes her edgy. Now, she is thinking of Miller.

"You know, they say every man hopes that his woman will never change, and every woman hopes that she will change her man, and both are disappointed. In reality...." She pauses. "In reality" is her favorite prefix clause, in the way others might say "the truth is" or "actually" or "in point of fact." It is as though this shuttlecock between the Rezidentura and the FBI was, and remains, in search of elusive reality.

"In reality," she says, "Miller needed me more than I needed him, so I tried to make him what I wanted. And I was angry with John for using me as a prostitute with Richard, and I wanted, you know, to get back at John. And so I thought: What if Richard succeeded where John had failed?"

She laughs at the thought of what is coming next.

"And Richard wanted so much to 'penetrate the KGB'! It would change everything for him, in his job, he said. And he was so worried at the time about everything, his debts, his children. He was just like a Russian—always thinking of ways to make money on the side when the authorities aren't looking! When I think about it, it's funny. At the trial, Richard pretended that I had been a Russian spy whom he had used to get to the KGB, while the government pretended I was a Russian spy to prove that Richard was guilty! Ah, Mr. Russell, if I'm a Russian spy, then the KGB's in a bad way, don't you think?"

The brittle laugh fades. The cigarette pack on the picnic table is acting like a magnet on her right index finger.

"Listen, I want to repeat: I loved John. Richard, I felt sorry for. He seemed so lonely. He was a human being. But the FBI were so anxious to get a case against him, they turned everything upside down. They reported night for day and bottoms for tops. They lied about Richard. They said he gave me his badge and a secret paper."

"But you said that yourself, when you pled guilty."

"They made me say it—I told you. They even said Richard wanted to go into the consulate-general. In reality, by the time we arrived, it was too late, and we were too drunk. In any case, it was John's idea, to start with, not Richard's idea, to show them some ID."

Now, she is thinking of Hunt. She seizes the cigarette pack and puts the phallic pacifier into her mouth.

"John said the FBI would protect me. As I told the judge, John told me everything I was doing was not only for him but for the government, so he said I had to do it. He said they knew in Washington what I was doing. He said he would introduce me to a CIA man from Washington, but I said it was enough that he was FBI.

"Richard said the same. He would lie on me in the car, you know what I mean, and tell me he worked for the CIA as well as the FBI, and that the CIA would protect me also. And then suddenly, at the end, Richard was saying that nobody would help me. Even now, I don't understand completely. But Richard did say that I never understood everything of what I was doing with him, that I never paid attention, he said. And in reality, that's true. But then he lied, under interrogation, and said he gave me some paper to give to Mr. Belyakov. He never did. I never read any paper. Later, he agreed that he never did. He said he only said he did, so that they would stop the interrogation. He said he would have admitted anything.

"You know why? Because never in his wildest nightmares did Richard ever dream that they were going to arrest him. Arrest an FBI agent? He thought they were going to *fire* him. They were always threatening to fire him. He told his boss that he had been meeting me, against orders, and that he had not written reports of many of the meetings. They said at the trial that Richard had always been bad about writing reports. When he lied about giving me the papers, he was emotional. He *is* emotional. But in reality, he is not stupid as they say. When you're in trouble, everybody tries to blame you for everything and anything."

She draws on the cigarette. Two birds in a tree a hundred yards away make a noise, take off, fly into prison and then out again.

"By the time I met Richard, I was drinking too much. I had gone back to live with my husband, but in reality I had broken with him. I went back because I could no longer be sure of John. I said to myself: What will happen to me? I was becoming, you know, paranoid. I went to see Dr. Jeikov for my nerves. He gave me pills. Something was broken in my relationship with John, and something was broken inside me. John had been fighting with his wife—about me. My beautiful dreams—all fucked up. I was worrying, and drinking. I was going crazy."

She stubs out her cigarette and looks her interlocutor in the eye.

"But after I was arrested, I was never able to tell my story. In the court, my lawyers said one story. The prosecutor told another story. I was never able to explain the truth. Nobody wanted to listen, even in the court. They tell you to answer yes or no. I was never able to speak at my own trial, anyway—only at Richard's. They didn't want me to say what they had told me—either you lie and say Richard gave you the paper, or you go to prison forever. If you lie, we only give you eighteen years."

It is the trigger for more emotional sobs. When she cried before the camera for Mike Wallace, the tears looked forced. Now, they look that way, too. It is part of the old Asian culture, which is the same in this regard as Africa's: A woman appealing to a man for understanding doesn't just throw open her arms and direct his glance toward her bosom, as a Western woman would—instead, she forces tears, and there is the spurious break in the voice of the old blues singers.

"I will never get John Hunt out of my loins, you know? He is in my cunt forever. We would swim in the ocean. We would do something wild every day. This was all new to me. In Russia, men do these things, not women. And then, after two years, he told me it was all over. I knew in my soul that what he was saying was that he had never loved me, that he had used me, that he had played games with me. He had told me that I had to get information for him or he would lose his job. Now, I don't believe it.

"The worst day in my life was the day I met John Hunt. He knew that I was unhappy in my marriage. He took advantage of me. They say in the papers that I fit the 'profile' of someone easy for the FBI to recruit. I was not satisfied with life; I needed money; I was meeting with Russian officials. Really, the problem was the marriage. My husband and I are very different people. He is a hard worker. He works all the time. Me, I like to meet people, and I met a *lot* of people. Nikolaiy never wanted to go out, and I wanted to go out. So I became involved with John Hunt. My mistake was that I believed him.

"For most of those two years, he wasn't really asking me for much information. He was going to other Russian immigrant people; some were people I had introduced to him, and he was writing down what they said, and then telling his boss that this came from Svetlana. He was always saying that he couldn't go out with me without permission, and that our meetings were supposed to produce 'information.'

"Before the trial, they showed me John's notes. You would think I was the greatest American spy in the world, Mata Hari of the FBI! It was all untrue. I only gave him scraps or took him to others who gave him scraps so that he could meet me. But his notes! What imagination! I said to one of my lawyers: 'Is this possible?' And he said: 'You'd better believe!' and he laughed. And my lawyer told me that I was a Russian, and that no one would believe I was not a Russian spy if the FBI said I was, and that if I didn't plead guilty, I could get a life sentence, or several life sentences, or natural life. For what? For thinking that John Hunt was in love with me! What a fool I was.

"I was worried about my son and my husband, because of my involvement with John. I was feeling some guilt, you know? My husband was working all the time, and sometimes, back in 1982, he would ask me where I was going. But I never told him John's name.

"So, anyway, after two years, that was in May 1984, I told Nikolaiy that I wanted a divorce; I said I wanted to marry an American. Matvei knew who it was. He didn't like the idea. He said: 'Mama, I don't like this man. I don't want to live with him.' I told Matvei to be patient, that John would be a good father to him.

"I told John that I had asked Nikolaiy for a divorce. A few days later, John told me that he had been ordered not to see me any more, because I was not productive enough for the FBI."

She stubs out a cigarette.

"In the end, they dropped everything against me except conspiracy, but I still don't understand what conspiracy is. With Richard? But it was John who ordered me to do whatever Richard asked me to do!"

As her thoughts go from Hunt to Miller, the smile returns. A listener gets the sense that if Hunt walked in on the conversation, she would be torn among three options: copulate with him, cut his throat, or both. Hunt brings out the Carmen in Svetlana. When she thinks of Miller, however, she becomes pitying in the heavy-handed babushka manner. But now she is thinking of her telephone conversation with Grishin.

"Even the FBI were laughing at the transcript—at me, at the man at the other end of the line saying: 'Do you understand?' But nobody in the court believed me. They thought I was a spy! Even my lawyers didn't understand. And they fired John from the FBI because of his affair with me! The FBI said it was retirement, but they fired him. In court, John testified against me, to save his skin, and because of his wife. He lied. He even said he had not seen me for months.

"But the court believed nothing, because I am Russian."

She stops and watches the two birds who keep wheeling into prison and out again, like reality.

"Mr. Russell, I was foolish. But even when I asked questions, John wouldn't tell me clearly what he wanted to do. Richard was the same. In reality, neither said he would work for the KGB. Richard said: Penetrate it. And so much of the evidence was sealed by the court. All I knew, or thought I knew, was that Richard was going to Vienna to do his work for the FBI, and that the Russian consulate-general wanted him to come, and that both of them would pay me for bringing them together.

"I never read spy books. I suppose I was working for the FBI; that was what Mr. Christensen thanked me for. In reality, in my own mind, I wasn't working for any organization. I was working for John. And John had told me to do whatever Richard asked. I had thought John was my lover, but he was only my seducer, you know? Now, he was my pimp! And I had to hold onto Richard, because he said he was going to help me. I had no choice. I knew I could not go back to Moscow. What could I do? The Russians knew I had an FBI man. Moscow knew; I mean, Anatoliy knew. So in reality my home is here, not there. But I didn't hurt nobody, did I? But John said that if I didn't do what he told me to do, the FBI or the KGB would hurt me.

"Now I think it would have been better if the KGB had arrested me, over there. I could speak for myself in my language."

This is perhaps the point in the narrative to add once more that John Hunt assiduously maintains that the assumptions of his superior, Don Stukey II, were wrong—and therefore that Svetlana is untruthful. He insists that he always behaved like an officer and a gentleman with his "asset," never going beyond a peck on the cheek on a moonlit beach or pressing his solar plexus against 'Lana's pendulous breasts on the night club dance floor. What seems harder to refute is Svetlana's emotional involvement with him and her anger at being "jilted."

A reporter conducts all interviews differently, according to the person being interviewed and his or her response. You stroke the afflicted, weave with the deceitful, shadowbox with the former president until his jaw comes into view. You talk to prisoners as you talk to those in the hospital and in pain. To the prisoner, any interview, even with authority, is a lifeline to the reality of the world outside, where even mosquitoes enjoy liberty. Svetlana is getting tired, but she wants to make sure that she has hit the key points.

"Even now, I'm not sure I understand everything. A couple of times, the judge asked me: 'Do you understand?' And I said: No. Surely the judge must know the truth. How could a grown-up, intelligent man, who knows the law, not see what happened? Sometimes, I think the door will open, and someone will say: It was all a mistake; I'm sorry.

"And how could the people at the consulate not know? First, John wants to meet someone. Then, it's not John, it's Richard, who was taking John's place. And then John was saying *he* would take Richard's place, it was *his* operation. How could gentlemen like Mr. Belyakov believe this nonsense?

"Another thing I don't understand was John's reaction when I told him I had admitted to Richard that I was involved with him—with John. And John said did I mean that I had told Richard about love and sex and everything, and I said: Yes, because you told me to do everything he asked me to do, and he wanted to make love to me, so I had to tell him about you.

And John said that I was stupid, that I should never have done that. John said Richard's plan was crazy. I was frightened. I thought Richard maybe really was doing something without permission, that he was not telling me the whole truth. No one was telling me the whole truth. I thought I might be in trouble with Mr. Belyakov, that I could lose the film business. I thought about what Mr. Anatoliy had said. I wanted to end all this nonsense.

"So in court I never knew what to say. There were so many things I could not understand. I am not stupid, as they say, but I am perhaps not very intelligent. You know? I tried to protect everybody—John, Richard, Mr. Christensen. And I didn't want to make the Russians any more angry, because of my mother and my son. And I was on the witness stand for three weeks! And sometimes they asked me the same questions, over and over, and they said that all my answers were not the same. I think everybody does that, no? The more you try to explain, the more you use different words. It was the same thing at the FBI. I signed the FBI interrogations without looking at them. I was so tired. They said if I signed, they would let me go to a hotel to rest. But they never let me go.

"In the end, I told my lawyers: Do what is best for me. If you want to win the case, win the case. If you think it is better to plead guilty, plead guilty. I don't even know to what it was that I pleaded guilty. What is conspiracy? I was tired. I was in the Metropolitan Detention Center in San Diego, and I had to get up at three o'clock every morning to be in court at Los Angeles by eight o'clock.

"Now, I am told I must protect my lawyers. That is why the warden has taken away my correspondence with them—so that you can't see it. My lawyers said over and over again that the jury would find me guilty anyway. Of following orders from two FBI agents! They said my husband would get life too, unless we both pled guilty.

"What finally made me give way was when they tied me to my bed. In the morning, I felt so down, having to go to court in Los Angeles after no sleep; I could not resist them anymore. That was in 1985. Now the newspapers say I will probably do twelve years, because it was a "security" offense. *Ai!* Nikolaiy still believes in American justice and the American flag, but I don't believe in it. Yet now I have no other country.

"I only pled guilty for my husband. My family is destroyed. My life is not worth anything, any more. I am finished. Yet all the Americans involved in this know I am not guilty. They asked me if we withdrew our pleas of guilt to please the KGB, so that we would be exchanged! I do not want to be exchanged, because the Russians are not fools; they would put me on trial! What worries me is the shame. All they are writing about me is sex and sex and sex."

She goes back to Miller.

"They say that Richard is guilty—that he would have worked for the KGB because he needed money. I don't know. In reality, I believe that, as he told me, he was trying to do his job for the FBI. Did they think I should not believe him? But what was in his mind, in reality I don't know. I just did what he asked me to do, and as John had asked me to do. At Richard's [second] trial, I said I did not believe that Richard intended to betray the United States any more than I wanted to betray the United States.

"But my lawyers said: Nobody wins against the United States in a spy case. So how do I prove that I am innocent? The judge sealed some of my evidence [in his chambers] for one hundred years. My love life is Top Secret! Maybe John wanted those papers sealed, to cover himself, the lying sonovabitch.

"They could accuse me of many things, but not espionage. They could accuse me of sex. Maybe I deserve ninety days for stealing John from his wife. But nobody believes I am not a spy, because I am Russian. They even think Nikolaiy is a spy. A Russian spy!

"I think to be KGB in America you would want a lot of training. It would have been much better for me if I had really worked for the KGB, because then they would have exchanged me long ago, and set me free, and called me a Soviet heroine. Instead, they called me a CIA whore.

"How could John Hunt do this to me? My lawyer's investigator, Dale Kelley, told me he could prove that I was innocent by showing that John Hunt was lying about not being my lover. But my lawyers told him to shut his mouth, that they were going to plea-bargain instead. Now, how do all these people feel? I am guilty of only one thing. Sex. I am guilty of falling in love with John Hunt, and I am also guilty of being unfaithful to my husband with Richard Miller. It was the Year of the Spy, the papers said. The jury looked shocked when I pled guilty.

"One day, somebody is going to pay for this! Somebody is going to confess. I think John will confess. He wants to come to see me, because he is scared. But I don't want to see him. I want only to see my son. Meanwhile, I try to smile. Even here in prison, people shout at me that I am a Russian spy. I don't care, anymore."

In 1988, Svetlana's mother in Yefrimov, who listened to the Voice of America, heard a news bulletin saying that the Ogorodnikovs would be deported back to the Soviet Union after their release. Neither had Soviet citizenship any longer, but a case might have been made for returning them to the last country from which they entered the United States—although that argument is usually used only for people who arrive at a U.S. port or airport without visas. An attempt to deport Nikolaiy to Kiev was blocked by federal court in January 1990, then restarted in late 1991.

Svetlana says: "I don't think any country can be forced to accept me. I do not want to go to the Soviet Union. I will *not* go there. They would put me before a military court. If I have to leave, I want to go to some country where I will be safe. Switzerland, perhaps. Or France. Or India. None of us have Russian passports—Nikolaiy, Matvei, or I. Matvei is in Russia on a tourist visa. If he were Russian, he would be doing military service."

Svetlana looks at her watch, lights another cigarette. She goes back to the circumstantial aspects of her case:

"The prosecutors made so much of the fact that I went to Russia in June and July of 1984. Would I do such a thing, and come back, if I was a secret spy? They say visiting my sick mother and my sick grandmother is not a sufficient reason." Both women have since died. "John told me I could have trouble in Russia because of my work for the FBI." Mentioning Hunt makes her reach for a Kleenex again. "At the consulate-general, they think I am a traitor to Russia. I think they have decided to punish me.

"Even for me, my case is still mysterious. In reality, I made one big mistake in my life. I got involved with the FBI. That was so stupid! I wanted love. I wanted romantics. Now, I dread all that! So many lies! This is a beautiful country, with a beautiful constitution, but each prosecutor wants only to win a case, for his career. The constitution wants justice, but a prosecutor doesn't want justice, he wants promotion.

"If I had to make the decision again, whatever the threats, I would never plead guilty. I would rather die. But when I pled guilty, the judge had no choice. I think the judge knows I am not guilty.

"If I live, it is for Matvei. Sometimes, they let me speak to him on the telephone, but my mother has no telephone. Has she read all they write about me? Always, sex. In reality, I know nothing about sex. In Russia, the woman kneels, and the man comes into her like a bull. A woman is like a cow. How could I ever seduce anybody, in America? Yet even the judge asked me how many men I had had in my life!

"My life! Anyway, I am not frightened anymore. Even if the sun doesn't rise in the morning, what is there left to be frightened of?"

So what of Hunt, the key figure in the Miller/Ogorodnikova tragicomedy? Donald Spatny, a California jack-of-all-trades who has been of considerable assistance, quotes Hunt as saying to him: "There's a lot of money in this if it's done right. I know more about her than anyone else." He apparently wanted to co-write a book with Spatny about the case. Spatny says that, when he turned Hunt down, the old G-man approached at least two other writers.

When I first spoke to Hunt on the telephone in 1987, he said bluntly: "I don't see any advantage for me in answering questions." When I politely suggested that he reconsider, pointing out that I was talking to everyone else, he said: "What's there in this for me?" I said that there were so many differences of opinion about his role in this drama that he should want to set the record straight, from his own viewpoint, and thus "save your honor". He retorted sharply: "You can't buy groceries with honor." I suppose I should have said that he could buy those with his generous FBI pension, but I wasn't quick enough off the mark.

Since Hunt had said that he did not like talking on the phone, I offered to visit him in Seattle. I was turned down. Over a year later, I wrote to Hunt, asking him to reconsider an interview. There was no reply.

I was able to slip a couple of questions into the 1987 conversation, anyway. Unlike the prosecutors or the internal security sources at Justice, Hunt told me he *did* believe that Svetlana Ogorodnikova was "*trained* and controlled by the KGB" (emphasis mine). He did not give me a chance to ask him why, in that event, she had not been "traded." He was presumably trying to whet my interest in his value on the auction block, because, not long after, he wrote a letter to his old boss, the director of the FBI, explaining at considerable length that neither she nor Miller had had any idea what they were doing.

I did ask Hunt about the surgical operation that Svetlana and her late doctor's secretary say Hunt paid for in January 1984, and that Svetlana says was an abortion.

"She should come up with the evidence," he said. (The doctor's records, of course, have disappeared, along with the L.A.P.D. Motor Traffic Unit's report on the late-night accident Hunt and Svetlana shared.)

The issue of Hunt's relations with Mrs. Ogorodnikova are of more than prurient interest, since they speak to the degree of control that he exercised over her, to the nature of her loyalties, and—had Hunt been less than truthful on that score—to the credibility of the rest of his testimony.

Hunt's request that Stukey (who initially oversaw the Miller-Ogorodnikova investigation for the FBI, while John Martin rode herd on it for Justice) remove from his in-house report all references to a sexual relationship between Hunt and Mrs. Ogorodnikova was fulfilled. Stukey declines to say whether this was because he changed his mind about the nature of the relationship, or simply couldn't prove it, or decided that it was embarrassing to a colleague. Questions remain unanswered as to why Hunt suddenly retired at the time he did—just after Miller and the FBI informant he and Hunt had shared was arrested, and Hunt himself was interrogated.

In February 1989, I tried again to get Hunt to spill the beans. At first, I left messages, which he did not return. I then did what I presume an FBI agent would do in like circumstances—I called him at 7 the next morning, in the hope that he was still in bed. I pointed out that I had now read his confidential letter to the director of the FBI.

"How much are you going to pay me?"

I snapped on the "Record" of the answering machine of my telephone, and went into a coughing fit to give the gadget time to go into the requisite mode.

"You mean you're not interested in justice, only in making a buck?" I asked.

"You're darned right I'm only interested in making a buck," said the retired special agent of the FBI.

Said one of the investigators, like Hunt a retired agent himself: "The only way there's going to be justice in this case is to prove that John Hunt committed perjury at the Miller trial. Period. He was feeding bullshit into the [Svetlana] file. But when I wanted to check hotel records and things like that, I was ordered to cease and desist."

Nikolaiy Ogorodnikov spent the pre-trial and trial period at Terminal Island. "Holding facilities" are in many ways worse than maximum-security prisons. Because no one is expected to be there for long, there are no amenities. Cells are crowded. New, traumatized prisoners come in all the time, often drugged, screaming and vomiting. For a "Russian spy" like Nikolaiy, with his squeaky, querulous manner, life was harder than for most. One day he was talking to some semi-sympathetic guards; being black, they did not entirely identify with Washington in the Cold War. Of course, like all prison staff, they were used to pleas of innocence; since these were usually untrue, their attitude was normally a cynical nod. But the notion that a Russian had been framed by the FBI did not seem unlikely, so they listened. So, one of them asked, why had he pleaded guilty when he had done nothing?

"Because they put my wife in prison for life otherwise, and I not chicken. I not let her die in prison."

Nikolaiy's probable innocence somehow got through to the least likely audience, metropolitan jailhouse screws. They advised Nikolaiy to appeal. He called Randi Pollock. She said she had always believed in his innocence, but since he had made her plead him guilty he would have to get a different lawyer. Nikolaiy kept repeating himself, and Miss Pollock told him what she had said before: That the prosecutors had approached him without her permission, that Svetlana's lawyers had brought undue pressure on him to help Svetlana.

Nikolaiy got a new lawyer, Terry Amdur, but Judge Kenyon refused to allow the Ukrainian to withdraw his plea. Amdur pursued other alternatives, but without much hope. Nikolaiy went off to serve his term at the modern medium-security facility of Black Rock in Phoenix. It was a long way from California. Matvei had had to go home to Nikolaiy's mother. At Black Rock, Nikolaiy made uniforms for seventy-five cents an hour and sent money each month to his mother for Matvei. Amdur lost the appeal.

Nikolaiy was interviewed by two reporters from the *Los Angeles Times* and of course complained that he had been railroaded; so when orders came to relieve overcrowding in federal prisons by use of the rent-a-cell program with some under-used state prison networks, Nikolaiy was on the first list to be moved from Black Rock. He suspected that another reason he was singled out was because of his correspondence with this writer and a former U.S. attorney general. He was sent to a state prison at Walla Walla in Washington State; at Walla Walla, which is maximum security, the wage for the mindless work that "inmates" do is only eleven cents an hour.

Theoretically, there are formalities for overcoming any grievance—forms to be signed. They have to be read, and answered. But of course they are rarely answered affirmatively. Nikolaiy asked, as a federal prisoner, to be sent back to a federal prison. How could he help his son, on eleven cents an hour? The response was to send him to another state prison, Clallam Bay, on the Canadian border. He went on a hunger strike for a few days, during which time he earned nothing; then he accepted that he was in a no-win situation, and he would just have to serve the rest of his five years and two months to parole.

Nikolaiy is more mature, more responsible than his spouse. A professional convict, he is also more of a survivor. He is not the sort of person with whom to be stuck on a desert island, but he is a pleasant companion for an evening. The author will not try to correct Nikolaiy's English, since it conveys the flavor of his soul. He speaks about two octaves higher than most men. His principal concern was to get parole for Svetlana, and to recover Matvei. But the teenager was now a man, a student, and although anxious to visit his parents he was determined to do no more than that. He had no other use, he had said, for his U.S. re-entry permit. By 1988, Matvei was living with Svetlana's mother, because his paternal grandmother had finally become too ill to keep him. That year, the elder Mrs. Ogorodnikova died.

Nikolaiy says that, in prison, "They wouldn't even let me telephone her, just before she die. So now my life is only Matvei, and Los Angeles, and my piano, and perhaps one day Svetlana. I would like to live with her again, in spite of everything."

In December 1990, eleven months after his release, Nikolaiy borrowed money from Mrs. Mathison, against his wages, to come to Washington and seek official help to get his wife's fate taken up again as a human rights matter. Needless to say, if Nikolaiy had really been a Soviet spy, he would probably not have been at liberty in the United States. Just how unlikely it is that Nikolaiy could be "KGB" is illustrated by the fact that it was this writer who picked him up at National Airport to bring him to his interview with the Soviet ambassador, Aleksandr Bessmertnykh, who later became the foreign minister, and to take him on to Tass for an interview with the bureau chief. Nikolaiy even wanted the writer to be present during his thirty minutes with Bessmertnykh, to function as his advocate. His aim then was to remain in the United States until he is sixty-five, then retire to Kiev, where his social security pension would go further, he thought, than in Hollywood. Now, he wants to stay in Los Angeles for good.

Nadya Mathison, Svetlana's "serious" friend, lives in Los Angeles with her Scottish husband. They are into every liberal cause, and their walls—even in the kitchen—are decked with posters. A typical northern European, she wears severe clothes and the sort of neck brooches one associates with Bette Davis in her character parts. She has an aristocratic, flute-like voice. Although she and Svetlana are about the same age, she sees her prison inmate friend as a sort of errant junior sister.

Talking to the author, Mrs. Mathison put some of Svetlana's ambiguities into perspective:

"My acquaintance with Svetlana was off and on. I would see her every other day for a couple of months, then I wouldn't see her for a while. I think I was the woman to whom she came when she had a problem. I never met Richard Miller. She talked to me about John Hunt, but I only met him a couple of times, and that was after her arrest.

"Guilty of espionage? Of course not! She was guilty of stupidity. Of course she was not a spy. She is simply not capable of the work. She doesn't have the education or the knowledge, or the knowledge of English. She absolutely couldn't carry out the task. She was convicted of conspiracy, which means that she did things Miller asked her to do, as she had done things Hunt had asked her to do, which forced her to do things the consulate-general asked her to do.

"Perhaps stupidity is too strong. She is not really stupid. Foolish. Both Miller and Svetlana were foolish. Both were pretending to play a role which they shouldn't have played. They were play-acting—acting out the theater of their fantasies. They were not thinking of the seriousness of what would happen. What she was worried about was only that the Russians would be angry because she was running messages for the FBI, and that they would take away her film work. Miller was afraid only of being fired. He never thought of being arrested.

"Yes, it is absolutely possible that he intended or wanted to be a double agent. He wanted money from the Russians and glory from America. . . .

"Of course her relationship with Hunt went on much longer. I am not sure what I think about that relationship. When she talked about it and said he wanted to marry her, I asked her questions and she denied that it was a sexual relationship. It was just kissing and embracing, she said, nothing more—just watching the sun set over the sea. In court, she admitted that she had been Hunt's mistress, but she had never told me that. I suppose she thought I would have disapproved. I think she misunderstood me. I would certainly have disapproved if she was being unfaithful to her husband just to be taken to nice restaurants and night clubs. But I would have thought it was okay if she loved him. Sexual relations are a part of love. I don't think she understood that I would have made a difference between love and lust.

"I don't know what to think about the pregnancy and the abortion. Hunt says she told him that she was going to the doctor because she had a rare blood disease. She didn't, but because she had been a cardiology technician, it was the sort of thing she could talk about convincingly. Actually, I think she was probably pregnant; the doctor's secretary more or less confirmed that in her testimony. Was she pregnant by Nikolaiy and didn't want to admit it to John Hunt? She says she doesn't know who the father was, but that she believes it was Hunt because she rarely slept with her husband. But she never told me she was pregnant at the time, so perhaps she didn't want me to know that she was pregnant by her lover. Sometimes I wondered if perhaps the pregnancy never took place; but Dr. Jeikov's receptionist said she had an operation and that Hunt paid for it.

"I don't think sex played a big role in her life. The number of times she and Hunt went to bed together, or whether they ever went to bed together, is irrelevant. The result would be the same whether she was his mistress or not. Svetlana was certainly hoping to marry Hunt. She said that he had told her that he would retire from the FBI at fifty-five, divorce his wife and marry her, and that they would buy a house in northern California. She told me about this in February or March of 1984. Hunt has told me it isn't true, that she has a 'disturbed imagination.' Mrs. Hunt says her husband told her about his meetings with Svetlana, and asked her to select gifts for Svetlana to reciprocate the gifts Svetlana gave to him. Of course, that wouldn't prove for a moment that he wasn't having an affair; in fact it's just what a *deceptive* person would do—and he *was* a professional policeman. He certainly told Svetlana to tell the consulate-general that he was her 'boyfriend,' to see how the consulate-general would react. That's his version, of course, but it's also hers.

"Perhaps because of the on-and-off nature of my acquaintanceship with Svetlana, I never saw her and Hunt together. And by the way, in spite of all the talk about her drinking like a fish, I only saw her drunk twice. She wanted to show her best side to me. She yearns for respect. She insists very strongly that she was sexually forced by both Hunt and Miller—not to accuse them, but to show that she's not promiscuous. Sex itself is not very important to her. I don't see her falling madly in love, physically, with anyone, and certainly not with either or both of those middle-aged policemen. Hunt says he cultivated Svetlana mainly in order to run her to pass disinformation to the consulate-general. He says this was more important than the gossip about the Russian community he was always asking her for. Of course, I'm a member of the Russian community, so you have to use a grain of salt and wonder if that isn't disinformation too.

"I don't think that anything she did looked suspicious; but some of the things could be twisted that way—not to get justice, but to get a conviction. A lot of Russians have their U.S. reentry permits doctored by Beverly International Travel. Jewish emigrants cannot revisit Russia—hence the necessity to pretend that they are not Russian-born. Nobody is deceived. It's just bureaucracy. And it's safe—can you see some congressman having the guts to criticize Russian Jews?

"The FBI misunderstood, or purposely misunderstood, Svetlana's relationship with the consulate-general. The fact is that the consulate people didn't take her seriously—and they were saying that long before she got into trouble. How could they have taken her seriously? The reason she couldn't get good films was because they didn't trust her. She was like a mosquito, always bothering them, asking them to give her something to do. She wanted to feel important, and to be able to go back and visit her mother, and to get Matvei into summer camp. Now, I suppose she can never go back.

"So, she's innocent. But she doesn't always tell the truth. For instance, she says she saw Hunt many times after her last return from Moscow; perhaps she has convinced herself that she did; but he says he spoke to her only on the telephone, and I have the feeling he's telling the truth about this. She also said at first that she never introduced Miller to Nikolaiy, but both Miller and Nikolaiy agree that their meeting took place. So, she tells lies, which means that even when she tells the truth it's easy to say that's untrue, too. And she confuses events and times.

"On the other hand, the prosecution lied. They said Miller went to Christensen only because he had just noticed that he was being watched. But he knew about the surveillance long before that—even though he also lies about that. Even Svetlana knew about the surveillance. Even little Matvei had spotted it. Perhaps the FBI didn't want to admit that an eighth-grader could spot their surveillance. Or perhaps they just wanted to show that Miller never intended to tell anyone about what he was doing with Svetlana and the consulate-general, to help their case."

Mrs. Mathison was no stranger to the consulate herself. What was its attitude to the double-agent scam?

She says: "I think the consulate-general didn't know at first what to make of it all. Then they found her 'boyfriend' was two different people, and apparently they both wanted to join the KGB! On with the motley!" Mrs. Mathison squeals with delight. "So obviously they went for the kill."

She returns to the question of the allocation of responsibility and says: "Svetlana blames Hunt for everything, but she also blames herself. Obviously, Hunt and Miller are not men to be trusted; but they wouldn't have been able to cause the trouble that they caused to themselves, and her, if she'd been a more sensible person. She was mentally disturbed—is that too strong? I mean mentally restless—does that make sense? It's true that Hunt approached her, but she sort of exaggerated her importance to the FBI. But of course Hunt was to blame, too; he was logging her in his file as though she were some sort of brilliant Mata Hari. And he was going out with her constantly, as though she were just that.

"Unfortunately, she would never ask for advice until it was too late, because she lacked confidence in herself. And if she got advice, she didn't listen, or didn't take it. And when they arrested her, and put her on trial, she never knew how to handle lawyers. She behaved like a sick peasant with a doctor, and left it all to them! Maybe, after all, stupid is the word; the stupid learn things the hard way. Poor Svetlana! She needs help."

# Chapter Sixteen

# Witnesses II: The Counterspy & The Gumshoes

*"R.W. was the all-American boy: The only things that interested him were screwing and money. . . . But I feel sorry for Svetlana. . . . I think she got railroaded and that her attorneys belong in prison."*

The decision to go after Miller could not be taken solely in Westwood. It was ultimately the prerogative of Washington. After John Martin, the head of internal security at Justice, had decided to drop suspicions of Miller, why was the case revived? Martin, after all, had an established reputation for pragmatism. Unlike Gene Hackman in the film *Mississippi Burning* Martin had solved the murder of the three northern students by buying irrefutable evidence from a high Ku Klux Klan official for thirty thousand dollars—about what the field operation was costing per day. So why was Martin, like Bretzing, overruled by Webster? Prosecutors were to argue later that Miller had, after all, confessed to passing a document. They denied that he had been under particular stress when he admitted this. Miller and Christensen were fellow Mormons, they pointed out; the two special agents were on friendly terms. It was Miller who had approached Christensen, saying he needed help with the operation he had undertaken. He asked only that his sexual relations with Svetlana be omitted from the report, to which Christensen had tentatively agreed. Miller did not say anything then about passing on documents, a very high-ranking official at Justice pointed out to the author later. Miller had essentially asked only for permission to go to Vienna on a double-agent operation.

This official, to whom the writer agreed to give anonymity, conceded that the Miller case was not a major security breach. Then the following exchange took place:

Q. The Russkies weren't exactly going to walk away with Silicon Valley.

A. Well, we were very concerned with where all this might lead down the line. Miller was hoping they'd pay him for chicken feed, but obviously they were going to say: 'This isn't enough,' and then they could blackmail him into getting more.

Q. Even if you were running his show?

A. Well, we were not convinced at all that that's what he had in mind—Miller, I mean. It looked very much as though he'd just tried to find a way of raising some cash on the side to pay his bills, and that he'd be kind of dragged along from there. . . .

Q. Now, what's your evaluation of John Hunt, and the way he ran Svetlana?

A. John Hunt was an agent with a respectable record. He had been a Treasury agent for two years, then in naval intelligence for four, then fourteen years with the Bureau.

Q. He seems to have taken an unconscionably long time to discover that Svetlana wasn't going to be of much use to the United States. Was he having an affair with her?

A. He says not. I couldn't put my hand on the Bible and say I know for sure.

Q. I understand that the FBI case officer, Donald Stukey, concluded that something was going on there, I mean something beyond a little dancing and cuddling.

A. Well, Stukey drew that conclusion from his evidence. I think you have to take Hunt's word. When Svetlana was arrested, naturally she tried to blacken his reputation.

Q. Well, she was in love with him.

A. Perhaps.

Q. She was expecting to marry him, no?

A. Possibly. That's what she says.

Q. Isn't that what she told her husband?

A. Apparently. I'm not trying to cover for Hunt. It's just his word against hers, and hers against his, and her word's not very good. She contradicts herself. She fabulates. Frankly, your guess is as good as mine.

Q. Or Don Stukey's.

A. Or Stukey's.

Q. I'm asking this because it speaks to her loyalties. A woman might betray her husband, but probably not the man she loves and hopes to marry. And I'm asking it also because I don't have the impression that the Russian Squad in Los Angeles was exactly a major-league counterintelligence outfit.

A. Let me explain. There are what the FBI calls "established" counterespionage sections in those cities where the Russians have a diplomatic or consular mission—Washington, New York, Chicago and San Francisco. Then, there are "non-established" sections in cities where there are no Soviet bloc missions at all, but where there is some activity because of defense industries, Cubans, shipping—places like Miami, Dallas and Baltimore. The Los Angeles office is in that category because of the enormous defense industry complexes in California. So, L.A. is not geared up to be in the same category as Washington or San Francisco, but they're not a bunch of duffers, either. They've cracked two or three cases, including one famous one—the "Falcon and Snowman" affair.

Q. I thought a uniformed Mexican police patrolman did that!

A. Well, yes, he saw one of them behaving suspiciously, but then there had to be an investigation back here. My point is that L.A. has had more than its share of espionage cases; but because it did not have the daily diet that established offices did, it did not have the same status.

Q. It was sufficiently downgraded to get people like Miller.

A. Sir, I'll say quite frankly: R.W. should never have been in the FBI in the first place.

Q. To come back to Hunt: Why was he taken off being Svetlana's handler? Was it because she was pressing him to marry her? Why was he encouraged to take early retirement?

A. He wasn't dropped as her handler. *She* was dropped as a Bureau informant because she was unreliable. Retirement? Well, lots of agents take early retirement. He had a medical problem, a heart condition. He had only two years to go, in any event. He officially retired on November 27, 1984, I think it was. His pension was secure.

Q. Why did he recruit Mrs. Ogorodnikova in the first place?

A. Well, initially she was considered to have some potential. She got around. By the time Miller got involved, she had been adjudged to be unreliable.

Q. Meaning what?

A. Unproductive.

Q. And it took fifty-five substantive meetings, and heaven knows how many unsubstantive ones, restaurants, night clubs, telephone conversations, exchanging gifts and so on, to determine that?

A. An FBI agent doing counterintelligence work with the *émigré* population must get to know the people. The only reason he had contact with her was to use her as an FBI informant and perhaps as a channel for disinformation to the other side.

Q. But no sexual relationship?

A. Not that anyone could prove.

Q. You're grinning.

A. Okay, I'm grinning. Look, Hunt was a mature, competent agent. Hunt was not, repeat not, a bad agent. But we are certainly prepared to admit that it was a goddamn poor management decision to put Miller into there.

Q. Into where? Into Svetlana?

A. Into counterespionage.

Q. Was Miller's approach to the consulate-general related to Hunt's earlier approach—his telling Svetlana to tell them she had a "boyfriend" in the FBI?

A. Miller took her on, on his own.

Q. But did Svetlana propose that Miller replace Hunt in trying to get a reaction from the consulate, or was this his idea?

A. She says he asked her. He says she brought it up at the Charthouse restaurant in Malibu. I'm not sure it makes too much difference which came first, the chicken or the egg.

Q. But surely it does. If she brought it up, she was their swallow, and guilty as charged in some degree. If he brought it up, as he admits he did even before she went to Moscow, he was either planning to break the law, or break some FBI rules and try to become a double agent.

A. The squad had no more use for her. If Miller hadn't taken the initiative, she would have been dropped as being of no value to us. She'd already been dropped.

Q. And it took fifty-five substantive meetings to decide she didn't make the grade? If Hunt wasn't just having an affair, and hyping his log—if he was a competent, mature agent as you said—then she must have been useful for a while. Fifty-five meetings! A year and a half!

A. You sometimes continue to see people for a while to see if they work out.

Q. But you still say you don't know whose idea it was for Miller to be in contact with the consulate-general?

A. Either he started it or she volunteered to put him in contact, I don't know which.

Q. But you have no doubt that she was run by the KGB?

A. No doubt at all.

Q. Wittingly?

A. Yes.

Q. And Nikolaiy?

A. Oh, of course.

Q. You're saying they were KGB agents.

A. Well, they weren't the most qualified agents, not the best trained.

Q. Do you think they had any training at all, any courses?

A. I don't think so.

Q. Did Hunt know, or suspect, that Svetlana was KGB?

A. No.

Q. Then why did he say that she didn't know where her loyalties lay? I guess it was Auer who actually said that, but he was going on what Hunt had told him, wasn't he? Didn't that mean Hunt suspected her?

A. I think maybe you're reading too much into what Gary Auer said.

Q. So, you're saying that Hunt handled her for a year and a half and did not suspect that she was what you have just told me she was, a KGB agent! And you still say Hunt was a good agent doing a serious job?

A. Well, maybe she wasn't KGB when she was working for Hunt.

Q. Oh, c'mon!

A. Well, she says Hunt sort of jilted her. That could have made her change sides. The point is, there's no doubt in our minds that when she was in contact with Miller she was controlled by the KGB.

Q. By "KGB" you mean Grishin.

A. Yes.

Q. But you don't think she fooled Hunt by working for Grishin when she was working for Hunt.

A. Maybe Grishin used Svetlana for the single purpose of bringing Miller in.

Q. You say "maybe."

A. Look, she was not a highly trained, highly skilled, long-term sleeper operative. But she was co-opted as a KGB operative.

Q. When?

A. I don't know.

Q. Tell me about her phony reentry permit showing that she came from Czechoslovakia.

A. The Los Angeles office knew she had it. They knew she went to Moscow on it.

Q. You never went into how she got it?

A. I don't think so.

Q. You mean "one of ours" was doing those permits?

A. All I know is we weren't concerned about it. *Émigrés* like the Ogorodnikovs had to have these things to visit Russia.

Q. Did Miller have an intent to betray, or was he just reckless? Was he interested only in money?

A. Miller was interested in money and in, well, balling Svetlana.

Q. Was he disloyal?

A. That depends what you mean. He didn't have the brain to be an ideologue. His motive was money. He wasn't a Marxist, he was a Christian. No one's suggesting he loved Russia more than America, but their money's the same as anyone else's.

Q. Surely Miller, especially since he was in the counterespionage section, knew when he went to San Francisco with Svetlana that goings and comings at the consulate were photographed by a surveillance camera? He must have seen such pictures.

A. I can't confirm that Miller knew that.

Q. But assuming that he must have done, doesn't that prove he wasn't concealing his act, whatever the motive?

A. No comment.

Q. Surely Grishin knew about the camera surveillance. He was a professional.

A. I just don't know what Grishin knew.

Q. Did the recordings indicate that Miller told Svetlana to show them his badge?

A. Yes.

Q. How come? The audio surveillance didn't start until a week later.

A. Well, if not the recordings, he himself said he gave her his badge.

Q. He said he gave her two documents, before he recanted. It was she who said he offered her his badge, if it should be needed to prove that he was an FBI agent; but that was some days after San Francisco.

A. Well, that was the recording I meant. He offered to supply his badge.

Q. What happened to the reporting document?

A. Since he admitted he gave it to her to take into the consulate, he must have done so.

Q. But it was found in his house—his father's house.

A. He could have had more than one copy.

Q. And the fact that he stood in full view of the camera doesn't mean that he was *not* concealing?

A. No comment.

Q. What was Nikolaiy's role, in your scenario?

A. Well, he knew what was going on. We didn't say he had a major role. He might have had a more important role if Miller had been a homosexual!

Q. Why do you think the Ogorodnikovs were never exchanged?

A. The Soviets never asked for them. They don't consider them tradable. They're expendable trash for the KGB. If they'd been trained spies, the Russians would have asked for them. They're not the only Russian spies in captivity here.

Q. They're not? Who are the others?

A. There's a Hungarian. There is an East German.

Q. We're talking about Russian spies.

A. Okay, correction. They are the only Russian spies whom Moscow hasn't traded recently. But there was a much earlier case, Sarkis Pascalian, whom they didn't ask for. He finished his term.

Q. Did they leave him to rot because he was cooperative with the prosecution?

A. I don't know.

Q. Why did Grishin leave without being declared *persona non grata* by the State Department? If he'd waited to be expelled, Moscow could have retaliated.

A. He left because the Russkies realized the organization was compromised. It's not unheard of for someone to bail out before we p.n.g. him.

Q. But Grishin was a First Chief Directorate man.

A. He was S division of First Chief Directorate, yes.

Q. They'd let you bounce one of their castles without making it legitimate for them to bounce at least one of your pawns? Surely, he was manipulating you into being obliged to arrest Miller and the Ogorodnikovs.

A. Not that I know of.

Q. To go back—did Hunt arrange for her to get that reentry permit saying that she had been born in Czechoslovakia?

A. That, I don't know.

Q. Wouldn't that indicate to them that she had the FBI's seal of approval?

A. Perhaps.

Q. Correct me if I'm wrong, but I get the impression that the guys in the squad room thought Hunt was having an affair with Svetlana, which helped him to run her against the consulate and the *émigré* community, which put her in the line of fire, so to speak, and made her vulnerable to the Russians saying: "Look, girl, we know where John Hunt is at, so if you want to go on visiting the old babushka in Yefrimov and have the kid going to summer camp in the Crimea, you'd better remember where those little goodies come from."

A. The last part's quite plausible, but perhaps I should point out that when Svetlana's lawyers, out of court, told reporters that Hunt had been her lover, Hunt set a lawyer on them and they retracted.

Q. (laughing) Good for them.

At this point another senior Justice official, who had been instrumental in setting up the interview, joined us. The interviewee's manner, until then friendly and even jocular, suddenly stiffened, as though he wanted his colleague to be able to confirm that the interview had been treated as adversarial.

*

Q. Let's get back to Grishin. He *must* have known of the camera surveillance of goings and comings at the consulate.

A. Maybe.

Q. He must have presumed that the consulate lines were bugged.

A. Maybe.

Q. Didn't the government suggest in court that that was why he used pay phones to call Svetlana? Pay phones away from the consulate area? Even from the airport?

A. Well, he was going to some trouble to avoid calling from the office.

Q. He must have assumed that Hunt and Miller were up to no good from a Russian point of view.

A. I don't think he knew what Hunt and Miller wanted. I think he played it by ear.

Q. Was his ludicrous imitation of "plain code" in his calls to Svetlana intended to create suspicion about her? He must have known that her line was bugged.

A. Not necessarily.

Q. Then why would he use "plain code"?

A. But you're saying, Mr. Howe, that he used a caricature of plain code to create suspicion. Why would he do that?

Q. To set up Miller and this FBI swallow so that "their own" would take care of them.

A. That's an interesting theory.

Q. It was said that Miller, with his career and emotional and financial problems, was an ideal target for the KGB. Wasn't Svetlana an ideal FBI target with her dreams of a more romantic life, her bad marriage, her access to the consulate-general and the *émigré* community?

A. For sure.

Q. But you're sure that, at least in Miller time—sorry about that—she was a KGB agent.

A. She was an agent of opportunity for Grishin—a utility agent, that was the phrase we invented for her.

Q. But would it be fair to say that you don't really know why she and Nikolaiy were never traded?

A. Yes.

Q. It could have been because they thought Svetlana was *your* swallow.

A. By the time of the contacts with Miller, she was their swallow.

At this point the author remarked that the case seemed principally to have shown how inadequate was the Los Angeles Russian Squad, whose language skills alone would have made it a laughingstock in, say, Berlin, Belgrade or Bombay. Surely, the writer suggested, this implied a similar inadequacy in similar squads in other cities that had no "established" units because there was no local Russian diplomatic or consular mission.

Q. Does the FBI give counterespionage in the area of Puget Sound, where the first line of nuclear defense—strategic submarines—is based, a lower priority than San Francisco? What about Anchorage? Surely the huge defense industry in southern California makes that even more of a target than northern California?

A. Well, we've learned a lot of things from this case.

Two of the investigators associated with the defense spoke with the author. Both had FBI backgrounds. Both thought they had uncovered proofs of innocence for at least one of the defendants, or had been prevented from doing so, and their broad analyses of the case were not unlike Nadya Mathison's. For obvious reasons, I agreed to conceal their identities.

One of them said:

"I spent a whole career with the FBI, so I'm not defense-oriented; but I'm not so dumb that I can't see when someone gets the shaft. It's happened before and it'll happen again. . . .

"How R.W. Miller ever got into the FBI beats me. He got in because he was a Mormon, and J. Edgar Hoover had a thing about Mormons, and because he did a minor in Spanish in college, and J. Edgar had a different thing about Spics. R.W. had about as much qualification to be a law enforcement officer as Fawn Hall had to handle ten million dollar checks. I'll go further: Miller was a no-good individual.

"I think he was guilty of passing information to the KGB. Don't misunderstand me: I don't doubt his loyalty. I'm sure he was doing it only for the money. I doubt if he'd ever have given them anything of any importance. Where would he have *gotten* anything of importance? To say that the document which he at one point admitted to passing over was *trivial* is to overstate its importance by a factor of about ten.

"Sure, for a thousand bucks and expenses you can get a superannuated general or author to fly out West and climb onto the witness stand in a starched shirt and swear it was the equivalent of Eisenhower's D-Day blueprint. But all it really was, was the sort of guide which bubble-brained policemen with no sophistication might need in dealing with foreigners— I'm thinking of the sort of flatfoot who doesn't know which countries produce uranium or what country Allende was the president of. The fact is that Miller was much too petty a person even to think of betraying his country: He was guilty of wanting to sell classified chicken feed to the enemy for bonzo bucks. His hero wasn't Karl Marx; it was Harpo. . . .

"Miller deserved to be fired from the FBI; not for being a traitor—for being a jerk. . . . R.W. was the all-American boy: The only things that interested him were screwing and money. . . .

"Okay, I'm not a defense-oriented person. My whole training and experience is against it. But I feel sorry for Svetlana. A lot never came out at the trial. Especially about her relations with Hunt. She had a couple of turkeys for attorneys. I think she got railroaded, and that her attorneys belong in prison or worse. They weren't criminal attorneys, they were fancy parasites of the litigation industry. People like that don't give a shit about justice. In the litigation industry, there's a little vomit in the trough for everyone to chew. A civil lawyer only loses *on points*.

"Hunt set Svetlana up as a low-level informant about the consular people. Then he got in over his head, and gave her to R.W., who was born to get in over his head. So she was out there in no-man's-land, and so of course she came under their— Russkie—control. So, sure, she was guilty of something: I think there was probably conspiracy between Miller and her, or an attempt to commit a felony.

"The KGB tried to get Hunt on their payroll through her. There's no question but that he had an affair with her. The defense wouldn't let the investigation dig for this, because the dumb clucks had talked about him as her lover *to the press* and he threatened a slander suit. Now that wouldn't have looked tidy for a couple of cadets in a fancy firm, so they rolled over on their backs and paddled their paws in the air and said they wouldn't dig. Justice?

"Nikolaiy? Nikolaiy is just a poor dumb Russian peasant. I don't think he had cowdoop to do with it. He went down with Svetlana because the U.S. attorney said it was both or nobody for the plea bargain. Either Nikolaiy chanced his luck with the jury, in the hope that, since there was no evidence against him, they would even let a Russian go free, and she got a couple of life terms, or he stuck by her for better or worse. . . .

"Of course Nikolaiy and Svetlana were never KGB agents! They had no espionage training. The consulate-general wanted to use them as agents of opportunity. But that dumb chick didn't know how to defend herself. To begin with, she's a lawyer's nightmare: She has a propensity not to tell the truth. Let's put it nicely: She's just not a well-grounded person. It wasn't just the booze and her nerves; it was not understanding what was happening to her—the American-justice-system roller coaster. And it was in her lawyers' interest *not* to help her; because, the worse she looked, the better their eighteen-year 'deal' made *them* look.

"She was over three weeks on the stand and they *never prepared her*. They never told her what questions to expect, what not to do. And she was too loopidoop to ask—she didn't even like having an interpreter!

"Above all, I believe she was the victim of perjury. I believe the guy who committed perjury was John Hunt. But who can prove it? Hunt's file on her ran to two volumes. *First thing I thought when I read it was that it was a fake!* I've written the length of a dozen Bibles of those things, and I do know shit when I read it. He was having fun, and the Bureau was picking up the tab. He was feeding bullshit into the file. He claimed he was running her against the consular officials, and up to a limited point he was—just enough to keep her on a string, with her legs spread out, I guess. . . . He was saying in his file that she was probably the greatest informant that ever walked down the street. Then— oops! He suddenly says they must 'close' her because she's unstable. Well, fancy that!

"She was unstable to begin with. If she became more unstable, it was because John Hunt had taken up most of her life for a year and a half. That would make me unstable! He played her along . . . .

"All this babe did was follow Hunt's orders, then Miller's orders, which it seemed to me *involved her doing whatever she could to have some credibility, which would mean following some orders from the Rezidentura.* She thought she was helping the FBI, and of course she got caught in the middle. Wasn't she supposed to set up something between Hunt and the consulate-general? Then between Miller and the consulate-general? Inevitably, the consulate had a certain hold on both her and Nikolaiy, to begin with. Of course they were homesick. Of course they had to keep 'in' with the consulate-general in order to get their Inturist visas. Hunt hyped her stuff, so that the FBI would allow him to go on meeting with her, but the fact is she *was* still giving him information during their endless nights on the town.

"Miller testified that she never asked him anything about the FBI. She complained about being passed from hand to hand, from Hunt to Miller, and he promised he wouldn't hand her on to any other agent. That's in the intercepts. Obviously, she knew, or thought she knew, that she was working for the FBI. Sure, she's inventive; she fantasizes. I don't think she's lying when she says she had an affair with Hunt, but she may have built it up in her mind into something more romantic and less sordid than perhaps it was. She fantasizes about sex, anyway. I mean, she's on record with boasting to Christensen that she was one of the mistresses of Yuri Andropov!

"Nikolaiy is even further removed from guilt. Just as Svetlana went looking for Karine Matevossian, so I can believe Nikolaiy helped the consulate-general in its efforts to trace Levchenko, or at least gave them an appearance of doing so. I'm glad he failed, but it wasn't something illegal, and it wasn't what he was charged with. He was railroaded into pleading guilty to something—by the threat that she'd go to prison for life if he didn't. Of course they weren't going to let him stand trial alone!

"He didn't have a chance, either. As his lawyer, Randi Pollock, said, no one ever gets acquitted of espionage.

"He made it clear that he didn't like his wife meeting every night with someone from the FBI, getting sloshed with this cop, having his son guess that his mama had a 'boyfriend.' When he knew she was going to Vienna with an FBI agent, he advised her to let the agent carry any documents, so that, if anything went wrong, the agent couldn't put the blame on her. That's the nearest he seems to have gotten to wondering whether Miller's operation was an FBI one or a KGB caper.... He advised her to get cheap tickets—why would he have said that, if he knew the

KGB were paying? The one and only time Nikolaiy met Miller, he was half-asleep, and Miller only remembered him saying 'Ya, ya' to everything. But because he had never actually forbidden his wife from becoming involved in this FBI comedy, or whatever it was, he finally said: 'I feel I am guilty of something'—leaving it to the judge to figure out what it might be. As he said: 'I became a sacrifice!' He was given an opportunity to take back his plea of guilt, but of course he didn't because he had heard his wife crying in the next room and saying she didn't want to spend the rest of her life in an American prison.

"He was angry that the judge didn't recommend early parole, because he felt the Court had violated some sort of gentleman's agreement—that it owed him something for having simplified things for the prosecution. . . .

"The whole Russian Squad in the L.A. office of the FBI was the KGB's best friend. After this mess blew up, they say Washington ordered the Chinese Squad to take over the Russian Squad's work! They say now it was a signal improvement, but I wonder how many in the Chinese Squad speak Russian, eh?

"Both the Ogorodnikovs were stupid, and unfortunate. Hunt had Svetlana over a barrel. Or a mattress, or something. She was an obvious set-up for the FBI. She had delusions of grandeur. Okay, I'll agree it was not unusual or improper for him not to tell her exactly what he was doing with her; but he should have ensured that she remained under FBI protection. It says in his file on her that she had been promised protection. Christensen testified that he'd told her they knew the risks she was taking for the FBI, and that they'd do their best to protect her. Then, as soon as the KGB makes waves, they pull the lifebelt off! Why? So that John Hunt can run for cover?

"I mean, think about it! Christensen said he met Svetlana in a coffee shop and 'commended her' for helping the FBI. He said she'd reported on her most recent trip to the Soviet Union and 'detailed' her contacts with the KGB, and that he 'indicated' that 'we appreciated her sacrifice, appreciated the effort she was making on behalf of the FBI.' I would think so! Then she found out what 'sacrifice' for the FBI meant!

"You ask if Hunt sort of passed her on to Miller. There's no 'sort of'! *He absolutely set her up with Miller because he had to get rid of her.* Danger! She wanted marriage! So, she was shafted.

Believe me, the government could allege espionage against *any* Russian citizen, and an American jury would believe it."

Another investigator gives a different picture, including recollections of Miller in the FBI:

"He was a below average agent; above all, he was uneven; but then he'd be afraid he was going to lose his job and he'd straighten up and fly right and win a commendation. His best skill was in handling informants, especially Spanish-speaking informants. But every time he did a good job, he'd sit back and relax and screw up again. It certainly cannot be true that he suddenly went over to the enemy in 1984 because for the first time he faced a threat of dismissal. He'd faced threats like that constantly since 1971.

"I'll go along with his own lawyers' characterization of R.W.—that he wasn't really bright enough ever to be a really good FBI agent, and that there was an aura of Jackie Gleason about him, that he could be dishonest. He had a messed-up private life. . . And whether R.W. should have been doing counterespionage work is another matter.

"I think R.W. is guilty of breaking FBI rules, but I just don't see him as a Russian spy. I think he went fishing in forbidden waters and hooked a big'un—Grishin. I think the question is: By then, or at any time, was Svetlana R.W.'s swallow or Grishin's?

"But either way, I think Svetlana was our boy's undoing. I think she was closer to the Rezidentura than she admits, perhaps closer than she realized, because she had to be. The fact that the anti-Soviet *émigrés* had it in for Svetlana and Nikolaiy tells you something. Whether it's important or not that Nikolaiy took photos of anti-Soviet demonstrators at Hollywood High School, or that he sent his son to the Crimean camp, I don't know. I agree that he would never have done attention-getting things like this if he'd been a real KGB sleeper operative; but I think the consulate had a certain hold on both of them.

"I think she may have set out to lay Hunt because the consulate-general suggested it, and that, when Hunt himself came up with the idea that she tell the consulate-general that she had a 'boyfriend' in the FBI, she realized he was counting on her loyalty to him—that he didn't suspect her, then, of perhaps being more loyal to the Rezidentura than to the FBI. By then, anyway, it really looks as though she had high hopes about her relationship with Hunt; that was when she was telling her friend Nadya Mathison that she was going to marry him. Okay, I know Hunt says the whole relationship was platonic, just a little cuddling on the dance floor like teenagers; but when anyone at Justice or the FBI tells you that, watch their eyes!

"I think she's angry with Hunt now, just as Marta York is teed off at Miller. Hell hath no fury like it, right? Mrs. York's not very bright, either. She's a Portland waitress from El Salvador, or Ecuador, or somewhere, and she's excitable. She spent two weeks with Miller that September, in Los Angeles, going to movies and cafeterias and the county fair with him. She was shopping for a new breadwinner.

"Then he jilted her—or at least that's how she says it looked to her. So she's angry, and she thinks about the surveillance she spotted, and she figures that he must have been doing something wrong, so she testifies against him, and says he'd told her he'd given the Russians a classified document because he thought he had a 'good deal' with them. But she varied her story so often . . . that it's hard to know *what* he told her. Whichever version you take, it doesn't sound like the sort of admission a real Russian spy or American turncoat would make.

"The prosecution's notion that all this happened because R.W. was head over heels in love doesn't grab me either. He was spending more time with Marta York. And because the document he was accused of passing *is* secret, it wasn't admitted in evidence, and the judge wouldn't allow witnesses to describe how trivial its contents were. I'm not saying Kenyon was wrong: I think he followed the procedures on classified documents correctly. What I'm saying is that nobody is suggesting that the document was worth fifty gees in Krugerrands!

"I just can't see what 'two life terms' has to do with all of this."

Lawrence Grayson was introduced to the reader in the first paragraphs of this book. A former special deputy in the Riverside sheriff's department, he had done work for Miller in the 1979-81 period. Readers will recall that he was interviewed in a hostile manner by the FBI, and plainly scared, a few hours before Miller was arrested, and that he tried to pass a warning to Miller—the "flowers on his mother's grave" tip to Paula. At Miller's trials, he refused to be interviewed by the defense attorneys or their investigator and had to be put on the stand "cold."

Grayson, it will also be recalled, told the author that if he had doubted Miller's patriotic motives in planning the Mexico meeting, he would have gone to the FBI, and that he was surprised that he had not been asked that point by either side on the witness stand. In conversations with the author, Grayson confirmed that he owed Miller a favor because of the FBI papers he had made available to the investigator, which Grayson said were on "mobsters." The earlier description of the Corona meeting with Miller, down to the details of the coffee, the hovering waitress, and so on, come mostly from Grayson.

Behind the bluff, friendly manner, Grayson is a cagey person to interview. In 1989, after Miller had won a retrial, the author questioned him again on the Denny's meeting:

Q. What did you think were Miller's intentions?

A. I didn't know what his intentions were.

Q. Did you think he intended to betray the country?

A. Not at the time.

Q. You mean you didn't think it at the time, or he didn't have treasonal intentions at the time?

A. I didn't think he had those intentions, but I didn't know what his intentions were. I didn't think he would go through with it.

Q. Did you think he had permission from the Bureau to go to Mexico?

A. Yes, I thought he had permission.

Q. But when you asked him why he was using you for the surveillance, you say he said that it was because his credibility was shot with the Bureau and they wouldn't approve him going.

A. Well, then I could see he was acting on his own. Frankly, I thought it was just another of R.W.'s wild ideas.

Q. But you agreed to help him if he went through with it.

A. I owed him a favor, but I didn't think he'd go through with it. I told him he'd be cutting his throat, for money.

Q. What did he say he was going to give the Russians in Mexico?

A. An illusion.

Q. What illusion?

A. The illusion that he was trying to create with the Russians was that he had access to important documents.

Q. At the [second] trial, you were obviously a reluctant witness.

A. No, I wasn't reluctant!

Q. Well, a cautious one.

A. Okay.

Q. The government must have warned you that they could try to get you for misprision or conspiracy.

A. Never. They never mentioned anything like that.

Q. Are you asking me to believe that there was nothing in what they said, the tone—that there wasn't anything that didn't imply that they could make life difficult for you?

A. Well, what the FBI and the U.S. Attorney's Office did say in a roundabout way was: "It's kinda hard to believe that if you had knowledge of this, you're not perhaps involved in it."

Q. That sounds ominous.

A. Well, they did say national security was involved. And I said: "You mean this is not just a song and dance?" I agreed that I had owed Miller a favor, and I agreed to turn over my notes about paying him for info on mobsters. In exchange, I said if a crime had been committed, I wanted a letter stating that, under their guidelines, there would not be any charges against me.

Q. And did you get such an undertaking?

A. Yes.

Q. Have you talked to Miller since?

A. I called him at Terminal Island, just after his arrest, and he said: 'I thought I could get away with it.'

Q. How did you manage to call a prisoner? Only lawyers can do that.

A. You have to know the right people out there at Terminal Island.

Q. Just a moment. Did the FBI ask you to call Miller and arrange for you to be able to call? Was that part of your understanding with them?

A. No. And I never talked to the other side.

Q. When you say "the other side," do you mean the prosecution or the defense?

A. The defense.

Q. I see. You mean that, having heard the evidence at the trial, you think R.W. betrayed the country?

A. Yes.

Q. Really? Intentionally?

A. Yes.

Q. You think, now you've heard the trial evidence, that he was prepared to sell the country for money?

A. Yes.

Q. You don't believe he planned to become a double agent, and sell "illusion"?

A. I'll never know if he did this to become a double agent, or with personal greed involved.

Q. But you just said, in effect, that the trial proved that he deceived you, and that he intended to deceive the United States.

A. Well, I think that, to begin with, he meant well, and was trying to perform his duty and his job to the best of his ability.

Q. But now you think he's guilty.

A. I think he was guilty of not informing his superiors that he had laid the foundations for this charade. If he's guilty of anything, he's guilty of stupidity.

Q. Just now, you went further than that. You said he had betrayed the country.

A. Well, he admitted passing those documents, without permission.

Q. So you think the prosecution did a good job.

A. No, I think they did a poor job. Why did they put on that *Reader's Digest* man? He said there was no double-agent program. My evidence contradicted that. Christensen contradicted that. William Webster contradicted that.

Q. Gary Auer testified that Miller had asked him if he knew where those three Russian defectors were living—if he could contact the CIA to find out. Would Miller have asked those questions if he'd been planning to work for the Russians, not just deceive them?

A. I agree. Why would he ask me to go to Mexico if my video would be testimony *against* him?

Q. There was a double-agent program, and Miller was a part of it. Are you saying that by exceeding orders, he broke the law *and* intentionally betrayed the country?

A. Look, his plan was crazy. I told him so. I doubted if he would have the nerve to go through with it. It was dangerous. It wasn't authorized. The chances of success—setting up an effective double-agent scam to stiff the Russians—were pretty slim. Once they had him, out of the country, they could have forced him to do something to damage the United States. We know that he was not prepared to go to Vienna without permission. I don't believe he would have had the guts to go to Mexico without permission, and I don't think he would have gotten permission. Was his motivation professional? Yes. Was it venal? Yes. It obviously wasn't ideological. Was he technically guilty of espionage, for giving them secret documents? Yes.

Q. Do you think the Rezidentura saw through his game?

A. I don't know. Probably.

Q. Do you think they set things up so that he would be arrested by his own people?

A. I suppose that's possible. No one's ever asked me that question before.

Q. Let's suppose that Miller had been invited to Mexico by the Russians, and let's suppose you got your pix and your sound, then what? Miller as hero? How could the FBI have taken it from there?

A. I don't know. I see what you're saying—even if he'd succeeded, he would have failed.

Q. Let's suppose you're not discreet enough in Mexico, and the Russkies grab your camera, and they rip the recorder from Miller's back. The mission would have failed, and the FBI might have fired him for the caper; but your presence would have proven he was spying on the Russians, not for them.

A. You're saying R.W. went down because the Russians said no to Mexico and insisted on Europe. Maybe that was it—just Irish luck. It was not his week.

Nearly a year later, on the eve of the third trial, Grayson called the author to say he was about to leave for vacation in Britain, his father's adopted country. He confirmed what Miller's attorneys had told the writer the day before—that Grayson had refused to be interviewed, in other words, that the lawyers still had no idea what he might say on the stand. Grayson said he expected to be subpoenaed for the defense. Knowing that he would probably not remember all his sometimes confusing answers of the year before, and other conversations before that, the author again asked him, in slightly different words, the question Grayson had complained that both sides had failed to ask him at the previous trials:

"Do you think Miller was trying to serve the United States, or simply trying to get money from the Russians?"

Said Grayson: "I think he was trying to help the United States *and* make money. But I never believed for a moment that he'd go through with his plan."

# PART IV

## *Justice*

# Chapter Seventeen

# *Third Trial: Mitigation*

*The case hung not only on evidence but on how evidence was interpreted.*

## *i*

In the spring of 1989, a federal Court of Appeal granted Miller a retrial, finding that Judge Kenyon had committed three errors. He should not have admitted the hearsay evidence of a polygrapher; he should not have prejudiced the jury by allowing the prosecution to introduce evidence of Miller's petty dishonesties in the FBI; and, having allowed a *Reader's Digest* editor to testify for the prosecution on KGB methods, he should have allowed Miller to call an intelligence expert for the defense.

In its summary, the Ninth Circuit Court of Appeals said:

> We conclude that the district court abused its discretion in admitting extensive testimony concerning the polygraph examination that Miller failed. We also conclude that the district court improperly admitted the evidence concerning Miller's alleged bribe of Grayson to be used to establish intent for all of the charges for which Miller was tried. Lastly, we hold that the prosecution improperly invited the jury to use expert testimony as character evidence. In light of these errors, we conclude that Miller's conviction on all counts must be reversed.
>
> The conviction is reversed and the case remanded for a new trial.

Kenyon refused bail, but was overturned again. Relatives put up three houses as collateral, and bail was set at $675,000. Miller, now just an innocent citizen awaiting trial, went home to Los Angeles. Kenyon, saying that "this is turning into a trial of me," recused himself. With a new judge needed, the luck of the draw gave the case to Robert Takasugi, who is regarded as especially fair by defense attorneys. He is the only federal judge to have known incarceration—as a Nisei child prisoner in an Arizona concentration camp during World War II. He's also famous as the judge who acquitted John DeLorean, the automobile manufacturer arrested in an FBI drug "sting."

At first, Miller went home to his sister, Mary Ann Deem, and was reluctant to discuss his case, even with his attorneys. Finally, they found him a job, as assistant to Al Sayers, who had once been his supervisor in the FBI and who was now a private eye. Sayers was also Miller's attorney's gumshoe on the Miller case. Later, Miller moved to a job as graphics editor of *Downtown News,* a supermarket giveaway newspaper—known as a "shopper" in the profession.

Now three hundred pounds, and as rumpled as ever, Miller was still not an ideal client, but he was "getting there." And Levine and Greenberg were quite convinced of his innocence— so much so that they were considering asking for a non-jury trial, something a guilty person pleading innocent virtually never does.

Just before the Moscow summit in the summer of 1988, Matvei Ogorodnikov, now seventeen, went to the capital, where the teenager was granted a brief audience with Eduard Shevardnadze, the Soviet foreign minister. As noted earlier, Shevardnadze agreed to try to take up his parents' case, under the human-rights agenda, at the meeting between Gorbachev and Reagan and their advisers. Matvei wrote to his father, then in Walla Walla, and Nikolaiy sent the letter on to the author, who had it translated.

Nothing, apparently, came of this filial initiative.

In January 1990, Nikolaiy was released. He had served two-thirds of his time, with a few weeks more taken off for good conduct. But instead of freedom, he faced a prison worse than the one he was leaving at Clallam Bay. As recounted earlier, the INS clapped him into the immigration "facility" in Seattle, "pending deportation." These modern dungeons, intended to be used for only a few days by arrested "wetbacks," have the worst overcrowding of all, and—since no one is supposed to be there for long—no classes or recreation. Knowing no Spanish, Nikolaiy was in a prison within a prison—a babble in which he could not join. His reaction was typically that of a city boy from the Ukraine. He called the author and cackled: "This is like a fucking gypsy camp!"

As also recounted earlier, Levine and Greenberg soon won an order from Takasugi saying that the Ogorodnikovs could not leave the United States because Miller's team might need them as material witnesses. Lawyers noted that Nikolaiy's chances of freedom had perhaps been diminished by this, since there might be more official concern that a witness in an espionage case would abscond than about just another wetback disappearing into the landscape. Ramsey Clark generously interested himself in the case again, and found a young human-rights lawyer in Seattle to help Nikolaiy without payment. At first, the young lawyer found Nikolaiy more grouchy than helpful. Then, both defense and government attorneys agreed that they had no objection to Nikolaiy going home to West Hollywood and back to work.

Said Greenberg: "After all, Nikolaiy's only guilty of being Svetlana's husband."

That was what the prosecution had concluded as well. They had now learned of the Occidental Research report making Svetlana out to be a real KGB major, with Miller as her dupe. The federal attorneys had, however, not been told that Nikolaiy was supposed to be her "support agent," a sort of KGB private, because the intelligence community didn't want Nikolaiy expelled or re-imprisoned. They wanted to see if Soviet intelligence would approach him first, and they didn't want to be cheated by the clumsiness of the FBI or Justice.

By then, "O.R." itself had been disbanded; Mrs. Ayres had been startled to find that her army of researchers had disappeared overnight. Joint Intelligence Center in Washington had decided that Merman's operation was too high-profile, too red-baiting for the sake of it, too kooky by half. The news had deprived Merman of his desire to die in a tunnel under a Rezidentura somewhere. Instead, the Washington decision gave him a fatal heart attack.

Next, there was trouble about Nikolaiy recovering his former job at Hoffman Brothers. A routine medical exam had turned up back trouble—the usual crunching together of the vertebrae that goes with the aging process, producing a diminution in height and the occasional "bad back." The author intervened, and Joseph Russo promised to find Nikolaiy a less strenuous job at lower pay. Later, Nikolaiy found a job more to his liking— courtesy bus driver at a hotel near the airport.

By then, Levine and Greenberg had found that Svetlana's talk of Hunt having a bad conscience was at least partly true. They learned that, after Miller had won a retrial, Hunt had written to the new FBI director, William Sessions, in July 1989, a ten-page letter asking for a meeting. He had complained that the FBI had withheld crucial information from the defense in the Miller case. Sessions responded icily that a meeting would not be "appropriate."

The defense then discovered that there were more letters. Greenberg told the author: "Hunt's position [about not cooperating with the defense] hasn't changed, but he's been talking to a lot of people about information the prosecution wouldn't let us get to, before. He's telling them Miller and Svetlana were unfairly convicted to shield higher-ups and conceal their incompetence." The reason lawyers employ gumshoes becomes at once apparent.

Judge Takasugi, over government protests, ordered Hunt's new lawyer, Lynn Sarco, to hand over eleven of Hunt's letters, and later a twelfth.

The cases of Miller and the Ogorodnikovs are and are separate. Proving Miller innocent would not necessarily exculpate the Ogorodnikovs, who might still have tried to recruit him for the KGB. But the growing possibility that Miller would be acquitted, or might be reconvicted on largely technical grounds, naturally raised hopes for his "conspirators," especially Svetlana. At the least, it might help Svetlana—by then sick from apparently psychosomatic causes in the Lexington prison hospital—plead that her inexperienced attorneys had mishandled her case.

At the time, it was assumed there would be a jury trial for Miller, which might mean another "hung" panel. Should that have happened, it would have been questionable whether the U.S. attorneys would have put the taxpayers to the expense of yet a fourth process. If charges against Miller were withdrawn, what would his conspirators be guilty of? They could, of course, still be guilty of *trying* to subvert him—and they *had* been persuaded to plead guilty.

Miller's former chief prosecutor, Robert Bonner, had become a judge. The prosecution was taken over by Adam Schiff, with Russell Hayman continuing as assistant. Then, Bonner was appointed to head the Drug Enforcement Agency in Washington, and he recruited Hayman to assist him. Shortly before the retrial started, Hayman was replaced by John Libby. (For the judicial record, the lead prosecutor was Lourdes G. Baird, the U.S. attorney for Los Angeles.)

Miller's lawyers had by then taken the plunge and asked for a non-jury trial. As noted, guilty persons pleading innocence (who are inevitably a majority of all defendants in all criminal trials, everywhere) ask for a jury, because they *want* a miscarriage of justice. Truly innocent defendants also sometimes ask for a jury because they or their lawyers have misgivings about a judge (as Levine and Greenberg had had about Kenyon) or because they feel that in certain cases (treason, espionage, major crimes in which the defendant is an ex-convict or is actually serving time for another offense), the judge will be psychologically conditioned to convict. To observers of the judicial system, Levine's and Greenberg's decision to convince Miller that he did not need a jury indicated that they were confident that the government's case was weak. (A defendant, be it noted, doesn't actually have to prove that he is innocent; the prosecution has to prove that he is guilty beyond a reasonable doubt. The defense sets out to prove that this is not so—that he is not guilty, which is not quite the same as being innocent. For instance, someone who is insane is obviously innocent by definition of *everything*, regardless of whether he has actually committed an unlawful act.)

Grayson, despite the statute of limitations on conspiracy, remained unwilling to cooperate with Miller's attorneys. He talked to the author, knowing that some of these conversations would be passed on and would form a basis for questions when he returned to the stand. He went on vacation to England for six weeks, the day before the retrial opened, but expected to be called for the defense as soon as he got back. Hunt continued to be elusive also, but was to be called once more as a prosecution witness.

When the trial opened, Miller's lawyers had still not decided whether to put Miller himself on the stand, where he would face cross-examination. R.W. was still maintaining that he had known nothing of Whipworm until Christensen told him of it—thus leaving it to the prosecution to *prove* that he had finally spotted a colleague in a car behind him, and that this awareness had induced him to *invent* a story of trying to infiltrate the KGB for the FBI.

As with Grayson, the defense had not informed Nikolaiy or Svetlana whether they would be called. The usual practice is to call such witnesses at the last moment, so that they are less likely to plan how to thwart attorneys' questions.

As the opening shots were fired in Judge Takasugi's courtroom on August 21, 1990, Levine exuded confidence, apparently not worried by the fact that Greenberg had other cases that would take him away from the Miller trial for much of the time. Miller had told Levine and Greenberg that he did not want to "do a deal"—to save the government's case by pleading guilty to a lesser charge of carelessness with security. Miller wanted as much vindication as he could get.

## ii

There had been eleven counts in the original grand jury indictment. With the conviction of the Ogorodnikovs, and the elimination of the most minor count (Miller "receiving" the Burberry raincoat from Svetlana), the counts for Miller had long ago been reduced to six, four concerning espionage (of which two were conspiracy charges) and two counts of bribery. With some summarization, mostly to avoid repetition, they were as follows:

Count One

Miller did. . .knowingly and willingly communicate. . .documents. . .relating to the national defense of the United States [in conspiracy with the Ogorodnikovs]. . . .

The objects of said conspiracy were to be accomplished as follows:

Miller would obtain [the documents].

Miller would provide [them] to Ogorodnikova.

Ogorodnikova and Ogorodnikov would arrange [*sic*] with unindicted co-conspirator Grishin for a meeting outside of the United States at which defendant Miller would provide classified and national defense materials and information to other representatives and agents of the U.S.S.R. . . .in eastern [*sic*] Europe in mid-October 1984.

The conspiracy:

a. In the third week of August 1984, Miller and Ogorodnikova met in Malibu to discuss the sale of FBI documents and information to Soviet agents.

b. Around the same time, Miller met Ogorodnikov at 1155 Gardner Street in Hollywood to discuss the sale.

c. Around the same time, at 5953 Josephine Street, Lynwood, Miller showed Ogorodnikova a document entitled "Reporting Guidance: Foreign Intelligence Information," dated July 27, 1984, and marked "Secret."

d. On or about August 24, Miller and Ogorodnikova went to San Francisco.

e. They [*sic*] visited the Soviet consulate [*sic*].

f. On September 11, Grishin telephoned Ogorodnikova to discuss a meeting between Ogorodnikova's unnamed friend and Soviet agents.

g. Ogorodnikova called Miller to arrange a meeting.

h. The next day, Miller and Ogorodnikova met in the parking lot at the intersection of Sepulveda Boulevard and Ohio Avenue in Los Angeles.

i. At the same time, Miller gave Ogorodnikova documents in an envelope.

j. Ogorodnikova went home, then walked around outside for about fifty minutes with Ogorodnikov.*

k. The next day, Miller and Ogorodnikova met again in the same parking lot.

l. Ogorodnikova went home, then walked around outside for about seventy-five minutes with Ogorodnikov.*

m. On or about September 16, Miller called Ogorodnikova to arrange a meeting.

n. On September 18, Grishin telephoned Ogorodnikova to discuss a trip by her and her unnamed friend to Poland.

o. Ogorodnikova and Ogorodnikov left their building and walked around for two hours.*

p. On September 20, Ogorodnikova tried to call the Austrian consulate [*sic.*]

q. On the same day, Miller and Ogorodnikova met at the Café Casino in Santa Monica.

r. The next day, Miller telephoned Ogorodnikova.

s. On September 24, Ogorodnikov went to the Soviet consulate [*sic*] in San Francisco.

t. The next day, Ogorodnikova telephoned Beverly International Travel to make airline reservations for two to Vienna.

u. On the same day, Grishin telephoned Ogorodnikova from a pay phone at San Francisco International Airport to discuss travel arrangements for Ogorodnikova and Miller to meet Soviet agents in Europe.

v. After the call, Ogorodnikova and Ogorodnikov left their apartment and walked around outside for an hour.*

w. On or about September 26. . .Miller and. . .Ogorodnikova shopped for clothes.

x. Ogorodnikova and Miller arranged to purchase a Burberry's trench coat. . .for Miller.

y. The next day, in the Federal Building at 11000 Wilshire Boulevard, Miller applied for a passport, falsely stating that he was going to Mexico and that his occupation was translator.

z. On October 2, Grishin telephoned Ogorodnikova.

* Suspiciousness is attributed to the Nikolaiy-Svetlana walks because they could imply a desire for secrecy. Knowing their home was bugged, the prosecution indicates, the Ogorodnikovs had to go into the street to get privacy.

Count Two

Miller, having reason to believe that it would be used to the injury of the United States and to the advantage of. . .the U.S.S.R., did knowingly and willfully copy, take and obtain [the reporting guidance].

Count Three

Miller, having reason to believe, etc. . . ., communicated the document to said foreign government.

Count Four

Miller did willfully. . .communicate to a person whom he had reason to believe to be an agent and representative of. . .the U.S.S.R. [classified information].

Count Five

Miller asked. . .for fifty thousand dollars in gold to copy and remove documents and writings from the offices of the FBI and to provide them to Ogorodnikova and other Soviet agents.

Count Six

Miller asked for fifteen thousand dollars to induce him to travel outside of the United States and to deliver to them official FBI documents.

Like the juries before him, the judge had to decide the answers to seven main questions:

1. Did Miller offer himself in a "dangle"—baited with documents or the promise of them—with the intention of trying to become a double agent for the United States, while pretending to the Soviet Union that he would be a mole within the FBI? Or was he setting up a paid relationship with the Soviet consulate-general in San Francisco that he intended to keep unlawfully secret from his FBI superiors?

To resolve this question, the judge had to reach conclusions on two other questions: Did Miller know he was being tailed before he went to Christensen, and did he not know that the consulate-general was under camera surveillance by his San Francisco colleagues? Or, conversely, did he think that his actions were entirely secret from his superiors?

The defense counsel were to argue that, had he spotted Operation Whipworm, he would have gone to his supervisors earlier to explain what he was doing, or—were he planning to become a Soviet mole—he would have ceased seeing or contacting Svetlana and "laid low."

2. Did Miller give Svetlana the document referred to in the statement that he recanted, with the intention that she give it to the consulate-general? When he made the admission after the long grilling, was he in a state of hysteria, consonant with his FBI psychiatric profile of 1982? Or, conversely, is it inconceivable that he would ever have signed any admission if it were not true?

3. Did he offer to go to Vienna with the intention of somehow keeping his journey secret, and did he inform Christensen only because he thought Christensen already knew about his "secret" plan? Or did he inform Christensen of the invitation to

Vienna because he needed authorization and back-up to proceed with a double agent scam against the Russians?

4. Were Miller and Grayson telling the truth when they testified (or when Miller's attorneys asserted) that Miller wanted photographic and sound proof of his projected meeting with KGB or GRU representatives in Mexico, in order to prove to his superiors that he had initiated a successful "charade" (Grayson's term), or was this a subtle, Machiavellian ploy by a mastermind of intrigue to cover his traitorous tracks?

5. Was Svetlana telling the truth when she said that John Hunt was her physical lover; that she was as useless as an FBI swallow or informant as he eventually proclaimed her to be; and that he kept up the handler-informant relationship for over a year for his sexual convenience, which would mean that Hunt was a perjurer whose evidence should be discarded? Or was Hunt telling the truth when he insisted that they were never lovers, and that he spent so much day and night time with this married woman over such an extended period because he was credibly trying to develop her as a disinformation channel against the Rezidentura?

6. Was Svetlana a Soviet agent, either willingly or under duress, in order to preserve her privileges of visiting Russia, sending Matvei to youth camp in the Crimea, and showing Russian films? Or, conversely, was she entirely at the beck and call of Hunt, Miller and the FBI, with the motivation of marrying an American and becoming independent of Nikolaiy? Was she genuinely in love with Hunt and expecting to marry him? Was Nikolaiy a Soviet agent? If one or both of them were enemy agents, was Miller aware of this? If they were, or Miller believed they were, does this validate or invalidate his claim that he was trying to deceive the U.S.S.R. to the advantage of the United States?

7. If Miller is guilty on all or some of the counts, are there attenuating or extenuating circumstances, and what should the sentence be? Do his responsibilities as an FBI special agent enhance his guilt and justify a harsh penalty? Is espionage a more serious crime than premeditated murder, child murder, etc., or does this depend on how far the security of the country is prejudiced and on whether the country is at war or not? Would passing the reporting guidance be as serious an offense as passing nuclear secrets or NSA codes?

*

The case hung not only on evidence but on how evidence was interpreted. In assessing the credibility of Miller's claim to be doing with the KGB what his famous colleague Joe Pistone had done with the Mafia, the court had to consider the prosecution's case that he had sought to conceal his activity from the FBI. Miller claimed he had not made initial reports because he had been disobeying instructions in continuing to meet Svetlana— the "Bernard Samson defense"—and because he feared his superiors would adjudge him incompetent to carry out a double-agent operation of such magnitude and temerity.

Miller clearly knew about the camera surveillance across from the entrance to the consulate-general, because he had reminded Svetlana of it. Was it possible that he had been unconscious of the Whipworm surveillance, as he had said, despite the camera in his workspace, and even though Svetlana, Nikolaiy and Marta York all testified that they had spotted that they were followed? We must remember that the Ogorodnikovs had said that their thirteen-year-old son had done so also—and Svetlana and Mrs. York had testified that they had told Miller about it. But since the prosecution claimed that he had suspected a surveillance only after he had spotted the DeFlores car, the judge would not have to consider if he knew about it earlier. If Miller had realized that both cars were bugged, would he have discussed meeting General Mikhail of the GRU in Svetlana's car rather than in the street? This tended to support both defense and prosecution claims that Miller's ignorance was blithe.

Miller should have known that the first response of any intelligence service to a volunteer "defector" is to assume that the offer is a scam. Did Miller's behavior prove the defense assertion that Miller was a fool, a Walter Mitty patriotically trying to be Bernard Samson, or did it prove, as the prosecution claimed, that "there are no double agents in this case"—that Miller hoped to get gold and dollars from the Russians for trivia such as the reporting guide, the FBI phone book, and so on?

The prosecution accepted that Grishin's phone calls implied that he and Miller had never met. But that could demonstrate caution, on either part. Was Miller, as the prosecution said, a man with so many professional and character defects that he was circumstantially likely to get "out of line"? The defense, on the other hand, said Miller wanted to save his career and retire in a "blaze of glory." How relevant, the court had to wonder, were Miller's defects, either way? His philandering, of which the prosecution was to make much, was irrelevant; he was spending more time with Marta York than with his swallow, and showed no signs of wanting a permanent relationship with Svetlana. That some people have more sexual needs than others is no more despicable than the physical continence of the impotent is virtuous. Each human is dealt his deck of cards and lives with it. So to what extent did his colleagues, like those of the fictional Samson, "have it in" for him, suspect him unjustly, hector and harass him unduly, and give him the "third degree" until this emotionally and psychologically damaged man had broken down, so that they could go for the kill? Or were they just doing their job?

How much importance could the court attach to Svetlana, with her tiresome contradictions, fuzzy-mindedness and memory lapses? Could it buy a used car from John Hunt? The judge would not know that Hunt had told this writer that he was more interested in selling a story than in justice, but there could perhaps be honest and justifiable reasons Hunt does not wish to speak to an author, such as having competing authorship plans. The court had to consider who had started what. The government did not question that Hunt had recruited Svetlana, and did not suggest that it was she who had made an offer. It did not contest that Miller, with or without authorization, had renewed to her the offer of being an FBI asset. So how did that make her an agent of the Soviet Union? Or did she become a Soviet agent *after* being recruited by Hunt, and re-recruited by Miller, for the FBI? How relevant was her status in regard to the guilt or non-guilt of Miller?

The judge would have to decide whether the Vienna trip—which Miller said was intended to be a Miller (or FBI) sting, and which the prosecution said was a blatant offer by Miller to be recruited, to which the Soviet Union had favorably responded—was anything more or less than a Soviet "sting" response to Miller's sting; that is, a Soviet sting for which the perhaps inadequate Russian Squad in Westwood couldn't wait to fall.

Grishin clearly set up a pattern of Tuesday calls, between 7:30 and 8 p.m., which Svetlana clearly expected. This procedure—

making things easy for the FBI—would be consonant with a Russian scam, although of course it might not be conclusive courtroom proof of it. The government said, in recounting the conspiracy, that the Ogorodnikovs held talks in the street because they knew their apartment was bugged; therefore, Grishin knew; therefore, the implications were that Grishin wanted his calls intercepted. Did Svetlana accept the telephone relationship with Grishin for Grishin's sake, or for Miller's? If Miller was in control of her, her contacts with Grishin on a bugged line could be seen as solely on behalf of the FBI, thereby proving, in part, Miller's defense. If Svetlana was in control of Miller, would this mean that he had "gone over" (i.e., was guilty), or simply that, while his heart was in the right, patriotic place, he was really being manipulated?

One car intercept seems clearly to show her pleading with him to "come to work" for the Soviet Union ("Please!"), and has him saying: "Well, we'll see." The court would have to consider whether that meant that, by that time, perhaps from fear, perhaps in reaction to being "jilted" by Hunt, or for other reasons, she was herself working for Soviet intelligence—as Miller's defense also asserted. Or does the exchange simply refer to Miller's intention to penetrate Soviet intelligence, to "play the game" (the words which she says he used), since this would involve remuneration from Soviet intelligence, which Svetlana might assume Miller would be able to keep.

Depending on how he testified, and on his credibility, Grayson could be regarded by Judge Takasugi as the most important witness for the defense. If his testimony was believable, and if Miller was not following an arcane scam of Philby-like ingenuity, with or without Grayson's awareness, this would indicate more than anything else that—at that point, anyway—Miller was entirely on the side of the angels. Should the bench become aware of Grayson's fear of government retaliation if the investigator helped Miller's defense, this could also perhaps point to the weakness of the government's case and therefore to Miller's non-guilt. If Grayson's evidence were to prove Miller not guilty, beyond any reasonable doubt, at the time of the Corona meeting, had anything transpired afterward that would have induced Miller to be a turncoat? Had he, in fact, turned his coat? The other key point of the prosecution case would be its attempt to convince the judge that Miller had indeed spotted DeFlores in his car. If unable to prove that, much of the prosecution's "cock and bull story" theory would fail.

During Miller's first trial, Judge Kenyon had told the lawyers, on October 10, 1985, that he would instruct the jurors that they *need not find that Miller actually passed a document to anyone in order to establish that a conspiracy existed.* A conspiracy to commit an offense is a felony, even if the offense itself is not committed—hence the intense importance, to prosecutions, of conspiracy counts.

Both on the conspiracy and other espionage counts, intent was obviously an issue. One of the best reporters covering the first trial, Linda Deutsch of the Associated Press, wrote toward the end of the process:

"The key matter under debate when the court recessed on Wednesday was the issue of specific intent. Defense attorneys want the jurors to be told that Miller cannot be found guilty of espionage unless he is found to have acted willfully, with specific intent to violate espionage laws. Prosecutors argued that only 'general intent' need be proved, and that commission of certain acts can lead to conviction regardless of specific intent."

It was the old question of the difference between murder and manslaughter, or rape and seduction.

As is invariably the case in trials involving national security, the prosecution won the contest. When instructing the jury on October 18, 1985, Kenyon said that "Good motive alone is never a defense where a crime is committed." Thirty-six years before, Judge Michael Roche had sealed the fate of Iva Toguri d'Aquino (accused of being "Tokyo Rose") by the same instruction. Laymen are instinctively offended by this, but in the abstract it is not much different from the axiom that everyone knows, that "ignorance is no defense."

Two days before the judge's instruction, Joel Levine had tried to balance what he feared was coming by reminding jurors of the doctrine of "beyond a reasonable doubt"—a factor which, now, Judge Takasugi would have to take into account. What it would come down to would be—as Judith Cummings of *The New York Times* explained in her reporting of that same first trial—whether the court believed Levine's assertion that Miller had "virtually achieved his goal of ensnaring Soviet spies, but was cheated of his achievement by a bureau hierarchy that disapproved of his methods and of him." Yet, because of the "intent" doctrine, if he passed a document "illegally," he would be as guilty as the speeding ambulance driver who "recklessly" runs over a pedestrian; and if he merely planned to do so, he could be guilty of conspiracy.

To sum up, what it came down to was this: If Miller planned to go to Vienna and give security documents *without permission*, he was guilty. If he would have done nothing without permission from Christensen and his other superiors, he was not guilty on that score.

If he gave documents to Mrs. Ogorodnikova, believing her to be a Russian agent, without authorization to do so, he was guilty, even if this was a "dangle." He was equally guilty if he never gave documents without authorization, but "conspired" to do so in the future. He was only not guilty if he never intended to part with intelligence without FBI permission.

If he had acted illegally, but with the best of patriotic and loyal intentions, he was still guilty, even though good motivation would be an attenuating factor in the sentencing.

The relative triviality of the documents involved would also be a consideration in sentencing, unless there was proof that Miller plotted or "conspired" to pass on more meaningful documents later.

## *iii*

The third performance of this outrageously expensive contest, *United States v. Miller*, was much shorter (seven weeks) and more to the point. Fewer trees fell in the forest to record it for posterity.

The new chief prosecutor, Schiff, seemed to match the new dispensation—a ponderous, unflamboyant, conservative man of medium build who would be Central Casting's choice for a prosecutor without a jury.

In the opening arguments, the prosecution sought to establish motive by again stressing Miller's need for money, his failing marriage, his "infatuation" with Svetlana, his growing dissatisfaction with the FBI. It announced that John Barron—"probably the foremost authority on the KGB in the United States"—

would again be called to attest to the significance of the reporting guidance.

Schiff said that the prosecution "will prove that Miller's brand of espionage was not ideological. . . . For [him, it] was a crime of dollars and cents, of lust, of dissatisfaction; it was even a crime of boredom."

For the defense, Levine emphasized that "the only evidence of soliciting bribes that you will [hear] at this trial. . .are Mr. Miller's statements. There will be no other evidence of it."

Miller had asked for deposits in three different deposit boxes, and receipts. "He was attempting to gather evidence of who it was that had paid him."

Levine pointed out that all the accounts of what had taken place on the San Francisco trip came from Miller's own report to Christensen. Miller had helped in the searches of Lynwood and Bonsall. He was admitting only to "unauthorized contacts" with Svetlana, and sexual relations with her.

The defense would agree that Miller had always been bad about doing reports. Medical evidence would be produced to show that, like many obese people, he had a sleep disorder, apnea, and that he was also an audio-dyslectic; he had genuine difficulty in distinguishing, in memory, between fact and what others say is fact.

Because Bretzing was accused by his staff of having coddled Miller for religious reasons, he had had to go to the opposite extreme and scapegoat him. The key to Miller's intentions lay in his approach to Grayson, but Grayson had been "grilled ad nauseam by FBI agents in October, 1984, in an effort, we submit, to get him not to testify to what you are going to hear in this courtroom," Levine said.

What would the three defendants say? In the event, neither the Ogorodnikovs nor Miller would be called.

Levine said the prosecution had exaggerated Miller's financial problems. He had been "tight," not bankrupt. Hunt, as his "134" file on Svetlana showed, had asked her to tell Belyakov that her FBI "boyfriend" had financial problems, and Miller had laid out the same bait.

"Mr. Miller received no money and there will be no evidence that he received any money from anybody related to the Soviet government," Levine said. "He conveyed no documents, even though he made a statement to Bureau agents that he did."

Levine noted that Grishin, in his phone calls, had told Svetlana to tell Miller to "bring the baggage," not to "bring more baggage," or "the rest of the baggage."

The principal difference between the third trial and the earlier processes was in the testimony of John Hunt, who supported Svetlana's contention that she had done only what the FBI had asked her to do, and had faithfully reported to the FBI what the KGB had asked her to do.

The prosecution was to allege again that Svetlana took the guidance and "other classified documents which have never been identified" into the consulate-general inside a film canister, but it once again produced no proof of this conjecture. She was also said to have taken his FBI credentials. The FBI were to testify that, when Richard and Svetlana left San Francisco, they initially drove north into Marin County—which was interpreted as an attempt to throw off followers, Russian or American. The FBI, because of the camera surveillance, had followed the couple to Livermore.

The lead weapon in the prosecution's case was, of course, the chief burden in the defense's: Miller's admission about the guidance under questioning, his repeat of this to Marta York, and to Bretzing in the car between Bonsall and San Diego on the night of his arrest, when he had even seemed to admit to "documents" in the plural.

Schiff said the Ogorodnikovs had been forced to do services for the consulate-general to win the right to visitors' visas to the Soviet Union. He also hypothesized that Nikolaiy had hoped to make money out of doing odd jobs for the consulate. He said curiously that for emigrants to be able to make visits to the Soviet Union was "unheard of."

Special Agent Ronald Durkin testified that he had removed a Nagra tape from Svetlana's Lynx at about 2:30 a.m. on September 27, 1984, and put in a new recording unit. The tapes were activated by a pressure switch, which was itself engaged when someone sat on the front passenger seat of the car. This raised the point that if Miller had been aware, or suspected, that he was under surveillance, he would have known what precautions to take—sitting on the edge of the seat—or would have implied that he had declined to take them because of the suspicions such precautions would arouse in his colleagues.

Hunt was on the stand for two days. He testified that he had left the FBI because of a "heart condition." He recalled how he had opened a "134" and a "105" on Svetlana—the latter being a counterintelligence unit report. He explained the procedures involved in recruiting an asset, including getting approval from headquarters in Washington. All contacts with an asset should be recorded, he said, and the insertion in the file had to be approved by a supervisor.

Hunt said he had first approached Svetlana on June 18, 1980, because of her contacts with the consulate-general and her reported encouragement of emigrants to return home to Russia.

Hunt: She told me that all her contacts at that time were efforts to obtain visitors' visas for her and her husband, to return—at least for a visit—to the Soviet Union.

Schiff: Did she indicate [*sic*] her visit was also connected to a movie film enterprise?

Hunt: Yes. . . She told me. . .she had never returned since emigrating to the United States and had been unsuccessful so far in obtaining visas. . . .

Schiff: Did you ask Mrs. Ogorodnikova which Soviet officials she had been in contact with, in San Francisco or in the embassy?

Hunt: I did.

Schiff: And would she identify those individuals for you?

Hunt: Not at that time.

Hunt related that here had been surveillances of Consul Viktor Zenov when he had been chauffeured by Svetlana. She had told Hunt that "her association with him was solely. . . helping him set up an Olympic Games display at USC in February of '80." Hunt had also questioned her about Soviet attempts to persuade Vasiliy Ripak, a merchant seaman who had jumped ship, to return home. Ripak had been too frightened to do so.

Hunt said he had "made kindova preliminary approach to her to determine if she might be willing to meet again, of course with the idea of developing information from her about her Soviet official contacts and all that." She had "immediately realized what I was saying, and cut me off and said: 'I know what you want and I'm not interested [in cooperating] with the FBI at all.'"

He had not, he said, renewed acquaintance with Svetlana until about two years later—February 11, 1982. His version of this contact is different from hers and makes it clear that, however unwelcome his approach, it did not come as a surprise.

Schiff: Did you call her and ask her whether she would meet with you?
Hunt: Yes. I telephoned her at her apartment.
Schiff: What was said in the telephone conversation?
Hunt: Very brief. I identified myself and asked her if she remembered me from two years earlier. She said she did and she agreed that she would then meet with me. . . . I went to her apartment and. . .we drove to a nearby coffee shop.

There, Svetlana recounted her first return visit to Russia, which had taken place the year before.

Hunt: She told me that this was the first time. . .since her emigration that she [had] felt that her future was in the United States and that she should really look toward establishing herself here and possibly becoming a citizen. . . . She indicated [*sic*] that [her husband] was not in full agreement with her on this, that he still wanted to go back, but she had talked to him about this, [about] how impractical this would be.

She had also said that she had spent about four thousand dollars entertaining Soviet officials in her home, to promote her film business, with little success; she had felt that "she was being taken advantage of—that's the way she expressed it to me."
Hunt identified his four-page "105" report on the conversation.

Schiff: Did you think at that time that she had potential as an asset?
Hunt: Yes, I did. . . . I met her on March 5, April 14 and April 20 in a series of, really, get-acquainted meetings in an effort to determine if she could be used as an asset for the FBI. . . . [On April 20] she volunteered some information. . .about the consul-general, a man by the name of Chikvaidze. And then she said that she was having a lot of marital problems, and that if she left her husband, as she planned to do, she might consider meeting

with me in the future and maybe furnishing information that she knew would be of interest to me, or felt would be of interest to me. . . .

Schiff: Was this the first time she had discussed her unhappy marital situation?

Hunt: Yes, I believe it was.

Schiff: And, until she resolved that, she didn't want to meet with you again?

Hunt: Yes, she said that she just didn't have time and didn't want to get involved, but that, if that came about, she would consider it. . . . [But] she told me at the end of that meeting that she didn't want to see me again, and she requested that I not recontact her.

Schiff: Did you still feel that she had asset potential?

Hunt: Yes, I certainly did.

Again, with Hunt apparently covering himself with the FBI, and Svetlana protecting her film and visa privileges at the consulate-general, their versions of how they resumed contact differs. He says that she called him at the office on May 19 "and indicated [*sic*] that she wanted to see me." They had met in the Sears and Roebuck parking lot on Western Avenue.

Hunt: She told me that she was aware that I was attempting to contact her close friend, Nina Thomas, and she said: "I want to warn you about my friend Nina. Nina is promiscuous. She has been known to compromise men in an attempt to blackmail them. I just wanted you to know this." I said: "Well, thank you very much for the information," and I accepted it. . . . [Mrs. Thomas] was a former Soviet citizen who had gained U.S. citizenship through marriage. . . .

Schiff: When was the next meeting?

Hunt: It was around May 23 or 24 [at the] same parking lot. At that time, I made a rather direct appeal to her that I would be interested in talking to her about Soviet officials that she knew and was in contact with. . . . She said she'd have to think about it. . . . And so I said: "Fine. Think about it and let's meet again." And I set up another meeting at Sears and Roebuck for two days later.

Schiff: About this time, did you submit a memorandum requesting permission to open up a 134 file?

Hunt: Yes, I did.

Christensen had approved, Washington had approved, and John and Svetlana had met in Hunt's car on May 26. They had driven to a shopping center parking lot off Sunset Boulevard. Because Svetlana had said she supposed that John's car was bugged, she had insisted on there being no conversation until they were out of the vehicle. They had walked around for "a couple of hours at least."

Schiff: Did the matters that you discussed pertain to foreign counterintelligence?
Hunt: Yes, all of them.
Schiff: Did she tell you about her association with Viktor Zenov?
Hunt: I believe that was the meeting where she told me that she remembered the 1980 surveillance that led. . .to Anaheim, and remembered me as part of the surveillance team. She said that on that occasion she had met Consul Zenov at USC and had driven him to a Soviet exchange student's house in Los Angeles, and then to Anaheim Police Department, where Mr. Zenov made arrangements to bail another exchange student who had been arrested for shoplifting. She had driven him to these places.
Schiff: Did you attempt to take notes?
Hunt: I tried. . . . She said: "No, no notes [or] I'm going to quit talking to you." So, I put my pencil away. . . .
Schiff: Did she indicate [*sic*] that Mr. Zenov knew who you were?
Hunt: Yes. . . . Not only from that surveillance, but from a high-speed chase [in which] I had been involved with him on another date.

Hunt said he had questioned her about her involvement in the Karine Matevossian case, when she had accompanied a vice-consul called Kurov, whom she "believed was a high-ranking military officer, involved in intelligence work," the retired agent said.

She had told Hunt that she had refused a Soviet check for one thousand dollars for her work in finding Mrs. Matevossian. But when *émigrées* who had been interrogated by the FBI gave her the FBI calling cards they had received, Svetlana said she had passed them on to the consulate-general. Then, Hunt conceded that the conversation had not been as amicable as he had hinted.

Hunt: We concluded the walk around the block and I took her back to my Bureau car and drove her back to her own car, and as she was getting into her car, she started to cry. And she said: "I don't know why I told you all these things. I'm sorry I did it, and I don't ever want to see you again. If you [try] to contact me again, I'm going to call my lawyer." She drove away.
Schiff: Did she tell you that she was going to tell her lawyer that you were harassing her?
Hunt: Yes, she did.
Schiff: Did you expect to have any further contact with Mrs. Ogorodnikova?
Hunt: No, I really didn't.

However, Svetlana called him again. Like drug pushers, they again met in a parking lot, and John took her off to dinner. She had been carrying a briefcase, which she said had been given her by a Soviet vice-consul and which she had put in Hunt's trunk when they went into the restaurant. Then, back in the car, putting the briefcase on her lap, she had suggested they go to Simply Blues for a drink. There, she had gone to the toilet, and said: "While I'm gone, why don't you take a look at what's in the attaché case?"
The case contained "four wooden dolls. . .of Russian women in traditional costume. . . . She said that Vice Consul Prischepa had told her to deliver the attaché case to—these were her words—a U.S. businessman."

Schiff: Did you ask her what U.S. businessman?
Hunt: I sure did.
Schiff: Would she identify him for you?
Hunt: She would not. . . . [But] shortly after that, she took one of the dolls out of the case and said: "I want you to have this as a present from me." I said: "No, I don't want to accept it. And, furthermore, I don't want to get you [into] trouble. This appears to be a set, and you can't take one out of a set [without] some problems for yourself." But she insisted: "No, I can handle it." She insisted that I accept one.

Schiff: Did you?

Hunt: Yes, I did. . . . Then, we were a little ways on the sidewalk [at] Hollywood and Vine, and she threw her arms around me and said: "I love you. Can't we go some place?"

He had shaken her off, he said, and driven her back to her own car and followed her home. But she had driven past her apartment building to Mischa's Club. The next day, the FBI laboratory had found no hidden electronic device in the doll.

Schiff: The incident where Mrs. Ogorodnikova threw her arms around you and said she loved you and wanted you to "take me some place"—is that . . .in the written reports [of] June 6?

Hunt: No, it is not.

They met again on June 24, he said. In the meantime, she had been to the Soviet embassy in Washington to try to "salvage" her Soviet citizenship, while remaining in the United States.

Schiff: What did she tell you occurred [in] the Soviet embassy?

Hunt: She said she [had been] questioned for several hours by two officials and [asked] to do some unspecified work for them in the Los Angeles area. She indicated to me that she didn't know their names. . . . She told me she had turned them down.

Schiff: Did there come a time when Mrs. Ogorodnikova again brought up that visit to the Soviet embassy?

Hunt: Yes. . .on July 7, 1982.

Schiff: Did she give you the name of either of the Soviet officials?

Hunt: Yes. At that time, she told me a great deal more about the meeting [and identified] one of the two men. . . . She gave me the last name of Pukolov. . . . She told me that they had promised her that if she would cooperate and do some work for them in Los Angeles, they would take care of her citizenship desires and that they would also allow her son. . .to attend a. . . youth camp. . . .

Schiff: Did she tell you whether she was shown any photographs?

Hunt: She said they showed her several photographs and that. . .one of the people photographed could very well have been me. . . . She [had been] asked if she was "seeing" an FBI agent . . . .She said she [had been] shocked when they [had] asked her this and she [had] immediately assumed that her "good friend" Nina Thomas had reported her to the Soviet consulate [*sic*] as "seeing" me. And so she was frightened, and . . .said: "Well, yes, . . . .but I just know him socially. . . ."

Hunt said they had told her to "go home and think." If she changed her mind about working for the embassy, she should send them a signal by requesting three visas. They would then know that she had agreed to do something for them. "On July 7 . . . .she told me she [had] sent the signal."

Schiff: What did she say about that?
Hunt: Well, she said. . .that, based on my comments on the 24th, she immediately [had] sent the signal. . . .
Schiff: Were you seeing her on a social basis?
Hunt: No, I was not.
Schiff: Why had she told them that?
Hunt: To cover herself. She felt that she couldn't make a total denial because of what Nina Thomas perhaps had said. . . . I told her that. . .knowledge of [her] friendship with an FBI agent was certainly going to cause a stir at the. . .KGB [and] they were going to [try to] capitalize on this association.

It was at this point that Hunt, trying to turn his own rather ham-fisted attempt to "penetrate" the KGB through Svetlana into a Soviet initiative, became unwittingly hilarious as he related how he had advised Svetlana to "react."

Schiff: Did you give her any advice about how she might respond if she was contacted by the Soviet officials?
Hunt: Yes, I told her. . . "You shouldn't have said that. You should have just made a complete denial. . . What you should do now is tell them this is very infrequent. You don't really get along with the guy [and] it's probably not going to continue at all."
Schiff: Was this an effort to de-escalate the situation?
Hunt: It was.

\*

How improbable all this was is reflected in Hunt's testimony, a minute later, that Svetlana had called him on August 11 to say she had received two calls from Belyakov.

Hunt: He made some reference to her FBI friend and indicated she should come up to the consulate right away. . . .
Schiff: Did you find her aggressive and intelligent?
Hunt: Yes, she was.

Belyakov, however, had postponed her visit while Moscow evaluated the situation, Hunt said. This, of course, was the point where Grishin and Myshkov, the new consul-general, were puzzling over Hunt's initiative, before finally deciding against trying to turn the obvious scam to their own advantage, while possibly encouraging him to think that he had made his mark.

Hunt: She told me she could still go if she wanted to. . . . By then, I was rehearsing her on things that she could say, [but] finally I said: "Svetlana, I don't think you should go." And she said: "I don't want to go." So I said: "Let's stop this right now." I didn't think she was prepared. I thought, quite frankly, she'd screw it up, to be honest, [that] she'd go. . .there and say the wrong thing. So I made the decision [to stop], and she immediately agreed. . . . On August 24, 1982, she told me about discussions she had had with [Belyakov] that she had not yet told me about. . . . [He had] chastised her for getting involved with an FBI agent in any manner. . . . [He thought] she was acting as an informant for the FBI. [She said he] instructed her to disassociate herself with [*sic*] me.

Belyakov, unbeknownst to Hunt, had thus set the ground for making Svetlana feel that she had done something wrong for which she would have to atone; when she reported this to Hunt, he would be expected to reveal his hand more clearly, and San Francisco could play it by ear from there.

Schiff: Now, at that time, did you feel that she had divided and shifting loyalties?
Hunt: Oh, yes. . . . I recall a significant meeting [with her] on September 14. . . . She told me about receiving a telephone call

from a consulate official indicating [*sic*] that she should come to
. . . San Francisco right away. . . . It was at that meeting or a
subsequent meeting [that] she indicated [*sic*] that she had
agreed with them that she would report to the Soviet consulate
in San Francisco, although she still had a lot of reservations in
her own mind that we discussed at some length. . . . [I said that]
if she was interested in pursuing this film business or visitors'
visas, she would probably have to respond, [and] if she did, I
said we would try to help her arm herself for the type of
questions that she would get from them, and to try to protect
her as best we could along these lines, to see that she was not
uncovered as an FBI informant. . . . She told me she was going
to go on the 23rd of September. . . . She told me that during the
call on the 14th with Belyakov, he had asked if she was still
seeing her FBI friend. . . . He said: "We find this hard to believe,
and we want you to bring a photograph with you of the two of
you together." Well, I told her we weren't going to do that.

Schiff: During this conversation of the 17th, was she set on
going or was she still somewhat hesitant?

Hunt: Well, she was hesitant up to the moment she stepped
on the airplane on the 23rd.

Schiff: What advice did you give her with respect to. . . what
. . . to say?

Hunt: Some things. . .that would help her explain how she
could be seeing an FBI agent [while] not being an informant for
the FBI. . . . I told her that it was all right with the FBI if she said
that I initially contacted her on a routine follow-up investigation
concerning her trip to the Soviet Union, and that thereafter I had
contacted her a few times, taken her out for lunch or a coupla
drinks.

Schiff: Did you tell her that she could also tell them that you
enjoyed getting around, enjoyed having drinks. . .and things of
that nature?

Hunt: I told her to say: "He's the kind of guy that seems to be
getting out a bit. . .and he's always good for a coupla drinks or
dinner or something like that." This was the way that she could
explain how she could be meeting with an FBI agent who was
married—and I told her it was all right to say that, too, that they
probably knew it.

Schiff: What were the purposes. . .in telling her what. . .to say?

Hunt: Well, there were three or four goals. . . . One, as I mentioned, [was] to try to protect her a bit. . .because I wanted to keep her as an informant. Another was to assess her further . . . . The other goals. . .were. . .that. . .if they asked questions about either the FBI itself, the Los Angeles office, or me in particular. . .we could be in a position to determine what their interests really were. . . . This is always an intelligence goal, to find out what the other side thinks they want, or what they don't have. . . .

Schiff: Was part of your purpose to determine how the Soviets might target an agent?

Hunt: Yes, that's correct.

Hunt had thus downplayed the significance of his ultimately unsuccessful mission, just as Belyakov had reacted by initially pretending that he was annoyed with his compatriot and would punish her. The objective, Hunt had told the court, was to make the unschooled Svetlana the double agent—even though she was already known to be frequenting an FBI agent—and this Hunt plan had been approved by Christensen and by FBI headquarters in Washington. All that was needed now was for Belyakov to convince this simple woman that his superiors had decided after all that they were delighted, and that she could be used as a Soviet agent. But Svetlana apparently sensed that she was being used as a cat's-paw for both sides.

Hunt: She finally said that she was going to go, but. . .continued to express reservations right up to the door of the airplane, really.

Schiff: Did you offer to have the FBI pay for her plane fare to San Francisco?

Hunt: Yes. She refused it.

Schiff: After she went to the consulate on the 23rd, did you meet with her upon her return to Los Angeles?

Hunt: Yes. That was the evening of the 23rd.

Schiff: Did you, in fact, pick her up at the airport?

Hunt: I did. . . . [But] she refused to discuss [the trip] in the car. . .[so]. . .I drove from the airport to the marina and we went to a restaurant. . . . She told me she was interviewed by Vice Consul Belyakov for about, I think, three or four hours. . .and that there were questions asked about me. . . . She said that

Belyakov instructed her to do nothing further until they got back to her. . . . The only thing she was cautioned about was not to lose this friend in the FBI. . . . She was told: "If you fail in this duty, you will never see the Soviet Union again." She indicated [*sic*] that she had told [Belyakov] that she would be willing to work with them and do whatever they had in mind, and would stand by for further instructions. . . .

Hunt's testimony thus far had been more helpful to Svetlana than to Miller. Hunt had conceded that he had, in effect, urged Svetlana to encourage the Russians to believe that she would be *their* mole, and that she had obeyed his instructions. This, of course, throws any case against Svetlana into a totally different light from that of the 1985 process.

Schiff: How was her demeanor?
Hunt: She was calm, much calmer than when she went up .... I debriefed her then, took notes and talked about the trip. . . . She said: "I've done this much for you, the least you could do is to buy me a dinner." She says: "My friend, Lucy, is going to be up at Mischa's. I'd like to go there for dinner with her." [So, we] went in [and] sat down at a table with Lucy Privo and Lucy Privo's friend. We had a couple of drinks and dinner.
Schiff: Was Lucy Privo a Russian *émigrée* who also resided in Los Angeles?
Hunt: Yes. . . . [And] there was a photographer on the premises going from table to table taking Polaroid shots of customers. . .and I think it was Lucy who said: "Take their picture," meaning, you know, Mrs. Ogorodnikova and myself. And so I says to her, I says: "Get ridda this guy." So [Svetlana] . . .moved to another table [and] said: "Take my picture," and he did. . . . As the evening went along, I became a little nervous about being out. . .and I made a call to home, and there were some family problems. . . . So I said: "I've got to leave right now. Let's go." And finally she stood up and accompanied me outside to my Bureau car.

Schiff discreetly didn't ask what the "family problem" was when John called Earlene and said he was in a night club with Svetlana. Why Hunt denied having let himself be (or having been unable to prevent himself from being) photographed with

Svetlana at Mischa's isn't clear. The photograph had been discovered in the search of the Ogorodnikova apartment five years before.

Schiff: Did you meet her the next day, September 24, 1982?
Hunt: I did.... I picked Svetlana up and took her over to Santa Monica where I was joined by my supervisor, Bryce Christensen. . . . We discussed her trip to the consulate the preceding day. . . . Mr. Christensen certainly was pleased, and. . .he gave that impression.
Schiff: Did you have any further contacts with Mrs. Ogorodnikova in 1982?
Hunt: At one time, September or October, I called her one morning to set up a coffee meet [*sic*]. . . . In talking about where to meet, she says: "Oh, let's make it a hotel today." She says: "I'll even pay." I says: "Oh, c'mon. Cudditout."
Schiff: During the period of time in which you met with Mrs. Ogorodnikova, did she begin to form what appeared to be an emotional attachment to you?
Hunt: I would say: Quite possible.
Schiff: Did she become affectionate with you at times?
Hunt: Yes.
Schiff: Was that manifested by her putting her arm around your shoulder and that type of thing?
Hunt: Yes, it was.
Schiff: Did she confide in you, at some point, problems that she was having with her husband?
Hunt: Well, she had right along mentioned problems with her husband from, I think it was April 20th; she had mentioned that, you know, she was not getting along well with her husband and wanted to leave him, but just didn't know how to do it.
Schiff: Did you ever meet her husband?
Hunt: I never met him.
Schiff: Did you report to your supervisor her growing emotional ties to you?
Hunt: Yes, I did.
Schiff: Did you specifically report the two occasions at Simply Blues [when] she threw her arms around you and said: "I love you"? And the [remark about going to a hotel room at her expense] on the phone?
Hunt: No, I didn't.

Schiff: At some point, did you recommend that another agent be assigned to Svetlana Ogorodnikova because of her growing affection for you?

Hunt: Yes, I requested in writing that another agent be assigned to take over the further handling of Svetlana. That was in October of '82.

Instead, Hunt said, he had held on to his lovelorn asset, and also introduced her to his wife and other members of his family. After that, he said, contacts had become less frequent; it had been Svetlana who had wanted to preserve the relationship.

Schiff: At some point in late '82, was a decision made between you and your superior, Mr. Christensen, that you should discontinue contacts with Mrs. Ogorodnikova and [that] her role as a potential asset should be closed?

Hunt: Well, yes.

Schiff: Did part of that decision relate to concerns you had about where Svetlana Ogorodnikova's loyalties really lay?

Hunt: That was part of it. And then, also, just a lack of good intelligence information being reported to me. . . . I told her [about breaking the contact] then and on several other occasions, as early as October and November.

Schiff: In late '82 or early '83, was her file formally closed?

Hunt: Yes. I. . .closed it. . .formally on the 23rd of January of '83.

Schiff: You mentioned that she gave you that doll. Did she give you any other gifts?

Hunt: Yes, she did. . . . Three *velours* shirts. . .a couple of dress shirts. . . .And then there was some Russian candy, and. . .a couple of ounces of caviar. And she gave my granddaughters each a little Russian doll. There might have been a few other things like that.

Schiff: Did she give you a phonograph record?

Hunt: She gave me a couple of phonograph records, yes.

Schiff: Did you report any of these gifts to Mr. Christensen?

Hunt: I told him about the *velours* shirts. . . . But I didn't report them all. . . .

Schiff: Did you give her some gifts?

Hunt: Yes. . .I gave her a silk scarf and. . .my wife and I picked out a little gold pendant. . .and I gave that to her. . . .

Schiff: Did you ever become physically involved with her?

Hunt: No, I did not.

Schiff: Is becoming physically involved with an asset permitted by the FBI?

Hunt: I don't believe it is. . . .

Schiff: Did you ever offer her money, Bureau money?

Hunt: Frequently.

Schiff: Would she accept?

Hunt: Never. . . . I assured her there [would be] no problem; it would be cash. And she just said: "No, I don't want to do that." I definitely wanted her to accept money. I wanted to get her involved in the FCI program as a paid informant. This was, you know, a high priority for me. . . .

Schiff: Did you meet her on October 20, 1983?. . . Was that the last time?

Hunt: I did. [It was] the last time. . . .

Schiff: How many contacts were there after her file was closed in January 1983?

Hunt: There were exactly six.

Schiff: And were these contacts that she initiated?

Hunt: Each one, yes.

Schiff: When was the first contact after the file was closed?

Hunt: January, 1983, when she telephoned my supervisor, Bryce Christensen. . . . She was requesting to meet with him to complain about me.

Schiff: And did you accompany Mr. Christensen to [the meeting]?

Hunt: I did, yes. . . . We walked down to Westwood. . . . She was upset that I was there, and told Mr. Christensen that she wanted to see *him*. . .and so I left. . . . The next meeting was around the 12th or 14th of March, 1983.

Schiff: Was that also based on a call. . .from her?

Hunt: Yes. . . . She called me at the office and said she wanted to say goodbye; she was going to the hospital in San Diego and might not make it out again. [She said] she had a rare blood disease. . . . She called me back the next day.

Schiff: At some point thereafter, did you meet her to go to the doctor?

Hunt: Yes. . . . It was, I think, the next day. . .around the [middle] of March. . . . I questioned her about her medical problem and found out where the doctor was located, and had her drive me by and show me the doctor's office. And I said: "Well, let's go in and talk to him." She said: "No, I'll call and make an appointment." I said okay. . . . And that brought on the second meeting. . . . We went into the doctor's office. She went in and talked to the doctor, and then I was called in. . . . [The doctor] said she did not have a rare blood disease [but] a chronic blood condition.

Schiff: Was that anemia, essentially?

Hunt: Yes. . . . He said it was not fatal.

Schiff: Did you report the visit to the doctor?

Hunt: No, I didn't. . . . I looked at this, really, as a personal thing. . . .

Schiff: Did you have a phone conversation with her after this?

Hunt: Yes. . . . The next morning, March 16, 1983. . . . She called me at the office. . . . She was screaming. . . . I assumed she was intoxicated. . . . I was having trouble following her. . . . I tried to find out where she was calling from. She was yelling. Finally, another person came on the line. . .a woman by the name of Raisa Buketova. Raisa said: "Everything is okay. I'm here with Svetlana at my house and she's been drinking," or something like that. . . . Later on, I got a call from Raisa, who said: "Can you come over and help me? I can't control the woman. . .and I don't know what to do." And I could hear [Svetlana] screaming in the background. And I said: "Yeah, I will."

Schiff: Did you get Mr. Christensen's approval to go over there?

Hunt: Yes. . . . I suggested [that] perhaps my wife and I should go over and talk to her. And [Christensen] said: "That's a good idea, and also take [Special Agent] Nancy Smith with you. . . ." When we arrived, my wife and I went inside, and [Svetlana] was as calm as I am right now. . . . I said: "What in the world is going on here?" And she said: "Well, you know, my husband hates me, my son hates me, they hate me at the Russian consulate-general, and it's all your fault, you know." And I think she made some reference to her trip to the Soviet Union. . . . She told me she was Premier Andropov's daughter. . . . My wife had been talking to Raisa. Then, my wife was talking to Svetlana. . . . All of a sudden, Svetlana says to my wife: "Let's see if we can get John to take us both out to dinner at the marina."

Schiff: During the conversation of the 16th, did Mrs. Ogorodnikova say anything about her son and her husband's plans?

Hunt: Yes. I forgot that. She said that one of the other things that was bothering her was that her husband wanted to send her son to school in the Soviet Union, and she opposed this. And he wanted her to use her existing contacts at the consulate to bring this about.

Schiff: Now, you mentioned some irrational things she said about being the daughter of Andropov. . . . Did it appear to you in late or mid-'83 that she was having some emotional problems?

Hunt: Yes, it did.

Schiff: I think you mentioned [that] she was also intoxicated at times?

Hunt: Well, yes. . . . I ended up taking her and Raisa and Raisa's daughter, and they stopped and picked up Matvei at Svetlana's house, and we all . . . met down at the marina and had dinner.

Schiff: When was the next contact with Mrs. Ogorodnikova?

Hunt: September 11. . . . I came home, on a Sunday, and there was a call from the duty agent at the office. . . . He had been contacted either by Mrs. Ogorodnikova or Raisa [who had asked] that I give them a call at Raisa's house. I did. She asked if I could come over and talk to her. . . . She said: "I've got a lot of problems, and I need your advice. . . . Please—both you and your wife—would you come over?" After contacting my supervisor, Mr. Auer, and receiving his concurrence and permission, we did.

Schiff: At Raisa Buketova's house?

Hunt: Yes. . . . Svetlana told me that she had gone to the consulate on September 8th . . . three days earlier. She made some reference to a five hundred dollar debt, and being beat [*sic*] up. I wasn't quite sure whether she meant at the consulate or somewhere else in San Francisco. And she also told me that she had been questioned by a consular official and [asked] to make some contacts in the Los Angeles area of people whose names she had been given by the consular officials.

Schiff: Was she supposed to do this to earn some kind of treatment for her son?

Hunt: Yes. She said that Nikolaiy had been to the Soviet Union in, I think, August or September of '83, and she said the purpose was to enroll Matvei in a school. She also said that she was advised [*sic*] by the consular people . . . to go to Moscow herself in October to receive some type of training. . . . It was my general impression that it was some kind of intelligence-type training, but I'm not clear enough to—I'd have to refresh my memory.

Schiff: When was the final meeting?

Hunt: October 20, 1983, just a little over a month later. . . . She called me at the office on the 19th, and she was again screaming and yelling at me, and demanding that I meet her. And I said: "I'm not going to do anything. . . . Call me back when you can be decent on the phone." And I hung up. . . . I think it was the next day [that] she called back, the 20th, and said that she had to talk to me about a trip that she had made to Moscow. And I said: "Well, fine, we'll come out and talk with you." And she says: "I want you to come out alone." And I says: "No way." And she says: "Okay, I agree." And so Special Agent Nancy Smith and I drove out to West L.A. and met with her.

Schiff: Did you go to a coffee shop there?

Hunt: Yes. . . . She did most of the talking. . . . She said that she had spent about a week in Moscow and had just returned. And I said: "Well, what was the purpose of the trip?" And she said it was to enroll Matvei in school. And she went on to say that while she was there, she was questioned four or five different times by an individual whom she assumed was a KGB officer. She was questioned about the United States and about her knowledge of the FBI and about me.

Schiff: Did she tell you who questioned her?

Hunt: Yes. Vladimir Mikhailovitch is the name she gave me
. . . .

Schiff: Turning ahead to October 1984, were you interviewed by FBI agents assigned to the inspection staff at that time?

Hunt: Yes, I was. . . . [They wanted] to discuss with me allegations that Svetlana Ogorodnikova had made about me to my supervisor a year and a half earlier. . . . In July, 1983. . . .

Schiff: Were you advised of your rights?

Hunt: Yes.

Schiff: Was this a criminal or administrative advice?

Hunt: It was a criminal advice.

Schiff: Did you read and sign rights?

Hunt: I did.

Schiff: Did you describe to the interviewers the course of your FBI meetings with Svetlana Ogorodnikova, as you've described them today.

Hunt: Substantially, yes.

Schiff: Did you address accusations by Svetlana . . . when she indicated [*sic*] that she was sleeping in churches because she had nowhere to stay, that you had threatened to kill her, that she told you when Brezhnev was going to die, that she had slept with Premier Andropov, that you [had] promised to marry her, that she was dying of cancer—these allegations and others?

Hunt: Those and others, yes.

Schiff: And [after] this interview, were you given a statement to sign?

Hunt: Yes.

Schiff: Did that interview result in a twenty-page, single-spaced report?

Hunt: Yes. A "302". . . .

Schiff: In the "302," was it recorded . . . that in one of your teletypes you had suggested that Svetlana might [become] a double agent, but that you didn't rule yourself out as a possible double agent?

Hunt: That's one of the passages I took exception to.

Schiff: Did the "302" also record that Svetlana Ogorodnikova wanted to turn the relationship into a purely sexual relationship?

Hunt: Yes.

Schiff: Was that an accurate statement?

Hunt: No, that was an absolutely inaccurate, misleading statement.

Schiff: During the last trial, in connection with the interview by Stukey and Torrence, were you asked if you could take a polygraph examination?

Hunt: Yes.

Schiff: Were you able to take a polygraph?

Hunt: I was not . . . because of my arrhythmic heart condition, that would influence the machine.

Schiff: Did the heart condition later require the placement of a pacemaker?

Hunt: Yes.

*

Levine did not ask for proof of Hunt's arrhythmia. Perhaps Miller and other colleagues knew about it. More curiously, he did not require proof that an arrhythmia would jeopardize a polygraph test. Given the doubts that Levine, Miller and the investigators Sayers and Kelley—both former FBI agents— entertained bout Hunt's veracity, this would perhaps seem to have been a lapse of judgment on the defense team's part. Could not an arrhythmia (irregular heartbeat) be monitored at the same time as a polygraph test? If the pacemaker had since corrected the condition, this would mean that Hunt could take a polygraph test as well as anyone else. Perhaps it was decided that the courts had little faith in such tests, anyway.

Schiff: Moving ahead to July 1989: Did you at any time ask your attorney to write a letter to the director of the FBI?

Hunt: Yes, I did. . . . The primary purpose was my concern about things that had happened on the squad while Mr. Miller was employed. . . . I wanted . . . an in-depth, serious investigation. . .into these matters, and I offered my assistance.

Schiff: Was one of [your] concerns with allowing Mr. Miller access to classified documents?

Hunt: Yes, it was.

Schiff: Did your letter express your opinion about the FBI's handling of the investigation?

Hunt: Well, I think the general tone of the letter was that there [had been] things that [had] not [been] done properly, and some things that, in my opinion, have not been done yet, and that there were problems yet to be acknowledged and corrected.

Schiff: Did your attorney's letter also make reference to evidence which you believed may have been withheld from the defense?

Hunt: Yes. . . . That would be information in the "134" file that I was thinking about, as well as the information developed during the course of the FBI investigation of Miller. . . .

Schiff: Turning to. . .the "134" file, what evidence do you believe was improperly withheld from [that] file? Your Honor, we may get into a classified area.

The next thirty-one pages of the transcript are missing, suggesting that the court was then *in camera* for more than an hour. Then, the questioning resumed as follows:

\*

Schiff: Were you a participant in a meeting on May 24, 1984, in Mr. Auer's office?

Hunt: Yes. . . . I returned to the office one afternoon, and I was called [in] either by Mr. Auer or Mr. Miller or both.

Schiff: Had you ever had a [prior] conversation with the defendant about Svetlana Ogorodnikova?

Hunt: No. . . . One of the first things. . .Mr. Miller. . .said [was]: "Guess whom I saw today?" And then he went on. . .that he had met with Svetlana Ogorodnikova. . . . He said: "Well, I received a telephone call a couple of months [ago] from a woman with a heavy accent who wouldn't identify herself, but [who] indicated [*sic*] she wanted to furnish information or help the FBI." She agreed to meet. So he says: "I proceeded [*sic*] to Westwood and met her and learned that it was Svetlana Ogorodnikova."

Schiff: Now, he said that [in] approximately March 1984, he received a call from what appeared to be the same woman?

Hunt: Yes.

Schiff: Had she identified herself in the prior call?

Hunt: No. He said he made the identification of the first call on the basis of the second call, when he was able to identify her positively. . . . He said he had made a meet [*sic*] with her in Westwood. . .and learned who it was. . . . She identified herself by name and showed him her driver's license. . . . I said: "Well, what did she say about me this time?" He said: "Nothing, really." He went on to explain that she [had] started talking about some of her personal problems. And he said: "When I started telling her about mine, she forgot all about her own." He [said they had] had lunch and she had even offered to pay. . . . [The conversation lasted] roughly fifteen minutes.

Schiff: How did the meeting conclude?

Hunt: It was my general sense of things. . .that she had been instructed by Mr. Miller to call back and contact him if she made some final decision as to whether she wanted to continue meeting, and maybe [doing] something for, the FBI, and that he was waiting for this incoming call before anything else was to be done.

Schiff: Did Mr. Auer indicate [*sic*] that he would decide what would happen if she called back?

Hunt: Yes. I think that was a decision yet to be made. It would depend somewhat on what conversation Mr. Miller would have with her in the future.

Schiff: After that conversation in Mr. Auer's office, did you have a further conversation with the defendant on May 24, 1984?

Hunt: Yes, I believe it was the same day. . .in his office on the 16th floor. . .[for] at least a half-hour, perhaps longer. . . . I discussed with him the pitfalls of handling Svetlana Ogorodnikova.

Schiff: Did you tell him at one point that you thought she had excellent potential as an asset?

Hunt: Yes, I did.

Schiff: What did you tell him that the problems were?

Hunt: Well, I don't remember everything I said, but I did specifically refer to the allegations she'd made against me. . . . I said: "You could end up in the same spot that I'm in."

Schiff: Did you ever discuss the San Francisco proposal that you mentioned earlier?

Hunt: No, not that I can recall.

At this point, Hunt seems to an observer to be loyally not wishing to load the unfortunate Svetlana, who would not be serving a long term of imprisonment if she had not been forced to meet with Hunt. Since Schiff's questions relate in part to hearsay—what Hunt says Miller told him—and also to what Hunt had told Miller, Hunt has been allowed to express opinions that would not otherwise be evidence. At the same time, Hunt implies that Miller had not been told about Hunt's own attempted "dangle" of the year before, although this was obviously generally known to the double-agent team of FCI-1, and therefore to Miller.

Schiff was more concerned with trying to show that Miller "knew" that Hunt's swallow was actually the KGB's:

Schiff: Did you express an opinion to the defendant [about] whether. . .Svetlana Ogorodnikova might currently be working with the KGB?

Hunt: Yes. Referring to the allegations that she made against me, I believe I mentioned that "for all I know, these were inspired by the KGB. . . ." He confirmed my general impression from the earlier meeting by telling me that he was going to wait for her call. . . . And I said: "She'll call."

Schiff: Did he tell you that he had already made plans to meet her later that afternoon?

Hunt: He did not.

Schiff: Did Mr. Miller ever tell you that he saw Svetlana Ogorodnikova again?

Hunt: He never did [although] I had several very short conversations with him over the next week or so.

Schiff then led Hunt through testimony about another *émigré*—the so-called Sasha Memo. Svetlana, Hunt said, had brought up Sasha during one of Miller's two authorized meetings with her. She had seemed to be threatening Sasha, to whom she owed money, to "lay off her" (Hunt's words) because of her friendship with an American counterintelligence figure— Miller. Hunt recalled telling Miller: "Look what she's doing already. You've got to be careful of this woman. You're getting in over your head." Hunt recalled that he had opposed assigning Miller to Svetlana.

Hunt: I did offer some words of advice to Mr. Auer. . . . I said: "Gary, how can you be thinking of opening and assigning this case to anybody after what you've written yourself, and what the rest of us have said about her?" And I says: "And particularly Miller."

Schiff: Did Mr. Auer thereafter ever reopen the file [of] Svetlana Ogorodnikova?

Hunt: No.

Schiff: Did he ever reassign that matter to the defendant?

Hunt: No.

Hunt testified that Miller had apparently taken a memo Hunt had written about Svetlana's shortcomings from Hunt's desk and later returned it without telling him. (In cross-examination, he was to be caught short on this later, by Levine.) Hunt said he had mentioned Svetlana to Miller "four, five, six times at least" in late May 1984. "I'd say: 'Has she called yet?' He'd say: 'Not yet.' And I would always say: 'She will.'"

*

Schiff: Did he ever tell you that he was meeting with her at this period?
Hunt: He did not.
Schiff: Sleeping with her?
Hunt: He did not. . . .

Hunt said he had had two telephone calls from Svetlana in 1984; but these do not appear to be the calls that she unwaveringly recalls making to Hunt before and after every meeting with Miller, on his instructions—in one of which he supposedly complained about her discussing him (Hunt) with Miller, and in another described Miller's and Svetlana's plans to go to Vienna together as "crazy." The defense knew nothing of these calls, or alleged calls—and the opportunity to call Svetlana, then reexamine Hunt, was missed. From Miller's point of view, anything that showed that Hunt's evidence was defective or selective would have been useful. Referring to the two calls Hunt admitted receiving, Schiff asked if these were both in August. Hunt said they were, and that they related to Svetlana's emotional breakdown because he had dropped her.

Hunt: The first was [on] August 2. . . . She said she was calling from her "boyfriend's" house, and she pleaded with me to help her. . . . I said no, I wouldn't do that. . . . I told her I was real busy . . .and could she call me the next day, and I specified a time. She said she would. . . . Well, she called, and I had already alerted Shelby Durr, the agent who sat right behind me [in the squad room], to expect the call and tape it on my behalf, which he did . . . . Then, three or four days later. . .she called me back. . .[on] roughly the sixth, seventh or eighth of August, 1984. And it was a very strange conversation. . . . She would be conversing with two different people [at her end]. It was quiet; there was no background noise [and] there were no answers coming from anybody else. And she was yelling and berating one of these two people. . . . And she would pose questions, and I was listening and there would be nothing coming back! It was an empty room, or at least that was my impression. And then she finally said: "That's right! Get out of here and don't come back!" And then she turned to the other—I think, mythical—listener and said: "Jimmy, close the door, please. Thank you very much." And there was some conversation to Jimmy, but never a response.

Schiff: Did she sound intoxicated on the phone?

Hunt: I'm not sure [she] was intoxicated. She sounded disturbed.

Schiff: Between October of '83 and these two calls in August of '84, did you have any other telephone contact with her?

Hunt: There were a coupla calls from her. . .in November [and] December of '83.

Schiff: What was discussed in the November call?

Hunt: That was also an unusual call. . . . She was talking very rapidly and, I think, mentioned that she was going to the embassy in Washington, to the hospital in San Diego [and] to Russia. And it was all in the same sentence. And as I remember now, I hung up on her. . . .

Schiff: Did she ever mention the defendant to you in any of your meetings and telephone calls?

Hunt: Never.

Having thus specifically denied Svetlana's insistence that she reported all her contacts with Miller to Hunt, on Hunt's instructions, and stressed that all efforts to reestablish contact between Svetlana and the FBI had been hers, Hunt had helped lay the foundations of the prosecution's case that her efforts were for the KGB rather than for emotional reasons—despite Hunt's evidence earlier in the day about her hysterical calls and her blaming him not only for jeopardizing her relations with the consulate-general, but also with her husband and son.

Hunt said he had marked the transcript of Svetlana's call—which Special Agent Durr had monitored—for routing to Miller.

Hunt: At that time, Mr. Miller had been temporarily reassigned to Santa Ana for the Olympic Games. And I, again thinking of this situation where he was supposed to wait for a call from her, thought that he should know about this—what appeared to be, to me—erratic pattern of behavior. I thought this memorandum should be routed to him in Santa Ana so he would be up to speed on what's going on, in the event he received this telephone call. . . . I told Gary that I [had] added Miller's name to this [memo]. . . .

Schiff: Did he at any time indicate [*sic*] that he had been in contact with Svetlana Ogorodnikova, after he returned from Santa Ana?

Hunt: No, he did not.

## *iv*

The next day, Hunt returned to the stand to be questioned by Levine for the defense. He said he had had "probably thirty hours" of consultations with Schiff before appearing, and that he had earlier been questioned about his conduct in the case by Stukey and Torrence. The questioning soon came to Hunt's angry letter to the FBI director, William Sessions, in July 1989, which Levine wanted offered in evidence. Schiff objected, on the grounds that opinion is not evidence. Takasugi agreed.

Hunt was then questioned about a discussion he had had with Gary Auer about Miller's suitability for handling a Russian asset.

Hunt: I said [to Auer]: "You're going to put a paper trail on this thing. The man doesn't belong in the squad, and he's going to be moved. I think you're going to have to take some formal action and start writing him up." [Auer] said something like: "My memo has walked back to me." [The memo] had been walked back and was not wanted in the front office, which meant that it was to be destroyed. . . . That was my impression . . . .

Moments later, Levine turned to the questioning of Hunt by Miller's investigator, the avuncular Al Sayers, and Svetlana's investigator, the Sam Spade-ish Dale Kelley, both former FBI special agents. Hunt agreed that he had tried to bar his two former colleagues from his home. Levine came back to the subject of Hunt's letter to Sessions.

Levine: Yesterday, you told us that among the things that you were criticizing was something to do with a psychiatrist or psychologist coming here to Los Angeles; do you remember telling us that, yesterday?

Hunt: I remember my testimony.... It was my understanding that it was a psychologist. ... I would say [he came] a couple of weeks before the arrest, approximately....

Levine: Did you ever see or talk to that person?

Hunt: Yes, I did.

Levine: Did that [man] sit down and talk to you concerning Mrs. Ogorodnikova?

Hunt: Yes, that's how I knew he was there. ...

Levine: Did [he] tell you he was here to assist the interviewing agents?

Hunt: That was my sense of why he was there. ...

Judge Takasugi: I think the concern I have is whether the psychologist suggested a method of interrogating Mr. Miller.

Levine: Or any suggestions on how to approach him or...what his weaknesses might be [under interrogation], which were things we argued to two juries that didn't know about it. ... I would also like the name of the psychologist so that we can interview him in this court.

Takasugi: What is the psychologist's name?

Schiff: I have no idea. And I have no idea whether any psychiatrist [*sic*] played any role in the interviews.

Schiff then began to raise objections, asking that the court summon the interviewing agents, instead, which had Levine bristling.

Levine: Your Honor, what Mr. Schiff is asking the court to do is to rely on witnesses whom we have alleged are biased, whom we now know omitted something important from a "302" report relating to Mr. Hunt. And we're not to be told what potential input a psychologist had on various people who interviewed Miller over five days, [when] we have argued to two juries that he was manipulated into making statements that weren't true. Psychologically [harmed]—not physically harmed; we didn't allege that, [except] by the length of the interviews.

Schiff: That contention has been rejected by two juries—

Levine: —who never heard from the psychologist.

Schiff: There is no evidence the psychologist played any role.

Takasugi: Let's do it this way. Please ascertain the name of the psychologist and submit it to the court *in camera*, what instructions the psychologist gave to the interviewing agents, if any, as it related to Mr. Miller.

Schiff: Very well, Your Honor. . . .

Levine: And at or around the time you had this meeting with the psychologist, the impression you had was that the arrests of both Mr. Miller and Mrs. Ogorodnikova [were] contemplated?

Hunt: We were generating information and evidence at that time that has subsequently been presented in these proceedings. And it was my opinion that there was probably—or [that] certainly this could result in the arrests.

Levine: You knew that the name of the operation was Whipworm, didn't you?

Hunt: I knew that, at some point. . . .

Levine: In connection with some of the criticism that you had of how the FBI had handled Mr. Miller, [you said] that you considered him to be a classic recruitable person. Do you remember that?

Hunt: Yes, I remember that.

Levine: In other words, in the 1983-84 time frame [when] Mr. Auer was the squad supervisor, you considered Mr. Miller a security risk. Is that right?

Hunt: Well, probably the entire time. That would include Mr. Christensen's time. . .as squad supervisor.

Levine: Did you ever discuss with Mr. Auer the impression you had. . .regarding the things you told us about yesterday: That he was in debt, that he wasn't a good agent, that he shouldn't have access to classified information, things of that nature?

Hunt: I [told] him things such as: "He's a bad agent; he's not a productive agent; he's not anyone the Bureau can rely on; he's a person who should not be an FBI agent," that sort of thing.

Levine: Did he tell you he had discussed those things with Mr. Christensen?

Hunt: [He said] he wanted. . .to get him off the squad if he could. He was agreeing with me. . . .

Levine: Do you know that Mr. Christensen, Mr. Bretzing and Mr. Auer have stated that they did not consider Mr. Miller a security risk?

Schiff: Objection, Your Honor. There's no relevance as to whether this witness knows what other people may have said.

Levine: There's relevance if it affects his opinion.

Schiff: We're not asking his opinion. That's not evidence.

Takasugi: You may answer that question.

Levine: Do you know that they have expressed that?

Hunt: No. . . .

Levine: Yesterday. . .you told us about some memoranda that you felt we didn't receive—the defense—and some information that your "302" reports that Mr. Stukey and Mr. Torrence wrote that was omitted. Do you remember, generally, that subject matter?

Hunt: Yes, I do. . . .

Levine: With respect to the three memoranda that you told us about yesterday, did you, in 1984 while you were still an FBI agent, see those three memoranda in Mrs. Ogorodnikova's "134" file in their unredacted [i.e., unedited] form?

Hunt: Yes, I did. . . .

Levine: Were there any discussions in 1984 or 1985 with the first group of prosecutors?

Hunt: There was some discussion, at least about one of the documents. . . . The third one.

Levine: With whom?

Hunt: Mr. Kendall.

Levine: Did you tell Mr. Kendall. . .that the document was no longer in the "134" file?

Hunt: No. There was a reference that it had been excluded from the information being used at the trial. . . . I made that initial assumption because it wasn't in my copy of the "134" file that was being used for trial purposes. It had been removed from that set of files. . . .

Levine: Did Mr. Kendall discuss with you, or did you discuss with him. . .the removal of the document?

Hunt: My comment generally was that I thought this was an important document and I was wondering what action, if any, the defense would take or how they would use this.

Levine: What did [Kendall] say? Did he say whether or not it was going to be disclosed to the defense?

Hunt: I'm not sure that I pinned him down on that, exactly.

Levine: Did you have discussions with anyone else in the U.S. Attorney's Office, either Mr. Bonner or Mr. Hayman, in the

'85-'86 time frame, concerning whether the memorandum was disclosed to the defense?

Hunt: Yes, I did. . . . I recall talking at least to Mr. Hayman and possibly Mr. Bonner.

Levine: Was this prior to the second trial or during the first trial?

Hunt: I think it was prior to the second trial.

Levine: What was said?

Hunt: Again. . .I just made the comment that. . .I [had] noticed in the [first] trial that there seemed to [have been] a great deal of effort expended by the defense to get me to acknowledge that I had operated or wanted to operate Svetlana as a double agent.

Levine: Don't go into contents [of the classified memorandum]. Tell us what else you said, without going into contents.

Schiff: Your Honor, it may be advisable. . .to have an *in camera* hearing on this. . . .

Levine: Mr. Hunt, do you think you can answer the question adequately without revealing some classified information?

Hunt: No, I think there might be some classified information revealed, to my knowledge. I don't know what's been declassified since.

After another *in camera* session, the cross-examination of Hunt resumed.

Levine: Yesterday, you told us that you had made several efforts to recommend against reassigning Mr. Miller to Mrs. Ogorodnikova—is that correct?

Hunt: I did make some effort. . .to stop the consideration that he might be given the case.

Levine got Hunt to agree that he had spent six years, 1978-84, on the FCI squad, and had been the "coordinator" of double-agent operations from 1982 until his retirement. Hunt said that there was "a general responsibility placed on every agent on the squad to be aware of the possibilities of [double-agent] operations" and that there were weekly or bi-weekly meetings on the subject.

Now, the defense moved into another sensitive area—Hunt's sudden departure from the FBI.

*

Levine: When you submitted your resignation request in mid- to late-October, did you ask that it be effective at the end of November?

Hunt: Yes. . . . That completed the twenty years I needed for retirement.

Levine: You were interviewed by these inspectors. . .[and] Mr. Stukey and Mr. Torrence, for about three days?

Hunt: Yes. . . . I think it was October 15, 16, 17 of 1984.

Levine: Was it they or the inspectors [who] had the discussion with you about the request for the polygraph examination?

Hunt: Both.

Levine: And your response was the same for. . .both groups—is that right?

Hunt: That's correct.

Levine: When, in relation to the interviews with Torrence and Stukey, was your resignation letter submitted?

Hunt: I don't know. A few days later, I think. . . .

Levine: Let's refer back. . .to 1982. . .[when] you were evaluating Mrs. Ogorodnikova. Tell us what period of time that evaluation [took].

Hunt: About eight or nine months.

Levine: Approximately how many meetings were there with her during the eight or nine months?

Hunt: About fifty.

Levine: I think you told us that they began to trail off toward the end of '82; is that right?

Hunt: Yes. The last couple of months, I tapered them off quite drastically.

Levine: Would it be a fair statement that the bulk of the fifty meetings. . . . occurred within a four-month period?

Hunt: Within about a six-month period. . .counting the initial meetings. . .in April and May, even before I opened the "134" investigation.

Levine: Yesterday, you told us that making her an asset was one of your goals; is that right?

Hunt: Yes.

Levine: And I think your actual words yesterday were that it was a "high priority item" for you—is that correct?

Hunt: It was, yes.

Levine: On what did you base that conclusion?

Hunt: Well. . .on her potential that was, you know, really obvious if she could be controlled, and if she was willing and loyal and able to perform for the FBI.

Levine, of course, was aware that Svetlana's investigator, another former FBI agent, had concluded that her potential would have been nil, and that Hunt had "fed bullshit" into her file to have a pretext for continuing a relationship with her.

The lawyer went on to question Hunt further about Mrs. Ogorodnikova:

Levine: Did your evaluation of her potential include the fact that she had contacts [with] high officials in the Soviet consulate [general] in San Francisco?

Hunt: That was one of the reasons, yes.

Levine: Was it also because she had contacts with persons in the Russian *émigré* community?

Hunt: Yes.

Levine: Was it also because she told you. . .that she had been asked to do things by KGB officials?

Hunt: That all figured into the overall evaluation of her potential.

Levine: And the fact that she told you things about her activities with KGB officials presented a potential to you, did it not, that you would be able to learn some things about those officials—correct?

Hunt: Yes.

Levine: Did she also tell you anything about what she did for a living?

Hunt: When I first met her, she was attending a technical school. . .to learn the operation of some hospital equipment. I think it was some kind of heart-monitoring machine that she was learning to use so that she could obtain employment at hospitals as a specialist in this area. This is something that she had claimed that she had also done in the Soviet Union. . . .

Levine: Did you use her in any operations before the evaluation period was completed?

Hunt: Well, I was accepting information from her during that entire period and I would sometimes request that she try to develop some information [where] she would be able to do so without going out of her way.

Levine: You were also attempting, were you not, to derive some benefit for the FBI from her trip to the consulate in September?

Hunt: Yes.

Levine: In fact, I think you told us yesterday that one of the benefits you were attempting to derive was to measure the response [to] anything that she would be saying [on your instructions]—is that right?

Hunt: Yes.

Levine: And you told Mr. Christensen what. . .Mrs. Ogorodnikova was going to say when she got to the consulate?

Hunt: Yes.

Levine: Was Mr. Christensen in favor of her doing that?

Hunt: Yes.

Levine: Did Mr. Christensen agree with you that there was some benefit. . .for the FBI [from] her imparting those things to somebody in the consulate?

Hunt: Yes, he was [*sic*].

Levine: What exactly was it that you and she discussed that she would say when she went to the consulate?

Hunt: Well, as I testified earlier, I told her that she could say that I was assigned to the Foreign Counterintelligence squad, handling Russian matters, and that I was married; I had contacted her on a routine assignment for the FBI and then had invited her out for lunch, dinner or a drink, or something like that, and [I] told her also to tell them that I was someone who apparently [liked] just to get out a bit, spend a little money.

Levine: What do you mean by "get out a bit"?

Hunt: Just to go out. . .after hours. . .and have a drink, something like that. [It was] an effort to justify why she could be seeing me. I also told her to tell them that I was always still attempting to get information from her, but that she was to tell them that she was not cooperating with me in that regard.

Levine: Did you tell us yesterday that you and she rehearsed, a number of times, what it was she was going to say?

Hunt: Yes.

Levine: How many times?

Hunt: I probably met with her two or three different times where we would just sit down over a cup of coffee and I'd say: "Okay, now what are you going to say if they ask you this; what are you going to say if they ask you that?"

Levine: Were you attempting to convey to her the notion that the Soviets, if they heard these things, might be interested in approaching you?

Hunt: What I was attempting to convey is [*sic*] that the Soviets would probably show some interest in her FBI contact [by] asking her to ask me questions about the job or about the FBI in general.

Levine: Do you recall a prior statement that you made in writing in 1984 where you [said] that you looked upon it as an opportunity to see if they would approach you through her?

Hunt: Yes. . . .

Levine: You did allow her to tell the Soviets some things about you which would entice them into whatever it was you were seeking to do—correct? You told her to tell them certain things about you—is that right?

Hunt: Yes, I did. . . .

Levine: Is that why you told her to say that you were a married man who likes to get around?

Hunt: Well. . .she had to have a reason to be seeing me that would make her look innocent to a KGB [officer], but when she also said: "He still keeps pestering me for information," they would know what's going on. . . .

Levine: Did you also consider. . .some form of a disinformation program?

Hunt: I did not.

Levine: I'm going to make reference to the transcript of August 14, 1985, and ask the witness if he [made the following responses] in Trial One?

Q. Did you consider the disinformation program aspect of her trip to be a unique opportunity for the benefit of the FBI?

A. Well, I'm always considering. . .a disinformation program . . .with any assets that I work with. . . .

Q. It was one of your considerations?

A. This was always a consideration with [whomever] I work[ed] with.

Hunt: As I testified in '85. . .this is always a consideration....

Levine: Did Mr. Christensen meet with her after the trip to San Francisco?

Hunt: Yes.

Levine: Did he thank her for what she had done?

Hunt: He was obviously pleased with her job, and I'm sure that she understood that.

Levine: Did he tell you why he was pleased?

Hunt: Well, because of the way that she apparently conducted herself and was able to. . . relay the information that we wanted relayed and [come] back and report it.

Levine: During the time [when] you were evaluating her, she told you about things that the KGB had asked her to do?

Hunt: Yes.

Levine: And she identified that person as either a military or KGB official?

Hunt: She identified him as a high-ranking military officer assigned to the San Francisco consulate.

Levine: And she gave you his name?

Hunt: Yes.

Levine: And that was a Mr. Kurov?

Hunt: Kurov. . .

Levine: And she also said that it was the Soviets who wanted her to have this picture taken with you at the Century Plaza Hotel—is that right?

Hunt: No. . . . She said that they wanted me to take her there so someone could look at us.

Levine: Did she tell you who the someone was?

Hunt: No.

Levine: Did she tell you why they wanted this done?

Hunt: As proof that she was seeing me—was her explanation . . . .

Levine: Did there come times during the two years that you knew her [when] she would tell you that she had been contacted by Russian officials to get in touch with you?

Hunt: There were two or three times when she received calls from Belyakov, who would ask: "Are you still seeing this fellow?" He'd say: "Don't lose him. This is something unique to [us]." There were conversations like that.

Levine: When you conversed with her about these things, did you frequently tell her that "If you ever hear from these people, call me and let me know"?

Hunt: I told her that many, many times. . . particularly in October, November, December, when I knew I was going to be closing her out. That's the one residual that I wanted to preserve.

Levine: Did you also have a discussion with her about that same subject matter in November 1983, when you and Nancy Smith met with her?

Hunt: We met with her in October. . . .

Levine: Are you aware that in March 1984, she attempted to contact you again?

Hunt: Yes, I'm aware of that.

Levine: And two other agents were dispatched to see her—is that right?

Hunt: That is correct.

Levine: Valdez and Fuentes—is that right?

Hunt: Yes. . . .

Levine: And were you also aware that she was [saying] either before. . .or at that meeting that she had been told by the KGB to recontact you?

Hunt: If it's in the memo, then I'm aware of it.

Levine: Did you make any effort to contact her after [that]?

Hunt: No, I did not.

Levine: In 1982. . .during the fifty-some-odd meetings, did you tell her anything about what your squad did, what the business of the FCI-1 squad was?

Hunt: Just in general terms, to give her a rough idea of the sort of things that we were looking for and wanted from her.

Levine: What did you tell her?

Hunt: I told her I was interested in information about her contacts among the Soviet officials assigned in the United States, and. . .about certain *émigrés* living in Los Angeles.

Levine: Are the objectives of the FCI-1 squad that you just told us about. . . classified in any way?

Hunt: I would think, probably. Yes. . . .

At this point, if Levine had asked if elements in the reporting guidance were sensitive, Schiff would surely have objected that this was asking for the opinion of a retired agent of relatively modest rank. But Levine would perhaps have been allowed to ask if any of the classified objectives Hunt was talking about were included in the guidance.

The lawyer then returned to the question of Hunt's relations with Svetlana.

\*

Levine: You also told us yesterday that you and she exchanged gifts from time to time.

Hunt: That's correct.

Levine: In the typical relationship between an asset and an FBI agent, that's not usual, is it?

Hunt: It's unusual. . . . I would say that this is not done often.

Levine: But you didn't consider it unusual in this case—correct?

Hunt: I considered it appropriate in this case because of her unwillingness to accept money, and the problems that I was having gaining some *rapport*, and keeping her on an even keel so far as wanting to cooperate with the FBI. . . . This was an unusual situation all the way along. Nothing was too typical about this case.

Levine: And the receipt of gifts by you was also for the purpose of building *rapport*, right?

Hunt: Yes.

Levine: You didn't want to [offend] her by [refusing]?

Hunt: That's right.

Levine: You told us yesterday that you told your supervisor about the dolls that she gave you. Were the other gifts reported?

Hunt: I think I. . .mentioned the *velours* shirts and. . .maybe something else to Mr. Christensen. My feeling was that that was sufficient. . . . As long as she wasn't giving me anything expensive, I didn't see any need to go into it.

Levine: You also didn't see any need to put anything about it [into] her file—correct?

Hunt: That's correct—I didn't.

Levine: Did she ever introduce you to any of her friends using a different name for you?

Hunt: She introduced me to Lucy Privo, of course, under another name.

Levine: What name did she use?

Hunt: I can't remember. . . . It was a first name.

Levine: Did she introduce you by some different last name?

Hunt: I don't think she used a last name. I'm sure she didn't.

Levine: You preferred that she use a different name—correct?

Hunt: Well, that was to protect her and. . .to try to avoid any connection between the FBI and Svetlana. I mean, my name was known around the *émigré* community. . .and I think my name has probably been in the paper a few times. So we didn't want to use the name John Hunt.

Levine: It was also, apparently, after December 1982, known in the Soviet consulate—correct?

Hunt: That's right.

Levine: Did you tell her it was okay to use your name when she went on the trip?

Hunt: That's right.

Levine: But in the *émigré* community, when you met with one of her friends socially, then you told her to use a different name?

Hunt: Absolutely.

At this point, Levine had thus more or less established that Miller's *modus operandi* with Svetlana was broadly similar to the one used by Hunt with the FBI's seal of approval. The lawyer now pressed the similar emotional link.

Levine: She told you that she loved you—correct?

Hunt: She said that.

Levine: And she told you that her marriage was failing?

Hunt: Yes.

Levine: On how many occasions did she tell you that?

Hunt: I think she made reference to it maybe half a dozen times over eight or nine months. . . . In fact, even after that, I think in. . .March of '83, when my wife and I and Nancy Smith talked to her, she made reference to it again.

Levine: In 1982, did you prepare a memorandum [with] a recommendation by you that no one else be assigned to her?

Hunt: I wrote the teletype.

Levine: At the bottom of page ten to the top of page eleven, it says: "Because of her currently overriding concern for her safety and that of her family, it is felt it would unduly alarm Asset if contact were to be made with her by another agent at this time." Did you write that?

Hunt: I wrote that. . . . At that time, I had told her that I was the only FBI agent that knew about her association with the FBI. [She had requested] that it not become generally known in the office that she was cooperating with the FBI. And I, of course, assured her that it was our secret. . . .

Levine: With respect to this San Francisco trip that she took in September 1982. . . would it be an accurate statement that several teletypes were prepared by Los Angeles?

Hunt: I prepared several teletypes, personally.

Levine: Would it also be correct that several teletypes were prepared by other offices of the FBI involving the information imparted by your teletype?

Hunt: Teletypes were prepared by the San Francisco office and probably by FBI headquarters.

Levine: Would that series of teletypes indicate to you that there was interest in what she was doing with respect to her contacts with the consulate?

Hunt: Yes, it would.

Levine: In fact, it was more than the average interest [in] other things that you did with her—is that right?

Hunt: That's correct.

Levine: In the two years that you knew her, was there any other thing. . .that you did with her that [generated] as many teletypes as this one incident?

Hunt: No.

Levine had thus further established Miller's "blaze of glory" reason for taking on Hunt's dangle, while exposing Hunt's earlier lie that the Bureau as a whole didn't know about Svetlana's work for U.S. counterespionage. Now, the defense attorney dived into Hunt's personal relationship with Svetlana.

Levine: During the time that you knew her, from '82 to late '83, did you see that she had emotional problems?

Hunt: I commented in my [memoranda] and teletypes. . .to headquarters in 1983 that I could see what appeared to be a radical change in her personality, indicating emotional problems and/or a serious alcohol problem.

Levine: Did the emotional and alcohol problems manifest themselves to you more, after you told her that you were dropping her as a potential asset?

Hunt: I would say there was no indication of an ongoing alcohol problem during 1982, when I was seeing her. . . . As far as any display of emotional problems, I would say that probably the first time that anything like that came to my attention was in mid-March 1983, when she was hysterical and screaming on the phone.

Levine: That was after you [had] told her that she was no longer being considered as an asset by you?

Hunt: That was probably five or six months after the time when I first told her that I was probably going to be closing the file and not meeting her any longer unless she could produce some better information.

Hunt had, in effect, thus confirmed that Svetlana had had what laymen call a nervous breakdown because of her unrequited love for the special agent.

Later that morning, Levine tackled the point that Hunt had made the day before—that Miller had sneaked the Ogorodnikova file off his desk.

Levine: Take a look, please, at Exhibit 19. This was the sign-out sheet on the "134" [on] Mrs. Ogorodnikova's case. On the entry of May 31, it appears to have your signature and [the] name of "R.W. Miller" written next to it. Do you see that?

Hunt: Yes.

Levine: And the file was out from 8:15 a.m. to 4:50 p.m. Do you see that?

Hunt: Yes, I do.

Levine: And you are, I believe the person—tell me if I'm wrong—who initialed it in and initialed it out. Is that right?

Hunt: No. I'm the individual that initialed it out and somebody else initialed it in.

Levine: Can you see whose initials those are?

Hunt: I can't decipher them. I don't recognize them. . . .

Levine: Can you recognize it as [Miller's] handwriting?

Hunt: No, I can't.

Levine: Do you have any recollection of having taken the file out that day for about eight hours, nine hours?

Hunt: No, I don't.

Levine: Do you have any recollection of having provided the file to Mr. Miller?

Hunt: I have no recollection. . . .

Levine: Do you know what the procedure is in the FBI when one agent who is the case agent wishes the file to be taken from the room for use by another agent, who is not the case agent?

Hunt: That could vary. It's possible that if another agent wanted the file, I would simply pull it and give it to him.

Levine: Looking at the entries of May 31, does that refresh your recollection as to what you did that day with that file?

Hunt: Well, there's an explanation for the second name.

Levine: Go ahead. What is it?

Hunt: But I have no recollection as to what happened.

Levine: What's your explanation for the second name?

Hunt: The explanation is that, sometime during that day when the file was out for eight hours, I went in and told the custodian of the files that Mr. Miller had the file and that, when they wanted the file back, or if he failed to bring it in at the end of the day, they should go to him for the file rather than myself. That's one explanation. . . .

Levine: In that scenario, you would have been concerned that Mr. Miller maybe would be the kind of person who wouldn't return it on time—isn't that right?

Hunt: That certainly would have been a consideration.

Levine: All meetings with an asset are supposed to be recorded in a "134" file?

Hunt: Yes, in some way.

Levine: And all contacts with an asset are supposed to be recorded in a "134" file even if they are not meetings?

Hunt: Yes, I generally would even record a telephone contact.

Levine: [So] there was a memo in the "134" file for each [1982] meeting—is that right?

Hunt: No. . . . There might be just a notation on the FD209. There would only be a memo in the file if some substantive information was furnished, and it would then be written up; it would be a memo or a copy of a teletype or some other communication with that information.

Levine: The visit to the doctor is not recorded in the file—correct?

Hunt: Correct. It is not.

Levine: The sexual overture she made outside Simply Blues Restaurant is not recorded—is that correct?

Hunt: Right. For the reasons I mentioned.

Levine: How about the two telephone calls you had with her in August 1984—are they recorded in the "134" file?

Hunt: One of the two is recorded.

Levine: That's the one that you tacked [on as] an addendum to Mr. Durr's memo?

Hunt: Yes.

Levine: What about the other one?

Hunt: No, it isn't, because it was so similar to Mr. Durr's [monitoring] that I just figured he had it covered and I just didn't even bother to include it.

Levine: Did you become aware, after you discontinued Mrs. Ogorodnikova from consideration as an asset, that she began making accusations against you?

Hunt: Well, yes. She called my supervisor in July of '83.

Levine: She made no such accusations, to your knowledge, while you were still considering her—is that right?

Hunt: Not to my knowledge.

Levine: Let me refer you again to the events around the end of May of 1984. Mrs. Ogorodnikova's name, [at] that time, wasn't a secret in the squad room, was it?

Hunt: No, it wasn't.

Levine: Would it be a fair statement that it was a pretty well-known name in the squad room?

Hunt: That would be an accurate statement.

Levine: In fact, when Mr. Miller first walked up to you, he made a statement [that] "Guess who I saw today?"—didn't he say something like that?

Hunt: He did.

Levine: And that would indicate to you that he and you both knew the name—correct?

Hunt: Yes.

Levine: And you responded: "Well, what did she accuse me of, now?"—isn't that right?

Hunt: That's right.

Levine: When you talked with Mr. Miller about her that day, you told Mr. Miller, didn't you, about her potential?

Hunt: Yes.

Levine: What did you tell Mr. Miller?

Hunt: I told him I thought she had a lot of potential.

Levine: In what respect?

Hunt: To furnish information to the FBI. . . .

What all this questioning has been designed to draw out is that Hunt had mis-testified about not giving Miller the Ogorodnikova file. It indicated that Miller had a legitimate role in handling her, even if Hunt thought Miller unsuitable for FCI work. Hunt had also admitted that he had encouraged his burly colleague by stressing that Svetlana had "a lot of potential." The testimony also showed that Hunt, while assuring Svetlana that her association with the FBI was "our secret," had, in fact, made her name a common subject of gossip in the Westwood squad room. Levine had also succeeded in reminding the court that even an averagely good agent like Hunt made his own decisions about what contacts with an asset to report and what to leave out of memoranda.

The lawyer now pursued Hunt's "briefing" of Miller further.

Levine: At some point after that, Mr. Miller and you had a discussion about a DMV [Department of Motor Vehicles] check on Mrs. Ogorodnikova—is that right?

Hunt: Yes.

Levine: When, in connection with this first meeting on the 24th, did you have that discussion?

Hunt: I'm not positive.... I do recall that I ran that DMV check the day he gave me the license number. There was a discussion about the license number some time prior to that date.

Levine: Then you submitted that to Mr. Miller?

Hunt: I routed it to him, yes, or just put it in his assignment box.

Levine: You wrote a little note on it, didn't you?

Hunt: Yes.

Levine: Do you remember what it was?

Hunt: I think I said: "R.W., it looks like this is the registration on her new car," and I signed my name....

Levine: Did you frequently utilize that kind of document?

Hunt: A lot of times, I'll run license numbers for my own information, and then I'll not enter the printout in the file itself.

Levine: The call that came in from Mrs. Ogorodnikova in August 1984 that was answered by Mr. Durr and reduced to a memorandum—did you make the decision to route that document to Mr. Miller?

Hunt: Yes.

Levine: Why did you do that?

Hunt: At that time, it was still my belief that he was going to be contacted by her.... I thought that she was going to call him and. . .he should know about this information that had just come in.

Levine: In other words, you felt that you still had some interest in her. Is that right?

Hunt: Well, it was my belief that he was still waiting for a phone call from her, and so I felt that he should be advised of her latest state of mind.

Levine: You saw [Miller] from time to time in the summer of 1984—is that right?

Hunt: Occasionally, yes.

Levine: Although he never told you about his contacts with Mrs. Ogorodnikova, did you notice that his mood had changed in the summer?

Hunt: No, I don't think so.

Levine: You didn't notice him to be a little more upbeat?

Hunt: I don't think so. . . .

Levine: Mr. Hunt, have you ever entertained thoughts about writing a book about your experiences with Mrs. Ogorodnikova?

Hunt: I have.

Levine: Have you taken [*sic*] any efforts with respect to that?

Hunt: I have not.

Levine: Did you never contact any persons to discuss with them the possibility of a literary project?

Hunt: My attorney has made a couple of inquiries and it is not—

Levine: Have you yourself ever talked with anybody else about it?

Hunt: No.

Levine: Have you ever had a conversation with a Mr. Overton* of the *Los Angeles Times*?

Hunt: Yes, I have.

Levine: Tell us about that.

Hunt: Mr. Overton was thinking about writing a book—in fact, presented a manuscript to one or more publishing houses to write a book himself.

Levine: Did he ask you to participate in the effort if he was successful?

---

Actually, Overend—*Author*

Hunt: No, he didn't, although I mentioned to him that perhaps we should discuss further some sort of collaboration on a book.

Levine: At some time you employed legal counsel to intervene on your behalf with respect to exploring this possibility [of] literary rights—is that right?

Hunt: Not with Mr. Overton.

Levine: I mean in general.

Hunt: Yeah, there were just some general inquiries made to see if there would be any interest in this sort of book.

Levine: Did you ever discuss with anybody in the United States government—either the U.S. attorneys or the FBI—your desires with respect to this subject?

Hunt: I don't believe so.

Levine: You mentioned the name of a friend of Mrs. Ogorodnikova's yesterday, Nadya Mathison.

Hunt: Yes.

Levine: Have you seen or spoken to Mrs. Mathison in the last year?

Hunt: Not in the last year. . . . I contacted her some time after the second Miller trial. . . . I gave her a phone call.

Levine: Did you discuss with her wanting to get together with Mrs. Ogorodnikova?

Hunt: No.

Levine: What did you discuss with Mrs. Mathison?

Hunt: I told her who I was. At that time, I was interested in pursuing a lawsuit for slander. . .against Mrs. Ogorodnikova's lawyers.

Levine: That's Mr. Bryant and Mr. Stone of the firm of Munger, Tolles, and Somebody and Somebody and Somebody?

Hunt: Correct. . . . I was aware. . .that Svetlana, who was her close friend, had made statements to her that our association was strictly platonic.

Levine: Did you ask her to intervene on your behalf to arrange a meeting between you and Svetlana?

Hunt: No. . . .

Levine: You mentioned something about pursuing a lawsuit. Did you ever file it?

Hunt: No, I didn't.

Levine: Was there a pre-filing settlement of your claim?

Hunt: The dispute between myself and the lawyers was settled to the satisfaction of all parties.

Levine: Were you given money as a result of that settlement?

Hunt: I'm not authorized to make any further statements.

Levine: Your Honor, I'm going to ask the court to order the statement made. It goes to the issue of a stake in the outcome.

Takasugi: Was there an agreement not to disclose?

Hunt: Yes, Your Honor.

Levine: That agreement may be binding between the parties, but if it's irrelevant to these proceedings—

Takasugi: I'm aware of that.

Schiff: The government has no objection.

Takasugi: All right. Please disclose it.

Hunt: Do I have to answer, Your Honor?

Takasugi: Yes, please.

Hunt: Your question, again?

Levine: How much?

Hunt: Fifty thousand dollars.

*v*

There was a brief re-direct examination by Schiff. Then Levine, on re-cross-examination, briefly re-explored the question of double-agent policy.

Levine: Are you telling us, then, that the FBI can authorize the use of an asset in the double-agent operation?

Hunt: That's correct.

Levine: Are you also telling us that the FBI would permit the conveyance of classified information to somebody outside the FBI?

Hunt: With proper prior approval, there could be situations where classified information would be turned over in that manner.

Levine: In fact, isn't there literature that is distributed amongst agents in your squad, that squad that you belong[ed] to, which basically covers the two subject matters I just questioned you about?

Hunt: I'm sure there is, but I just don't remember any particular instruction about these matters.

Levine: Is that because, in your years in the Bureau, you understand they had something about everything—is that correct?

Hunt: I think that would be what I'm trying to say.

Under further re-direct, Hunt backed off slightly from his testimony of the previous day—that FBI special agents were never used as double agents.

Levine revealed that the Lexington Women's Prison, to which Svetlana had been moved, had said she was too ill to come to Los Angeles for testimony until after an operation. The court would have to wait until November. Judge Takasugi suggested telephone testimony, but Levine clearly doubted the coherence of that. (In the event, as noted, neither Miller nor either of the Ogorodnikovs were called.)

The Hunt testimony had revealed that it had been Hunt who had contacted Nadya Mathison about Svetlana, not the other way around—even though he denied having sought to use her to visit Svetlana. Levine never asked if there was an application on file at Pleasanton (there was) for Hunt to visit his former asset.

Above all, the tougher questioning of Hunt (than had been the case at the previous trials) established—despite all Hunt's wriggling—that he had begun to use Svetlana as a double agent; that on his instructions she had pretended to be sympathetic to the consulate-general's goals and had pretended to reject Hunt's "pestering" of her for information as an FBI informant— while apparently faithfully telling Hunt everything she had from San Francisco. Hunt had conceded that she was "emotionally involved"—i.e., in love—with him, and that they had exchanged a number of gifts, only a couple of which he had recorded officially, and that he had failed to record the doctor's visit, at which he had received a receipt for eight hundred dollars. He had admitted that he had involved Miller in the controlling of Svetlana. In brief, Hunt had damaged his own credibility to some extent, while to some extent helping Miller's. But overall, his testimony had served to exculpate Miller only partly—while exculpating Svetlana more or less entirely.

\*

Howard Teten testified that he was the behavioral scientist who had served out a career with the FBI, mostly composing profiles of suspects or advising the FBI on how best to grill them when they were arrested. He said he had devised profiles of Miller and Svetlana, before their arrest, to facilitate FBI interrogations, concentrating on their weaknesses and such tactics as interrogating fat men like Miller at night, when they would be more fatigued than most people.

## *vi*

On October 9, 1990, Miller's third court ordeal came to a close. The chief prosecutor, Adam Schiff, began his closing arguments by quoting Miller himself:

"I've got everyone yelling at me. I've got my job yelling at me, my wife yelling at me, my church yells at me, and I'm just to the point where I'm rebelling." (In reality, the crucial last clause in the sentence was hype; Miller never said it.)

Schiff went on: "Those were the words Miller used to describe his state of mind in the fall of 1984, in conversation with Marta York. . . .

"Although the defendant did not begin to rebel until the summer and fall of 1984, the seeds of that rebellion were planted earlier. . . . In 1983, the defendant was isolated from his church when he was excommunicated for adultery; he was isolated from his wife and family, living in a separate apartment [*sic*] in Lynwood, complaining to his colleagues about his relationships with his wife, contemplating divorce, and seeking in other women to find what was absent in his life at home.

"In addition to his isolation from his church and his family, as early as 1983 he began being isolated at work. His field assignments were taken away from him in early 1983. He was relegated to listening to a wire tap forty hours a week. Problems that he had had throughout his career became much more significant: The weight problem that had plagued him throughout his twenty years in the Bureau was now being addressed forcefully by the new S/A/C, Richard Bretzing. . . .

"Well, in '83, these problems. . .were dealt with by Mr. Bretzing in the form of a censure—suspension—in September, without pay, and in the form of another suspension without pay in April of 1984. These were the strongest actions that had been taken to date with the defendant's weight problem, and he felt that they were unjustified. As he lamented to Rudy Valdez when he was suspended: "They didn't have to do that to me. The hell with them! They're just trying to fire me, anyway." He came back after two weeks of suspension. He had hoped that the agents would have taken up a collection for him, which was a Bureau tradition, and no one had taken up a collection. As Nancy Baker-Smith and John Justice testified, he was teary-eyed, disappointed and upset, and the reaction of the other agents. . .was to walk out of the room.

"It was during this period of isolation, dissatisfaction and difficulty with the Bureau that the defendant's financial burdens became most oppressive. He had a wife and eight children to support on an agent's salary, which was a feat in and of itself. His [other] income was dwindling. His mortgage payments were late. [His] checks were returned for insufficient funds. He had to open up charge accounts. . . .

"Also at this time, he began accepting odd jobs to supplement his income. . . . As he summarized [*sic*] to Marta York, at the time he was almost obsessed with the idea of making money. But it was the two-week suspension without pay that was, I think, the straw that broke the camel's back. It not only set him back $1,400 to $1,600, but he felt that it was patently unfair, to himself and to his family."

Faced with disloyalty by the FBI, Schiff argued, Miller felt justified in being disloyal. He went on:

"It was precisely at that time, May of 1984, when the defendant came back from suspension, that Svetlana Ogorodnikova came into the defendant's life. And from the very beginning, the evidence, I think, has demonstrated that he was infatuated with Svetlana Ogorodnikova. . . .

"He ignored the direct instructions of his supervisor, met with her and slept with her, knowing, as any agent would know, that to do that, not only the insubordination, but sleeping with an asset, would result in his immediate termination from the Bureau. . . .

"Svetlana Ogorodnikova fed the seeds of Miller's private rebellion. She offered him money; she offered him sex; she offered him consideration. And on an evening of August of '84, the defendant accepted those offers when he provided classified documents to her, and in so doing, betrayed his job, his family and the entire community that placed its trust in his hands."

Schiff maintained that in order to get visas and youth-camp "perks" for Matvei, the Ogorodnikovs had become "utility agents of the KGB." Their "tasks" had "broadened" to include locating defectors, as Donald Levinson had testified. Miller had been brought in, and had told Auer he wanted to find three of them for a training program—a "bald and unequivocal lie."

Schiff continued: "How, then, has the government proved that his isolation, his financial debt, and his infatuation with Svetlana Ogorodnikova caused him to provide classified information to the Soviets, caused him to solicit money and gold, proved the events it set out to prove? The court has received a number of stipulations, telephone toll records, surveillance observations. . .to show, I think, the pressing weight of the circumstantial as well as the direct evidence in this case. . . . The calendar begins in March of '84. . . . Nikolaiy Ogorodnikov travels to Vienna and Moscow. . . . April 2, the defendant admits taking diuretics. His property taxes from '83 remain unpaid ....April 5, S/A/C Bretzing recommends that the defendant be censured, suspended from duty, and continued on probation for failure to bring his weight within Bureau limits. . . . It's clear at this time that the FBI is leading up to the termination of Miller."

Schiff was building, once more, the case that all these misfortunes created Miller's willingness to "go over" for money, and that all that Miller thought he faced would be dismissal. In May, the Ogorodnikovs had hired Donald Levinson to find the defector Levchenko, and had begun a "continuing pattern" of leaving their apartment to hold talks in the street.

Continuing with the chronology, Schiff said: "[On] May 23, Svetlana Ogorodnikova visited the Soviet consulate in San Francisco. . . . The very next day. . . [she] calls the FBI and asks for the defendant by name. . . . The defendant meets Svetlana in Marina del Rey. . . . He informs Auer of the meeting and he's told not to initiate any further contact and to report immediately if Svetlana Ogorodnikova calls. . . . We also know from John Hunt's testimony that each time he asked Miller: 'Have you heard from her yet?' Miller lied to him and said: 'No, nothing yet. . . .'

"On June 18, the defendant writes a check for his April and May mortgage payments, later returned for insufficient funds....On June 24, Svetlana Ogorodnikova leaves Los Angeles en route to Vienna and Moscow. Two days later, Grishin leaves for Moscow. . . .

"On July 23, Svetlana Ogorodnikova returns to the United States from the Soviet Union. . . . On July 26 [she] visits the Soviet consulate in San Francisco. . . . On August 1, [she] makes the first call to the defendant in the Santa Ana office of the FBI."

Why Schiff mentioned this is not clear, since if Svetlana's task was to "recruit" Miller as a mole, she would hardly have called him at the office; but it is a legitimate part of the chronology.

"On August 2, defendant meets [her] in East Los Angeles for dinner, tells her that he is unhappy at work, has great financial problems, weight problems; he's considering a divorce. He realizes that Svetlana Ogorodnikova is trying to recruit him. We know this from the admissions he makes [under interrogation] and from telephone toll records. . . . [There was a] second meeting on August 5 at the Charthouse restaurant. . . . She requests a personnel list. . . . The defendant demands fifty thousand dollars in gold in three safe deposit boxes in exchange for the classified documents. . . . On August 7, [he] meets [her] again in East Los Angeles for dinner. He tells [her] that he reviews intelligence reports from the CIA, the DIA and other agencies regarding the Soviet Union, edits the information and prepares a report for distribution."

For the reader's recollection, we are now just before the point where Miller is telling Grayson that what he is offering as a dangle to the KGB is the "illusion" that he has access to real secrets. Schiff went on to recount how Svetlana had told Miller that she would introduce him to "an important man in the KGB," and had taken him to meet the sleepy Nikolaiy, to whom Miller had offered "information for money," only to discover from the FBI computer that Nikolaiy was Svetlana's husband.

"He calls her and berates her for the deception. . . . The 1984 Positive Intelligence Reporting Guide has now been received in the L.A. office. . . . [Sometime between] August 12 and August 21, the defendant makes a Xerox copy of the...guide at the office on a Sunday afternoon and brings it home." Neither Svetlana's nor Miller's prints had been found on the photocopy, because the heat of a photocopier takes prints off, Schiff explained. A secretary had made copies for the whole unit, and that in turn had taken all prints except hers off the original.

"August 15 was the date he actually met Larry Grayson. He tells Grayson that 'they' have asked for a personnel list. . . . His request for that list was a product of Svetlana Ogorodnikova's request. Defendant brings [her] to the Lynwood residence for the evening, shows [her] the guide in the bedroom doorway.... Aleksandr Grishin returns to the United States from Moscow.... On August 25, Svetlana Ogorodnikova [leaves] the defendant at a [cafeteria] near the consulate. The defendant gives [her] his credentials so she can demonstrate to the consular officials [that] she's dealing with a real FBI agent. . . . We know from testimony both of Mr. Barron and Mr. Kennedy that recruitment requires proof of *bona fides*. . . . [The next day] toll records indicate calls from the [Livermore] hotel to Boris Belyakov's residence."

Schiff now came to the first Grishin telephone call, on September 11, and Svetlana's frantic search for Miller, whom she hadn't seen for two weeks, then to their meeting of the next day, and the Whipworm tapes of their conversations. Miller is heard asking: "How did you get my number?" and Svetlana says: "You gave it to me." Miller says: "I thought you didn't want to see me anymore."

At this point, Judge Takasugi interrupted Schiff to ask: "Why would he quiz her as to how she got his phone number if you're contending that in August he provided the personnel list to her?" Said Schiff: "Well, I think the defendant didn't realize that that's where she got the number from."

The prosecutor recalls Miller's meeting with Svetlana on September 12, at which Miller is overheard saying: "I almost thought you weren't going to show up. . . . I didn't think you were going to come." Recounting more of the tape, Schiff went on: "And later he says...his car...'needs some work on the front end, on the wheels. Maybe when I get back from Mexico, I'll—' and he never finishes the sentence. It's clear he thinks he's going to have the money to fix the car or get a new car when he returns from Mexico. At this point, he still thinks the destination is Mexico. . . .

"As the defendant has explained continually, she is always asking for paper, meaning classified documents. We know this not only from the [interrogations, but also] from the Grishin tapes."

Schiff then quotes excerpts from the Whipworm tapes: "[On September 17] he explains to Marta York, 'My wife handles every problem through yelling and screaming, and I disagree with that. She says: 'Well, you know. . .it gets the job done,' and Marta York explains: 'No, it doesn't. The children hear so much yelling and screaming, they don't believe it anymore.' Miller responds: 'Well, exactly. It's already come to that. . . . Nobody likes to be forced. . . . I've got my job yelling at me, my wife yelling at me, my church yells at me.' She says: 'I'm not yelling at you.' And he says: 'Well, you're next.'

"On September 18, the defendant calls Svetlana Ogorodnikova to confirm the meeting on the twentieth."

Schiff then recounted the next Grishin call, but implying that Grishin did not know he was being monitored, although he was said to be using "plain language code."

Schiff continued: "Grishin says: 'What shall I convey to your acquaintances?' [She says:] 'Well, I'd like to come by tomorrow at five or six for the films, because I'm afraid of losing the movie theater. The movie theater I have is cheap. So, at least to take one or a couple of films.' Plain language code translated, meaning: 'What should I convey to the KGB?' and 'Well, I'd like to come by tomorrow at five or six for the classified documents, because I'm afraid of losing Mr. Miller. Mr. Miller is cheap, so at least to take one or a couple of classified documents.' Also in this conversation, Svetlana says: 'Because I must give back these films. The director of the movie theater is also worried, you understand.' Translated, [that's] 'Because I must give back these classified documents. Mr. Miller is also worried, you understand.' Also in this conversation, Svetlana says: 'Well, better that he'—referring to Nikolaiy Ogorodnikov—'does visit the Soviet consulate, because I am worried about this director of the movie theater. It's too bad; the movie theater is cheap. It would be a shame to lose [it], you understand.' Finally, in this conversation, Grishin says: 'Well, what would be most convenient for you [is] that you and your friend could go together. . . . Have him bring all the baggage with him. I mean that which will help him on his vacation.'

"On September 20, the defendant calls [Svetlana's apartment], again introducing himself as Boris; [he] calls to confirm the meeting at Café Casino. . . . [They] meet [there]. . . . They go to the Palm Motel and have sex. . . . When they're in the Café Casino [a cafeteria], Special Agent DiPretorio was right behind them in line and he overhears the defendant saying, 'Well, I guess you're not very happy with me,' and they walk out. [Later] Miller says [under interrogation] that 'It was Svetlana's idea to go to the motel.' It's clear he's having cold feet, and it's clear they go to the motel at Svetlana's suggestion so she can further entice him to go on this trip. . . . The defendant and Svetlana discuss the dates for travel to Vienna. The defendant makes a calendar on hotel stationery. We know this not only from the defendant's admissions, but [also] from the conversations between Svetlana and the travel agent setting up these same dates. . . .

"[On] September 21, the defendant calls Svetlana Ogorod-nikova from a phone booth and tells her: 'I will bring the rest of the stuff from my house. . . . Also, I went downstairs this morning and got an application for that item.' Why is he talking in vague terms?. . .The only concern he could have is that the FBI is tapping his [*sic*—Schiff presumably meant 'her'] phone.... What would that expression be used for—'The rest of the stuff'? It refers to documents, in the plural. . . .

"[On] September 24, Nikolaiy Ogorodnikov travels to the Soviet consulate in San Francisco with one film canister. . . . We know that Svetlana and Matvei Ogorodnikov drive to [Los Angeles] airport [for Nikolaiy]. They recognize the surveillance car. We know that from the envelope that was found in the car; we know from Agent van Bockern's testimony that the number on the envelope is [that of] his license plate. . . . Nikolaiy and Svetlana Ogorodnikova go for a long walk in the park and converse. . . . On September 25, Svetlana Ogorodnikova calls Diana Baskevitch and orders tickets for herself and Miller. . . . Grishin calls—it's again Tuesday night—from the phone booth and asks if the arrangements have been made to travel on the tenth. He again indicates he'll call back in exactly a week. . . . From Miller's testimony, we know. . .that that evening, Marta York tells the defendant that they are being surveilled. On September 26, the defendant and Svetlana Ogorodnikova cross paths with FBI Agent DeFlores in the parking lot at Ohio and Sepulveda. . . . I submit that the defendant was able to see [DeFlores] accurately."

Schiff paused to drink water, but it seemed to be for refreshment, not effect.

"The defendant has been meeting with Svetlana Ogorodnikova for four months, and until this date he says nothing to anyone. The defendant and Svetlana Ogorodnikova go shopping for clothes for the trip. She places a hold on the Burberry coat. . . . [She] instructs the defendant to bring FBI credentials and paper on the trip, and informs the defendant he'll receive fifteen thousand dollars in cash, which he agrees to, and [she] will receive twenty-five thousand in cash. . . .

"[On] the tape recording in the car. . .Miller says: 'Every two weeks they give me eight hours of vacation time,' and Svetlana says, 'Oh,' and Miller says, 'My vacation time is very low. . . . Two eight-hour days is sixteen hours—should be [a] Thursday and Friday. I'll just put down that I'm at my father's house or something, so if they call, I'm not here. They won't call.' We know he's planning on using annual leave for this trip; why would he do that if he was planning on reporting the trip? He also tells her: 'I put down on my passport application Mexico, six to twelve months. Okay? It doesn't say I'm going to Europe or anything like that. Okay?' Why does he have to put Mexico on his passport application? Svetlana Ogorodnikova is never going to see that application. [The destination] doesn't appear on the passport [itself]. . . . Miller also says: 'I'm worried about doing this.'

"Later, he's talking about the [impending sale of the] Lynwood residence. . .and she says: 'You're not tired of living like that?'. . .and 'Well, when you come and work, you know, you go rent a good apartment.' And he says: 'Well, we'll see.' And she says: 'Please!' And he says: 'Well, let's see if your people want to see me, because they may not even want to use me.'

"[On] September 27, he goes into Bryce Christensen's office. He admits having unauthorized contacts with Svetlana Ogorodnikova and that he has had sex with her. . . . He claims to have been trying to infiltrate the KGB. . . . He admits that he was to receive fifty thousand in gold and fifteen thousand in cash. . .[and says:] 'This affords the FBI a unique opportunity ....There could be some real benefit to the FBI.' It's clear from the context [that he means]: 'This is the situation I've gotten myself involved in, but it can be turned to the advantage of the FBI.'

"After he is polygraphed, he is told by Murphy that he has failed the [examination]. He admits that he may have allowed Svetlana Ogorodnikova to bring his credentials into the consulate in San Francisco on the trip, something he had never even mentioned to Bryce Christensen.... [On] September 29, defendant tells the [interrogators] he believes [she] took his credentials into the consulate.... He admits that he copied the guide [and] thought about showing it to Svetlana.... Not only do we know this from the admissions, we [also] know that the document was copied, that copies [*sic*] were in his residence, and we know that Svetlana Ogorodnikova spent the evening there....

"[On] September 30, the defendant admits Xeroxing the Positive Intelligence Reporting Guide on a Sunday on the fifteenth floor of the FBI office, after informing Svetlana Ogorodnikova that he would get her some paper.... He admits...[that] he was angry and upset when she told him that they had been followed and photographed [supposedly by the KGB] and indicates [*sic*] he was not trying to be recruited by anyone.... He admits he gathered documents in his residence to serve as a pool from which he could furnish materials to the Soviets.... [Under interrogation] he admits placing [the guide] in a woven bag on the trip to San Francisco. He admits this to Larry Torrence....

"On October 2, the defendant states that the classified documents to be provided to the Soviets did not exceed the new PI Guide.... He goes outside...[and] tells her [the same thing]—he 'did' only one, and that he thought he had a good deal....

"[On] October 3, following the defendant's arrest for espionage, he waives his right to remain silent. He again admits giving the new PIG Guide to Svetlana Ogorodnikova, knowing it was secret, because all of the documents that crossed his desk were secret....

"The first [interrogation] testimony of Larry Torrence indicates [*sic*] that on the first day [Miller] said he had absolutely no classified documents in his residence, that if the Positive Intelligence Reporting Guide was in the 'Svetlana' file, he didn't know how it got there and it must have been an accident.... [On] September 29, he admits copying the [guide] and [thinking] about giving it to Svetlana, and he requested a new polygraph examiner. [On] September 30, he admits copying the [guide]....  [On] October 1, he tells Larry Torrence and Graham van Note how he [had] showed her the [guide]; he draws [a] diagram...."

Schiff is getting worked up, and sometimes confuses the present and past tenses.

"During the first [pre-polygraph] interview with Jim Murphy on September 28, the defendant said it was possible Svetlana Ogorodnikova took his credentials into the consulate. . . . [The next day] he tells Murphy [she] probably took [them]. . . . [On October 2] the defendant recognizes the need to investigate an incident of espionage and the need to do a damage assessment. He. . .wants to tell his wife what he has done. He assures the interviewers that the damage doesn't exceed documents in his residence and the new PI Guide. . . . On October 1. . .he explained to [polygrapher Paul Minor] that he wasn't really going to be paid for this document; it was going to be used to establish his [*bona fides*]. . . . [On the night of] October 2- 3, in the car with Agent Bretzing. . .he states he gave classified documents, in the plural."

In a play or a film, the author or the scenarist decides the dramatic breaks. On television, their role is usurped by advertisers for flea collars or computer toys. In court, it depends on the endurance of His Honor's bladder. After a ten-minute recess to allow everyone to go to the toilets, Schiff began to summarize:

"I think the defendant gave the best indication of his view of the interview process [i.e., interrogation] when he described during the suppression hearing how he had tried to be completely truthful with the interviewers, that he had made all the admissions that the government asserted he had made, and that 'It wasn't until eight months later, sitting in Terminal Island [Prison], going through all this disclosure material, that I knew I didn't.' I don't think that's an uncommon reaction of people in custody. . . .

"The indictment before the Court is in six counts. The conspiracy, I won't bother going through. . . . The second count is copying and obtaining national defense information. . . .with intent, or reason to believe, that it would be used to the injury of the United States or to the advantage of the Soviet Union. . .

"He does not have to have the intent to do it, only reason to believe it would be injurious and helpful, [only] one or the other. All we have to prove is [that] he had reason to believe that the . . .guide would be of help to the Soviets. . . .

"Moreover, for the purpose of this count, all we have to prove is that he copied and obtained the documents, which is really uncontested, not that they were transmitted or conveyed to anyone.

"The third count, delivering national defense information to a foreign government, has two [parts]: communication. . .[and the] intent, or reason to believe, that it would be helpful or hurtful. . . . [Miller] explained in detail to Mr. Minor how he chose this particular document.

"The fourth count in the indictment, communication of classified information, requires three elements: That the defendant was an official or employee of the government [and] that he communicated the information to a person he had reason to believe was an agent of a foreign government. . .and that he knew the information was classified. . . .

"Finally, the fifth and sixth counts, the solicitation or agreement to receive bribes. . . . Again, we don't have to prove that he solicited, merely that he agreed to receive [and] that [he] was an employee of the United States [and that] he was going to be receiving the fifty thousand in gold and the fifteen thousand in cash."

Schiff then responded to the defense case:

"The first phase of the defense case was the Grayson phase. Grayson testified that he met with the defendant on August 15 at Denny's [cafeteria and] outside in the car, [and] discussed what was involved in the defendant's proposition. . . . The money and the gold was [*sic*] not discussed until they had moved to the car. . . . Grayson testified that his response [had been that Miller] would need more money than that. . . . The defendant's response was: 'There'll be more that I'll get after that.' Not 'The FBI will protect me.'. . .but 'There will be more money later.'

"Mr. Levine asked Larry Grayson: 'Did the defendant tell you he was planning on keeping the fifty thousand in gold?' Grayson's answer was [that] he might have. He might have! Mr. Levine followed up: 'Well, you were going to go down there with him. You were going to take photographs, weren't you?' And Mr. Grayson's response was: 'Well. . .I'm just the photographer. I wasn't involved in the documents. That's his business, and I'm just there as a photographer.' It was clear Mr. Grayson knew what was going on. . . .

"What happens when the FBI goes to talk with Larry Grayson for the first time? He calls the defendant's residence that evening, and he says: 'Two people came by to put flowers on Mother's grave.' Although he was reluctant to admit it, he admitted that he was trying to warn Miller that the FBI was on to him."

Schiff referred to testimony by a Mrs. Osman about Miller's learning disabilities, and counter-attacked: "Somebody with a severe auditory dyslexia problem could not listen [to] and transcribe tapes [and] remember. . .the sequence of numbers. I would also submit that his mastery of Spanish. . .is inconsistent with someone who has a severe auditory problem. . . .

"The defense in this case—the double-agent, penetrate-the-KGB defense—is a common defense in espionage cases. . . . If the defendant was trying to redeem his career, why did he purposely disregard supervisor Auer's instructions and clandestinely meet and 'sleep' with Svetlana Ogorodnikova, when that alone would result in his immediate termination from the FBI?. . . If the defendant was trying to be recruited by the KGB, why was he upset that he had been followed and photographed by her [Svetlana's] government during the trip to San Francisco?. . . Why was he planning to take annual leave on the dates of his travel?. . . If the defendant was acting to benefit the FBI instead of in his own self-interest, why did he tell Marta York: 'I thought I had a good deal.' If the defendant was acting to benefit the FBI, instead of acting in his own self-interest, why was he trying to use the CIA to locate three Soviet defectors for the KGB?"

## *vii*

At the defense table, Levine nodded confidently in Miller's direction. Virtually the only solid part of the government's summation had been Miller's own admissions under interrogation. That remained the burden to overcome.

Levine, a slim, athletic man with a nervous manner who frequently makes malapropisms, began by setting his theme of exasperation: "Three days from now will mark the sixth anniversary of my involvement in this case. . . . My client has waited that period of time, five years of which were spent in prison. . . . We've waited that period of time [for] the government to present its case through evidence of events that actually occurred. As we stand here today on October 9, 1990, we're still waiting. . . . The dominant portion of the government's case rested on statements obtained from Mr. Miller during five days of intense and questionable interrogation. . . .

"We do not contest that Mr. Miller made these statements...or that Marta York did not hear what Mr. Miller said. What we contest is what got Mr. Miller to make those statements, whether the statements he made were true depictions of events that occurred. And remember, one of the things that was admitted from the pretrial hearings was Mr. Miller's statement to Mr. Christensen: 'I don't know if I'm admitting what they told me I did or what I did. . . .'

"Instead of tape-recordings or videotapes of the [interrogations], so that we could really see what Mr. Miller's demeanor was, we had a different method: '302s' were taken [and] agents would get up on the stand and recount those, six years later, from their memory—that, as a substitute for real evidence!

"The defense, during this trial, produced expert testimony that Mr. Miller suffered from auditory dyslexia. . . . The court, at the suggestion of the government, gave [the government] extra days to prepare for the examination of these witnesses.... And also at their request, if they chose to do so, to make a motion upon the court to have Mr. Miller examined by another expert to see whether or not any of these deficiencies—the sleep apnea or dyslexia— existed. No effort was made by the government, despite the fact that we also agreed to it, to ask for such an examination. . . .

"We told you during the opening statement that Mr. Miller came forward voluntarily on September 27, 1984, to report to Mr. Christensen what he had done. . . . It was not because he spotted Paul DeFlores in a parking lot. . .but. . .because on a shopping trip taken with Mrs. Ogorodnikova that day [of] which Your Honor heard a tape of approximately one and a half hours, Mrs. Ogorodnikova told Mr. Miller that she had obtained the tickets for the trip. His response was—and I'm going to try to imitate the inflection of his voice, which Your Honor has heard—'You did?' After which, one day later, he reported these events to Mr. Christensen, and told Mr. Christensen he felt the

thing had gone to a point where he could take it no longer alone
. . . .

"You saw a number of witnesses come before Your Honor who had what we would call a bias, or a stake in the outcome of what Your Honor would decide. Some had a stake because of their careers or their reputation, some because of their dislike for Mr. Miller, some because of internal FBI disputes, some because they had it in their mind to write a book or receive money as a result of their involvement in this case. . . .

"One of the things that occurs in a trial like this is that events which seem innocuous or innocent beforehand take on added importance, and some of those were brought up during Mr. Schiff's argument this morning. He continually refers to the significance of conversations regarding three defectors. That event appears suddenly important. In 1984, to the FBI, it apparently did not. Mrs. Ogorodnikova met with two FBI agents in March of 1984, a Mr. Valdez and a Miss Fuentes, whose testimony was brought to Your Honor by stipulation. She told these people that the KGB had told her to help find three defectors for them. It was not such an important event when she told them this. They wrote a memo to the file. . . .

"Something as innocent as the use of the word 'stuff' now becomes a *cause célèbre*. . . . Mr. Miller did use it in a number of conversations, and in some we could conclude that he referred to classified documents. He also used it to refer to diesel additive; he used it to refer to fingerprints. And I think for the court to convict Mr. Miller on the assumption that every time he used that word he was referring to classified documents [would be] stretching imagination beyond belief. . . .

"[One day] Mr. Miller is seen walking in a parking lot carrying an envelope. The assertion is that Mr. Miller is conveying classified information to Mrs. Ogorodnikova. Just like you heard [that] in the Café Casino the next day, he's looking at a little pink card in his pocket. They don't even ask him for the pink card, but the agent tells you that it was a very serious business conversation that they were having. I'm sure the implication is that he's reading something of a very secretive nature to her. . . . Now, other evidence had been produced...with respect to what happened on September 12. At 5:30 in the afternoon, Mr. Miller is walking across the parking lot. Over the hour or two hours before that, from video and audio tapes, you see Mr. Miller talking on the telephone, making notes on a piece of paper, and then you hear him talking to various banks, taking down information. And what is that information? It's information relating to a bank application that he's making out, which is precisely what he told Mr. Torrence he was doing. You then also have the file of Santa Barbara Savings & Loan. . .to illustrate to Your Honor that, in fact, that institution did receive documents from Mr. Miller shortly thereafter. Now, we cannot prove beyond all certainty [*sic*—presumably, "doubt"] that in fact those documents were the documents Mr. Miller was working on that day at the telephone. But certainly, we came closer to proving the event circumstantially than anything that the 'Whipworm' agents could do or even [tried] to do."

Levine then laid heavy stress on the fact that there was no independent evidence that Miller had ever "transmitted documents." For the purpose of the defense, he took the line that Grishin and Ogorodnikova "did not know they were being recorded" during their telephone conversations. He noted that on September 11, Grishin had said that Svetlana's "friend" should "bring the baggage with him," noting: "There was absolutely no reference. . .to anything having been transmitted before. . . . More importantly than that, Mr. Miller is then called by Svetlana shortly thereafter. . .the same evening. And his reaction to her is: 'I didn't ever expect to see you again.' He doesn't say: 'Did they like the baggage?' 'Did they like my gift?' 'Where is my money?' 'I gave you the game plan for counterintelligence.' Instead, Mr. Miller says to Mrs. Ogorodnikova: 'Gee, I thought you didn't want to see me anymore.' [And why would he] say the next day: 'I thought you weren't going to show up.'

"Now, the next day, Mr. Miller goes on a shopping trip and, as Mr. Schiff points out, one of the things he says to Mrs. Ogorodnikova. . .is: 'I don't even know that your government wants to use me.' Now, this is a fellow who [has] supposedly already given away documents [and] should be expecting money. We don't have any evidence that he ever received any. In fact, if anything, we have evidence that he's still financially distraught. The government introduced testimony that he couldn't even pay a forty-two dollar jewelry bill. . . .

"And then we have the 'business' about Mr. Grayson telling us that even in his conversation with Mr. Miller, the exchange of the documents for the gold was to occur on the foreign trip, which was either going to be in Mexico or some place overseas. It was something that was to occur in the future, which coincides with the agenda Mr. Grishin expressed on the tape-recording."

Levine poured scorn on the "elaborate explanation" as to why there were no Miller fingerprints on the "guide that he supposedly copied," and went on: "There's another reason. [He] never touched them."

It was time to turn to the argument about R.W. Miller as victim:

"He certainly was not a typical FBI agent of twenty years' vintage, and it is this person who enters the four days of interrogation, not Efrem Zimbalist Jr. And the best evidence we have of what I am now stating to you is the psychological profile, which we didn't even know existed until this trial, conducted by [an FBI psychologist]." Levine said the profile drawn "was useful to the interrogators in attempting to manipulate Mr. Miller. . . . The psychological profile really assists the interrogators to choose which interrogation techniques to use. . . .

"Mr. Miller was not only entering this phase of the interrogation as a person who had exhibited a fair degree of ineptness over twenty years in the FBI, but. . .with defects, which until this trial we did not know. One, Mr. Miller suffered from sleep apnea."

(This is a condition that affects about three million Americans—a majority of obese women, and nearly all obese men. Virtually all such people sleep on their backs. Muscles depress the bronchial tubes and, to resume breathing, the sleeper awakes, sometimes for less than a second, sometimes a thousand times in a night. Getting little or no "deep sleep," they are never really alert during the day.)

Levine said: "Sleep apnea would have an effect, we submit, on his abilities to function in a setting late in the day, after many hours of interrogation, so that his abilities to make rational and believable statements would be impaired. We know from surveillance logs and video tapes. . .that he fell asleep during the day. We know from his wife that he fell asleep often in places where persons who suffer from this kind of malady would.

"We also know from Mrs. Osman that Mr. Miller suffered from auditory dyslexia. And I think her answer to Your Honor's question probably put the whole subject into the most. . .understandable terms: A person with his disability wouldn't be able to understand questions in a stressful situation. This is basically the person. . .who went through four or five days of interrogation, along with religious overtures, time-consuming discussions with agents who weren't believing him, misleading statements about who the people were, not being given information regarding. . .the search of his home, never being given documents to refresh his recollection, even though he said: 'I may have documents somewhere which can do this.' This was the person who was hanging in the wind, and was ripe for plucking. And, Your Honor, these agents knew that, because their boss, three days earlier, after Mr. Miller came forward with his statement, told them that he was getting on a plane [and going home because] they didn't have a case. And they knew they needed to make one, and they went ahead and did that...."

This was a reference to John Martin, the head of internal security—counterintelligence—at the Justice Department, having concluded that no criminal case existed.

Levine went on: "Did Mrs. Ogorodnikova contact Mr. Miller by name, or did she contact him two months earlier and then call him back in May 1984? . . . He [made] different statements regarding that. The government [has pointed] to this as evidence. . .that he's inconsistent and lying. You might conclude that it's evidence of a confused state of mind.

"He told the agent that he gave her a document in San Francisco to give to the Soviets at the consulate, but that the same document was shown to her in his home two weeks earlier [when she had] thumbed through it, didn't think it was particularly important, but he doesn't know if she kept it or not.... And he made those statements on the very same day. Now, how can a person give somebody a document, not know whether she had it, and then give it to her again two weeks later on a trip to San Francisco?

"This is a case, Your Honor, where the government is capable of bringing you. . .hours upon hours of taped conversations [from] a wire tap kept going twenty-four hours a day for thirty days, but what you don't have are any recorded comments of Mr. Miller during those days of interrogation, not only to see what his demeanor was, but what the questions were.... We've already learned from Mr. Hunt's testimony that this method [of recording interrogations] is susceptible to editorializing [*sic*—

presumably "editing"], to leaving out, to putting in only what the [interrogator] thinks is important."

Levine insisted that Miller had no knowledge of Whipworm. Marta York, he said, had testified that Miller had shown no concern when she complained that they were being followed.

"You've also seen videotapes of Mr. Miller performing his daily functions in his office during the month of September, 1984. And we would ask Your Honor to attempt to evaluate whether that looks like a person who thinks he's being followed, and is under surveillance. . . . It is not the burden of proof of the defense to show you that he had no knowledge; it's the burden of proof of the Government to show you that he did. . . .

"We also have testimony that Svetlana not only told Miller that she was being followed, but she told Hunt many times she was being followed; she told Mr. Valdez many times she was being followed. And even in Mr. Miller's verbatim statement to Bryce Christensen, he says that 'she told me many times she was being followed, and I just told her to forget about it: nobody cared about my activities.' Well, if Mr. Miller ever told anything that was truthful, that was it. Nobody ever cared about his activities."

The government had maintained that Miller intended to keep his "op" secret, and had gone to Christensen only because he had spotted DeFlores in a parking lot and had suddenly woken up to the notion that he was under surveillance. Levine set about demolishing the DeFlores evidence:

"Mr. DeFlores told the Court that both Miller and Svetlana were out of the car and that Mrs. Ogorodnikova was carrying something. Nobody else who was conducting surveillance that day saw anything like that. Mr. DeFlores told you that the car... was a Mazda wagon, when we know it was a Mercury Lynx. Mr. DeFlores tells you that the woman was wearing light-colored clothing, and from the pictures and the surveillance testimony we know that that wasn't the case. And then he tells you that the car drove out of the Ohio Street side of the parking lot and went [off] in a westerly direction, when everybody else who came to testify on this subject saw them on Sepulveda. Mr. DeFlores also told you that he was making these observations, including the one about Mr. Miller's surprised look, while he was backing into a space, taking notes, and Mr. Miller was supposedly looking in the direction of the sun, for a grand total of seconds. And you are being asked to conclude, based upon that testimony, that a little light went off in Richard Miller's head and said: 'I am under investigation; I'd better do something about it.' So let's look at what Mr. Miller then did.

"He went on a shopping trip to go to Europe with Svetlana Ogorodnikova, creating yet more evidence if, in fact, he was guilty of a crime. On that shopping trip, you heard his voice; you heard the tone of his voice. Did he sound like a worried man, talking to Mrs. Ogorodnikova about Eliza Doolittle and *My Fair Lady*? He spent hours with Mrs. Ogorodnikova that day and, according to the testimony of the surveillance agents, not one effort was made while Mr. Miller was driving the car that day to 'dry-clean himself'. . . . After the shopping trip is over, Mr. Miller is supposedly alerted to the fact that somebody in the parking lot saw him. So what does he do? He goes back to the same parking lot! He's overheard by an agent. . .having a conversation with Mrs. Ogorodnikova. . . .

"But something else did occur on that shopping trip. . . Mr. Miller heard that the tickets were available. They may not have been actually bought, but he was told that they had been. The little light did go off. . . . He was in over his head; the trip was about to occur. He could not carry forth his double-agent plan any more without the assistance of the Bureau.

"On the morning of September 27, after the supposed light went off from [the] DeFlores contact, Mr. Miller goes to the passport office to apply for a passport, and he keeps the copy of that passport [sic—presumably 'application'] in his desk. . . . One would think that if Mr. Miller had been alerted to this investigation, one of the last things he would be doing would be creating additional documentary evidence of his guilt. He went out and joined a health club right after speaking to Mr. Christensen. He went out on another date with Marta York after joining the health club. Now, if he thinks he's being followed, it would seem kind of odd that he wouldn't cancel that meeting as well.

"A number of things that Mr. Miller did not do are also indicative of the fact that he did not know he was under investigation when he came forward. We have this issue about documents being in Mr. Miller's home. Why didn't he get rid of them? One, he doesn't know the documents are there; two, he doesn't know he's under investigation. Also, he had not told

Christensen or Torrence on the first two days of interrogation about his conversations with Grayson and another friend, David Reid.

"Now, if these conversations were a plant for the defense... you would think that one of the things Mr. Miller would [say] to Mr. Christensen is: 'Do you believe me?' And if he doesn't get the direct 'Yes,' his response would then be: 'Well, go talk to Larry Grayson in Riverside.' But Mr. Miller doesn't do that because he does not have a guilty state of mind....

"If you employ the presumption of innocence, and you give these facts and the evidence a fair evaluation, you come to the conclusion that Mr. Miller came forward because he [had been] told the tickets were available."

Levine compared Miller's behavior to that of police who penetrate the drug world.

"Many of the statements that he made to Mrs. Ogorodnikova could be viewed...as carrying out the role he was playing... If there's one thing we've learned about Mr. Miller through all of the witnesses who have testified about his career, it's that he spent an entire career not following FBI regulations in virtually every category they write them.... You can't judge Mr. Miller and how he was performing and what his intentions were by the same method [by which] the ideal FBI agent is judged... Mr. Christensen told Mr. Miller in Mr. Miller's wife's presence, on the night of September 29, that 'if it's just a failure to report contacts, it may not even be a prosecutable offense'.... John Hunt... reported those contacts he wished to report.... There were some that he didn't choose to report.... He didn't report a visit with Mrs. Ogorodnikova to a doctor; he didn't report when she made a sexual overture to him."

Levine referred again to Miller's little plot with Grayson and his conversation with the garage-owner friend, David Reid. "What he told Mr. Reid—in response to a question—was that he had been frustrated in his years in the FBI, [that] he loved his country, that he hadn't really been given the opportunity during his career to excel, and he hoped that before his career ended he could go down [*sic*—presumably 'out'] in a blaze of glory instead of going down in flames.... Then he meets with Mr. Grayson—also before there's any investigation... The Government would have you believe...that Grayson and Miller were really talking about a crime.... Grayson testified that Miller told him that the FBI would cover the [Mexico] expenses. . . If it's a clandestine crime, how do we reconcile that with the FBI paying for it, and with Mr. Grayson agreeing to go?. . . When Grayson said to him: 'How can you give them the personnel list that they asked for?' Miller said: 'I can handle this.' And the reason. . . [was] because he wasn't going to exchange documents for money until after his trip, and he was going to be getting proof of that to show to his superiors. . . .

"Mr. Miller and Mr. Grayson were concerned about secrecy, so they adjourned from the coffee shop to the parking lot so that they wouldn't be overheard. These concerns were [Grayson's] . . . . It was Mr. Grayson who said: 'Let's step outside.' It was Mr. Grayson who said: 'Let's give it a code name: *Mother*.' "

Levine then came to the "Svetlana" file found at Lynwood:

"Now, it's true, a short version of the Positive Intelligence Reporting Guide was inside this file, with nobody's prints from this case; not Mrs. Ogorodnikova's, nor Mr. Ogorodnikov's. Also within this file were Mr. Miller's leave records, an invoice from a psychiatrist, partially written reports, lists of dates, and a copy of the note which Mr. Auer wrote to John Hunt, and numerous other sundry documents which, we submit, are evidence of one thing: That Mr. Miller is a pack rat who throws documents into files. If he was truly intending to be a spy, and if that's what his actions were depicting, why would he keep a file marked 'Svetlana' in his home, and why would he not destroy it if he knew he was under investigation?. . . .

"This file, and other documents in his home, and the documents in his desk, which are inches high, involve old outdated documents, some classified, some not; old outdated investigatory files [in] some of which Mr. Miller was the case agent and [in] some [of] which he was not; old interview forms, waiver-of-rights forms."

Levine said the expert witnesses had agreed that Soviet intelligence usually paid for classified information in cash, and that they did not reveal true identities.

"So what does Mr. Miller do in what the Government thinks is the intent to be a spy? He requests that fifty thousand dollars in gold be paid, with the payment in three separate safety deposit boxes in three different banks. And he further requests that he know the identity of the person that he's dealing with.... If he's hungry for money, and he's selling documents, obviously

he wants cash and he wants it hidden! He doesn't want a trial
. . . .

"Why would he request the identity of the person that he is seeking to do business with? Because he's an FBI agent who has developed an undercover plan, possibly not by the book; he wants to know, so he can report to his superiors whom he's dealing with. If the object of this scheme was to get rich quick, then it would be cash—and he wouldn't need to know the identity of anybody. . . .

"He met with Mrs. Ogorodnikova repeatedly in broad daylight, within eyeshot of the FBI office building. Now, that is significant. Your Honor was there; you could turn around and see the building in the distance. When Mr. Hunt was meeting with her, it wasn't there, and whatever Mr. Hunt's motives were in establishing *rapport* with this woman for fiftyfive meetings in six months, he certainly met with her in locations other than the shadow of the FBI building. Why does Mr. Miller meet her there? . . . . Because he's unconcerned. He's unconcerned because his intentions are innocent. . . .

"The passport application: Mr. Miller doesn't attempt to travel under a false name. . . . He does it on September 27. That's the day after he supposedly knows he's under investigation. And then he keeps a copy of [the application] in his desk and it's found there after his arrest. . . .

"Mr. Hunt testified that in 1982, among the duties he had was to be in charge of double-agent operations on the FCI-1 squad in Los Angeles. And during that year, he authorized Mrs. Ogorodnikova to make a trip to San Francisco, to talk about Mr. Hunt and say certain things to the consular officials about Mr. Hunt which, as Mr. Barron says: 'If they heard something like that, they would salivate.'. . . . Whatever it was that Mr. Hunt did in 1982 was done with the approval of the FBI. What that means is that plans such as this are conceptually valid, and that a person like Mr. Miller working on the FCI-1 squad would have the right to conclude that, in concept, such a plan was valid.

"Mr. Miller's plan was procedurally flawed; but everything Mr. Miller did in the FBI was procedurally flawed.

"One of the things that you might conclude is that the Hunt/Svetlana scenario. . . never really ended. . . Numerous times in 1983 and 1984, Mrs. Ogorodnikova is reporting to the FBI that she wishes to see Mr. Hunt and that the KGB has been meeting with her and that she needs to tell him what's happening. . . . Earlier [in 1984] she met with two other agents [to say] that she had just come from Moscow [and that] the KGB wanted her to talk to John Hunt. . . . Hunt took out [her] '134' file several times during 1984. He took it out on the 24th of May and the 31st of May, and Mr. Miller's name appears on the long day when it was out for eight hours. But Hunt also took the file out three other times in 1984: March 27, July 19 and August 2. That suggests that there is activity going on between Hunt and Mrs. Ogorodnikova." As late as August, Levine said, she was reporting that Hunt's "dangle" of the previous year was now drawing a positive response from Moscow.

"What really happened," Levine went on, "is [that] Mr. Miller retrieved the torch that had been lit by Mr. Hunt. . . [and] that he went further than John Hunt and actually allowed himself to be 'recruited' instead of merely assessing how the Soviets might react; that he became, in the words of Colonel Kennedy, a 'target of opportunity'. . . [Miller] differs from John Hunt in that he did not deny having a. . . sexual involvement with Mrs. Ogorodnikova. Mr. Hunt may or may not have; the resolution of that is not important to this case. We know that Mrs. Ogorodnikova, six months before she ever met Mr. Miller, went to [her] lawyer, Donald Levinson, to report that she had a problem in the form of an affair with an FBI agent and she wanted some legal advice. But the outcome of that resolution, we submit, is between Mr. Hunt and his maker. We do know that Mr. Hunt ended this scenario after four years with fifty thousand dollars in his pocket, and Mr. Miller ended it with five years in jail. . . .

"My client is not a perfect man. He was more or less a bad FBI agent. He was probably more or less a bad husband. He was a good father; he was good with informants, but bad in many other ways in the performance of his career in the FBI. But what you're being asked to do is to say that, based on the quality of the evidence before you, he was also a spy. And if you analyze [the evidence], Your Honor, you cannot draw that conclusion."

In his rebuttal, Schiff sought to downplay Levine's points about actions indicating Miller's innocent intentions. At one point, Judge Takasugi interrupted him to ask: "What's your explanation of payments in gold in three deposit boxes?"

Schiff stressed the unlikelihood that the Russians would accept this method, and added: "Why in particular Mr. Miller asked for gold instead of another form of payment is something we will never know."

Later, Schiff said: "The salient point is: After four months of clandestine meetings with Svetlana Ogorodnikova, it wasn't until September 26* that he decides to go to Bryce Christensen and lay out an alibi. This raised the Government's claim that Miller had gone to Christensen because he had spotted DeFlores in the parking lot.

Judge Takasugi interjected: "I believe it's impossible, from... where Mr. Miller was standing, to see who was the occupant of that FBI car except, perhaps, by recognizing the type of car used by the FBI at that time."

Said Schiff: "Mr. Miller had a chance to see that car on a number of occasions. . . . It is, I think, by anyone's estimation, an unusual-looking car."

Schiff said the prosecution hadn't called Grayson "because the Government cannot be satisfied that Larry Grayson is telling the complete truth." He returned to Hunt's assertion that the FBI uses assets as double agents, but no FBI agents as double agents. Curiously, the defense had not raised the example of Agent Joe Pistone, whom Miller admired. The Government's view of Hunt, as Schiff expressed it, was similar to Levine's in one important respect:

"Mr. Levine is right. Whether Mr. Hunt was [sexually] involved with Svetlana Ogorodnikova has no bearing on this case . . . The prosecution would fully concur with the defense contention as far as that is concerned. . . It's not really questioned, I think, that she had an attachment to John Hunt. . . I don't think that there's any question about the feelings that she had for John Hunt."

Takasugi had already made it clear that he rejected the Government claim that Miller only went to Christensen with a "cock and bull" story because he had seen DeFlores in the parking lot. He ignored the expert testimony of Barron and Kennedy as to what the KGB did or did not do in the cold war

---

Actually, September 27—*Author*

battle of intelligence. But he rejected the defense's contention that the confession to actually giving a document had been extracted from a basket case by manipulation. In layman's terms, the judge found Miller guilty, but with the best intentions. He did not question Miller's loyalty, but he strongly questioned his common sense. In an impressively short verdict statement, Takasugi said:

"Some difficulty experienced by this trier of fact was to place in proper perspective the possible emotional bias of the FBI in investigating one of its own."

He went on: "Mr. Miller, aside from his social relationship with Svetlana Ogorodnikova, did intend to utilize her as an asset of the FBI and retire from the FBI in a blaze of glory."

But "following Svetlana's return from Moscow in July, 1984" he had lost control of her to Grishin. "In the battle of wills, Mr. Miller. . .begrudgingly. . . compromised his obligations to the FBI. . . . The Court does find Mr. Miller guilty of Counts One through Six."

Schiff asked for Miller to be remanded, but bail was continued. Schiff asked that Miller be obliged to wear a tracking device, but this also was refused. Everything pointed to a much reduced sentence for the would-be Bernard Samson of Los Angeles.

# Chapter Eighteen

# *Trial and Error: The Principal Victim*

Judge Takasugi, aware that a really short sentence would be an indirect reflection on his colleague, Judge Kenyon, seems to have stopped short of giving Miller less than Miller's "accomplice," Svetlana Ogorodnikova. On February 4, 1991, he reduced the "two consecutive life terms plus fifty years," (in effect, 110 years) to twenty years, with a recommendation of parole after one-third of the term. As Miller had already been incarcerated for five years, this left him at least twenty months to serve. Unless the parole board ignores Takasugi's recommendation, Miller is due for release in the near future.

By October 1993, Svetlana will have been uninterruptedly in prison for nine years; she is then due for consideration for parole. (Even prisoners with multiple consecutive life sentences have a chance at parole after ten years, provided they show convincing proof of remorse and rehabilitation.)

Miller received his sentence in the presence of his sister, Mary Ann Deem, and his third son (nicknamed Tres, but pronounced Trace). He was somber but resigned, no longer the weeping wreck that he had been when put on the griddle by the FBI. The following week, aided by a new lawyer, Greg Nicolaysen, he filed another appeal.

Said Charlie Bates, fourteen years into his retirement: "Damn fool thing! They should have just told Miller: 'You resign, y'hear? If you don't resign, you're fired.' Those damn trials brought disgrace on the FBI."

In the final analysis, the most unfortunate victim of this *farce macabre* is Svetlana, who is accused of having decided that she could trust the disembodied voice of Aleksandr Grishin more than she could trust John Hunt, who had "jilted" her; she was, of course, persuaded not to present her case—to plead guilty, or go to jail "forever"—so hers is a case that has never been tried. Is Svetlana a totally or only a partly innocent victim of an FCI-1 unit's ham-fisted attempt to play MI-5?

Much goes to the question of Svetlana's credibility. Her account of how Hunt recruited her as his swallow differs from his. For instance, she says he invaded her graduation party and swept her off for a "night on the town." He says it was her suggestion that they go to a restaurant and a night club. Her memories are disorganized; he has logs. Her recollections are self-serving. His are selective, and he dissimulates. Are the time variations in John's and Svetlana's respective stories relevant, or unimportant?

She is anxious to appear not to have taken the initiative in the link with Hunt. She is also anxious to appear to have been virtually a non-drinker before Hunt "taught" her "booze." She stresses determinedly that she had always been sexually faithful to her husband until she met Hunt and Miller. Proceeding from the hypothesis that she is not entirely truthful on "moral" matters such as alcohol and adultery, is there a criminal or a *psychological* explanation for this? Mata Hari, who was similarly arrested for espionage, not adultery, was equally prissy about her early life under questioning. Did Mrs. Ogorodnikova have a freer and perhaps more promiscuous lifestyle than she wants to see reported in the press, or in a book? Why would a woman with an unhappy marriage limit her infidelities to two not particularly attractive, middle-aged policemen, the younger of whom (Miller) she described to a friend as being "too old" for her, while the other, she claimed to her fellow prisoners at Pleasanton, made love like a raging bull? Is any of this relevant to her guilt or innocence of espionage?

Like Mata Hari, to whom she compares herself, she has a tendency to tell unnecessary lies, especially when she is trying to be her own lawyer and to invent her own defense strategy. At one point in this writer's discussions with her, she claimed that the September shopping expedition was "for Matvei," although Miller himself admits that the shopping was mostly for him. Nikolaiy admits he chose Miller's new shoes, as part of the Ogorodnikov family effort to make the shabby, shambling

G-man presentable in Europe. Do her inaccuracies suggest that she is trying to distance herself from her role—whether her role as part of a Miller "sting" or as part of a Soviet recruitment effort—or is she simply trying to distance herself from the whole fiasco? Again—is this relevant?

Then still again, if she is not being honest when she says she was Hunt's mistress, what does this imply? Does it have any bearing on her guilt or innocence? As this writer has noted earlier, a woman might betray her husband (if she no longer loved him), but she would be much less likely to betray the man she loved. Is she telling the truth about a liaison with Hunt, or is she lying to conceal her guilt? Or is she lying to preserve her moral reputation and her relations with her home country, in the same way that she fought to retain her film business?

The reader is also entitled to question whether Hunt's interest in her was purely professional, whether as an informant she was worth so many hundreds of hours of his time, especially after-dark overtime, and especially if we accept his testimony that he had only limited uses and intentions for her as a low-level informant and unwitting "double agent" disinformation channel. Svetlana gives great detail about their sexual involvement; she says a woman friend allowed them to use their apartment for sex. Just as the reader is entitled to suspect that she exaggerates her role as a seduced housewife to protect her "name," so the reader is entitled to suspect that Hunt was her lover, not just a dance-floor cuddler, and who also needs to protect his "name," and his marriage. What relevance does this have? Of particular relevance, of course, is the degree of "hold" he had over her. Would she tell Nadya Mathison and her husband that she was going to marry Hunt if this was not her intention? Or was this just one of her fantasies? There is objective evidence, with which Hunt agreed on the witness stand, that she was emotionally upset when Hunt ended their relationship. At the same time, he is angry that the Bureau has impugned his moral behavior.

Whenever Svetlana talks about Hunt now, she cries and rages. Is she trying to fool the author? Is she fooling herself? Or are her emotions what they appear to be—i.e., as one investigator noted, demonstrative of the fact that hell hath no fury like a woman scorned?

Why are the traffic records for the day on which she had a road accident with John Hunt in the car missing? Why are Dr. Jeikov's records missing for the day on which Hunt took her to him? Are these simply two amazing coincidences? Or does it mean, as she put it, that there was an "FBI cover-up" to protect Hunt? Why did he not "log" his visit to Dr. Jeikov with her, if the trip was an "innocent" one so far as he was concerned?

Svetlana Ogorodnikova gets dates and sequences of events mixed and confused. This may be genuine. Interviewing her is like, as the saying goes in the profession, trying to pinch mercury. Unlike John Hunt, she has no log to refer to, and appears to have a genuinely poor memory. For instance, when this writer first talked to her, she had the meeting between Nikolaiy and Miller, the drive around Lynwood with Nikolaiy's nephew to find Miller's house, and the shopping expedition with Miller all running together. A reader may wonder whether, on events about which she is nervous, she is not genuinely confused in her memories. As one investigator sympathetic to her plight said, she has a "propensity not to tell the truth." How relevant is this to her guilt or innocence? When a colonel like Oliver North or a president of the United States like Richard Nixon tells lies, we are entitled to suspect this as implying consciousness of guilt. It is more difficult to reach such a hard and fast conclusion with a "scatterbrain" like Svetlana.

Is the FBI, as she claims, covering up for Hunt—for instance about his alleged willingness to part with his identification? Have we been told all the reasons he left the FBI so suddenly? Hunt says he never saw her again after early 1984—only spoke to her on the telephone. This implies that he obeyed Auer's orders to cease his involvement with her, but is it credible? (The author isn't saying it isn't, but if Hunt wanted to keep a continued connection with her secret, actual meetings would probably be easier to conceal than telephone calls.) There seems no reason to doubt that he instructed her to keep him informed of all her dealings with Miller. If you doubt this assertion (that there were no face-to-face meetings), does this damage his credibility further? Or does it have little or no relevance? Bear in mind that Svetlana's confidante and friend, Mrs. Mathison, who despises Hunt as an unprincipled seducer, believes Hunt's version here and disbelieves Svetlana's.

In the climate of deceit that goes with espionage and counterespionage, who was fooling whom? Did Svetlana hype her relationship with the consulate-general to make herself more attractive to Hunt, or did she hype her relationship with Hunt, on his instructions, to tickle the fancy of the KGB? Remember that Svetlana denied to Nadya Mathison that her relationship with Hunt was sexual, and that Mrs. Mathison is unsure of the truth—that maybe Svetlana was concealing her "adultery," or maybe Hunt really did have an adoring Svetlana "begging for it," but not getting any. The reader may feel that Nadya Mathison's insights into Svetlana's character are more profound than Svetlana's own, rather spacy self-analysis, or than those of two rather naive American policemen. What exactly was Svetlana's role with the consulate-general? Remember Mrs. Mathison's remark that she was always buzzing around the place "like a mosquito," asking for something to do. How much of a role would a highly qualified intelligence professional like Grishin, stationed in the heart of enemy territory and in charge of Soviet intelligence for half of the entire country, confide to Svetlana Malutina of Yefrimov? Reversing Greenberg's metaphor, the author is satisfied from the evidence that Grishin used her as live bait to hook not only Miller but Bretzing.

The crucial questions about Svetlana come down to two:

Was she loyal to one side—and, if so, which one—or neither?

Who controlled the Miller/Ogorodnikova relationship? Judge Takasugi said that, in the end, it was she. The author believes that the fisherman controls both the bait and the catch. Grishin had them both on his line.

Grishin's September 11 telephone call was clearly related to the instructions Svetlana had received in Moscow from "Anatoliy." (Grishin says "in the special house," while she says "in my hotel"—are they the same thing?) This was the prickly meeting that Svetlana apparently faithfully reported to Hunt on her return. This Moscow meeting is also reflected in Grishin's comic use of the "clear code" that she admits Anatoliy told her about—such as references on the bugged line to "the acquaintances," a formula Grishin clearly used to attract suspicion. There can surely be no doubt that the Vienna trip, which Miller says was intended to be a Miller (or FBI) sting (and which the prosecution said was a blatant offer by Miller to be recruited, to which the Soviet Union had favorably responded) was nothing more nor less than a Soviet sting.

Grishin clearly set the alarm-bell pattern of Tuesday calls, between 7:30 and 8 p.m., which Svetlana clearly expected. This procedure—making things easy for the FBI—is consonant with the Russian scam, which it was neither in the interest of the defense or the prosecution to present in court, since it makes fools of both. Did Svetlana accept this "telephone relationship" with Grishin for Grishin's sake, or for Miller's? Or was she just the shuttlecock?

One car intercept seems clearly to show her pleading with Miller to "come to work" for the Soviet Union ("Please!") after he had said: "Well, we'll see." Does this mean that, by that time, perhaps from fear, perhaps in angry rejection to being "jilted" by Hunt, or for other reasons, she was herself working for the KGB (or the GRU)? Or does it simply refer to Miller's intention to "penetrate" Soviet intelligence, to "play the game" (the words she says he used to her), since this would involve remuneration from Soviet intelligence, which she may have presumed he would be able to keep?

One of the prosecutors at her 1985 trial asserted that "like most spies in fiction, she was only working for herself. It was who was in control of her that counts." Was she conscious of being controlled, or was she just "on a roll," as Mrs. Mathison imagines?

Whether or not she was romantically and perhaps sexually involved with Hunt is clearly important in determining her allegiances—at the time of her involvement, and after being, as she claims, jilted—but how important, if at all, was the nature of her sexual relationship with Miller? Wasn't he just your average American cop doing what came naturally—humping a promiscuous female informant? Or are there any grounds for thinking—as the prosecution claimed—that (although he was considering marriage to Marta York) he was actually "infatuated" with Svetlana and that she "controlled" him?

What should one make of the statement that Miller says Svetlana made to him—that "if anyone becomes aware of [this], you'll get the first bullet"? If this was in fact said, was it a threat or a friendly, concerned warning? Did it mean that if the Rezidentura discovered that he was running her as an FBI asset, his life would be as cheap as hers? Could the remark have any other meaning? Was it just hype—since the KGB had never killed anyone in the United States?

It is easier to believe Nikolaiy and Miller and the prosecution than it is to credit Svetlana, because she is contradictory and tells unnecessary untruths. Is Nikolaiy, however, entirely innocent? He admits he took a report on *émigrés* to San Francisco and gave it to a mysterious man in a café. He was given the report by Svetlana, and it appears to have been a "dangle" from Hunt; but of course, there is no proof of this. Was Nikolaiy acting as a courier for Hunt—who would have thought that his "swallow" Svetlana would be doing the delivery herself—or were Nikolaiy or Svetlana (or both of them) courier(s) for some low-level informant of the Rezidentura? Nikolaiy was not accused of this, but would such work be relevant to his guilt or innocence of the charges of which he was accused?

If Mrs. Ogorodnikova acted solely for the FBI (as the KGB concluded), she is innocent. If she thought she was acting solely for the FBI, and consciously did nothing for the KGB, she is innocent. If she was engaged in a conspiracy to recruit Miller for the GRU or the KGB, she is guilty. Theoretically, Ogorodnikov could be guilty even if his wife were not, but only if he acted independently of her. If she is guilty, he is guilty in the measure that he consciously abetted her.

Judge Takasugi imposed a much less controversial sentence on Miller than Kenyon had done, because Takasugi had recognized, as Kenyon had not done, that Miller's original intentions were good. Miller was like an aberrant child who does something to impress his parents and make some candy money as well. Joel Levine described his client in court as Inspector Clouseau played by Jackie Gleason, but he was really Bernard Samson played by a middle-aged Dennis the Menace. Compared to the cases of, say, Walker, Pollard or Pelton, the Miller case was also of staggering triviality—which is what makes it so human and understandable to law-abiding citizens. When Edward Howard, the Soviet mole in the CIA, made his 1985 escape, under the noses of the FBI around his house, the hunt for him was followed not only by America's intelligence chiefs, but also by such interested parties as Viktor Mikhailovich Chebrikov, then the chairman of the KGB, and General Sir Frederick Figures, then the director of MI-6. It was unlikely that either of these gentlemen knew who Richard Miller was when he was arrested. There seems little likelihood that Miller's retrial won the attention of Vadim Kryuchkov, the KGB's head at the time.

Takasugi, however, had to face, within the sentencing guidelines incumbent on him, the question of how security offenses—and specifically security offenses in peacetime but in the context of the Cold War (Gorbachev was not yet in power in 1984)—fit into the variegated gallery of crime. Most of us, with a basement apartment to rent, would rather have a spy down there than a thief or a drug-pusher. Yet clearly the gravity of an offense must also be a factor in sentencing. When he found Miller guilty, could Takasugi sentence him to less than Svetlana, an accessory? The British were presumably flabbergasted to learn that Kenyon gave Svetlana a greater punishment— eighteen years—than the fourteen years given at the Old Bailey to Klaus Fuchs, who passed the secrets of the hydrogen bomb to Stalin. Are spies such as the Rosenbergs, Fuchs or Kim Philby, who spied out of ideological conviction, rather more or less forgivable than a John Walker or a Miller, who did it for the cash—at least, the prosecution said that was Miller's motive. Is a Jonathan Pollard the worst of all, spying both from conviction and for hundreds of thousands of dollars? Certainly, it is harder for a court to be lenient with a traitor (an American spying on America, or a Russian spying on the Soviet Union) than with a patriot (an American spying on the Soviet Union, or a Russian spying on America).

The sentences imposed in the Miller case related as much to the *form* (in particular, the secrecy) of the alleged passage of information (or alleged conspiracy to pass it or sell it later) as to the (not particularly sensitive) *nature* itself of the information.

A source with substantial prosecutorial experience told the author in 1989 that his guesstimate was that John Walker, Jon Pollard and R.W. Miller (if his original conviction had not been reversed) would all do about the same "time"—roughly eighteen years. He thought Svetlana, if there was no special intervention, would do twelve. We are entitled to consider whether the notion of her doing two-thirds as much time as John Walker and Ronald Pelton, and nearly four times as much actual time as Ann Pollard, does not imply a certain irrationality.

This raises the question of the "level" at which one assesses espionage. Our own instinctive reactions are not necessarily a guide. We might be repelled by the neighborhood rapist, and the child molester—like the spy—even faces molestation by fellow convicts, but most of us would have welcomed a chance to meet Kim Philby. If the choice were between sharing a cell with a street mugger doing eighteen months and Jerry Whitworth doing twenty-five years, whom would you choose? Whom would the judge choose? As Ed Howard, the Soviet mole in the CIA, told the *Washington Post* in 1991, in his butlered dacha outside Moscow, even treason is only a white-collar crime—and white-collar crime *frightens* us less than smaller but violent crimes such as housebreaking. In espionage, also, clearly the importance of the "secrets" involved must be a factor.

One reason the Miller/Ogorodnikova caper took on an unwarranted importance was because of the cast: an FBI special agent of the "counterintelligence" unit, someone depicted in part of the press as a Russian vampire, the vamp's husband, and a shadowy KGB operative. When the long and outrageously expensive first and second Miller trials ended with the sort of sentence meted out to serial assassins, this put Miller in a spy class above that of Pollard and Whitworth and on a par with John Walker and Pelton (who got three consecutive "lifes" plus ten years—in functional terms, one hundred years, or ten less than Miller). Svetlana Ogorodnikova, who might perhaps be not unfairly described as the Daffy Duck of espionage, got eighteen years, whereas a cold-eyed and unrepentant Ann Pollard received only five. The Miller/Ogorodnikova case illustrates the capriciousness of justice and sentencing. The question is: Was Judge Kenyon unreasonably harsh, or were the judges who sentenced the Walkers and the Pollards unreasonably lenient?

Again, the form is as important as the nature of the crime itself. Miller could have passed the guidance information to the Rezidentura by simply giving it to an American reporter. If discovered, he would have faced in-house sanctions, perhaps dismissal, but no criminal charges; and he would not have been paid by the press, whereas he allegedly hoped to keep whatever he was paid for whatever he might have delivered to the KGB. What would the FBI have done, in such an event?

If the story had appeared in the *Anchorage News*, the Bureau would probably have decided that it would be best not to draw attention to it by saying anything. If the article had appeared in a major magazine, where the Soviet embassy would be sure to read it, the FBI director would probably have ordered an in-house investigation to determine the source of the leak. If the story had broken in the *Washington Post* or the *Los Angeles Times*, there would have been concern that Congress and/or the White House might criticize the Bureau's lax security. In this event, the director, who is not usually an intelligence specialist, might have rushed into print with a statement deploring the irresponsibility of the reporter and the press. If advisers had gotten to him first, he might have arranged for a leak to, say, the Evans and Novak column, saying that the document in question was a notional draft and that the final version had been totally different in every way. This, it would have been hoped, would confuse the KGB.

In any of these scenarios, it is extremely unlikely that the journalist would be bothered further, any more than was the case with the Pentagon Papers, a much more important document.

Do the huge disparities in sentencing in the United States—for almost all offenses—not imply a failure to eliminate judicial caprice, regardless of "guidelines"? These require the judge to consider three penological factors—protecting society, punishing and rehabilitating—and to compare the offense with other offenses of the same nature or the same degree of importance. Was the principal victim of this affair the bumbling Miller, the manipulated Svetlana caught in the crossfire, the bystander Nikolaiy—or justice itself?

Even when convictions themselves are not appealed, perhaps sentencing should be subject to a review panel, as in military justice.

The Miller tragifarce did not come out of the blue. The Falcon and Snowman case in the same bailiwick (which Miller's lawyer, Joel Levine, prosecuted) was cracked by the Mexican police, not the FCI. What, above all, the Miller case drew attention to was a level of professional and linguistic incompetence in U.S. counterintelligence—as illustrated by one of its largest FCI offices—that deserves a total investigation; not just an in-house whitewash, but a full-scale congressional inquiry. It is significant that all the agents concerned with the shortcomings of FCI in Los Angeles in "Miller time"—Bretzing, Christensen, Auer, Hunt—were all persuaded to take early retirement or given "Siberia" assignments; but the whole notion of allowing the FBI to leave counterintelligence to the spavined nags of Car Theft and Immigration is surely naive and irresponsible. Clearly, at this time, the United States has no real equivalent of Britain's MI-5 or France's DGST.

The bizarre linguistic inadequacies of FCI are a neon feature of its overall incompetence. No country has such a bank of linguists as America. Over six million Americans speak "difficult" languages such as Chinese, Japanese, Arabic, Russian, Korean or Vietnamese, either because it is the mother tongue of first-generation immigrants or the "kitchen language" of their often better-educated children. Of course, millions more speak Spanish or German and other facile tongues with syntaxes like that of English. Yet only one member of the nineteen-man Russian squad in Los Angeles could speak the language of the people they were spying on, and none of the eighteen deficient members were taking courses. (Needless to say, even Grishin's driver could speak fluent English.)

Because the CIA's domestic espionage is restricted by law, FCI is the humble equivalent of MI-5. Yet FCI is not a permanent assignment. Although a few members have been on brief intelligence courses, many at any one moment are just veteran agents serving out their time in a risk-free environment. (The KGB never physically targeted an FBI man in America, any more than the CIA would have targeted KGB personnel in Russia.)

Is there any reason intelligence and counterintelligence should not be grouped in a single organization, as is the case in other countries? Would the CIA be more of a threat to American civil liberties than the FBI? Couldn't Congress, as the watchdog, exercise oversight over the one as easily as the other? Certainly, investigative reporters would rather deal with a better breed of spook!

Although the cold war is over, the needs of political, military and economic intelligence remains. Anyone spying on the Chinese—one human being in every five—should not only be able to read the Xinhua file over breakfast but also, preferably, to speak unaccented Mandarin. Counterintelligence requires not only something better than Richard Bretzing, J. Bryce Christensen, Gary Auer, John Hunt, R.W. Miller and Svetlana Ogorodnikova, but also something totally different.

# Epilogue

The author has described Nikolaiy's first year after release in January 1990. Following his unsuccessful mission to the Soviet embassy in Washington at the end of that year, Nikolaiy went home to Los Angeles. One night, as he was waiting for hotel guests to come out for his next run to the airport, a husky young black man came running up. The youth was literally on the run from the police, and armed. He wanted the keys to the bus, to use it for a getaway. The five-feet-one, fifty-eight-year-old veteran of the Red Army spluttered: "No! No! Hotel guesti only!" and threw himself on the intruder. Somehow, the scrappy Nikolaiy managed to hold on to the rascal who wanted to steal "his" bus until the police puffily arrived and took over the arrest.

The story of the "Soviet spy" who had risked his life in the name of law and order made the local press and television. Nikolaiy was interviewed. The LAPD praised him and presented him with a citizen's commendation. Hampton Inns International made him "Employee of the Year" and hung his photo-portrait in lobbies from Vancouver to Valparaiso. Now, his principal thoughts were of Matvei, his son.

Both the grandmothers who had taken care of the boy were now dead, and the eighteen-year-old was following in his mother's footsteps by studying to be a medical technician. He wanted to be a doctor. But in the Soviet Union, it often wasn't what you knew so much as who you knew that decided a career, and the offspring of an old jailbird from Kiev didn't have much chance. By 1991, Matvei, who speaks unaccented American, decided to return to California. He went to the U.S. consulate-general in Moscow and said he wanted to rejoin "my dad."

The visa clerks soon recognized the name Ogorodnikov and began to make difficulties. He called his father.

Nikolaiy then called the author, who called the INS, which confirmed that Matvei's "green card"—which the boy had surrendered when his parents had been arrested—was still valid. INS had nothing "against" the boy. I got the number of the valid card and called the office of Senator Joseph Biden, Democrat of Delaware, who is chairman of the Senate Judiciary Committee, which holds the pursestrings of the judiciary, the FBI—and INS. One of Biden's staff sent a message to the consulate-general in Moscow, asking why the boy's return was being delayed. He didn't need a visa, only reissue of his valid card, it was pointed out.

Matvei arrived in Los Angeles and soon resumed his medical-technician studies, with a view to getting a job that would enable him to study to be a paramedic—which would enable him to get a better job and put himself through a medical degree at UCLA. Nikolaiy's lined, white-thatched face beamed with pride. Decades before, when Matvei had been born, he had dreamed of his son becoming a Red Army officer; seeing the boy become a doctor in California would have been beyond his dreams.

Television and the *Los Angeles Times* interviewed father and son. Father and son were happy. Nikolaiy's employers were pleased. But the INS wasn't pleased; it announced that, since the Miller retrial was over, there was no bureaucratic reason why Nikolaiy should not be expelled to "the Soviet Union," which had not yet disappeared. A local lawyer argued that Nikolaiy wanted a retrial, that he had a workmen's compensation suit going for the head injury he had acquired in the hotel tussle with the gunman, that Nikolaiy's son needed his father. To no avail. Nikolaiy mustered his friends in the local media, and when the black hats came to take Nikolaiy bodily to prison again, for deportation, the tiny apartment on Gardner Street was packed with videocameras, sound booms and stand-up reporters.

That was in October 1991. For the seventh time in his life, Nikolaiy entered prison, the notorious Terminal Island facility. Still refusing to go to Russia or the Ukraine, he was moved to Winchester County jail in Virginia, about fifty miles from Washington, so that Yevgeniy Antipov, the then Russian consul-general, could determine his wishes. Again, Ramsey Clark found a veteran immigration lawyer, David Carliner, to take on Nikolaiy's case. From the earnings from a part-time job, Matvei managed to pay the rent, do some simple cooking, and send the attorney a thousand dollars.

Antipov, an urbane gentleman, did not want to do anything to offend the United States, to which his government was looking for all sorts of aid. He transmitted to Moscow the INS request that Nikolaiy be given "travel papers"—all a stateless citizen could expect. He arranged for Carliner to have Nikolaiy brought from Winchester, and the old Ukrainian met his new lawyer for the first time in Antipov's office. Antipov asked

Nikolaiy if he was prepared to go to Russia. Nikolaiy, his high voice rising even higher, said he wasn't prepared to go to Russia or to his native Ukraine. He wanted to go back to work and support his son.

Antipov said the Ukraine—which the Russian consulate-general was temporarily representing as well—wouldn't accept its old convicted felon. The Russian government had authorized him to issue travel papers for Russia, but only if Nikolaiy asked for them. He was not, he explained, authorized to issue papers to anyone who didn't want them.

So Nikolaiy went back to the Winchester jail. As the six-month maximum that the INS can hold someone for deportation, while an "accepting country" is sought, drew to a close in May 1992, Carliner was told that Nikolaiy would be released, then immediately rearrested and charged with a felony: Refusing to ask for travel papers for Russia. Maximum: ten years.

A dispirited Nikolaiy called frequently. A distraught Matvei, now refusing to speak Russian to the other Russians on Gardner Street, and asking that he be called Matthew, also called frequently. "Have you any news about my dad?" Even Svetlana began calling and sending cards. "Why are they doing this to that poor old man? He was only punished because of me." Profiled behind her concern was the likelihood that, if Nikolaiy was successfully deported, her own chances of resisting eventual deportation would be almost non-existent.

It was at this point that Abdul Karim Abou Nasr, the Lebanese editor of the Middle East newsmagazine *Al-Wasat*, for whom the author is the Washington correspondent, called to say that he'd noticed that old hands of the KGB and the (East German) Stasi were beginning to talk to reporters. All the Russian talkers were defectors. Could I find a real, serving KGB officer in America with a Middle East career background and get him to agree to be interviewed? I said I thought it was unlikely, but that I would try.

Eventually, through contacts, I was given a name and a Moscow telephone number to call at the Russian Intelligence Service, which is what the First Chief Directorate of the KGB—Grishin's old shop—has become. I got through to this very senior officer at once. He had been expecting my call, and said I could interview a very, very senior person in Moscow, but not over the phone. I said I would check with my editor, to whom

I suggested that he pass this plum assignment to his Moscow correspondent. Abdul Karim said: "Can you do it yourself? This is dynamite."

So when Nikolaiy next called, I was able to give him the improbable news that I was going to Moscow. Of course, I didn't mention the nature of the assignment. Nikolaiy asked if I would take a letter.

It turned out to be a letter, in Russian naturally, to the next-to-next-to-last chairman of the KGB (Nikolaiy hadn't kept up with the news). It asked the Chairman to write a letter saying that Nikolaiy had never worked for the KGB. What a hope! And what a lucky chance—Nikolaiy didn't even know that I would be dealing with the ex-KGB.

The seventy-year-old spymaster with whom I spent a solid week of interviews in Moscow was Lieutenant-General Vadim Alekseivich Kirpichenko, the most senior serving career intelligence officer of his country. He had never been interviewed by any journalist, even a Russian, before. As veterans of—and allies in—World War Two, we got along well together; the three planned interviews were extended to five, plus a dinner under the chandeliers of the old First Chief Directorate VIP mansion in downtown Moscow, and even a dinner at his home, with his wife—the Russian translator of Nobel Prize for Literature laureate Naguib Mahfouz—doing the cooking, and the general playing the piano. There was a selection from *Mary Poppins* and an old Russian drinking song which became the theme tune of *Fiddler on the Roof*.

Kirpichenko had been persuaded to collaborate in what became a twenty-thousand-word cover story in *Al-Wasat* because he had made his career in the Middle East, ending up as Rezident in Cairo. Then came his elevation to the command of "S" directorate in Moscow, in charge of all the Walkers and Howards across the world, and the immediate boss of fellow-general and neighbor Kim Philby. He went on to accumulate this post with that of Deputy Chief Director of the First Chief Directorate, the highest post available to a career intelligence officer. When I saw him, he had become chief counselor to the political-nominee head of the new Russian Intelligence Service, Yevgeni Primakov.

Kirpichenko puckishly pointed out amusing mistakes in *KGB*, by John Barron—whom Miller's prosecutors had described as America's leading authority on Soviet intelligence—including getting the general's patrynomic wrong (Vasileiyvich instead of Alekseivich.) We discussed "active measures" (disinformation) which each side had played on the other, and he showed me how Frederick Forsyth, in his far-fetched yarn *The Fourth Protocol*, had fallen for a line from one of the general's "S" illegals and had said that Kirpichenko had died in a road accident in 1985.

"You are talking to a living corpse," the old spymaster chuckled.

On the last day, I brought up the Ogorodnikov letter, which I had handed to a senior official some days earlier. Had the Ogorodnikovs been "KGB", Kirpichenko would have been their ultimate controller. Had Miller "penetrated the KGB", he would have been getting his orders from someone under Kirpichenko's orders.

I asked the general if there was anything he could do about Nikolaiy's plaintive request. Kirpichenko said it would be totally impossible for him or for any other Russian intelligence officer to sign a letter saying that so-and-so worked, or had worked, or had not worked for the KGB. I said I understood that, and that such a document would probably have little or no convincing value in a U.S. court, anyway.

I then asked if I could ask him a question on the matter under the rules we had established. These were that everything he said would be on the record; if there were questions which he could not answer for reasons of security, I would neither push him nor mention the unanswered questions in my articles; but that everything he told me would always be the truth.

He agreed, and I said: "If either of the Ogorodnikovs had been officers or employees of the KGB, would you not have moved heaven and earth to get them exchanged and allowed to return to Moscow, once they were arrested?"

His response was: "If either of the Ogorodnikovs, or anyone else, had been officers or agents of the KGB or any other Soviet intelligence service, and they were in trouble overseas, we would always try to do everything possible to help them. We wouldn't want them undergoing interrogation or trial. We would naturally try to save them. We always did, in every such case."

He must have been expecting the question that day, because he leafed through some papers in his briefcase to refresh his memory. He went on:

"Svetlana Ogorodnikova was an adventuress. She offered her services to the FBI. She slept with this policeman. The FBI sent her to the consulate-general [in San Francisco], and we could see what she was doing. She saw herself as a sort of mata hari. Her husband was just a poor fellow who was subject to his wife.

"Neither of these individuals could even have been *thought about* [by us] as possible agents. They would have been completely unacceptable. They had neither the education nor the training, especially for working in what we then considered to be the 'main enemy'. It was publicly reported in our press that Svetlana went to bed with an American policeman on her own initiative, something a real KGB agent would never do away from Russia. As I said, she wanted to become a second mata hari. She was working for the FBI and pretending that she wanted to make a present to the KGB and come back to the Soviet Union.

"From what we have heard, she was the leading force. Her husband did nothing, really. [But] we have no obligations toward these people. They voluntarily gave up their citizenship in the Soviet Union when they said they were emigrating to Israel. If they want to come back to Russia, I think we will probably accept them, but we have no obligation."

I then asked: "To sum up, does the fact that you never asked for them to be exchanged mean, then, that they never worked for the KGB?"

He responded: "I think that is obvious, is it not? I can see that they are a humanitarian case, especially the husband. But we never asked for their release or exchange because they were never ours. They are not citizens of Russia or the Ukraine.

"I was director of the 'S' Directorate of the First Chief Directorate, in charge of all the illegals, all nondiplomatic intelligence officers and agents of my government throughout the world, from 1974 to 1991. I cannot answer all your questions, naturally, but I have promised that when I answer a question I will always tell you the truth. As a rule, we never say whether someone is working for us or not working for us. But I understand that you are moved by a humanitarian concern, and I recognize that there is a humanitarian element in this matter. So I will break the rule and say: Every Soviet illegal in the world worked for me, from 1974 to 1991, and these two people never worked for me; nor would I ever have considered them as potential for the 'S' Directorate or for any Soviet intelligence agency."

In 1991, Miller again appealed, asking for a fourth trial. Greg Nicolaysen, his new attorney, said Takasugi's conviction should be reversed for "abuse of discretion"—refusal to consider one motion for "untimeliness," and admitting tainted, coerced evidence.

The appeal says Hunt's actions with Svetlana, including a "romantic involvement," were essentially the same as Miller's; but the FBI had been "strikingly more punitive toward Miller than the benign, hands-off position displayed by the Bureau toward Hunt."

Nicolaysen notes that "By the end of September 1984, the FBI's investigation [of Miller] was far too inconclusive to constitute a prosecutable case. . . Surveillance of Svetlana . . .failed to yield any concrete evidence of any illegal behavior, let alone espionage activity connected to Miller."

Miller had tried to mount a scam on the KGB. He "acknowledged that his actions with Svetlana had clearly transgressed the FBI rules and regulations, [but] his statement to Christensen hardly amounted to an admission of espionage."

Miller had been ground down over five days of third degree, with Bishop Bretzing taking advantage of his religious ascendancy over the weeping Mormon. This had resulted in Miller's briefly agreeing with the FBI's version of events, which he had later corrected. However, assured that his fellow agents wished him well, that he was still "on the team", he had offered to sign anything they wrote: "The admissions made by Miller were the product of a will overborne."

In his fifty-six-page brief, Nicolaysen said: "Bretzing's goal was simple and direct: To make Miller confess to something." Miller had been falsely told that the FBI had "taped evidence" showing Miller passing classified information. "In fact, no such evidence existed."

Deception had been used to make Miller believe he had nothing more serious to fear from confessing than in-house sanctions. "While the search of the Bonsall residence was being conducted, Miller's wife, Paula, was informed by Christensen that the purpose of the search was to investigate her husband's failure to report certain conversations he had had with certain people, that those actions did not constitute a prosecutable offense, and that her husband would not lose his job as a result thereof. Paula later conveyed the result of this conversation to Miller, as she was expected to."

The Appeal Court's decision was awaited when this book went to press. After 15 months, Nikolaiy was still in prison in Winchester, in virtual solitary confinement, without charge or trial, awaiting return to Terminal Island prison in Los Angeles.

# Index